1983 SEASON
THE COMPLETE HANDBOOK OF PRO FOOTBALL

Super Sports Books from SIGNET

(0451)

☐ **THE ILLUSTRATED SPORTS RECORD BOOK by Zander Hollander and David Schulz.** Here, in a single book, are 350 records with stories and photos so vivid they'll make you feel that "you are there." Once and for all you'll be able to settle your sports debates on who holds what records and how he, or she, did it.

(111818—$2.50)*

☐ **SPORT MAGAZINE ALL-TIME ALL STARS edited by Tom Murray.** Profiles of 22 of baseball's greatest players by an all-star team of writers about the way each of them played the game, the way each of them lived his life, and what is takes to be the very best.

(091698—$2.50)

☐ **THE LEGEND OF DR. J: The Story of Julius Erving by Marty Bell.** An electrifying action-profile of the fabulous multi-millionaire superstar. "Graceful and admirable!"—*Dick Schaap*

(121791—$2.95)

☐ **EVERYTHING YOU ALWAYS WANTED TO KNOW ABOUT SPORTS* *and didn't know where to ask by Mickey Herskowitz and Steve Perkins.** Here is the book that answers every question a sports fan ever had in the back of his mind and tells the truth about all the whispered rumors of the sports world.

(124715—$2.75)

☐ **PB: THE PAUL BROWN STORY by Paul Brown with Jack Clary.** The personal story of a man, the men he led, and the game he loves. "Insightful . . . Paul Brown has something worth saying and he says it well."—*The Cincinnati Enquirer* (099753—2.95)*

*Prices slightly higher in Canada

Buy them at your local bookstore or use this convenient coupon for ordering.
THE NEW AMERICAN LIBRARY, INC.,
P.O. Box 999, Bergenfield, New Jersey 07621

Please send me the books I have checked above. I am enclosing $_____
(please add $1.00 to this order to cover postage and handling). Send check or money order—no cash or C.O.D.'s. Prices and numbers are subject to change without notice.

Name_____

Address_____

City _____ State _____ Zip Code _____

Allow 4-6 weeks for delivery.
This offer is subject to withdrawal without notice.

1983 SEASON
THE COMPLETE HANDBOOK OF PRO FOOTBALL

EDITED BY ZANDER HOLLANDER

A SIGNET BOOK
NEW AMERICAN LIBRARY
TIMES MIRROR

ACKNOWLEDGMENTS

With no visions of a strike but a new league to tempt the draftees and sign a few of the oldies, the NFL enters its 64th season licking its Al Davis wounds and without fear of destruction. And the coming of John Elway lends an aura of excitement for Denver and all of the NFL.

For this ninth annual edition of the handbook, we gratefully acknowledge the writers on the facing page, contributing editors Howard Blatt and Eric Compton, and Frank Kelly, Rich Rossiter, Pat Murphy, Judie Marks, Steve Wisniewski, Phyllis Hollander, Peter Hollander, Beri Greenwald, Dot Gordineer, Jim Heffernan, Joe Browne, Fran Connors, Roger Goodell and the NFL team publicists.

Zander Hollander

PHOTO CREDITS: Cover—Mitch Reibel; back cover—Ray Amati/Focus on Sports. Inside photos—CBS-TV, Malcolm Emmons, George Gojkovich, Marc S. Levine, Miller Lite, NBC-TV, Richard Pilling, Mitch Reibel, Bob Shaver, UPI and the various club photographers, including Nate Fine and Ed Mahan, and the college photographers from Georgia (Richard Fowlkes, Tim Gentry, Clate Sanders), Stanford (David Madison), Arkansas, Clemson, Florida, Oklahoma, Penn State, Pitt, SMU and USC.

Copyright © 1983 Associated Features Inc. All rights reserved.

SIGNET TRADEMARK REG. U.S. PAT. OFF. AND FOREIGN COUNTRIES
REGISTERED TRADEMARK—MARCA REGISTRADA
HECHO EN CHICAGO, U.S.A.

SIGNET, SIGNET CLASSICS, MENTOR, PLUME, MERIDIAN AND NAL BOOKS
are published by The New American Library Inc. 1633 Broadway
New York, New York 10019

First Printing, August 1983

1 2 3 4 5 6 7 8 9

PRINTED IN THE UNITED STATES OF AMERICA

CONTENTS

The Mystery of John Riggins........... By Paul Attner	6
Madden and Merlin: Who's No. 1?.................... By Mary Flannery	14
Mark Gastineau and The Hot Dog Controversy .... By Jim Smith	22
A Fantasy: If Herschel Walker Hadn't Jumped..................... By Joe Gergen	30
The Computer Takes Over The College Draft .... By John Clayton	38
Inside the NFC .... By Paul Attner	48

Atlanta Falcons	50	New Orleans Saints	109
Chicago Bears............	59	New York Giants........	118
Dallas Cowboys..........	67	Philadelphia Eagles	126
Detroit Lions.............	76	San Francisco 49ers	135
Green Bay Packers	84	St. Louis Cardinals	144
Los Angeles Rams	92	Tampa Bay Buccaneers .	152
Minnesota Vikings.......	100	Washington Redskins....	160

Inside the AFC .... By Dave Newhouse	170

Baltimore Colts	172	Los Angeles Raiders	236
Buffalo Bills	182	Miami Dolphins	245
Cincinnati Bengals	191	New England Patriots....	254
Cleveland Browns.......	200	New York Jets...........	263
Denver Broncos.........	209	Pittsburgh Steelers	272
Houston Oilers..........	218	San Diego Chargers.....	281
Kansas City Chiefs......	227	Seattle Seahawks.......	290

NFL Statistics	300
NFL Standings: 1921–1982............................	313
John Elway Calls His Shot	330
NFL Draft...	332
NFL Schedule..	348
NFL TV Schedule.......................................	351

Editor's Note: The material herein includes trades and rosters up to final printing deadline.

THE MYSTERY OF JOHN RIGGINS

By PAUL ATTNER

Minutes after he had become an instant Super Bowl legend, John Riggins stood in an interview room, television lights glowing around his head, and captured the moment in a few well-chosen words.

"Ronnie may be President, but I'm King for the day," Riggins deadpanned.

It was vintage John Riggins. Humorous, offbeat and right on the money. It also became the most-quoted remark from Super Bowl XVII, coming from the mouth of the man who caught the attention of America's football fans for three dramatic hours on Super Sunday last January in Pasadena, Cal.

If John Riggins wanted to, he could well become one of America's favorite athletes. Certainly, he could be a media darling, and that status usually leads to public adulation. He has all the right ingredients for fame: good looks, a quick mind, a wonderful sense of humor and talent. He also has a manner that makes him one of the boys, and not some polished, above-the-masses athletic star.

But the John Riggins I have observed, interviewed and quarreled with for the last half-decade isn't about to sell his soul to John Q. Public.

It's a cliché, sure, but John Riggins does march to the beat of a different drummer. A real far-out beat. Even his perky wife, Mary Lou, admits she doesn't know what he is going to do from one moment to another. Riggins seems to live on whim from day to day; if it's socially odd, then he views it as the right thing to do.

Yet he doesn't always purposely behave to be different. He

Pro football sleuth Paul Attner regularly investigates the unsolved case of John Riggins for the Washington Post.

John Riggins breaks away for the winning TD in Super Bowl.

The fresh-faced campus hero at Kansas.

just *is* different, different than any prominent athlete on today's sports scene.

Name another athlete who would walk away from an annual salary of $300,000 and sit out a season because he sincerely felt he had lost the desire to play anymore.

"At one point I felt John sat out a year because he wanted more money," said Redskin general manager Bobby Beathard. "But now I'm convinced that when he said he had lost his desire, he meant it. He just didn't think it was right to play a year at that kind of money and not give the team its proper return. He thought he was cheating the team."

That's exactly what Riggins said during that controversial summer of 1980, when he suddenly bolted after the second day of training camp and returned to his farm outside Lawrence, Kan. But in this cynical era of sports, when athletes are chasing King Dollar with a vengeance, who could believe that kind of indifference?

There was a catch. Riggins told the Redskins if they would toss in an incentive, say a one-year, $500,000 contract, he might reconsider, because the extra money could give him the zest to return. Right away, it sounded like a different twist to the old salary holdout game. Yet in his own unique way, Riggins apparently was searching for a way to be fair both to himself and to Washington.

Consider how many other athletes likely play game after game not caring if they produce or not. As long as the check comes every week, they'll take the money and run. Riggins, with his unusual set of principles, wanted no part of going-through-the-motions performances.

"I had lost my desire, my fire," he said near the end of last

As a Jet, Riggins went from an Afro to a Mohawk.

season, referring to those 1980 summer months. "I didn't know if I wanted to ever play again."

In our search to unlock the mystery of John Riggins, that's the first clue. Riggins means what he says. He isn't out to cheat or to sell anyone short. His word is good, his efforts first-class, even if the way he goes about his business is different than the accepted route.

Redskin coach Joe Gibbs says: "It took me awhile to even begin to figure out John, and I'm not saying I know him that well now. But I know this, when he says he is going to do something, he does it. He came to one of our minicamps out of shape but he told me that when training camp started, he would be top shape, and he was.

"When he came to me before the start of the playoffs this past season and asked me to give him the ball, because he didn't have many years left and he wanted to make the most of the next games, I knew he was going to play well. The man does what he says."

What he did will be recounted for years. In four playoff games, he rushed for more than 100 yards each time out. No one had ever done that before in NFL history. In the Super Bowl, against a tenacious Miami defense geared to stop him, he gained a record 166 yards and put away the Dolphins with a stunning 43-yard run that came off a play designed to gain a couple of yards and a first down. Rarely has there been a better pressure performance; rarely has an athlete responded so well, so dramatically under the spotlight of public attention.

Yet even in triumph, the Riggins mystery continues. He is the seventh-leading rusher in NFL history, no easy achievement, but it took that one game, 11 years into his career, to obtain the attention O.J. Simpson received in his rookie season.

"I never have been very spectacular," Riggins said after a 66-yard run against Dallas in the 1979 season finale. "I don't want to have many more of those runs. I almost died running the last 10 yards."

Everyone laughed, but there was truth in what he said. Riggins has moved into the ranks of the running greats through consistency, endurance and plodding. He ran a sub-10-flat 100 in high school, but he isn't quick. He needs a good step or two to get into decent gear and a few strides to move into high. So the blocks have to be sustained a bit longer while the man they call Diesel cranks up his gears. Hey, this is a prototype fullback at work here, not some greyhound.

Once Riggins gets moving, you are talking about pure strength and determination. He doesn't fall to arm tackles, nor to cornerbacks brashly charging up to make a quick stop. "It may not be noticeable," he says, "but I don't take many direct hits. I don't want to be punished for carrying the ball a lot. It takes me 20 carries to really feel into the game, so I have to make sure my body can hold up for a long time. I'm not trying to be a hero out there."

Because until the 1982 playoffs he hadn't been spectacular and because he hasn't always played on the best of teams, Riggins has crept up on many fans.

He joined the New York Jets in 1971 as a first-round draft choice out of the University of Kansas, where he'd broken all of Gale Sayers' records. As a rookie he led the Jets in rushing and receiving, and he played four more seasons before becoming a free agent and signing with the Redskins in 1976.

Riggins tells the story of his 1972 season with the Jets, when he thought Weeb Ewbank would pay him a contract incentive he nearly reached. Riggins had rushed for 944 yards, shy of the 1,000-yard target. When Weeb stuck to the terms of the contract, Riggins became a lot more cynical about life and football.

Unfortunately, the image most have had of Riggins is that he is an oddball, an eccentric, maybe a weirdo. And probably those tags are all true, to an extent. But they also have overshadowed a superbly tuned, determined, muscular athlete who became the guts of Washington's Super Bowl champs.

Understand this. The players love John Riggins. Not because of what happened in the Super Bowl. But because he is one of the boys. That's another key to understanding the John Riggins mystery. Riggins is not the super-polished superstar with a mini-conglomerate of businesses, a horde of agents and attorneys and an above-the-masses attitude. He'd rather go out drinking with his teammates than count his money. He'd rather show up for work in a hunter's camouflage outfit than ever be seen in a three-piece suit (although he owns a few). He lives hard, plays hard and *enjoys* himself. If it's not fun, Riggins wants no part of it.

Remember, in the past offseason he negotiated a $1-million-plus contract with Redskin owner Jack Kent Cooke, one of the world's shrewdest businessmen, without the benefit of an agent. That's right, he walked into Cooke's Virginia country estate and took on the big man himself, one-on-one. And he didn't walk away a pauper.

It's not that Riggins doesn't trust agents. He just doesn't think he needs one. That tells you something about the extreme confidence he has in his own ability and intelligence. It's fascinating to watch Riggins pull the leg of people who don't know him. He works very hard at trying to be the naive country boy from Kansas who is being overwhelmed by the big city and all the media attention. But this is a clever man, manipulating others at times to get his way, at the price he wants to pay.

Of course, his off-field shenanigans have done much to create a particular image. Why does Riggins do such unconventional things, like go to training camp with a mohawk haircut, or ride halfway across the country on a motorcycle, or walk out of camp for a day and then announce that he went fishing and the fish weren't biting?

"It's just John's way of being different," said guard Ron Saul, his closest friend among the Redskins. "He does things that he thinks he'll enjoy." And if that enjoyment isn't conventional, so what?

"He keeps to himself," Gibbs says. "He doesn't do very much talking to me at all. He may talk to Don Breaux [Redskin backfield coach] more but it's more like . . . just leave him alone and let him be and he'll do the job."

Says Riggins: "I'm not much for meetings and X's and O's. All that stuff really can't prepare you for a defense. You have to adjust to what they do from play to play. That's why I like to carry the ball a lot. It lets me get a feel for what the defense is doing."

That's another clue to Riggins. He is very football wise. He uses that sharp mind to get the most out of his skills. And he uses that mind to weave that wonderful path of his through life.

It's a shame that, for the most part, Riggins has cut himself off from the public the last three years. Since his yearlong walkout, he has banned media interviews, with a few exceptions. Once he ranked among the league's five most quotables. He was an original thinker who could say the same things in a different fashion. (Example: when he showed up at Redskin Park after the holdout

12 THE COMPLETE HANDBOOK OF PRO FOOTBALL

year, he said he was in uniform "because I'm bored, broke and back.")

He has never said why he went into a shell. The best guess is that many of the things he said to the press wound up being quoted by the Redskins during a lengthy and losing grievance hearing sought by Riggins in an attempt to regain his lost salary.

So he clammed up. He gave only rare chances to see inside John Riggins and find out what makes this intriguing man tick.

And when he does speak now, it becomes a major media event. Take the press conference he held last season, prior to the NFC championship game. It was one of the most fascinating media events I've ever attended. Riggins was going to break an 18-month silence and everyone who was anyone within the Washington sports press corps responded.

The Redskins staged the event in a large team meeting room. Eight television cameras recorded it. Some television stations broadcast it live. The radio station that carries Redskin games sent every word live over its airwaves. Reporters jammed the room, waiting for his grand entry.

Riggins finally showed up, wearing a nondescript T-shirt and giving, for the most part, nondescript answers. Some of what he said gives us some insight into his character, however. At one point he said he considered himself not a team leader, but a Sgt. York type. At another, he talked about how the fire had gone out in his mind after the Redskins lost to Dallas in the 1979 season finale. He refused to talk about retirement—he would be a free agent when the season ended—and he brushed off all the tough questions with off-color answers or tongue-in-cheek remarks.

Yet he held court for an hour. And he made the headlines and the newscasts, saying nothing new. But King John had spoken and eager fans were anxious to hear anything the man wanted to say.

It was even a bigger scene weeks later at the Super Bowl. Riggins became the first player in the game's 17-year history to hold a mass press conference. Usually, players sit at tables and are interviewed by groups of media. Riggins stood at a lectern and answered questions from 400 reporters. He was funny and irreverent. He said that in an early meeting with Gibbs, who took over as Redskin coach two years ago, he told him "you'll be a good coach with or without me." Riggins added, "So far I've proven one part of that to be right." Even Gibbs had to laugh.

Then, of course, Riggins enlivened Super Bowl Week even before his spectacular game-day demonstration. At a Redskin team party two days earlier, he showed up in top hat and tails. It brought down the house. The funny part is, no one thought it was strange

Railroads are on the wane, but the 1983 Diesel rumbles on.

that he did it. That's John.

I want to know more about what makes him function. I want to know why this family man, who has three young children, will go on day-long solo hunting trips during the offseason, staying at places where civilization can't find him.

I want to know why he will make commitments, like he has since the Super Bowl, and then not honor them. He has stiffed NFL Films, failing to show up for an appointment. He has stiffed the Larry King television show, appearing a week later than he was originally scheduled. He has gained a "don't-count-on-him" reputation, even going so far as to miss the Redskins' welcome-home parade through downtown Washington that was witnessed by 500,000 fans.

I want to ask him more about his obsession with injuries, and how he dreads leaving the game with permanent ailments. I want to delve into what motivates him to play better now, in his 30s, than he did in his 20s. I want to talk to him about his growth from a Kansas University great to a Redskin great.

But Riggins doesn't appear ready to let anyone crack that facade, to solve his continuing mystery. Agatha Christie, help!

John Madden's appeal is as broad as he is.

Madden and Merlin: Who's No. 1?

By MARY FLANNERY

Their styles are as different as the insights they bring to National Football League television viewers each fall Sunday. No, there's

Dick Enberg (left) and Merlin Olsen: NBC's Super team.

no mistaking the two best color commentators in the business for one another. However, separating them on the basis of ability is a much more difficult task. So the debate rages: Who's the best—CBS' John Madden or NBC's Merlin Olsen?

If you want the heights and the pits, the agony and the ecstasy, Madden is your man. The former Oakland Raiders' coach has lost none of his enthusiasm for the sport. He moans and groans. He carries on and cuts up. Even if you're not aware that the dial is on CBS, you can't help but realize that it's Madden behind the microphone.

The same instant identification can't be made with Olsen. He is the kind of analyst who makes you wonder, "Who is this guy?"

Mary Flannery lives close to the tube as TV sports columnist for the Philadelphia Daily News.

16 THE COMPLETE HANDBOOK OF PRO FOOTBALL

His comments, delivered without bombast, are on-target. Olsen's subtle but penetrating observations reveal how much he learned in 15 years as a defensive tackle for the Los Angeles Rams. Olsen's affection for the game is obvious, too.

Madden, of course, is the one with the memorable lines. Who else would describe a fan who was stripped to the waist in a frigid stadium as "a guy whose elevator doesn't go to the top?" Who else would predict with accuracy and humor that Renaldo Nehemiah's transition from running track to running NFL pass patterns would be like "going from driving on country roads to driving on the Los Angeles Freeway?"

Madden makes football fun. Olsen makes you think. During the Super Bowl XVII telecast, the cameras were alternating between shots of the Redskins celebrating John Riggins' game-winning touchdown and fans in the stands doing their own celebrating. But a deep, calm voice kept insisting, "Don McNeal slipped on that play." It took NBC four replays, but finally the cameras proved Olsen was correct. The Miami cornerback slipped in pursuit of a man in motion and it cost him one critical step in reaching Riggins. That's the sort of subtlety Olsen provides to enrich a telecast.

Olsen and Madden are regarded as the two most-prepared analysts. Before each game, they do extensive homework, and it shows. They also use their entree as former members of the NFL fraternity to learn a team's game plan. Coaches will tell Madden and Olsen what their teams are going to do on Sunday.

Madden, however, takes it one step further. During a game, he'll repeat something interesting that a coach said. Or he'll mention a little-known fact about one of the players. He makes more of an attempt to develop the human-interest side of football, which appeals to many viewers. Madden, for example, found out the ring sizes of the Cincinnati Bengals and San Francisco 49ers before Super Bowl XVI, so he could tell the viewers which winning player had the biggest finger. Now that is human interest.

Olsen can provide plenty of personality tidbits, too, but he uses them sparingly. Actually, Dick Enberg, his partner, is the one who usually mentions a player's background or personal life. Olsen has been reluctant to draw upon his own playing experiences because he feels that those associations are usually forced. But during Super Bowl XVII, he broke his own rule because he related to the pride shared by Washington's pit crew, "The Hogs." The positive response that Olsen's recollections received may convince him to be a bit looser this season.

Both commentators have their gadgets. Madden uses the Telestrator or Chalkboard. This is a monitor with a stylus attached, allowing Madden to outline on the TV screen which player to watch on a replay. First used in the 1981 playoffs, the Chalkboard lets the ex-coach act like a coach. These X's and O's are deep enough for the real football fan to appreciate and not too technical for most casual viewers.

The Chalkboard's purpose is to point out exactly why a play worked or failed. Madden can isolate the key block or tackle. But the device is not without its faults. After Madden used it to illustrate a touchdown pass during the Dallas-Green Bay playoff game last season, Pat Summerall quipped, "That looks like the menu in a Chinese restaurant."

"That was the soup," Madden replied.

That can be a problem. While Madden is drawing all those lines on the monitor, it makes perfect sense. But when he steps back to inspect his handiwork, it sometimes looks like scrawling in a foreign language to an untrained eye.

Olsen's innovation is Action Capsules, a feature which he has developed in association with the NBC production staff. These replay packages, often seen in baseball telecasts, had never been applied to football coverage until the Miami-New York Jets AFC championship game last season. Olsen suggested which plays might be appropriate for a Capsule and ex-NFL wide receiver Mike Haffner coordinated them in the production truck. The Action Capsule's most striking utilization provided viewers with a sense of how the effectiveness of Miami linebacker A.J. Duhe resulted from the freedom he had on the field.

No matter how high a skilled analyst can soar, he is tied to his play-by-play man like a kite to a string. So, it is no coincidence that Madden's partner, Pat Summerall, and Olsen's cohort, Dick Enberg, are esteemed as the most talented play-by-play announcers. These are the best *teams* in NFL announcing and, like love and marriage used to be, you can't have one without the other.

"This is a very overlooked part of Madden's success," says Terry O'Neil, NFL executive producer for CBS. "Pat provides the structure that allows John to be John. John can be effusive and have a stream-of-consciousness delivery. He can be emotional and sometimes wildly overactive. But he is able to be that way because Summerall is always providing the frame into which John's comments fit. Not only does Pat provide the nuts and bolts of who carried the ball or made that tackle, he does it in a very economical use of words. His play-by-play is very spare.

"Also, with these guys there is a great blurring of the traditional lines, where the play-by-play man calls the play and finishes talking after the tackle and the analyst picks up and talks until they break the huddle for the next play. You probably hear John's voice twice as often as Pat's. In most other situations between color

18 THE COMPLETE HANDBOOK OF PRO FOOTBALL

Olsen seems to be as wise and gentle as Father Murphy.

men and play-by-play announcers, it's 50-50. Sometimes when Pat is talking, he is actually assuming the role of commentator."

This is Madden's fifth year as a commentator. He worked with Vin Scully his first season and Gary Bender his second. When CBS decided to split up its Summerall/Tom Brookshier team, Madden catapulted into the catbird seat. Madden/Summerall chemistry works because they are such interesting extremes. Madden is emotional; Summerall is the cool professional. Madden is passionate; Summerall is restrained. Madden doesn't try to be anyone else but himself.

"The key to the whole thing is to be natural," he says. "When we're on, I talk and act like I would if I were talking things over with my quarterback or my wife."

Olsen and Enberg, who just completed their fifth season of broadcasting matrimony, operate in complete sync. They may not be able to finish each other's thoughts, because Enberg doesn't have as extensive a knowledge of the game as his NFL Hall-of-Fame partner, but they're smooth together. They blend. In the belief there was some merit to NBC's experimental announcerless NFL game in 1980, they deliberately leave space between their words to let the picture tell the story.

In fact, it was the special relationship that Olsen has with Enberg and the NBC brass that helped to persuade the baritone color man to sign a new contract last March. The four-year deal calls for Olsen to be deeply involved in football coverage and also to develop several made-for-TV movies.

"I wanted to continue the affiliation with Dick Enberg and with [NBC coordinating producer for football] Ted Nathanson," says Olsen. "I didn't want it to slip away. When I retired from the Rams, my initial feeling was that broadcasting was going to be a stepping stone to other things. But now I realize I don't want to throw away the things I do well. I'm not going to neglect my acting. But to walk away from broadcasting, which I enjoy and is a challenge, and where I have such a good relationship with Dick—that would be silly."

While the Enberg/Olsen team is certainly more reflective and generally quieter than Summerall/Madden, the NBC crew actually has much to say. Enberg and Olsen will begin talking about any and all topics when the score is lopsided by halftime. That's when they bring out "The Blowout List." Before each game, Enberg and Olsen compare notes and make a list of possible subjects for discussion should the game no longer be competitive enough to sustain viewer interest on its own.

"I want to have plenty to talk about," says Olsen. "If I didn't have all that stuff, I'd feel naked."

20 THE COMPLETE HANDBOOK OF PRO FOOTBALL

Madden brews excitement—in ads and in TV booth.

Olsen comes completely prepared and Enberg lets him shine. There is no ego problem in this broadcast booth. "The stars of television are the analysts and I've recognized that," says Enberg. "So I'm not frustrated by the fact that Merlin is the star of the football telecast."

He is only to a point. Olsen and Enberg have a commitment to remaining in the background. While Madden's comments, especially the outrageous ones, divert the viewers' attention from the game to that flushed face, we're seldom distracted by what NBC's No. 1 team has to say. Unless the game calls for "The Blowout List," the unblinking focus is on the field.

"Above all, Dick and I feel that we should only showcase and spotlight the action on the field, never take precedence over it," says Olsen.

It is all a matter of personality—Madden is one; Olsen has one. Their roles as football analysts are perceived in the light of their extracurricular activities. It is impossible to separate John Madden the analyst from "that crazy coach who used to roam the sidelines." He makes us smile in the Miller Lite commercials. He makes us smile when he says, "Pittsburgh is all-league in booing."

Occasionally, he seems as if he is caught up in playing John Madden—working too hard at maintaining his image as a disheveled but lovable redhead with a head for football. But the average viewer probably is unaware of any strain. To most people, Madden is the guy-next-door, explaining the game with just the right amount of insight and humor.

Olsen, too, is somewhat defined by his acting roles. In both "Little House on the Prairie" and "Father Murphy," he played a wise, gentle man. That is how we think of him and the image lends strength to his analysis. He's accurate and comfortable, but lacks Madden's flair.

Who's No. 1? Madden, by a fraction, in most people's eyes. Unless your tastes are more cerebral and you think football is a science. Then it's Merlin Olsen all the way.

22 THE COMPLETE HANDBOOK OF PRO FOOTBALL

Jet fans love Mark Gastineau's spotlight dance.

MARK GASTINEAU AND THE HOT DOG CONTROVERSY

By JIM SMITH

If Mark Gastineau did not dance, leap, flail his arms and play to the crowd after his sacks, he probably would be regarded highly by most fans, media and his National Football League opponents. After all, he is one of the best defensive ends in pro football. But "hot dogs" are accorded recognition grudgingly, if at all. That is the price Gastineau pays for his exuberance.

The same people who applaud high-fiving, spiking, and other displays of emotion on a football field shake their heads and bad-mouth Gastineau. They question his motives, his sincerity, his class. It is clear that Gastineau, who is entering his fifth season with the Jets, often violates an unwritten rule of the NFL's code of conduct: "Thou shalt not humiliate thy opponent."

"I think a champion should be gracious and humble," Green Bay Packers' wide receiver James Lofton says. "Over-played theatrics dilute the spirit of the game. I think a few people are perturbed with Mark Gastineau, because there is an arrogance to what he does. Like, 'I'm King of the Hill!'—beating his chest. But you can't get inside a person and feel *his* emotions."

Gastineau says that he isn't trying to embarrass opponents. He just always was an excitable boy. He was a tall, clumsy kid from Springerville, Ariz., who lacked self-confidence. A late bloomer, Gastineau spent a year at tiny, isolated Eastern Arizona Junior College and a year at Arizona State. He was not even on Frank Kush's traveling squad at the end of his sophomore season. Then, he started to blossom.

Through hard work, Gastineau emerged two years later as the Most Valuable Player in the Senior Bowl. He had moved with his

---

As a pro football writer for Newsday, *Jim Smith is a gourmet of NFL hot dogs.*

family to Ada, Okla., and transferred to East Central Oklahoma State. He thrived in a small-time program. The Jets took Gastineau in the second round of the 1979 draft. He started only one game as a rookie and totalled only two sacks, but he improved rapidly and led the team with 11½ sacks in 1980. Still, the 6-5, 276-pound defensive end, who boasts 4.55 speed in the 40, said he felt like he was playing in a straitjacket.

"I had started [celebrating after a sack] in college in front of 2,000 fans," Gastineau said last March, as workmen renovated his Huntington, L.I., home. "I always got excited when I sacked the quarterback. I really didn't know why I was doing it, I just did it. Before I knew it, I was doing it before 60,000 fans.

"It's something I did, not knowing it was going to get me publicity. It's a true feeling, not a fake feeling. I used to get a lot of trouble from my [Jet] teammates for it. I jumped up and down on half my sacks in 1980—about five. Then when I had 20 the next year I jumped up and down on every one. I guess it transformed me into a 'hot dog' in some people's eyes. I feel I'm just a player who plays with a lot of emotion."

Many of pro football's flamboyant players over the years have been wide receivers. The New York Giants feel that Homer Jones (1964-69) was the first to popularize spiking.

Harold Carmichael of the Philadelphia Eagles admitted he tried to "bust the ball" on some of his exuberant spikes in the early '70s. Carmichael also became well-known for dropping to his knees in the end zone and rolling the ball as if it were dice after scoring a touchdown. He learned to control himself in the last few years, under the disapproving eye of since-departed coach Dick Vermeil.

Other notable celebrants have included Elmo Wright, Otis Taylor, Rich Caster, Charley Taylor, Charlie Joiner, Butch Johnson, Duriel Harris and John Jefferson. Currently, there is "The Fun Bunch" in Washington.

Johnson, of the Dallas Cowboys, is universally accepted as the NFL's best active spiker. His "California Quake," in which he knocks his knees together and performs various other gyrations, is the most elaborate routine in the NFL.

Spiking has gained Johnson enormous publicity, considering he has caught only 91 passes and scored only 16 touchdowns in his seven seasons. Johnson has been a frequent critic of Dallas coach Tom Landry. Landry prefers to use Johnson as a third receiver—usually only on obvious passing downs. So perhaps Johnson's spikes are as much a sign of frustration as an expression of joy. Johnson seems to save his best spikes for nationally-tel-

Washington's Fun Bunch had plenty to high-five about.

evised games. And the Cowboys have not tried to curtail his showmanship.

In an article in *Newsday* in 1974, John Jeansonne wrote, "The basic receiver-defensive back antagonism seems to have nourished the spike. For a while, the gesture began as a sort of hallelujah. It is often used now as a derisive remark directed at a defender."

"You spike it near that defender's head," Harold Carmichael said, "and he can tell what it's for. But with me, it's more than that. It's to say, I'm doing it for me and the fans, to show them that I appreciate them being there to see my touchdown."

There have been some embarrassing spiking incidents over the years. In a 1971 Monday night game on national television, Pittsburgh Steelers' receiver Dave Smith spiked the ball on the five-yard line. It rolled through the end zone for a touchback and the Kansas City Chiefs beat the Steelers.

Dallas' Drew Pearson stretched knee ligaments when he came down awkwardly from a leaping spike in a 1979 game. The next week Pearson watched his streak of consecutive games end at 100.

26 THE COMPLETE HANDBOOK OF PRO FOOTBALL

In 1980, Miami Dolphins' receiver Duriel Harris hurt himself as he leaped to spike a ball after scoring on a 17-yard touchdown pass. "From now on," Harris said then, "I'll just look for the referee and hand it to him. That's the way Paul Warfield did it. When you don't get in the end zone very often, sometimes you forget how to act."

"It's a natural reaction," veteran Buffalo Bills' receiver Frank Lewis said of spiking. "As long as a guy does things with a certain amount of class, it's all right with me. When a receiver catches a ball, it's been in the air, he had to make a move to get it, and sometimes he gets tackled hard. So after it's done, a spike is just a little something to top it off. Most times, a scoring pass is a beautiful play. So, subconsciously, you might be doing something to rejoice."

Players have given vent to their emotions in various ways through the years. Hollywood Henderson, Fred Williamson, Jack Tatum and Johnny Sample were defensive players who enjoyed verbally taunting opponents. Steelers' defensive lineman John Banaszak and Dwight White were extroverted and demonstrative. Banaszak did a dance similar to Gastineau's after making a good play.

Pittsburgh receivers Lynn Swann and John Stallworth, during their heyday in the mid-'70s, would jump and clap hands after their touchdowns.

But the Washington Redskins' "Fun Bunch" probably gets more players involved in touchdown celebrations than any team in history. They received national publicity during last year's playoffs. Their celebrations began as a means of relieving the boredom of practice. Whenever any member of the group scored a touchdown in practice or in a playoff game last year, all the members celebrated with a group high-five. Those involved were receivers Charlie Brown, Alvin Garrett and Virgil Seay, tight ends Don Warren, Rick Walker and Clint Didier and running backs Otis Wonsley and Clarence Harmon.

The home fans at RFK Stadium were delighted to see the group do their thing in the end zone. The player who scored the touchdown waited for everybody else to arrive. They gathered in a circle. They brought their arms up to chest level twice, crossing themselves in a secret clubhouse signal that signified togetherness. Then, they all leaped as high as they could for a communal high-five. A few times they slapped each other's cheeks by accident.

"It's something different," Brown said. "Like Butch Johnson has the California Quake. What I like about ours is that it's not an individual thing. It's a team thing. And all the fans get into it, too. It makes us want to score, that's for sure, so we can get everybody involved and get RFK going wild."

"Billy [White Shoes] Johnson had his thing [an elaborate dance routine] with the Oilers in the '70s," Redskins' safety and player representative Mark Murphy said, "but what I like about the Fun Bunch is that it was a team thing. Football is a team sport. It was one guy who scored, but the work of the whole team got him there."

Murphy added, referring to Gastineau's dance, "I think it's getting a little carried away. But it's certainly got people interested. To each his own. I wouldn't do anything like that. But, of course, I've only had two sacks in my career."

The NFL leaves control of flamboyant displays up to its teams. An NFL source said that the league did put in a rule in the early '70s to prohibit spiking while the ball is in play. Violators are penalized for delaying the game. There also is a rule that prohibits taunting an opponent with gestures. But a league official who requested anonymity said the NFL has nothing against hot-dogging if it is done with good taste. And he indicated that Gastineau's antics enliven a telecast.

"I'd imagine if you talked to a television producer or director," the official said, "he'd probably say anytime he can get a good shot, he wants it. We want our games to be exciting. We are in the entertainment business. But we hope it's within the bounds of good judgment."

Although James Lofton objects to Gastineau's dance over a fallen lineman, Lofton has been considered a hot dog, too. He said, "I used to throw the ball in the stands in 1981, but when the league boosted the fine to $1,000 in 1982, I had to find a way to restrain myself. Now, it's back down to $100 for '83, so I'll probably start doing it again. If you can give a fan a memory for life, I think it's great. It makes them part of the game. Sometimes at home games I'll leap and slap the fans in the stands a high-five after I score."

Lofton said he thinks Gastineau goes overboard. "When you say hot-dogging," he said, "you're doing something derogatory to another player. It starts on emotion, but there's showmanship involved [with Gastineau]. In a playoff game, he was dancing and he didn't see that a ball had been fumbled. His may not be a celebration. It's not like an exclamation point. When a receiver does it, it's like an exclamation point...I don't think it should be outlawed, though."

In an article in *Inside Sports* Magazine, Marty Lyons, who plays alongside Gastineau on the "New York Sack Exchange" defensive line, told writer Gary Smith, "This is your living. You're supporting a wife and kids. It's embarrassing enough for an of-

28 THE COMPLETE HANDBOOK OF PRO FOOTBALL

fensive lineman when you beat him for a sack, let alone doing that... I'm not trying to be derogatory toward Mark Gastineau, but I wouldn't do it. It's not contagious. It doesn't pump me up. Apparently, it's doing something for him off the field [financially], isn't it?"

Gastineau reportedly earned $225,000 between the 1981 and 1982 seasons—more than twice his 1981 salary. He endorses sneakers, designer jeans and automobiles and is in constant demand for public appearances and speaking engagements. Gastineau even appeared with his mother in a television ad for a razor. So his antics on the field seem to have paid off during the off-season.

"His exuberance means quite a bit," said Gastineau's agent, Gary Wichard. "His showmanship has been his calling card. He's easily recognizable on the field. Everybody has helmets on. The only thing fans can relate to are players' feelings. He's got an identity. That means quite a lot as far as endorsements and commercials. But the most important thing is that he's an all-pro. He gets his sacks. He gets opportunities to do his dance."

By the end of the 1982 season, Gastineau said most of his teammates had come to accept his dancing. He had cleared it with since-departed coach Walt Michaels and team president Jim Kensil, who told him not to belittle an opponent with his gestures. And the Shea Stadium fans loved it.

"When I'm on the field, it feels like I have a different type of relationship with the fans," Gastineau told *Newsday's* Greg Logan. "It's like talking to each other when I get a sack. It's enthusiasm. They sit and freeze half the year and it's a pleasure for them to get out of their chairs and cheer."

But Gastineau admitted to Logan that there still seemed to be some lingering resentment from a few teammates.

"A couple of people," Gastineau said, "told me they'd be my friend if I didn't jump up and down. If that's what it takes, they're not my friends in the first place. I used to break my back to be friendly to people on this team. But you can't force them to like you. The more you try, the more you embarrass yourself. I don't have anyone on the team that I can tell all my problems to. My wife, Lisa, is my best friend. Both of us are loner types. We don't socialize much."

Gastineau's father Ernie, 72, still drives a bulldozer and takes part in team roping events in rodeos near the family's Ravia, Okla., home. "Gastineau's father," Logan wrote, "remains his alter ego. They still talk almost daily on the telephone. When the family sees Mark make a sack on television, says Ernie, they all get up and dance... Maybe Gastineau's sack dance is just his way of mugging for the cameras, his way of saying, 'Hi, Dad!'"

Maybe so. But there is ego and showmanship involved, too. The offensive linemen Gastineau beats have it rough. "I'm in a no-win situation," Packers' tackle Greg Koch said after the Jets beat Green Bay last November. "I block him on 50 plays, he makes a sack and everything he does is put up on instant replay."

The spike may be part of American folklore, but Gastineau's dance is not. The disapproval doesn't bother him.

"After three years and 40-something sacks," he said, "they [teammates] have gotten used to it because it isn't goin' to change. It's for real. A lot of people who used to tell me not to do it now come to me and say, 'Keep dancing; don't stop.' They pat me on the back... It's nice to know that when I'm out there, I don't have to worry about people not liking it...

"Before I knew it, people were saying I'm one of the more flamboyant players," he added, "I couldn't figure it out. I guess I was naive. But one time we played Green Bay and John Jefferson walked off the field with me. He said, 'I got a lot of spit for doing the high-five in Green Bay, you get it for doing your dance. Don't pay any mind to it. A lot of it is jealousy. Do it.' I don't see anything wrong with expressing your feelings and emotions on the field. I thought the 'Fun Bunch' was great. It showed that I'm not the only one who's crazy."

Gastineau said he thinks players in general are becoming less uptight these days and that most teams have a few players who make a spectacle of celebrating their triumphs. But he admits that his timing can sometimes be a problem. And he seems to have a somewhat self-centered perspective on the game.

"When I'm ahead," he said, "it makes it even better. When I'm behind, though, sometimes I forget we are behind. I try to get everybody fired up so we can come back and win." Instead, he sometimes gets blank stares in the huddle.

Gastineau said he hopes that someday he will be respected for his play rather than resented because of the way he celebrates his sacks. "There's no question in anybody's mind that Mark Gastineau is a good player," he said. "I've made the Pro Bowl. Twenty sacks is not too damn bad. My play speaks for itself. I don't have to prove anything.

"You know, I go around now and speak to different groups and people talk to me about the things I've done. People tell me their kids play like me. After a sack, they jump up and down, 'like Mark Gastineau.' That makes me feel good. I think I'm helping to mold some kids... [The dance] is something different, something nobody had done. I'm not a psychology major. I don't know why I do it. But I know I'm not going to stop."

A FANTASY: IF HERSCHEL WALKER HADN'T JUMPED...

By JOE GERGEN

This is the senior year that might have been for the most celebrated Georgia Bulldog of all time.

The irony of the situation was not lost on Herschel Walker or his teammates. For the first game of the 1983 season, the University of Georgia football team was dressing in the clubhouse of the New Jersey Generals. And there, over Walker's locker under the stands at Giants Stadium, several of the Bulldogs had created an elaborate cardboard sign featuring the five-star logo of the United States Football League team and the $5,000,000 figure the Generals had been prepared to pay the running back to forego his senior year.

"Who did this?" Walker asked, a wide grin playing across his face.

"Must have been Penn State," said fullback Barry Young. "No way they wanted to tangle with Herschel Walker again. Not after what you did to them in the Sugar Bowl."

Walker winced at the memory. In one of his most frustrating games on the stage of college football, he had been limited to 107 yards in a 27-23 loss on New Year's night in New Orleans. It had been only the third defeat for Georgia since Walker entered school and it had prevented the Bulldogs from annexing a second national championship in three years.

That's why Georgia was only too happy to accept an invitation for the first Kickoff Classic, a game matching two of the premier

---

To the joy of his readers, Newsday *sports columnist Joe Gergen sometimes has fits of imagination.*

Herschel leap-frogs into the senior season that never was.

teams from the previous season, in East Rutherford, N.J., almost in the shadow of the New York skyline. The opponent was Penn State, voted No. 1 by both The Associated Press and United Press International following the Sugar Bowl. And although stars Curt Warner and Todd Blackledge had graduated to the National Football League, the Nittany Lions represented a formidable obstacle to Georgia's plans for a national title.

The early schedule was particularly harsh. After playing Penn State on the unlikely date of Aug. 27, the Bulldogs would play their home opener against UCLA on the night of Sept. 3 and, two weeks after that, would meet Clemson in South Carolina. "It won't take long to find out how good we are," coach Vince Dooley said.

It took approximately 20 seconds. Penn State kicked off away from Walker, as it had in the Sugar Bowl, but Georgia anticipated that and ran a reverse, with Herschel taking the handoff and sprinting 95 yards down the sideline for a touchdown. The Georgia cheering section sang, "Glory, glory, Herschel Walker," and began barking, a most uncommon sound in the North, outside of dog pounds.

32 THE COMPLETE HANDBOOK OF PRO FOOTBALL

The Penn State defense, stripped of several seniors who had been so unyielding in the Superdome, wore down under the pounding of Walker and a huge Bulldog line. Walker broke loose for 36 yards and his third touchdown early in the fourth quarter, sealing a 27-13 victory.

"This may be the best team we've had since I've been here," he said after the game. "I came back because I like the guys on this team and I enjoy school and I want to be part of another national championship. I've never been one to base decisions on money."

A reporter asked Chuck Fairbanks, who watched the game from the press box, how he thought Walker looked. "He looked," said the president and coach of the Generals, "like five million dollars."

Georgia was featured in a second national television extravaganza the following week. But this time the game was played in Sanford Stadium, enlarged by 20,000 seats in Walker's sophomore year and lighted in time for Walker's junior year. Before a record crowd of 81,613 on the first Saturday night in September, the Bulldogs blasted UCLA, the defending Rose Bowl champion, 34-20. Walker accounted for 176 yards and two touchdowns.

On his first carry against Clemson, Herschel took a pitchout and ran seven yards around right end. The gain pushed his career total to 5,602 yards and enabled him to pass Charles White of Southern California as the second-most prolific rusher in NCAA history. The announcement was warmly applauded by the normally partisan Clemson fans, but the next play drew more vociferous cheers. William (The Refrigerator) Perry, the Tigers' massive middle guard, broke through to nail Walker for a five-yard loss. Suddenly, Walker was No. 3 again.

But on Georgia's next series, Walker firmly established himself as No. 2, behind Tony Dorsett of Pitt, gaining 48 yards on a 73-yard scoring drive, the first of two long marches by Georgia in a 17-7 triumph. None of it came easily against a Clemson defense that had forced two Walker fumbles in a victory at Death Valley two years earlier. In 1982, playing with a cast on his broken thumb, Walker had gained only 20 yards in 11 attempts against the Tigers. So Walker's big game—131 yards and two touchdowns—was particularly satisfying.

The Bulldogs were ranked No. 1 in both polls before the next game, against South Carolina in Athens. And when Walker broke two touchdown runs of more than 50 yards, the tailback became an overwhelming favorite to win a second Heisman Trophy. In addition, his 212 yards placed him within range of Dorsett's record. That was significant, because the Bulldogs had one home game before spending two weekends on the road.

It was against Mississippi State on Oct. 1 that Walker set the most memorable of 20 NCAA Division I records. On a delay late in the third quarter, Herschel ran 16 yards over the left side, surpassing Dorsett's four-year mark of 6,082. The quarter ended with Walker on the ground and, when he got up, it was to a standing ovation. He removed his helmet and lifted it to acknowledge the crowd. Then he jogged to the sidelines, his work done for the day, as the Bulldogs coasted to a 35-10 victory.

Georgia tore holes through the first half of the Southeastern Conference schedule, easily adding Mississippi, Vanderbilt and Kentucky to the victim list. Walker averaged 150 yards in those games and gained 125 in only one half against Temple. That left him strong for traditional rival Florida in the annual game at Jacksonville and he responded with a 205-yard effort in a 31-14 rout.

A driving rainstorm and a rugged Auburn defense combined to shut Walker down the following week. He was limited to 78 yards in a 10-10 tie. And there was some concern on campus after a second sub-par performance against Georgia Tech in Atlanta, although the Bulldogs won the game, 16-14, on the third of Kevin Butler's field goals.

When Walker flew to New York to accept the Heisman Trophy, the wire-service polls had Georgia ranked second, behind another SEC team. Under first-year coach Ray Perkins, Alabama had won all 11 games and finished first in the conference. The Tide would be the host team in the Sugar Bowl. The visitors? Why, Georgia, of course.

While it was rare for two teams from the same league to compete in a bowl game, there was no rule preventing it. Georgia and Alabama, the perennial SEC power during the long reign of the late Paul (Bear) Bryant, had never met during Walker's career.

"They're a great team," Walker said. "I consider us the underdogs. If I was a betting man, I'd have to put my money on them. But I think we have a chance."

The chance was named Walker. Making his fourth successive appearance in the Sugar Bowl, Herschel made his final college game a memorable one. Alabama keyed on his thrusts from the I formation, as had Auburn and Georgia Tech, but on the night of Jan. 2 Walker caught seven passes for 130 yards and two touchdowns and ran back a kickoff for another score. The fans barked for Herschel and the Bulldogs one last time on Bourbon Street after a convincing 27-17 victory.

"I think my hands are just as good as anybody's," Walker said. "I like to catch the ball on the run outside."

Now that Walker had added a second national championship,

Another Heisman for Herschel.

a career rushing mark of 7,144 yards and a pass-catching demonstration to his portfolio, the NFL was abuzz with rumors of impending deals for the rights to draft Walker. By virtue or vice of having gone winless for a second season, the Baltimore Colts had the No. 1 pick again. Walker said he wasn't getting involved in the controversy of where he wanted to play. Herschel directed all his inquiries to his attorney, Jack Manton, while he busied himself for the Olympics.

An Olympic gold medal had been a goal of his since high school and he went directly from the football season to the indoor track circuit in preparation for the trials to be held in Los Angeles in mid-June. "This is something I've dreamed of for a long time," Walker said at the Millrose Games in New York. "Pro football can wait another few months. I'll get by."

Walker worked hard on his sprinting technique as outdoor training began in the early spring. Meanwhile, Manton was busy, too. After a get-acquainted meeting with Colts' owner Robert Irsay and coach Woody Hayes, who had been hired after the resignation of Frank Kush, Manton held a news conference to announce he was advising the Colts to trade Walker's rights and to one of four teams: the Atlanta Falcons, the New York Giants, the New York Jets or the Dallas Cowboys.

Irsay was incensed. "He's not going to pull another John Elway on me," the owner said. "He'll play for us or he won't play in this country."

"May I remind Mr. Irsay of the USFL," Manton retorted. "The Generals are still very interested in making Herschel Walker comfortable for life."

The Colts listened to the offers of all four teams and a late proposal from Al Davis, who had earned the approval of Manton by offering to move the Raiders to whatever area pleased Walker, even Wrightsville, Ga., if necessary. But Irsay remained adamant. On draft day, while Walker flew overseas for a series of track meets, the Colts picked Walker.

"That's their privilege," Manton said, "but if they don't trade him before the end of the Olympics, they'll be the loser."

The competition in the 100 meters was fierce. And Walker, although he was as sharp as he had ever been since that day in Wrightsville when he finally outraced his sister, Veronica, could do no better than fourth in the trials. That precluded him from a starting position in one of the showpiece events of the Olympic Games, barring an injury, but it earned him an alternate status. As the fourth-best American at that distance, he would have a chance to run in the 4×100-meter relay.

The Memorial Coliseum was filled to capacity with more than 100,000 fans on Aug. 9 for a full day of track and field. Walker, who had played football in front of huge crowds all his adult life, was nervous nonetheless. "It's nothing," said Carl Lewis, the sprinter-broad jumper from Houston. "Just pretend you're playing Alabama."

"Certainly not Auburn," Harvey Glance said. Glance, the leadoff runner in the relay, had attended Auburn. Walker laughed. 'Remember," Glance cautioned as they limbered on the track, 'no fumbles."

"No fumbles," Walker repeated.

Glance had a two-step lead on the field when he handed the baton to Walker. There was no fumble. With a remarkable burst of speed, the 220-pounder extended the lead between himself and the Cuban team to almost five yards. That was exactly the margin at the finish as Stanley Floyd and Lewis closed out an American victory.

And Herschel Walker, All-American, got to stand on a crowded podium, listen to the Star-Spangled Banner and receive an Olympic gold medal. A solid block of fans wearing red hats and waving Georgia pennants started barking as Walker stepped down. He

Herschel makes tracks on the way to the Olympics.

smiled and waved to them.

Within an hour after the event, witnessed by some 100,000,000 Americans on television, George Steinbrenner was on the phone to Manton. "I'd like you and Herschel to come to New York as my guest," Steinbrenner said. "By the way, has he ever played baseball?"

"I don't know," Manton said, "but I'll find out."

A week later, Steinbrenner proudly presented Walker to the New York press. "Our baseball people tell me he's an excellent prospect," the owner of the Yankees said. "They are convinced he could be our right fielder for a long time to come. Later this week I intend to present Mr. Manton with a firm contract offer similar to what we were prepared to pay John Elway."

Walker found it quite amusing. "Well," he said, "I was pretty accurate throwing rocks when I was about nine or 10. But I never liked standing around in the outfield when I was a kid, so I didn't play baseball."

Manton said the Yankees' offer now gave Walker three alternatives to explore. He listed them this way: 1) the Generals, 2) the Yankees and 3) the Federal Bureau of Investigation. Walker, he said, has always wanted to be a G-man.

"What about the Colts?" a newsman asked.

"Who?" Manton replied.

Finally, Irsay got the hint. Two weeks before the start of the 1984 NFL season, in a transaction which came as a surprise to his coach, the Colts traded Walker's negotiating rights to the Falcons for Lynn Cain and two No. 1s. Walker signed a five-year contract before the day was out for $6,000,000, the largest in the history of pro football.

"I've enjoyed my trips," Walker said, "but the best thing about travel is coming home."

On the eve of the season, the Falcons announced plans to build their own stadium outside of town, adjacent to the airport. It would seat 80,000, according to the architects, and there would be two rows of hedges alongside the field. A statue of a powerful running back would be placed at the main entrance.

"We'd like to keep the identity of the back a secret until the unveiling," said Rankin Smith, the Falcons' president, "but you're free to guess."

Unofficially, of course, he did not object when a reporter called it "The House That Herschel Built." In fact, he barked loudly.

The Computer Takes Over The College Draft

By JOHN CLAYTON

Computers are programmed for perceptiveness. Two years ago an office computer in a New Orleans firm predicted an increase in the unemployment rate: it forecast its own firing. Advised that its new boss was a cowboy with a crewcut, the computer knew it would have to leave town by sundown. New Orleans just wasn't big enough for both the Saints' Bum Phillips and the computer.

Even when Phillips worked in Houston, a leading center in the computer revolution, he considered the machines disposable livestock. So naturally, when Phillips moved his lasso to the Superdome, the first victim was the in-house computer. Bum ain't no Silicon Valley cowboy. He's a football coach.

"I don't need to use a computer to have a bad year drafting," Phillips says. "We can pick our people better than computers."

"Bum said that he didn't want a lot of paperwork," recalls Dick Steinberg, who helped to install the Saints' computer. "He does his notes on legal pads. He doesn't care about the injury record, just as long as the guy is healthy."

But Phillips was never a trend-setter among NFL coaches. Contrary to Phillips' beliefs, most coaches are using computers to evaluate college seniors prior to the draft. Selecting college seniors may be an inexact science, but scouts are beginning to depend upon probability and statistics. These days, if a player

---

John Clayton of the Pittsburgh Press *feeds the computer as a football writer covering the Steelers.*

doesn't have a printout bearing his name in a scout's filing cabinet, then he isn't considered a prospect. In fact, a futuristic trend is taking hold on the league.

"Teams can operate without the computer, but they will be like mom and pop stores," explains Jack Butler, head of the Blesto Scouting Combine, which supplies player ratings for Chicago, Detroit, Philadelphia, Pittsburgh, Minnesota, Baltimore and Miami. "Computers may not be the answer, but they do amazing things. For a scouting combine like ours, they handle the output of a staff of 50. It all depends upon what you put in them. Like they say in computer talk—garbage in, garbage out."

To all of this, Phillips says garbage. For two seasons, his Saints have rebuilt their franchise around draft choices like George Rogers, Russell Gary, Rickey Jackson and Lindsay Scott—all picked without the help of automation. Phillips is so old-fashioned that he doesn't even use modern transportation to scout players during the season. The team's scouts stay in their offices.

"I can find a player without sending scouts on the road," Phillips says. "We have enough contacts around the country to find out who the good players are. And our scouts watch films of players eight hours a day, five days a week. We see more film than anybody else in the league. Then, we get to see the top 200 players when our scouting combine holds its pro day in Tampa. We also get to talk to the players in the college all-star games. If we can't get any idea if they are our kind of player by then, we never will."

Of course, most NFL coaches don't have crewcuts or wear cowboy boots and hats. Around the league, most coaches appreciate the work of computers. Some use them for bookkeeping. Some depend upon them for game plans.

"The computer is like the dollar bill; everyone has one," says Dallas Cowboys' player personnel director Gil Brandt. "Programming today is like driving an auto. Everybody is doing it. Computers are becoming so refined that a large one can process 100,000 payroll checks and answer a 150,000-question exam by the time it takes to draw a cup of coffee. With the Cowboys, it's a way of life for us."

If there is any question about the computers' impact on drafting, simply attend a pro draft day sponsored by scouting combines. Prospects no longer perform only for the scouts; they must please the computer, too. When Blesto assembles the top 100 players in Detroit each year, their individual efforts are recorded by a machine.

"The speed at which the computer can give back the information is amazing," says Dick Haley, the Steelers' director of player personnel. "We can watch all the drills, and then get a complete

COMPUTER 41

The Saints' Bum Phillips prefers critters to computers.

printout with all of the results that day. They can punch a button and give you all the medical information they recorded that day."

"Certain things can be brought out and marked down that might have been forgotten had we done things by hand," says Blesto's Butler.

Harry Buffington, who directs National Football Scouting, Inc. (formerly known as United), forecasts even greater benefits for teams using computers. Buffington sounds like a scientist. He knows computers react quicker than the human eye. So to find the "Six Million Dollar" player, he wants bionic scouts. Tech-

42 THE COMPLETE HANDBOOK OF PRO FOOTBALL

nology has supplied him with the equipment, but transportation hasn't cooperated.

"We have some timing equipment that reacts by laser beam, but the equipment is bulky and we can't carry it around easily," Buffington says. "You can see the benefit. When runners break the beam, the computer records the time. With this, you can determine leg explosion exactly. You would be able to time the 10- and 20-yard dashes precisely. You won't have to depend upon the 40-yard dash. The eye doesn't react quickly enough to count the 10-yard dashes exactly every time. You can get more beneficial times for linemen, who usually don't run 40 yards."

Patience, Harry, patience. In the last 23 years, computerized scouting has come a long way. Predictably, America's computer craze captured the imagination of America's Team, the Cowboys. Gil Brandt believes that though the Cowboys may not have been the first NFL team to use a computer, they were the first to depend on it.

Cowboy owner Clint Murchison and general manager Tex Schramm attended the Winter Olympics in Squaw Valley in 1960 and were impressed with the workings of a computer that was created by a subsidiary of IBM. Dallas had been in the NFL only one year at the time and Murchison and Schramm felt a computer might help. "We thought we could apply the computer to scouting first," Brandt recalls. "On a scale of 1-to-100, it was first thought to be used one-tenth of one percent of the time. When we saw how it would work, we just kept expanding on it. Now, everybody has a desk-top computer."

In many ways, Brandt views his computer the way Captain Kirk viewed the memory banks of the Starship Enterprise in Star Trek. When he negotiates a contract, Brandt can punch buttons on a desk-top computer and watch contract terms and breakdowns on every player in the league. The computer shows a history of every contract talk the player had. On top of that, it supplies breakdowns on salaries by position, by experience, by specific terms. Meanwhile, scouts and coaches can ask for a stereotype of the best player at a certain position. During the season, coaches can evaluate opponents' tendencies.

"You can get a computer to do whatever you want it to," Brandt says. "The classic example is law enforcement. When you used to go into police stations to identify five possible suspects, policemen would pull out piles of books. Now, they can punch a few buttons on a computer and a list of five possible suspects comes out."

One must concede the benefits of pro football's developing technology. The Cowboys have had 17 straight winning seasons and have made the playoffs 16 times, including five trips to the Super Bowl. Computers have helped. Conversely, the Steelers, winners of four Super Bowls, haven't relied on computers very heavily through the years. Haley, however, sees their potential.

"I know that this is the computer age," Haley says. "It's something that we might look into. It would be nice to have access to something that can review information that quickly."

That's one of the problems in scouting. Information becomes too plentiful. Each scout supplies reports on players. Scouting combines supply reports. As teams develop their techniques for evaluating players, file folders grow.

"We have 70 different factors we use to evaluate our players," Buffington says. For the 16 teams that pay for Buffington's NFS ratings, players are rated from one to nine, with nine being the perfect player.

Dallas shares information with San Francisco, Seattle and Buffalo, then each club makes its own player evaluations.

"Ask Gil Brandt what the computer said when it passed over Everson Walls, who wasn't drafted and made all-pro, and then picked Rod Hill in the first round," Phillips says. "Hill hasn't played a lick. What did the computer say, that Walls wasn't a player?"

In its early years with the Cowboys, the computer advised Brandt and coach Tom Landry to pick Mel Renfro, who became a Pro Bowl-caliber defensive back. "We took a long time to make the pick; some people thought the computer broke down," Brandt says. People were equally surprised when the Cowboys made an Ivy League running back, Calvin Hill of Yale, a first-round pick.

"Calvin had all the ingredients of success," Brandt says. "More than that, he had a great desire to excel. He was playing baseball and could have gotten a big contract."

Instead, Hill gained 5,009 yards with the Cowboys and didn't retire until a year ago. Still, most teams aren't as enthusiastic about the computers as Brandt.

"You can use the computer as a checking system," Steinberg says. "We read every report, but then you punch in the information into the computer. It gives you an average and helps eliminate some of the emotional judgments."

Computers simply devour information and make quick presentations. They chart production. They can provide information on catches and drops for wide receivers. They can evaluate numerous statistics for quarterbacks and running backs. They can list all players according to size and speed and rate their production.

"We have been using a computer at Blesto since 1963," Butler

44 THE COMPLETE HANDBOOK OF PRO FOOTBALL

Raiders' Marcus Allen should have been drafted higher.

says. "We have schools rated for the number of pro players they have produced. You can take that into account, say, when you are evaluating a player's competition. You can compare a player from Southern Cal with one who played at Carnegie-Mellon (Division III school in Pittsburgh). It grades reports from area, regional and national scouts. It compares positions so that you can get critical factors like weight, quickness and speed. You can get the 12 quickest players at a particular size. You can even incorporate the weather difficulties a player might experience in a drill or game."

Nobody escapes evaluation. "We can even check the checkers and give scouts personalized grades for their efficiency in evaluating players," Butler adds.

The computer, however, can't control the weather. Buffington remembers a day a year ago when a thunderstorm growled over his office in Oklahoma City. Oklahoma storms can be violent, and this one was exceptionally vicious. Buffington tried to ignore the noise outside, but he suddenly turned pale inside the office. His computer screen went blank. Later, he checked the computer and found its memory had been erased.

"Fortunately, we had enough files to be able to reprogram the computer," Buffington recalls.

Phillips chuckles at that story. That's the problem when people depend on machines. College drafts, he feels, don't need to be so sophisticated. All teams are trying to do is find 12 new employees.

Each year Phillips and Brandt grow further apart with their philosophies. Brandt believes the computer can grade aggressiveness and desire. Buffington agrees. "We are starting to be able to measure heart," Buffington says.

"It works in the insurance business, where the computer is able to show productivity," Brandt says. "Medical schools have been doing it for some time. I don't see why it shouldn't be able to do the same with football players."

Blesto tried to do that, but it found the experiment to be a failure. Now, it no longer grades players for intangible qualities.

"We tried various tests for desire," Butler says. "There are different types of testing that you can use, different than tests of just the players' physical training. We fooled with it for five years, but the results were only semi-valid. So we decided to discontinue it."

Buffington, however, remains optimistic that valid tests of the intangibles are possible. But his grading system has imperfection built in. Since players are rated from one to nine, there are no Bo Dereks:

"The only way to get a 10 is to put two fives together," Buf-

Joe Jacoby didn't compute, but starred with Super 'Skins.

fington says. "Instincts and intelligence go into our totals. We give an aggressiveness grade that goes into the personality of a kid. We are getting closer and closer to revealing the heart of a player. College guidance programs are getting better input on students."

Despite the debates about the validity of personality evaluation, mistakes can be made. Last year two running backs were taken before Southern Cal's Heisman Trophy winner Marcus Allen. Combined, Darrin Nelson of Minnesota and Gerald Riggs of Atlanta gained 435 yards. Allen, a first-round pick (10th overall) of the renegade Raiders, who typically have an independent arrangement for their computer input, rushed for 697 yards and was Rookie of the Year. Many scouting reports had Allen listed as a middle pick in the first round.

"That was incredible, that he didn't go higher," Steinberg says of Allen. "No matter what you put into a computer, he should have been the first back picked. He had all of the statistics, along with the Heisman Trophy. He was never hurt during his four years. He had all of the instincts and speed to run inside or outside. He was an excellent blocker who was a blocking back for Charles White, a former Heisman winner. What else could you want? I guess teams looked at how great the USC line was and devalued Allen. I guess they looked at how some of the USC tailbacks haven't had great success. But Allen had the definite skills. On top of that, he was a good person. We had him rated the best."

In recent years, certain positions have caused the machines greater difficulty. Numerous highly-rated defensive linemen haven't lived up to their advance billing. Leonard Mitchell, Keith Gary, Jeff Bryant, Glen Collins and Lester Williams are all defensive linemen who were first-round picks in the 1981 or 1982 drafts. Only Williams and Bryant became immediate starters. Gary defected to the Canadian Football League, where he spent a disappointing two seasons. The others have only been able to supply spot help.

"It's intriguing," Steinberg says. "Maybe it's the money, but there seems to be more mistakes with the defensive linemen. They look good on the computers, guys who are 6-6 and 249 pounds and can run the 40 in 4.9. They seem to have good attitudes. They come up with big plays on their college films. When they come in, they seem to lack intensity. Maybe it's because they step up a level from where they should be and get the big paycheck."

Computer rejects also defy their ratings. Redskin tackle Joe Jacoby, out of Louisville, wasn't even drafted, but last year he played at all-pro levels and capped his season by dominating Miami's Kim Bokamper in the Super Bowl.

THE COMPLETE HANDBOOK OF PRO FOOTBALL

INSIDE THE NFC

By PAUL ATTNER

PREDICTED ORDER OF FINISH

EAST	CENTRAL	WEST
Washington	Chicago	Atlanta
Dallas	Green Bay	New Orleans
St. Louis	Tampa Bay	San Francisco
New York Giants	Minnesota	Los Angeles Rams
Philadelphia	Detroit	

NFC Champion: Dallas

Okay, who is it going to be this year? Forget Washington, forget San Francisco, forget Philadelphia, forget Los Angeles. They've all been to their one Super Bowl. How about New Orleans? Don't laugh. Just think back to 1981. Did you pick San Francisco to win the NFC title? Did you pick the Redskins to prevail last year? Did you buy the Brooklyn Bridge real cheap?

Parity has played hell with these predictions. You might as well try to name the number of bees in a hive. You've got about that much chance of being correct. Both the 1981 49ers and 1982 Redskins came from nowhere to somewhere in a year. And the Rams and Eagles have returned to no-man's land almost as quickly as they ascended to the top.

But the boss says I've got to make the picks. He's a masochist, I guess. Maybe it's easier to say why some teams shouldn't win. Philadelphia doesn't have enough speed and Marion Campbell never has shown he can be a successful head coach. Dallas is getting used to being a runnerup. The Giants? Well, who can be No. 1 with a former defensive coordinator as head coach? Wrong era.

Paul Attner of the Washington Post *took a champagne bath with the champion Redskins last season.*

INSIDE THE NFC 49

Pro Bowler Dan Hampton helps make Bears a top contender.

That leaves Washington and St. Louis in the Eastern Division. It's hard not to pick the Redskins again, but how can they possibly stay so healthy again? And will John Riggins repeat his performance? The formal choice will be Washington; the hunch pick will be St. Louis. There's no great reason, other than the fact the Cardinals have improved every year under coach Jim Hanifan and seem capable of making the big jump.

Dan Henning will make the Falcons a legitimate power again, good enough to win the West Division in a surprising struggle with the Saints. The Rams have too many defensive holes and the 49ers still are reeling from GM-coach Bill Walsh's wheeling and dealing.

That leaves the Central Division. How about the Bears? Jim McMahon will mature at quarterback, Buddy Ryan will get the defense straightened out and Tampa Bay will find a way to blow a late lead again. Green Bay should be favored, but injuries will mess up the Packers' chances. Minnesota was hurt by a bad draft. Detroit remains Detroit—what player will want to bail out next?

50 THE COMPLETE HANDBOOK OF PRO FOOTBALL
ATLANTA FALCONS

TEAM DIRECTORY: Chairman: Rankin Smith Sr.; Pres.: Rankin Smith Jr.; Exec. VP: Eddie LeBaron; GM: Tom Braatz; Dir. Pub. Rel.: Charlie Dayton; Head Coach: Dan Henning. Home field: Atlanta Stadium (60,748). Colors: Red, black, silver and white.

SCOUTING REPORT

OFFENSE: When the Falcons went to the playoffs, but didn't win last year, that was all Atlanta's front office could take. The Falcons had lost their last two regular-season games, against Green Bay and New Orleans, and then fell to Minnesota in the first round of the playoffs. There was no snap, crackle or pop in this team anymore. So out went coach Leeman Bennett and in came Washington assistant Dan Henning, a thinking man's coach whose strength is offense.

Maybe Henning can restore Steve Bartkowski's confidence. The fans were booing The Golden Boy last year, and he couldn't silence them by throwing one of his famed long passes. He didn't connect with Alfred Jenkins on a single bomb all year. Bennett didn't help by sticking too much to ball control through short passes, thereby putting the wraps on one of the league's best deep throwers. Henning, an advocate of aggressive offense, will loosen the hold a lot, but don't look for the Falcons to become too wild.

The offensive line has good talent and William Andrews could become another John Riggins now that the Falcons will be running out of a one-back set. Henning can rest Andrews, too, by using talented Gerald Riggs in his place.

DEFENSE: For a while, it appeared Atlanta's defense was on an upswing last year after a poor 1981 performance. But it was a misleading impression.

By the time the season was over, Atlanta still was troubled by a lot of defensive difficulties. The Falcons gave up 103 points in their last three games, hardly an encouraging sign. They had no pass rush, and there were quickness problems in the secondary.

Henning has to find a way to generate more pressure on enemy passers. Atlanta had only 18 sacks last year—and seven of those were in one game. The Falcons' rushing defense fell to 10th in the conference and the secondary had only 10 interceptions.

Nose guard Don Smith remains a solid factor, but ends Jeff Yeates and Jeff Merrow can't shake injury problems. An injection of young talent certainly would help. Cornerback Bobby Butler and strong safety Bob Glazebrook are fixtures in the secondary,

ATLANTA FALCONS 51

but the Falcons need more speed at right corner and free safety.

Only at linebacker is the picture really pretty. And that could change if Buddy Curry can't snap back from a knee injury.

KICKING GAME: Dave Smigelsky couldn't do the punting job, so Atlanta turned to veteran George Roberts, who averaged 40.6 yards a kick. Mick Luckhurst was adequate, making 10-of-14 field-goal attempts. There are more glaring problems elsewhere.

William Andrews led the NFC in total yardage with 1,076.

FALCONS VETERAN ROSTER

HEAD COACH—Dan Henning. Assistant Coaches—Dan Sekanovich, John Marshall, Bobby Jackson, Jack Christiansen, Bob Fry, Steve Crosby, Bob Harrison, Garry Puetz, Ted Fritsch, George Dostal.

No.	Name	Pos.	Ht.	Wt.	NFL Exp.	College
31	Andrews, William	RB	6-0	200	5	Auburn
82	Bailey, Stacey	WR	6-0	162	2	San Jose State
10	Bartkowski, Steve	QB	6-4	213	9	California
99	Brown, Clay	TE	6-3	225	2	Brigham Young
46	Brown, Reggie	RB	5-11	211	2	Oregon
66	Bryant, Warren	T	6-6	270	7	Kentucky
23	Butler, Bobby	CB	5-11	170	3	Florida State
21	Cain, Lynn	RB	6-1	205	5	Southern California
89	Curran, William	WR	5-10	175	2	UCLA
50	Curry, Buddy	LB	6-3	221	4	North Carolina
59	Davis, Paul	LB	6-1	215	3	North Carolina
—	DeBruin, Case	P	6-1	176	2	Idaho State
34	Gaison, Blane	S	6-0	185	3	Hawaii
36	Glazebrook, Bob	S	6-1	200	6	Fresno State
83	Hodge, Floyd	WR	6-0	195	2	Utah
64	Howell, Pat	G	6-5	253	6	Southern California
85	Jackson, Alfred	WR	5-11	176	6	Texas
84	Jenkins, Alfred	WR	5-9	155	9	Morris Brown
81	#Johnson, Billy	WR	5-9	170	9	Widener
37	Johnson, Kenny	CB	5-10	176	4	Mississippi State
20	#Jones, Earl	CB	6-0	178	4	Norfolk State
78	Kenn, Mike	T	6-6	260	6	Michigan
14	Komlo, Jeff	QB	6-2	200	5	Delaware
54	Kuykendall, Fulton	LB	6-5	225	9	UCLA
51	Laughlin, Jim	LB	6-0	212	4	Ohio State
18	Luckhurst, Mick	K	6-0	180	3	California
75	Merrow, Jeff	DE	6-4	255	9	West Virginia
87	Mikeska, Russ	TE	6-3	225	5	Texas A&M
80	Miller, Junior	TE	6-4	235	4	Nebraska
15	Moroski, Mike	QB	6-4	200	5	California-Davis
53	Musser, Neal	LB	6-2	218	3	North Carolina State
71	Perko, Mike	DT	6-4	235	2	Utah State
27	Pridemore, Tom	S	5-10	180	6	West Virginia
56	Richardson, Al	LB	6-2	206	4	Georgia Tech
42	Riggs, Gerald	RB	6-1	230	3	Arizona State
12	#Roberts, George	P	6-0	186	6	Virginia Tech
33	Robinson, Bo	RB	6-2	225	5	West Texas State
77	Rogers, Doug	DE	6-5	255	2	Stanford
67	Sanders, Eric	T	6-6	255	3	Nevada-Reno
70	Scott, Dave	G	6-4	265	8	Kansas
61	Scully, John	C	6-5	255	3	Notre Dame
65	Smith, Don	DT	6-5	248	5	Miami
47	#Spivey, Mike	CB	6-0	198	7	Colorado
25	#Strong, Ray	RB	5-9	184	6	Nevada-Las Vegas
68	Thielemann, R.C.	G	6-4	247	7	Arkansas
57	Van Note, Jeff	C	6-2	247	15	Kentucky
52	White, Lyman	LB	6-0	217	3	Louisiana State
58	Williams, Joel	LB	6-0	215	5	Wisconsin-LaCrosse
79	Yeates, Jeff	DE	6-3	248	12	Boston College
63	Zele, Mike	DT	6-3	236	5	Kent State

#Unsigned at press time

TOP FIVE DRAFT CHOICES

Rd.	Name	Sel. No.	Pos.	Ht.	Wt.	College
1	Pitts, Mike	16	DE	6-5	255	Alabama
2	Britt, James	43	DB	5-11	195	Louisiana State
3	Provence, Andrew	75	DE	6-3	255	South Carolina
4	Harper, John	102	LB	6-3	234	Southern Illinois
5	Miller, Brett	129	T	6-7	275	Iowa

ATLANTA FALCONS 53

THE ROOKIES: Defensive end Mike Pitts of Alabama was one of the highest-rated linemen in the draft and the No. 1 pick should help the Falcon pass rush. Cornerback James Britt of LSU, a good second-round selection, could become an instant starter at another weak position.

OUTLOOK: The Falcons are considered by the rest of the league to be a sleeping giant. If Henning can wake them up, watch out. They aren't that many players away from being a legitimate contender. The key won't be the offense—it will be whether the defense can be tightened up considerably.

FALCON PROFILES

STEVE BARTKOWSKI 30 6-4 213   Quarterback

Front office wasn't sure if he still had his confidence by the end of the 1982 season... Another frustrating year for this Golden Boy, who has wonderful talent but usually gets blamed for everything the up-and-down Falcons do wrong... Be interesting to see his progress under new coach Dan Henning, whose specialty as an assistant coach was working with quarterbacks... Finished season with a personal-best completion average (63.4 percent)... Has improved that average each of the last five seasons... No one in football can throw the ball long any better... Threw for 1,905 yards, but was intercepted 11 times.... Born Nov. 12, 1952, in Des Moines, Iowa... Attended University of California.

WILLIAM ANDREWS 27 6-0 200   Running Back

Became a one-man offensive gang once again for the Falcons... When everyone else was faltering, he was playing wonderfully, good enough to make a third straight trip to the Pro Bowl ... Led the NFC in total yardage (1,076), rushing for 573 and amassing 503 more on 42 catches... NFC's fourth-leading rusher and third-best receiver... A third-round draft choice, mostly because of his blocking ability... Somebody at Auburn sure can recruit running backs... Born Dec. 25, 1955, in Thomasville, Ga.

LYNN CAIN 27 6-1 205　　　　　　　　　　　　Running Back

Was supposed to lose his starting job to rookie Gerald Riggs, but played well enough to force a shared-time situation... Now he'll probably have to contend with the Falcons' possible use of a one-back offense, with William Andrews being that one back... There's still room for an outside rusher in that set-up, but he'll have to have a fine training camp... Gained 173 yards on 54 carries in 1982, a long drop from his 915-yard output of 1980... A fullback at USC and that experience might help him this year... Born Oct. 16, 1955, in Los Angeles.

GERALD RIGGS 22 6-1 230　　　　　　　　　　Running Back

Considering that William Andrews does the bulk of the Falcon ball-carrying, he had a decent rookie season, gaining 299 yards on 78 carries... Big and strong and he can only get better... A surprise No. 1 pick for the Falcons, who really needed defensive line help last year—and still do... Could be a factor in a one-back offense, since he has better speed than most 230-pounders... Physical education major and standout player at Arizona State... Born Nov. 6, 1960, in Tulluha, La.... Only son among seven siblings.

MIKE KENN 27 6-6 260　　　　　　　　　　　Offensive Tackle

Meet one of the league's best offensive tackles... A three-time Pro Bowler, he now has established a reputation, so it will be difficult to keep him out of future all-star games... Could become a cornerstone of the Falcons' revised offense... Added strength to complement exceptional quickness, and that has made a difference the past few years... Had a streak of 26 penalty-free games two years ago... This first-round draft choice from Michigan has paid off handsomely... Born Feb. 9, 1956, in Evanston, Ill.... Has varied offseason interests, including gourmet cooking and real-estate investments.

ATLANTA FALCONS 55

JUNIOR MILLER 25 6-4 235   Tight End

Number of catches could increase greatly from last season's 20 if he can provide new coach Dan Henning with needed downfield speed at tight end... Henning won't be afraid to go to his tight end regularly... Has all-pro ability, but just hasn't demonstrated it often enough.... Another Falcon first-round choice at a time when they needed help at other positions, and that has added pressure to his career... Things came very easily to him in 1980, his rookie season, when he made the Pro Bowl... Born Nov. 26, 1957, in Midland, Tex.... Was a consensus All-American his senior year at Nebraska.

TOM PRIDEMORE 27 5-10 180   Safety

One of the league's most interesting personalities... A player in the regular season, a politician in the West Virginia House of Delegates in the offseason... That shows what his home-state fans think of him... Born April 29, 1956, in Ansted, W. Va., and still lives in that town... Attended West Virginia... He is a self-made player who has made yearly improvements through hard work... One year, he showed better peripheral vision, the next, better hands... His strength is his ability to tackle from his free-safety spot... Would benefit if the Falcons could strengthen their cornerback situation.

BUDDY CURRY 25 6-3 221   Linebacker

Coming into this training camp, he will be a major question mark... Sustained ligament damage to his left knee in final regular-season game against New Orleans... Ligament damage is more serious than any other kind of knee injury... Led the Falcons in tackling (60) last year and was showing the talent that made him one of the league's most promising young linebackers... Fits into the developing mold of league linebackers—quick and not very big, but good on pass coverage and blitzing... Born June 4, 1958, in Danville, Va.... A standout at North Carolina, where he was a teammate of another decent linebacker, Lawrence Taylor, now a Giant.

56 THE COMPLETE HANDBOOK OF PRO FOOTBALL
JOEL WILLIAMS 26 6-0 215   Linebacker

There is some question whether a history of bad knees will prevent him from fulfilling the promise he showed as a rookie in 1979.... When he was healthy, there appeared to be no end to his abilities... But when you're this small and you're trying to play linebacker in this league, you need to have quickness and that is where the constant knee problems are hindering him... Stayed healthy through only three weeks of the 1981 season... At least he lasted through the entire 1982 campaign... Was a free agent from Wisconsin-LaCrosse who was cut by the Dolphins... Born Dec. 13, 1956, in Miami.

FULTON KUYKENDALL 30 6-5 225   Linebacker

If nothing else, he has one of the eye-catching names in the NFL.... One of those veteran linebackers who has made a nice living, although he has never been very spectacular... Ironically, he first got the Falcons' attention with his play on special teams, where he earned nickname "Captain Crazy"... Been hindered throughout his career by an assortment of injuries... Former Eagle coach Dick Vermeil who had him at UCLA, says he has a near-genius IQ... Born June 10, 1953, in Coronado, Calif.... Likes to lift weights and dabbles in real estate.

COACH DAN HENNING: This is his first head-coaching job after putting in a long apprenticeship as an assistant coach in the pros and colleges... Comes to the Falcons from Washington, where he was Joe Gibbs' assistant head coach... Helped formulate offensive strategy department and aided in development of the passing game... Worked closely with the receivers and quarterbacks ... It'll be interesting to watch how he handles the pressure and his relationship with the press... "I've prepared myself for this opportunity and I'm looking forward to it," he says... Left Don Shula and the Miami Dolphins to go to Washington, because he wanted to be closely tied to administrative as well as coaching duties... Born June 21, 1942, in New York

Look for Steve Bartkowski to be throwing long again.

City...Attended William and Mary...Also coached with the New York Jets, Houston Oilers, Florida State and Virginia Tech...Played briefly as a quarterback in the Continental League.

GREATEST QUARTERBACK

The Golden Boy.

The very image projected by those two words is something special in the world of sports. Obviously, the Golden Boy has to be handsome and blond and big and strong and a hero. A football player, too. A quarterback. A Steve Bartkowski.

Like the song says he has it all. But it took him half of his pro career to funnel that talent into consistency, to make the Atlanta Falcons into bonafide playoff contenders. And then when the Falcons slumped last season and coach Leeman Bennett was fired, there were whispers about Bartkowski. Not the old ones about his fast life; he has given that up. No, these were about his guts. Maybe he didn't stay in the pocket as well, maybe he panicked on passes more, not waiting for patterns to develop.

For the only truly talented quarterback in Falcon history, those were tough words to handle. At age 30, after eight years in Atlanta, he has to prove himself once again, something he seems to have been doing almost yearly since coming out of the University of California. So much for the fun of being the Golden Boy.

INDIVIDUAL FALCON RECORDS

Rushing

Most Yards Game:	167	William Andrews, vs New Orleans, 1979
Season:	1,308	William Andrews, 1980
Career:	4.205	William Andrews, 1979-82

Passing

Most TD Passes Game:	4	Randy Johnson, vs Chicago, 1969
	4	Steve Bartkowski, vs New Orleans, 1980
	4	Steve Bartkowski, vs St. Louis, 1981
Season:	31	Steve Bartkowski, 1980
Career:	116	Steve Bartkowski, 1975-82

Receiving

Most TD Passes Game:	3	Alfred Jenkins, vs New Orleans, 1981
Season:	13	Alfred Jenkins, 1981
Career:	39	Alfred Jenkins, 1975-82

Scoring

Most Points Game:	18	Lynn Cain, vs Oakland, 1979
	18	Alfred Jenkins, vs New Orleans, 1981
	18	William Andrews, vs Denver, 1982
Season:	114	Mick Luckhurst, 1981
Career:	270	Nick Mike-Mayer, 1973-77
Most TDs Game:	3	Lynn Cain, vs Oakland, 1979
	3	Alfred Jenkins, vs New Orleans, 1981
	3	William Andrews, vs Denver, 1982
Season:	13	Alfred Jenkins, 1981
Career:	39	Alfred Jenkins, 1975-82

CHICAGO BEARS

TEAM DIRECTORY: Chairman/Pres: George Halas; VP: Edward McCaskey; Exec. VP/GM: Jim Finks; Treasurer: Jerome Vainisi; Dir. Pro Scouting: Bill Tobin; Dir. Pub. Rel.: Patrick McCaskey; Head Coach: Mike Ditka. Home field: Soldier Field (65,793). Colors: Orange, navy blue and white.

Walter Payton continues his chase of Jim Brown's record.

60 THE COMPLETE HANDBOOK OF PRO FOOTBALL
SCOUTING REPORT

OFFENSE: You have to start with quarterback Jim McMahon. Suddenly, you don't see anything being written about the Bears' quarterback problem. There's a good reason. There isn't one anymore. Coach Mike Ditka brought McMahon along slowly, not starting him at first. But even then it was obvious he was the class of the Bear quarterbacks and now it appears he should be in that spot a long time—if the Bears will pay him enough money the next time they talk contract.

Ditka needs to build up the offensive line to give McMahon more protection. McMahon showed he could throw on the run, but that's a dangerous way to live. It will help if Dennis Lick, Ted Albrecht and Revie Sorey can stay healthy and rookie tackle Jimbo Covert is a fast learner. Walter Payton would second that motion. He gained 596 yards behind a patchwork line that hardly resembled the Bears' strong units of a few years ago.

It also would help if receiver James Scott can play an injury-free season. He caught only two passes last year. Tight end Emery Moorehead made a fine transition from wide receiver, catching 30 passes. But he isn't much of a blocker.

DEFENSE: Defensive coordinator Buddy Ryan was retained by owner George Halas prior to Ditka's hiring, so no one will ever know if the new coach would have kept Ryan around if he had had a say. But now Ditka is having his say. He wasn't all that pleased with the way the Bears played defense last year. He didn't see enough zones in the secondary and he would like to see more 3-4 fronts. Ryan has always relied on a lot of man-to-man coverage and blitzes to confuse offenses, but all those tactics got the Bears last season was frustration, as opponents scored lots of points.

Dan Hampton is a standout as defensive tackle and both Gary Fencik and Mike Singletary had fine years to make Ditka at least a little happy. Anyway, according to Ryan, things aren't as bad as they look. A little patching there, a little pasting here and the Bears should be almost as good as old.

KICKING GAME: Ditka admits he made a big mistake by cutting Bob Thomas and keeping John Roveto as the placekicker. Ditka finally called Thomas back, but says his initial decision cost the Bears at least two early-season wins. He stayed with Bob Parsons as the punter, a good move.

THE ROOKIES: Payton should feel better about running behind Pittsburgh's Covert, a massive 280-pound No. 1 pick with good

CHICAGO BEARS 61

BEARS VETERAN ROSTER

HEAD COACH—Mike Ditka. Assistant Coaches—Jim Dooley, Dale Haupt, Ed Hughes, Jim LaRue, Ted Plumb, Johnny Roland, Buddy Ryan, Dick Stanfel.

No.	Name	Pos.	Ht.	Wt.	NFL Exp.	College
64	Albrecht, Ted	T-G	6-4	250	6	California
7	#Avellini, Bob	QB	6-2	210	9	Maryland
84	Baschnagel, Brian	WR	6-0	184	8	Ohio State
79	Becker, Kurt	G	6-5	251	2	Michigan
25	Bell, Todd	S	6-1	207	3	Ohio State
54	Cabral, Brian	LB	6-1	224	5	Colorado
59	Campbell, Gary	LB	6-1	220	7	Colorado
57	Chesley, Al	LB	6-3	240	5	Pittsburgh
72	Doerger, Jerry	T	6-5	270	2	Wisconsin
81	Earl, Robin	TE	6-5	240	7	Washington
8	Evans, Vince	QB	6-2	212	7	Southern California
45	#Fencik, Gary	S	6-1	192	8	Yale
24	Fisher, Jeff	S	5-11	188	3	Southern California
21	Frazier, Leslie	CB	6-0	189	3	Alcorn State
—	Frederick, Andy	T	6-6	265	7	New Mexico
29	Gentry, Dennis	RB	5-8	173	2	Baylor
99	#Hampton, Dan	DT	6-5	255	5	Arkansas
35	Harper, Roland	RB	5-11	210	8	Louisiana Tech
90	Harris, Al	DE	6-5	250	5	Arizona State
73	Hartenstine, Mike	DE	6-3	243	9	Penn State
71	Hartnett, Perry	G	6-5	275	2	Southern Methodist
51	#Herron, Bruce	LB	6-2	220	6	New Mexico
63	Hilgenberg, Jay	C	6-3	250	3	Iowa
65	Jackson, Noah	G	6-3	265	9	Tampa
62	#Jiggetts, Dan	T	6-5	270	8	Harvard
70	Lick, Dennis	T	6-3	265	8	Wisconsin
82	#Margerum, Ken	WR	5-11	170	3	Stanford
37	McClendon, Willie	RB	6-1	205	5	Georgia
67	McKinney, Phil	T	6-4	250	8	UCLA
9	McMahon, Jim	QB	6-0	187	2	Brigham Young
76	McMichael, Steve	DT	6-1	245	4	Texas
87	Moorehead, Emery	TE	6-2	210	7	Colorado
58	#Muckensturm, Jerry	LB	6-4	220	7	Arkansas State
52	Neal, Dan	C	6-4	255	11	Kentucky
68	Osborne, Jim	DT	6-3	245	12	Southern
87	Parsons, Bob	DT	6-3	225	12	Penn State
34	Payton, Walter	RB	5-11	204	9	Jackson State
—	#Saldi, Jay	TE	6-3	230	8	South Carolina
44	#Schmidt, Terry	CB	6-0	177	10	Ball State
89	Scott, James	WR	6-1	190	7	Henderson JC
50	Singletary, Mike	LB	6-0	230	3	Baylor
69	Sorey, Revie	G	6-2	260	8	Illinois
26	Suhey, Matt	RB	5-11	217	4	Penn State
16	Thomas, Bob	K	5-10	175	8	Notre Dame
33	Thomas, Calvin	RB	5-11	220	2	Illinois
78	Van Horne, Keith	T	6-7	265	3	Southern California
75	Waechter, Henry	DE	6-6	270	2	Nebraska
23	#Walterscheid, Lenny	S	5-11	190	7	South Utah State
80	Watts, Rickey	WR	6-1	203	5	Tulsa
88	Williams, Brooks	TE	6-4	226	6	North Carolina
43	Williams, Walt	CB	6-1	185	7	New Mexico State
55	Wilson, Otis	LB	6-2	222	4	Louisville

#Unsigned at press time

TOP FIVE DRAFT CHOICES

Rd.	Name	Sel. No.	Pos.	Ht.	Wt.	College
1	Covert, Jimbo	6	T	6-5	279	Pittsburgh
1	Gault, Willie	18	WR	6-2	178	Tennessee
2	Richardson, Mike	33	DB	6-0	190	Arizona State
3	Duerson, Dave	64	DB	6-3	202	Notre Dame
4	*Thayer, Tom	91	C-G	6-5	268	Notre Dame

*Signed with Chicago Blitz of USFL

62 THE COMPLETE HANDBOOK OF PRO FOOTBALL

credentials. The problem with receiver Willie Gault, a second-rounder from Tennessee, is that he is so fast, he may wait for the Olympic Games.

OUTLOOK: The Bears will go as far as McMahon and defensive improvement will take them this season. This isn't a great team, but it should be competitive. And a lot will depend on the coaching. Ditka has had a year to catch on to his new job, so he may improve, too.

BEAR PROFILES

WALTER PAYTON 29 5-11 204   **Running Back**

Settled into a pattern of good seasons and questions about his future in Chicago... Sometimes wonders aloud whether he wants to continue his career, at least as a Bear... May be the highest-paid player in the league... Was the NFC's No. 3 rusher last year, with 596 yards and an average of 4.0 yards per carry... Also became a more productive receiver in coach Mike Ditka's offense, with 32 catches for 311 yards... Now has career rushing total of 10,204 yards and hints that he wants to stay around long enough to make a run at Jim Brown's career NFL rushing record (12,312)... Born July 25, 1954, in Columbia, Mo.... Leading scorer in NCAA history with 464 points for Jackson State.

JIM McMAHON 24 6-0 187   **Quarterback**

Became the answer to the Bears' long-standing problem at quarterback... Mike Ditka finally handed the job to him and now the coach says the Bears are set there for years to come... Fifth player taken in the 1982 draft... Consensus All-American at Brigham Young, where he set 56 NCAA Division I records for passing and total offense... Finished as the fourth-rated NFC passer last season, with an 80.1 rating... Passed for 1,501 yards, with nine touchdowns and seven interceptions... "He has a great ability to avoid throwing passes that can be intercepted," Ditka says... Born Aug. 21, 1959, in Jersey City, N.J.... BYU was 22-3 while he was a starter.

CHICAGO BEARS 63
GARY FENCIK 29 6-1 192 — Safety

Closing in on Bears' all-time career interception record—he's five short of passing Bennie McRae (27) for second place... Not bad for this underrated former Ivy League star... Had a wonderful 1982 season... Led the team in tackles (82), including 30 assists... Now has been the team's top tackler five times in the last six years... All this from a former free agent... Works for a cable television outfit, is a member of the U.S. Volleyball Association and is studying for a master's in business... Born June 11, 1954, in Chicago... Graduated from Yale with a B.A. in history.

BOB THOMAS 31 5-10 175 — Kicker

Had to reclaim kicking job from John Roveto during the 1982 season... Roveto finished with more points (22-21), but look at the difference in accuracy: Thomas made 5-of-7 field goals, Roveto only 4-of-13... Remains the most accurate kicker in Bear history and is closing in on Mac Percival's club field-goal record (99)... Already the fourth-leading scorer in Bears' annals... Born Aug. 7, 1952, in Rochester, N.Y.... His 1981 season was marred by a pulled hamstring... Academic All-American at Notre Dame and law school graduate who is breaking into the commodities market.

EMERY MOOREHEAD 29 6-2 210 — Tight End

One of Mike Ditka's personnel moves that paid off... Here is a former wide receiver and kick returner—you know how they hate to block—playing tight end and earning a starting job... Provided the Bears with better receiving from that position, something ex-tight end Ditka thought they desperately needed... Added 10 pounds to his frame, but still might be the smallest regular NFL tight end... Caught 30 passes, second on the team, for 363 years, a team high... Also had five touchdowns, best among the receivers... Sixth-round draft choice of the Giants in 1977 after a decent career at Colorado... Also has played for Denver... Born March 22, 1954, in Evanston, Ill.... Hadn't caught a pass in two seasons.

BOB PARSONS 33 6-5 225   Punter

Still listed as "punter-tight end" although he hasn't caught a NFL pass since 1976... Wonder what position he would have played if Mike Ditka had been his original head coach in Chicago?... In shortened 1982 season, he enjoyed his highest pro average for punting (41.3 yards per kick)... It was third time he has averaged over 40 yards... Had a 81-yarder, breaking his old career-best mark by 19 yards... Former Penn State quarterback, who was switched to tight end as a senior, has completed seven of 12 passes from punt formation since joining the Bears... Born June 29, 1950, in Bethlehem, Pa.... Works with construction equipment company in the offseason.

MATT SUHEY 25 5-11 217   Running Back

Once again emerged as Walter Payton's backfield mate, becoming a maturing receiver out of the backfield... Caught a career-high 36 passes, which led the team... Had only 40 catches in his first two pro years... Gained 105 rushing yards, and the Bears would like that total to increase... Was the seventh running back taken in the 1980 draft after starting four years at Penn State... Left college as the second-leading rusher in Penn State history, trailing only Lydell Mitchell... Born July 7, 1958, in Bellefonte, Pa.... Father and two brothers have played for Penn State.

DAN HAMPTON 25 6-5 255   Defensive Tackle

Meet perhaps the best defensive tackle in the league last year... Probably leapfrogged ahead of Randy White during his first season since moving over from defensive end... Still made the Pro Bowl and many all-pro teams at his new position... Was second on the team in tackles (71), trailing only Gary Fencik... Had seven sacks, which placed him among the league leaders... Now has 32 sacks in four years... A quality first-round choice out of Arkansas who should get even better... Has outstanding quickness and desire to go along with great natural ability... Born Sept. 19, 1957, in Oklahoma City, Okla.... Plays six instruments and has a pet pig.

CHICAGO BEARS

MIKE HARTENSTINE 30 6-3 243
Defensive End

Regained starting position he had lost the year before, in part because his broken thumb healed with the help of pins... Wound up with 4½ sacks, the third-best total on the team, and 24 tackles in 1982... Durable player who rarely misses playing time... Considered one of the league's strongest players... Lifts weights daily in the offseason, with normal day including four hours of lifting 100,000 pounds... Born July 27, 1953, in Allentown, Pa.... A consensus All-American at Penn State, but a linebacker in high school... Has a 48-inch chest, 34-inch waist.

NOAH JACKSON 32 6-2 265
Guard

Seems he should be at the end of his career, but he continues to hold down starting position on the Bears' changing offensive line... Gained some fame during Walter Payton's glory years, when he was considered the glue that held together a very good line... Drafted by the Colts, he came to the Bears in a 1975 trade... Was a Canadian Football League player for three years and is one of few players to have started playoff games in both the CFL and the NFL... Born April 14, 1951, in Jacksonville, Fla.... Standout at University of Tampa, which he left after his junior year, in 1972.

COACH MIKE DITKA: Had a rocky and sometimes stormy first season as the Bears' head coach... But that was to be expected... Always has been known for his frankness and fire... Admitted he made some mistakes during his first season as a head coach on any level... But he is determined to do things his way with the Bears, which means restoring the team's toughness and hopefully its position among the league elite... May have brought some stability to the quarterback position by installing Jim McMahon... Previously, the Bears had refused to use a first-round choice to take care of obvious quarterback problem... Will get more involved with the defense, which used too many formations and changed too much for his liking last year... Born Oct. 18, 1939, in Carnegie, Pa.... Two-way performer for University of Pittsburgh... One of the NFL's all-time great tight ends for Dallas, Philadelphia and Chicago, he set a standard for that position.

COMPLETE HANDBOOK OF PRO FOOTBALL

GREATEST QUARTERBACK

The first time he lined up behind the center—behind the center, for God's sake, not seven yards deep in the backfield—Sid Luckman tripped over his own feet on the opening play. But he soon gained his sense of balance—and then some.

This was the quarterback who showed the world that George Halas' new T-formation could work. And in the process, he put to sleep the single wing, the offense which got him into the pros in the first place.

A product of New York City and Columbia University, where he'd been a single-wing quarterback in the era when college and pro teams played single wing, Luckman became the pioneer T-quarterback in the pros in 1939 when he joined the Bears.

In 1940 he quarterbacked the Bears to a 73-0 rout of the Redskins in a memorable NFL championship game. He was the NFL's MVP in 1943, when the Bears won the championship again, a season in which Luckman threw for seven touchdowns in one game. And he quarterbacked Chicago to the title in 1946.

He finished his brilliant career in 1950 with a total of 14,686 passing yards and 139 touchdowns.

INDIVIDUAL BEAR RECORDS

Rushing
Most Yards Game:	275	Walter Payton, vs Minnesota, 1977
Season:	1,852	Walter Payton, 1977
Career:	10,204	Walter Payton, 1975-82

Passing
Most TD Passes Game:	7	Sid Luckman, vs N.Y. Giants, 1943
Season:	28	Sid Luckman, 1943
Career:	137	Sid Luckman, 1939-50

Receiving
Most TD Passes Game:	4	Harlon Hill, vs San Francisco, 1954
	4	Mike Ditka, vs Los Angeles, 1963
Season:	13	Dick Gordon, 1970
	13	Ken Kavanaugh, 1947
Career:	50	Ken Kavanaugh, 1940-41, 1945-50

Scoring
Most Points Game:	36	Gale Sayers, vs San Francisco, 1965
Season:	132	Gale Sayers, 1965
Career:	541	George Blanda, 1949-58
Most TDs Game:	6	Gale Sayers, vs San Francisco, 1965
Season:	22	Gale Sayers, 1965
Career:	79	Walter Payton, 1975-82

DALLAS COWBOYS

DALLAS COWBOYS 67

TEAM DIRECTORY: Chairman: Clint Murchison Jr.; Pres./GM: Tex Schramm; VP-Player Development: Gil Brandt; VP-Administration: Joe Bailey; Pub. Rel. Dir.: Doug Todd; Head Coach: Tom Landry. Home field: Texas Stadium (65,101). Colors: Royal blue, metallic blue and white.

Dallas' ground game is named Tony Dorsett.

68 THE COMPLETE HANDBOOK OF PRO FOOTBALL
SCOUTING REPORT

OFFENSE: Ah, the fine scent of a quarterback duel. Nothing livens up training camp more or fills up newspaper space better than these battles. And there is no reason why the Cowboys shouldn't have a beauty, even though Danny White has been a wonderful replacement for Roger Staubach the last three years.

Waiting to take over his spot is young Gary Hogeboom, who always has had the potential, but never got a chance to show it until he played so well against Washington in the NFC title game after White was hurt. Now coach Tom Landry says they will get equal shots at winning the job.

That may be the spark Dallas needs to have more consistency. The Cowboys just couldn't roll on all cylinders after the strike, even though Tony Dorsett finished strongly. Landry hints that he may use more one-back offense this year, using Dorsett as the one back. Otherwise, the cast is so, so familiar: Butch Johnson, Tony Hill and Drew Pearson at end, Doug Cosbie and friends at tight end, no changes in the line.

Landry would like to get more from receiver Doug Donley, the fastest at the position. Otherwise, the action is at quarterback.

DEFENSE: The Redskins showed that teams can move the ball on Dallas, even when the Cowboys want to play good defense. And there are too many times that they aren't inspired at all. And that causes Landry concern.

Randy White was an all-pro last year who didn't have the best of seasons. He is working on new moves to work his way free from extra attention. It would help if John Dutton would remain healthy. When he is, it takes some of the pressure off White, who can't be double-teamed as easily. Another problem for the front four is age, since everyone but White is really getting on in years. But don't tell that to Too Tall Jones, who is playing the best football of his career.

Linebacking is the weakness of the defense. Landry loves Bob Breunig in the middle, especially his smarts, but there wasn't a lot of consistency on the outside last year. Mike Hegman has a lot of talent on one side and Anthony Dickerson failed to win the job on the other.

There may be a change in the secondary, where strong safety Benny Barnes will be challenged by Dextor Clinkscale and Monty Hunter.

KICKING GAME: Landry still is searching for a punter to replace Danny White to cut down on the risk of injury and take

DALLAS COWBOYS 69

COWBOYS VETERAN ROSTER

HEAD COACH—Tom Landry. Assistant Coaches—Jim Myers, Ermal Allen, Neill Armstrong, Al Lavan, Alan Lowry, Dick Nolan, Jim Shofner, Gene Stallings, Ernie Stautner, Jerry Tubbs, Bob Ward.

No.	Name	Pos.	Ht.	Wt.	NFL Exp.	College
62	Baldinger, Brian	C-G	6-4	253	2	Duke
31	Barnes, Benny	S	6-1	204	12	Stanford
76	Bethea, Larry	DT	6-5	244	6	Michigan State
53	Breunig, Bob	LB	6-2	225	9	Arizona State
59	Brown, Guy	LB	6-4	227	7	Houston
18	Carano, Glenn	QB	6-3	204	7	Nevada-Las Vegas
47	Clinkscale, Dextor	S	5-11	190	3	South Carolina State
61	Cooper, Jim	T	6-5	263	7	Temple
84	Cosbie, Doug	TE	6-6	232	5	Santa Clara
51	Dickerson, Anthony	LB	6-2	222	4	Southern Methodist
83	Donley, Doug	WR	6-0	173	3	Ohio State
67	Donovan, Pat	T	6-5	257	9	Stanford
33	Dorsett, Tony	RB	5-11	192	7	Pittsburgh
26	Downs, Michael	S	6-3	203	3	Rice
89	DuPree, Billy Joe	TE	6-4	223	11	Michigan State
78	Dutton, John	DT	6-7	275	10	Nebraska
27	Fellows, Ron	CB	6-0	174	3	Missouri
58	Hegman, Mike	LB	6-1	288	8	Tennessee State
25	Hill, Rod	CB	6-0	182	2	Kentucky State
80	Hill, Tony	WR	6-2	198	7	Stanford
14	Hogeboom, Gary	QB	6-4	199	4	Central Michigan
34	Hunter, Monty	S	6-0	202	2	Salem (W. Va.)
86	Johnson, Butch	WR	6-1	187	8	California-Riverside
72	Jones, Ed	DE	6-9	270	9	Tennessee State
23	Jones, James	RB	5-10	202	4	Mississippi State
57	King, Angelo	LB	6-1	230	3	South Carolina State
79	Martin, Harvey	DE	6-5	260	11	East Texas State
44	#Newhouse, Robert	FB	5-10	219	12	Houston
30	Newsome, Timmy	RB	6-1	231	4	Winston-Salem State
88	Pearson, Drew	WR	6-0	193	11	Tulsa
22	Peoples, George	FB	6-0	211	2	Auburn
65	Petersen, Kurt	G	6-4	268	4	Missouri
75	Pozderac, Phil	T	6-9	270	2	Notre Dame
64	Rafferty, Tom	C-G	6-3	259	8	Penn State
70	Richards, Howard	G-T	6-6	258	3	Missouri
50	Rohrer, Jeff	LB	6-3	232	2	Yale
68	Scott, Herbert	G	6-2	260	9	Virginia Union
1	Septien, Rafael	K	5-10	180	7	Southwest Louisiana
52	Shaw, Robert	C	6-4	261	4	Tennessee
60	Smerek, Don	DT	6-7	257	3	Nevada-Reno
55	Spradlin, Danny	LB	6-1	241	3	Tennessee
20	Springs, Ron	FB	6-1	210	5	Ohio State
32	Thurman, Dennis	CB	5-11	183	6	Southern California
63	Titensor, Glen	C-G	6-4	260	3	Brigham Young
24	Walls, Everson	CB	6-1	189	3	Grambling
66	Wells, Norm	T	6-5	261	2	Northwestern
11	White, Danny	QB	6-2	192	8	Arizona State
54	White, Randy	DT	6-4	260	9	Maryland
15	Wright, Brad	QB	6-2	209	2	New Mexico
73	Wright, Steve	G-T	6-5	263	3	Northern Iowa

#Unsigned at press time

TOP FIVE DRAFT CHOICES

Rd.	Name	Sel. No.	Pos.	Ht.	Wt.	College
1	Jeffcoat, Jim	23	DE	6-5	255	Arizona State
2	Walter, Mike	50	DE	6-3	230	Oregon
3	Caldwell, Bryan	77	DE	6-4	248	Arizona State
4	Faulkner, Chris	108	TE	6-5	253	Florida
5	McSwain, Chuck	135	RB	6-2	190	Clemson

70 THE COMPLETE HANDBOOK OF PRO FOOTBALL

pressure off the quarterback. Rafael Septien kicked well in the playoffs and has become a star, though he's not always as steady as Landry would like. Return-game mistakes hurt the Cowboys badly in the NFC title game.

THE ROOKIES: The Cowboys have not drafted particularly well lately when going after defensive linemen. But that didn't prevent them from taking three—Arizona State's Jim Jeffcoat and Bryan Caldwell and Oregon's Mike Walter—as their top three choices. Jeffcoat, the No. 1 pick, could help immediately, although he isn't that quick on the pass rush.

OUTLOOK: It always seems the same. With so many talented players and with the league so balanced, the Cowboys always are contenders, but they don't seem quite good enough to put teams away anymore. They've lost in the NFC title game the last three years, a string they'd desperately like to break.

COWBOY PROFILES

DANNY WHITE 31 6-2 192   Quarterback

Strange season for this talented Cowboy quarterback... Played well enough to make the Pro Bowl—he threw the winning touchdown pass to John Jefferson in the final seconds—but he still came under heavy criticism, some from within the team... Seems his inability to get the Cowboys into the Super Bowl has brought up questions about his leadership... He says some of the veterans on the team have to do a better job of leading the younger players... Finished with the highest rating of his career (91.08) and threw for 16 touchdowns and 2,079 yards... Was knocked out on his feet by a Dexter Manley sack in the NFC title game against Washington and didn't play in the second half... Born Feb. 9, 1952, in Mesa, Ariz., and attended Arizona State.

DALLAS COWBOYS 71
TONY DORSETT 29 5-11 192   Running Back

Finished the regular season in spectacular fashion with a 99-yard touchdown run against Minnesota, the longest in NFL history... Now is the NFL's 10th all-time leading rusher (7,015 yards) after gaining 745 yards last season... Only Steelers' Franco Harris has gained more career playoff yards... Yet Dorsett was inconsistent, especially after the strike ended... Sometimes seemed to lack the fire he showed in 1981, his best season... Still, which NFL team wouldn't take him?... Born April 7, 1954, in Rochester, Pa.... This former University of Pittsburgh star is called "the epitome of an artist" by Jim Brown.

EVERSON WALLS 23 6-1 189   Cornerback

A legitimate All-American success story... Nobody wanted him in the 1981 draft even though he had played well at Grambling, so he wound up signing with the Cowboys as a free agent... And he led the NFL in interceptions his first two pro years... No one had done that before in his initial two seasons, and only Philadelphia's Bill Bradley had ever led the NFL in back-to-back seasons... Picked off seven passes last year after intercepting 11 his rookie season... Has four interceptions in two Pro Bowl appearances... There is more to his story, too... Born Dec. 28, 1959, in Dallas, he was raised two miles from the Cowboys' practice field.

RANDY WHITE 30 6-4 260   Defensive Tackle

For the first time in his wonderful career, there were questions about his performance last season... Made all the all-pro teams and was named to the Pro Bowl for sixth straight year, but may not have played up to his usual standards... He is so good, he automatically makes the all-star teams... Usually considered the premier defensive tackle in the league... Came to camp last year at 270 pounds and perhaps that was too heavy to maintain his quickness... Cowboys tried to get him free of double-teaming by lining him up at linebacker during playoffs... Born Jan. 15, 1953, in Wilmington, Del.... Attended University of Maryland... Doesn't enjoy the spotlight... Would rather fish and hunt.

72 THE COMPLETE HANDBOOK OF PRO FOOTBALL

ED (TOO TALL) JONES 32 6-9 270   Defensive End

Since coming back from one-year hiatus he took to pursue ill-fated boxing career in 1979, he has played better than ever... Made the Pro Bowl and received all-pro mention for the second straight season... Has become the dominating force everyone thought he would be from the start... Imagine, a 6-9 defensive end... Has a rhythm-and-blues album on the market on which he sings... Dare you to tell him he is off-key... Another Jones record was entitled, "Do the Dip '81/Funkin' on Your Radio"... Born Feb. 2, 1951, in Jackson, Tenn.... Teammate at Tennessee State dubbed him "Too Tall"... Has done some acting.

RAFAEL SEPTIEN 29 5-9 174   Kicker

Holds NFL playoff records for field-goal accuracy and consecutive field goals made... Kicked a 50-yarder against Green Bay in the playoffs, the second-longest field goal in playoff history... Cowboys' all-time leading scorer with 462 career points, breaking Bob Hayes' mark of 456... Born Dec. 12, 1953, in Mexico City... Son of Carlos Septien, member of two Mexican World Cup soccer teams... A two-time NFLPA racquetball champion... Attended Southwest Louisiana and was signed in 1978 as a free agent, after he was cut by the Rams.

GARY HOGEBOOM 25 6-4 201   Quarterback

The Cowboys knew they had a fine talent when they signed him to a lucrative long-term contract prior to the 1982 season, though he had not yet thrown his first NFL pass after two years in Dallas... Finally had a chance to show his talents against Washington in last year's NFC title game, when he almost rallied the Cowboys to victory in second half... Was playing in place of Danny White, who had been sidelined with a concussion... Now there is some question whether White can hold off this challenger in training camp... Led Central Michigan to a conference title in 1979 and was a fifth-round draft choice in 1980... Born Aug. 21, 1958, in Grand Rapids, Mich.... Coaches a woman's softball team in the offseason and his players include Cowboy wives.

DALLAS COWBOYS 73

TONY HILL 27 6-2 198 — Wide Receiver

Make it five straight years as the Cowboys' leading receiver... An impressive string considering he is surrounded by talented pass-catchers... Caught 35 passes for 526 yards last season and added seven more in a playoff game against Green Bay... Adjusts to ball in flight like a great center fielder... Calls his TD celebration routine "Wings of Victory"... Considered the Cowboys' premier big-play man, even more so than Tony Dorsett... A standout at Stanford, he seems to be getting better with more experience in the pros... Born June 23, 1956, in Long Beach, Cal.... Started a sports camp for underprivileged children in Long Beach in 1981.

DREW PEARSON 32 6-0 185 — Wide Receiver

Cowboys' all-time leading receiver (442 receptions for 7,277 yards) and the NFL's second all-time playoff receiver... But you have to wonder how many more good years he has left... Was the Cowboys' No. 3 receiver last season, with 26 receptions... Overshadowed by Tony Hill and, lately, Butch Johnson... Yet the Cowboys still need him for his ability to perform under pressure... Succeeded Joe Theismann as high school quarterback in South River, N.J., where he was born Jan. 12, 1951... Tulsa grad who was signed as a free agent in 1973... Crusades against drug abuse and has done considerable television commentating work.

BOB BREUNIG 30 6-2 225 — Middle Linebacker

Coming off one of his best seasons and was named to the Pro Bowl for the third time... Became more decisive and did more gambling, after years of making sure he executed assignments precisely... Worked after practice on catching passes to improve his hands... One of his strengths is film study and he also does fine job quarterbacking the defense during games.... Only the third middle linebacker in club history (behind Jerry Tubbs and Lee Roy Jordan)... Born July 4, 1953, in Phoenix, Ariz.... Standout at Arizona State... Sells real estate in offseason.

COACH TOM LANDRY: Became a wonderful actor in televison commercials during the players' strike... Did a credit card bit built around the Cowboys-Redskins rivalry that had everyone laughing—even the people in Washington... It was a chance to see the humor of the man, who too often is miscast as a cold, cold customer... Certainly efficient after all these years, but is very approachable, contrary to his image... Working to regain the Super Bowl touch... Cowboys have lost the NFC title game three straight years and that isn't the kind of trend Landry wants to see continue... Could be faced with some interesting personnel decisions in the offseason, including one at quarterback... Born Sept. 11, 1924, in Mission, Tex... Graduate of University of Texas... This will be his 24th year as Cowboys' coach... Career record is 202-115-6, with 17 straight winning seasons, two Super Bowl triumphs... Ranks third all-time in victories among NFL coaches... And to think he almost was hung in effigy by Cowboy fans early in his career.

GREATEST QUARTERBACK

No question Don Meredith sings better. And he has a better sense of humor. And perhaps makes more money, too, but don't count on that. Still, you don't spell Dallas' best quarterback any other way but S-T-A-U-B-A-C-H.

Maybe the two-minute drill was invented for this 1963 Heisman Trophy winner out of the Naval Academy. If it wasn't, Roger Staubach sure made it his own. It got so incredible that the Cowboys kept stats on his heroics. Final count: 14 times in the final two minutes he rallied the Cowboys to victory. Another nine times, he brought them back earlier in the fourth period.

For 11 years (1969-1979) he was a Cowboy—four Super Bowls (two victories)—and he saved one of his greatest feats for his last game as a Cowboy, against the Redskins. Washington was two minutes from the NFC East crown when Staubach got untracked. He threw a pass to Drew Pearson in the final seconds to win the game after his team had once trailed by three touchdowns.

When Captain America, the symbol of America's Team, retired in the spring of 1980, he went out on top, the best way to leave.

DALLAS COWBOYS

INDIVIDUAL COWBOY RECORDS

Rushing

Most Yards Game:	206	Tony Dorsett, vs Philadelphia, 1978
Season:	1,646	Tony Dorsett, 1981
Career:	7,015	Tony Dorsett, 1977-82

Passing

Most TD Passes Game:	5	Eddie LeBaron, vs Pittsburgh, 1962
	5	Don Meredith, vs N.Y. Giants, 1966
	5	Don Meredith, vs Philadelphia, 1966
	5	Don Meredith, vs Philadelphia, 1968
	5	Craig Morton, vs Philadelphia, 1969
	5	Craig Morton, vs Houston, 1970
Season:	28	Danny White, 1980
Career:	153	Roger Staubach, 1969-79

Receiving

Most TD Passes Game:	4	Bob Hayes, vs Houston, 1970
Season:	14	Frank Clarke, 1962
Career:	71	Bob Hayes, 1965-74

Scoring

Most Points Game:	24	Dan Reeves, vs Atlanta, 1967
	24	Bob Hayes, vs Houston, 1970
	24	Calvin Hill, vs Buffalo, 1971
	24	Duane Thomas, vs St. Louis, 1971
Season:	122	Rafael Septien, 1981
Career:	462	Rafael Septien, 1978-82
Most TDs Game:	4	Dan Reeves, vs Atlanta, 1967
	4	Bob Hayes, vs Houston, 1970
	4	Calvin Hill, vs Buffalo, 1971
	4	Duane Thomas, vs St. Louis, 1971
Season:	16	Dan Reeves, 1966
Career:	76	Bob Hayes, 1965-74

76 THE COMPLETE HANDBOOK OF PRO FOOTBALL
DETROIT LIONS

TEAM DIRECTORY: Pres.: William Clay Ford; Exec. VP/GM: Russ Thomas; Dir. Football Operations/Head Coach: Monte Clark; Dir. Player Personnel: Tim Rooney; Dir. Pub. Rel.: Don Kremer. Home field: Pontiac Silverdome (80,638). Colors: Honolulu blue and silver.

Eric Hipple has passed Gary Danielson in race for QB job.

SCOUTING REPORT

OFFENSE: Okay, who is the quarterback? If we were talking about two all-pros, that would be one thing. But the subjects of this debate are Eric Hipple and Gary Danielson, who used a USFL bid to get a nice, fat contract from the Lions, even though he didn't finish the season as No. 1. Hipple did, which makes things very confusing, considering Danielson is older and has taken the Lions nowhere during his time in Detroit.

Coach Monte Clark has to sort out this mess—and fast. He says he wants one quarterback, the two quarterbacks say they want one, too. We'll see.

If Hipple starts, which is likely, he'll probably hope to see improved players around him. The Detroit offense went from No. 1 to mediocrity last year, even though Billy Sims gained 639 yards. Receiver Fred Scott fell from 53 to 13 catches and former No. 1 choice Mark Nichols contributed little again.

Clark benched linemen Russ Bolinger and Karl Baldischwiler during the season, leaving the offensive line in transition. No. 1 choice James Jones should be the power fullback the Lions need to go with Sims.

DEFENSE: Defensive coordinator Maxie Baughan, who learned his stuff under George Allen, left during the offseason to become head coach at Cornell. He left the Lions with questions about their ability to stop the big play and a susceptible secondary.

A key player, defensive end Bubba Baker, wants to be traded after slumping last season. He has the ability to be as good as anyone, but always seems to be hurt or complaining. The defensive signal caller, Stan White, was a free agent. He didn't stay around to listen to new offers from the Lions. Instead he left for the riches of the USFL, taking a lucrative offer from the Chicago Blitz.

The Lions are especially concerned about the secondary, where cornerback James Hunter was forced into early retirement by a neck injury. That leaves nothing but free agents and rookies. That combination proved totally ineffective against Washington in the playoffs last year and that won't help Clark's outlook on this season.

KICKING GAME: Before the strike, punter Tom Skladany and kicker Ed Murray staged a contract walkout, an unprecedented move in league history. The two came back after the strike to have decent seasons, with Murray making 11-of-12 field-goal attempts. A solid area for Detroit.

LIONS VETERAN ROSTER

HEAD COACH—Monte Clark. Assistant Coaches—Don Doll, Fred Hoaglin, Bill Johnson, Joe Madden, Ed Khayat, Mel Phillips, Ted Marchibroda, Larry Seiple, Jackie Simpson.

No.	Name	Pos.	Ht.	Wt.	NFL Exp.	College
60	Baker, Al	DE	6-6	250	6	Colorado State
76	Baldischwiler, Karl	T	6-5	260	6	Oklahoma
54	Barnes, Roosevelt	LB	6-2	220	2	Purdue
24	Bussey, Dexter	FB	6-1	210	10	Texas-Arlington
53	Cobb, Garry	LB	6-2	227	5	Southern California
16	Danielson, Gary	QB	6-2	195	7	Purdue
72	Dieterich, Chris	T	6-3	255	4	North Carolina State
58	Doig, Steve	LB	6-2	240	2	New Hampshire
70	Dorney, Keith	T	6-5	265	5	Penn State
61	Elias, Homer	G	6-2	255	6	Tennessee State
78	English, Doug	DT	6-5	260	7	Texas
—	Fanning, Mike	DT	6-6	255	9	Notre Dame
57	Fantetti, Ken	LB	6-2	227	5	Wyoming
65	Fowler, Amos	C	6-3	253	6	Southern Mississippi
79	Gay, William	DE-DT	6-5	255	6	Southern California
66	Ginn, Tommie	G	6-3	255	3	Arkansas
33	Graham, William	CB-S	5-11	190	2	Texas
26	Gray, Hector	CB-S	6-1	190	3	Florida State
67	Greco, Don	G	6-3	255	2	Western Illinois
62	Green, Curtis	DE-DT	6-3	252	3	Alabama State
35	Hall, Alvin	CB	5-10	184	3	Miami (Ohio)
51	#Harrell, James	LB	6-1	220	5	Florida
81	Hill, David	TE	6-2	230	8	Texas A&I
17	Hipple, Eric	QB	6-1	196	4	Utah State
28	Hunter, James	S	6-2	195	8	Grambling
32	#Kane, Rick	RB	6-0	200	7	San Jose State
25	#King, Horace	FB	5-11	205	9	Georgia
43	Latimer, Al	S	5-11	177	4	Clemson
64	Lee, Larry	G-C	6-2	260	3	UCLA
83	Martin, Robbie	S-WR	5-8	177	3	Cal Poly-SLO
29	McNorton, Bruce	CB-S	5-11	175	2	Georgetown (Ky.)
63	Moss, Martin	DT	6-4	252	2	UCLA
3	#Murray, Ed	K	5-10	170	4	Tulane
86	Nichols, Mark	WR	6-2	213	4	San Jose State
80	Norris, Ulysses	TE	6-4	232	5	Georgia
89	Porter, Tracy	WR	6-1	196	3	Louisiana State
75	Pureifory, Dave	DE	6-1	255	12	Eastern Michigan
84	Rubick, Rob	TE	6-2	228	2	Grand Valley State
87	Scott, Fred	WR	6-2	228	2	Amherst
20	Sims, Billy	RB	6-0	210	4	Oklahoma
—	#Skladany, Tom	P	6-0	195	5	Ohio State
50	#Tautolo, Terry	LB	6-2	227	7	UCLA
39	Thompson, Leonard	WR	5-11	192	9	Oklahoma State
38	Thompson, Vince	FB	6-0	230	2	Villanova
55	Turnure, Tom	C	6-4	250	4	Washington
27	Watkins, Bobby	CB	5-10	184	2	SW Texas State
59	Williams, Jimmy	LB	6-3	221	2	Nebraska

#Unsigned at press time

TOP FIVE DRAFT CHOICES

Rd.	Name	Sel. No.	Pos.	Ht.	Wt.	College
1	Jones, James	13	RB	6-3	235	Florida
2	Strenger, Rich	40	T	6-7	261	Michigan
3	Cofer, Mike	67	DE	6-5	227	Tennessee
4	Curley, August	94	LB	6-3	225	Southern California
5	Johnson, Demetrious	115	DB	6-1	190	Missouri

DETROIT LIONS 79

THE ROOKIES: The Lions made a wonderful first-round selection in Jones, the powerful fullback from Florida. He should pair well with Sims and he also catches well out of the backfield. Tackle Rich Strenger of Michigan, the second-round choice, will compete for a starting spot, while linebacker Mike Cofer of Tennessee may be a year away.

OUTLOOK: To some observers, this is a team in trouble. One thing about the Lions: they never seem to live up to expectations. Clark may have trouble keeping his job for much longer if the team stumbles again—Detroit has had only one winning record in his five years.

LION PROFILES

BILLY SIMS 27 6-0 210　　　　　　　　　　　**Running Back**

Has reached a level where excellence is expected... Name the best five running backs in the league and you'd be wrong if you left his name out... Stronger and faster than most of his rivals... Finished second to Dallas' Tony Dorsett in rushing among NFC backs last year with 639 yards on 172 carries, even though he held out for most of training camp... His contract unhappiness could hurt the Lions down the road... They'd better give him what he wants before he switches leagues... Born Sept. 18, 1955, in St. Louis... Won the 1978 Heisman Trophy at Oklahoma... Gained 1,303 and 1,437 yards in first two NFL seasons, scoring 13 TDs each year.

ERIC HIPPLE 26 6-1 196　　　　　　　　　　　**Quarterback**

The Lions entered training camp expecting him to win the starting spot from Gary Danielson... At least that is how the picture looked at the end of last season, when Hipple quarterbacked the Lions against Washington in the NFC playoffs... Couldn't handle the Redskins' complex coverages, but not many quarterbacks can... Got his break the year before, when Danielson was hurt and Jeff Komlo couldn't do the job, and threw for 2,358 yards, 14 TDs... A fourth-round pick from Utah State in 1980 who didn't throw a pass his rookie season... Born

GARY DANIELSON 31 6-2 195 Quarterback

Training to be a television sports announcer... Probably should learn the trade quickly, since his future may be limited, at least in the NFL... Couldn't keep his starting spot last year and watched as Eric Hipple guided the Lions in the playoffs... First lost job to Hipple in 1981 after breaking a wrist early in the season... Born Sept. 10, 1951, in Detroit... Prepared for the pros at Purdue... Was working on a car assembly line when the Lions signed him as a free agent in 1976... Set Detroit passing records for completions (244) and passing yardage (3,223) in 1980... Wound up last season as the lowest-rated passer among NFC quarterbacks, completing 100 of 197 for 1,343 yards, 10 TDs and 14 interceptions.

AL BAKER 26 6-6 250 Defensive End

Some of the luster is starting to wear off his superstar status... Not nearly as consistent or as explosive as he has been or should be... Maybe the new pass protection rules are getting in his way... Also has been bothered by nagging injuries... Has the athletic ability to be a great one and has played like one in the past... Had 10 sacks in 1981, but was sidelined five games because of a severe muscle pull... Born Dec. 9, 1956, in Jacksonville, Fla.... A second-round draft pick out of Colorado State in 1978 who had 23 sacks his rookie season.

KEITH DORNEY 25 6-5 265 Offensive Tackle

Many of those holes that Billy Sims runs through are opened by this giant of a man, who is the best of the Lions' linemen... And he wants to get better... He already was chosen "Lifter of the Year" among Lion players for his dedication to weightlifting... Coach Monte Clark says you build an offensive line around a guy like this... That's one reason the Lions used a 1979 first-round pick to take this Penn State All-American... Born

DETROIT LIONS 81

Dec. 3, 1957, in Macungie, Pa.... An insurance and real estate major in college who has relocated on the West Coast.

ED MURRAY 27 5-10 170   Kicker

How about this: a kicker holding a hold-out... That's what Murray did early in the 1982 season... When he came back after the players' strike, he wasn't any richer... Finished with 49 points, putting him way down in the scoring lists... Still had an accurate year, making 11-of-12 field-goal attempts and all 16 of his extra points... Had 116 and 121 points in his first two seasons... A seventh-round choice from Tulane who replaced Benny Ricardo and wound up in the Pro Bowl in 1980... Born Aug. 29, 1956, in Halifax, Nova Scotia... Wanted to be a pro soccer player.

DAVID HILL 29 6-2 230   Tight End

Was second on club to Billy Sims in receptions last year, with 22, for 252 yards... Gives him 245 in seven years in the league... People have stopped wondering when he will develop into a Pro Bowl player... Seems he will never live up to that billing... When he wants to play, he can be dominating, but he's too inconsistent to ever be spectacular every week... A second-round pick out of Texas A&I in 1976... He scored 21 TDs in his college days there and he's had 23 scores in his pro career... Born Jan. 1, 1954, in San Antonio... Replaced the great Charlie Sanders in Detroit.

FRED SCOTT 31 6-2 180   Wide Receiver

Not much of a 1982 season, with only 13 catches for 231 yards, but that still ranked him as the team's No. 2 wide receiver... The Lions just couldn't get the ball to the outside very much in an erratic season... He had 53 catches for 1,022 yards in 1981... Was a starter briefly in Baltimore before coming to the Lions prior to the 1978 season... Teammates call him "Doc" because he's enrolled in medical school in Michigan... A cum laude graduate of Amherst... Born Aug. 5, 1952, in Grady, Ark. ... Normally is the Lions' only dangerous deep threat, but could be losing a step.

82 THE COMPLETE HANDBOOK OF PRO FOOTBALL
DOUG ENGLISH 30 6-5 260　　　　　Defensive Tackle

Is he better than Dallas' Randy White or Chicago's Dan Hampton? No one else in the NFC other than those two comes close to matching his talents... Sat out the 1980 season and still came back to play better than ever... Never had been in the Pro Bowl before his year's absence, and now he's an automatic... Seriously involved in the Texas oil business ... Born Aug. 25, 1953, in Dallas... Just a big, strong player who once helped Texas to three straight Southwest Conference titles.

TOM SKLADANY 28 6-0 195　　　　　　　　Punter

Coming off a Pro Bowl year in 1981, he figured there was no better time to sit out and demand a new contract... That's what he did, but it did him no good... Came back after the strike ended, finished with second-worst season of his career, averaging 41.2 yards, 2.3 yards less than his 1981 average... Has a terrific leg which can boom Ray Guy-type punts at times... Not as consistent as the Lions would like, but certainly one of the team's better players... Born June 29, 1955, in Castle Shannon, Pa. ... All-American at Ohio State, where he kicked a 59-yard field goal.

COACH MONTE CLARK: With all the turnover in the coaching profession after last season, he probably wondered about his job... But he'll be back for sixth season after getting the Lions into the playoffs... So what if they had a losing record and played like it against the Redskins?... It still goes down as a playoff appearance... He is coaching a mystery team that may have been overrated all these years... If not, the Lions certainly haven't lived up to their potential... Gained his coaching fame with the job he did at San Francisco (8-6) in 1976... His records in Detroit have been 7-9, 2-14, 9-7, 8-8 and 4-5... Has pedigree as assistant coach, serving for six years under Don Shula at Miami, where he developed those great Dolphin offensive lines.... Has had problems with general manager Russ Thomas ... Born Jan. 24, 1937, in Fillmore, Cal. ... Attended USC... Played 11 years in the NFL as offensive lineman for San Francisco, Dallas and Cleveland.

GREATEST QUARTERBACK

Bobby Layne was a two-fisted player. With one hand, he could pass the pigskin out of a football. With the other, he wasn't too shabby lifting a beer. Or something stronger.

Layne loved the good life, the fast life, the night life. He trained on his own time, with his own rules, at his own pace. He was the first NFL quarterback with a memorable paunch. But they didn't make 'em any tougher or much better than Bobby Layne.

Wear a face mask? No way. That was for the soft-hearted. So what if his face got messed up a few times. He wouldn't wear rib pads or extra protection most other places, either. Once, Doak Walker said that Layne never lost a game in his life. "Time just ran out on him," Walker said.

From 1950 until early in the 1958 season, when he moved on to Pittsburgh, this fun-loving Texan was a clutch performer, leading the Lions to NFL crowns in 1952, 1953 and 1957 on his way to the Hall of Fame. Here was a man who, without question, did it his way.

INDIVIDUAL LION RECORDS

Rushing
Most Yards Game:	198	Bob Hoernschemeyer, vs N.Y. Yanks, 1950
Season:	1,437	Billy Sims, 1981
Career:	4,765	Dexter Bussey, 1974-82

Passing
Most TD Passes Game:	5	Gary Danielson, vs Minnesota, 1978
Season	26	Bobby Layne, 1951
Career:	118	Bobby Layne, 1950-58

Receiving
Most TD Passes Game:	4	Cloyce Box, vs Baltimore, 1950
Season:	15	Cloyce Box, 1952
Career:	35	Terry Barr, 1957-65

Scoring
Most Points Game:	24	Cloyce Box, vs Baltimore, 1950
Season:	128	Doak Walker, 1950
Career:	636	Errol Mann, 1969-76
Most TDs Game:	4	Cloyce Box, vs Baltimore, 1950
Season:	16	Billy Sims, 1980
Career:	38	Terry Barr, 1957-65

GREEN BAY PACKERS

TEAM DIRECTORY: Chairman: Dominic Olejniczak; Pres.: Judge Robert Parins; Sec.: John Torinus; Assts. to Pres.: Bob Harlan, Tom Miller; Dir. Player Personnel: Dick Corrick; Dir. Pub. Rel.: Lee Remmel; Head Coach: Bart Starr. Home fields: Lambeau Field (56,189) and County Stadium, Milwaukee (55,958). Colors: Green and gold.

SCOUTING REPORT

OFFENSE: There are two images that come to mind when one thinks of the Packers' offense in 1982. They both are of James Lofton. The first is a reverse that he ran for a touchdown against the Giants on Monday Night Football. The second is a reverse that he ran for a touchdown against Dallas in the playoffs. They were runs of beauty, runs that come only from a man—and team— with exceptional talent.

There is no question Green Bay has talent and striking power. But the Packers still always manage to mess things up somehow. But the botches are happening less frequently lately. Now if coach Bart Starr can only get John Jefferson more involved in the offense, so the team can make better use of his outstanding talents. If Lynn Dickey can find Jefferson more often, who will stop this unit?

Other than tackle Tim Stokes, the line is young and improving. It will get better if Ron Hallstrom, a No. 1 choice in 1982, gets better. The only worry centers around running back, where there is a big dropoff if Eddie Lee Ivery goes down with an injury.

DEFENSE: Once the Packers thought they had a weakness at linebacker. Oh, how they worried about it. But no more. You won't hear any complaints now, not as long as Mike Douglass plays like the all-pro he is, Randy Scott plays like he did in the playoffs (he led the team in tackles) and George Cumby keeps coming on like he did last year.

Now the key is to get the rest of the unit to make the same improvement. Certainly, Dallas showed in the playoffs that the Packers could give up points in a hurry. There is too much talent around to let that happen much longer. Mike Butler and Ezra Johnson have loads of ability at end, and Terry Jones has been a pleasant surprise at middle guard. The secondary is on the small side, but it is tenacious. There seems to be plenty of quickness, a vital asset in this speed-conscious league. And the addition of No. 1 pick Tim Lewis at cornerback has to be a plus.

James Lofton poses the question: How high is up?

KICKING GAME: Will he or won't he? Only Jan Stenerud knows for sure. We may not know if this veteran kicker is going to retire until shortly before the opener. Punter Ray Stachowicz averaged 40.2 yards per kick. Starr is worried about improving his coverage teams, which did an awful job down the stretch.

THE ROOKIES: After some spotty recent drafting, the Packers helped themselves this season with the selection of cornerback Tim Lewis of Pittsburgh in the first round. He was the best secondary back available and could become an instant starter. Mike Miller of Tennessee adds yet more speed at receiver.

OUTLOOK: Consistency is the only thing standing in the way of the Packers and playoff glory. Starr has been walking a tightrope

PACKERS VETERAN ROSTER

HEAD COACH—Bart Starr. Assistant Coaches—Bob Schnelker, John Brunner, Lew Carpenter, Ernie McMillan, Bill Meyers, John Meyer, Richard (Doc) Urich, Monte Kiffin, Ross Fichtner, Dick Rehbein.

No.	Name	Pos.	Ht.	Wt.	NFL Exp.	College
59	Anderson, John	LB	6-3	221	6	Michigan
73	Braggs, Byron	DT	6-4	290	3	Alabama
93	Brown, Robert	DE	6-2	238	2	Valparaiso
77	#Butler, Mike	DE	6-5	265	7	Kansas
19	Campbell, Rich	QB	6-4	224	3	California-Berkeley
88	Cassidy, Ron	WR	6-0	185	4	Utah State
34	Clark, Allan	RB	5-10	186	5	Northern Arizona
82	Coffman, Paul	TE	6-3	225	6	Kansas State
52	Cumby, George	LB	6-0	230	4	Oklahoma
96	DeLoach, Ralph	DT-DE	6-5	255	3	California-Berkeley
12	Dickey, Lynn	QB	6-4	210	13	Kansas State
53	Douglass, Mike	LB	6-0	224	6	San Diego State
31	Ellis, Gerry	FB	5-11	216	4	Missouri
85	Epps, Phillip	WR	5-10	165	2	Texas Christian
79	Fields, Angelo	T	6-6	314	3	Michigan State
57	Gofourth, Derrel	G	6-3	260	7	Oklahoma State
24	Gray, Johnnie	FS	5-11	185	8	Cal State-Fullerton
65	Hallstrom, Ron	G	6-6	286	2	Iowa
69	Harris, Leotis	G	6-1	267	5	Arkansas
23	Harvey, Maurice	S	5-10	190	5	Ball State
38	Hood, Estus	CB-S	5-11	180	6	Illinois
25	Huckleby, Harlan	RB	6-1	199	4	Michigan
74	Huffman, Tim	T	6-5	277	3	Notre Dame
40	Ivery, Eddie Lee	RB	6-1	210	4	Georgia Tech
83	Jefferson, John	WR	6-1	198	6	Arizona State
90	Johnson, Ezra	DE	6-4	240	7	Morris Brown
21	Jolly, Mike	S	6-3	195	3	Michigan
63	Jones, Terry	DT	6-2	259	5	Alabama
—	Key, Larry	RB	5-9	189	*1	Florida State
64	Kitson, Syd	G	6-4	252	3	Wake Forest
68	Koch, Greg	T	6-4	265	6	Arkansas
60	#Laslavic, Jim	LB	6-2	236	10	Penn State
22	Lee, Mark	CB-S	5-11	187	4	Washington
56	Lewis, Cliff	LB	6-1	226	3	Southern Mississippi
81	Lewis, Gary	TE	6-5	234	3	Texas-Arlington
80	Lofton, James	WR	6-3	187	6	Stanford
54	McCarren, Larry	C	6-3	248	11	Illinois
29	McCoy, Mike	CB-S	5-11	183	8	Colorado
78	Merrill, Casey	DE	6-4	255	5	California-Davis
62	Merrill, Mark	LB	6-3	234	5	Minnesota
37	Murphy, Mark	FS	6-2	199	3	West Liberty
51	Prather, Guy	LB	6-2	230	3	Grambling
35	Rodgers, Del	RB	5-11	197	2	Utah
58	Rubens, Larry	C	6-1	253	2	Montana State
55	Scott, Randy	LB	6-1	220	3	Alabama
16	Stachowicz, Ray	P	5-11	185	3	Michigan State
10	#Stenerud, Jan	K	6-2	190	17	Montana State
76	Stokes, Tim	T	6-6	252	10	Oregon
67	Swanke, Karl	T-C	6-6	251	4	Boston College
87	Thompson, John	TE	6-3	228	4	Utah State
75	Turner, Richard	DT	6-2	260	3	Oklahoma
30	Whitaker, Bill	CB-S	6-0	182	3	Missouri
17	Whitehurst, David	QB	6-2	204	7	Furman
50	Wingo, Rich	LB	6-1	230	4	Alabama

*Played in CFL in 1982.
#Unsigned at press time

TOP FIVE DRAFT CHOICES

Rd.	Name	Sel. No.	Pos.	Ht.	Wt.	College
1	Lewis, Tim	11	DB	6-0	192	Pittsburgh
2	Drechsler, Dave	48	G	6-4	250	North Carolina
4	Miller, Mike	104	WR	5-11	180	Tennessee
5	Thomas, Bryan	132	RB	5-10	195	Pittsburgh
6	Sams, Ron	160	G	6-3	260	Pittsburgh

GREEN BAY PACKERS

for the last few years, but if he can't whip all this talent into a legitimate contender, then maybe he should be looking for other employment.

PACKER PROFILES

LYNN DICKEY 33 6-4 220 — Quarterback

Another Packer who overcame injuries and settled in to produce a decent season last year ... His passing almost rallied the Packers past Dallas in the playoffs ... Has a terrific arm, but injuries have all but ruined his mobility ... Threw for 1,790 yards and 12 touchdowns, but was intercepted 14 times and that's too many considering the kind of receivers he has at his disposal ... Born Oct. 19, 1949, in Paola, Kan., where the high school stadium is named after him ... Set Big Eight passing records at Kansas State ... Likes to play golf in the offseason, which he spends in Lenexa, Kan. ... Drafted by Houston in 1971 and traded to Green Bay in 1976.

EDDIE LEE IVERY 26 6-1 210 — Running Back

The good news is that he made it through even a strike-shortened season in good health ... Previously, he had missed huge chunks of two seasons with knee problems ... Gained 453 yards on 127 carries last year and scored 10 touchdowns, ranking him fifth in the NFC in scoring ... Added 106 catches ... Has the kind of running ability and quickness to make any defender show respect ... Gained 356 yards in a game against Air Force as a star running back for Georgia Tech ... Born July 30, 1957, in Thomson, Ga. ... Still returns to his home state in the offseason.

JAMES LOFTON 27 6-3 187 — Wide Receiver

Who can forget that electrifying 71-yard run he had against Dallas in the NFC playoffs last year? ... A picture of beauty, a highly gifted athlete at the peak of his skills ... May not be a more talented, exciting player in the league, but sometimes his skills just don't seem to be tapped fully by the Packers ... Had 35 receptions, but his name should be at the top of the

NFC list, even with John Jefferson as a receiving mate... Averaged 19.9 yards per catch... Standout performer in the Superstars competition... Born July 5, 1956, in Los Angeles... A second-round pick out of Stanford in 1978... Dabbles in photography and whale watching, among other interests.

MIKE DOUGLASS 28 6-0 224   Linebacker

One of the four best outside linebackers in the league... He compares favorably with Giants' Lawrence Taylor and Tampa Bay's Hugh Green, and that is pretty heady company, especially for a mere fifth-round draft choice out of San Diego State... Should be annual Pro Bowl performer for seasons to come... Doesn't have the prototypical linebacker's height, but makes up for that with wonderful athletic skills and aggressiveness... Born March 15, 1955, in St. Louis... Nickname is "Mad Dog" and that probably says it all... Likes bowling, cars and skating.

PAUL COFFMAN 27 6-3 225   Tight End

If Green Bay continues to win, he'll get more recognition for what he is—a fine tight end who is getting better every season... Caught 23 passes last year on a team with a passing game dominated by its wide receivers, James Lofton and John Jefferson... Already holds single-season mark for catches by a Green Bay tight end (56 in 1979)... A free agent out of Kansas State, he talked a Packer assistant coach into giving him a tryout... Born March 29, 1956, in Chase, Kan.... Likes to play racquetball and ski... Coach Bart Starr says, "He's one of the hardest-working athletes I've ever been associated with."

JOHN JEFFERSON 27 6-1 198   Wide Receiver

Not as physically strong or as durable as Lofton, but there isn't much else separating the two... Packers have yet to adapt to him and vice versa... There were complaints last year that he didn't run his patterns exactly right, and he complained he wasn't being thrown to enough... Wound up with 27 catches for 452 yards... Much-publicized contractual holdout prompted San Diego to trade him to Green Bay in controversial 1981 deal... Former Arizona State star had three straight seasons of 1,000 or more yards receiving for San Diego... Amazing athletic skills... Leaping ability makes his receptions look so easy... Born Feb. 3, 1956, in Dallas... Has way of showing enthusiasm that turns on fans.

GERRY ELLIS 25 5-11 216   Running Back

Get different opinions on this explosive fullback... Some think he is getting better all the time; others believe he must be replaced if the Packers are to improve... He gained 228 yards on 62 carries as Eddie Lee Ivery's running mate last year... And coach Bart Starr remembers the years that this free agent bailed the Packers out when Ivery was hurt... Led team in rushing in 1981 with 860 yards... Played a year at Ft. Scott Junior College, then attended Missouri... Originally a seventh-round choice of Los Angeles in 1980... Born Nov. 12, 1957, in Columbia, Mo.... Name is pronounced "Gary," not "Gerry."

GEORGE CUMBY 27 6-0 230   Linebacker

Bart Starr was pleased with his linebackers last season, and this guy is one reason why... Has improved after being slowed by injuries and the adjustment to performing different duties than he did in college... Had to learn to be more disciplined... But what athletic gifts... No one has ever questioned his ability to seek and destroy ball-carriers... An All-American at Oklahoma, where he played so well his senior year he became a living legend... Has built himself up with an offseason weight program... Born July 5, 1956, in La Rue, Tex.... Was more of a rover back in college and there was a question of whether he would become a man without a spot in the pros.

RAY STACHOWICZ 24 5-11 185   Punter

When the Packers took him on the third round of the 1981 draft, some wondered if the team had lost its marbles... With all their other needs, why draft a punter so early?... And it didn't help when he got off to a unsteady start... But now he is firmly established as the team's punter, after turning in two straight years of 40-plus averages (40.2 in 1982)... Packers would like to see an increase in distance, but at least he is providing them with more consistency than they had enjoyed... Has unusual leg strength and a two-step style that allows him to get off punts quickly... Born March 6, 1959, in Cleveland... Big Ten's leading punter three of his four years at Michigan State.

MIKE BUTLER 29 6-5 265   Defensive End

Settled in to give the Packers the line play they had expected when they drafted him on the first round in 1977, out of Kansas... Has all the tools: 4.7 in the 40, good strength, elusive quickness... Only needed to improve consistency... Also has developed leadership ability the last three seasons, which is much-needed on the defensive unit... Born April 4, 1954, in Washington, D.C.... Was selected high school player of the year his senior season before going to Kansas... Had a 70-yard return of a recovered fumble, longest in Packer history.

COACH BART STARR: Has another one-year contract, although he led 5-3-1 Packers into the playoffs, where they nearly beat Dallas... "We obviously don't have the complete confidence of the people that we need, but we'll keep working toward that end," he said, voicing his disappointment... Has not enjoyed a comfortable reign his eight years as coach of Packers, and has survived this long only because he is the best quarterback and the most revered player in Packer history... That type of image will help you survive all types of sticky coaching jams... Career coaching mark is 44-68-3... Seems to have worked out the kinks in his coaching staff, and that has helped his team's development... Lots of young players are beginning to mature, but Starr admits the team still needs help in many areas... That also is called protecting your flank... Born Jan. 9, 1934, in Mobile, Ala... Drafted in 17th round in 1956, because of back injury that troubled him as a junior at Alabama... Wonder what three-time NFL passing leader would have done as a player if he had John Jefferson and James Lofton as receivers.

GREATEST QUARTERBACK

Green Bay's Starr rose in 1960, and how it did shine.

For an eight-year period, Green Bay was almost unbeatable, with a 82-24-4 record, six divisional championships, five NFL crowns and victories in the first two Super Bowls. Who else could have pulled that off but cool, calm, expressionless Bart Starr?

He was Vince Lombardi's coach on the field. He made mistakes, one suspects, but try to remember one in a big game. How could you melt an iceberg that refused to go away? And this from a former 17th-round draft choice from Alabama.

Just consider these achievements. He was a 57 percent career passer in a time when teams didn't depend so much on short passes. He once went 294 passes without an interception, 86 passes better than the No. 2 mark. He was never better than in Super Bowl I, when he completed 16 of 23 passes for 250 yards and two touchdowns in Green Bay's 35-10 win over Kansas City.

Quite appropriately, he was the game's first MVP, and, fittingly, he wound up as the Green Bay coach.

INDIVIDUAL PACKER RECORDS

Rushing

Most Yards Game:	186	Jim Taylor, vs N.Y. Giants, 1961
Season:	1,474	Jim Taylor, 1962
Career:	8,207	Jim Taylor, 1958-66

Passing

Most TD Passes Game:	5	Cecil Isbell, vs Cleveland, 1942
	5	Don Horn, vs St. Louis, 1969
	5	Lynn Dickey, vs New Orleans, 1981
Season:	24	Cecil Isbell, 1942
Career:	152	Bart Starr 1956-71

Receiving

Most TD Passes Game:	4	Don Hutson, vs Detroit, 1945
Season:	17	Don Hutson, 1943
Career:	99	Don Hutson, 1935-45

Scoring

Most Points Game:	33	Paul Hornung, vs Baltimore, 1961
Season:	176	Paul Hornung, 1960
Career:	823	Don Hutson, 1935-45
Most TDs Game:	5	Paul Hornung, vs Baltimore, 1961
Season:	19	Jim Taylor, 1962
Career:	105	Don Hutson, 1935-45

92 THE COMPLETE HANDBOOK OF PRO FOOTBALL
LOS ANGELES RAMS

TEAM DIRECTORY: Pres.: Georgia Frontiere; Asst. to Pres./Consultant: Don Klosterman; Exec. VP: Ray Nagel; Dir. Operations: Dick Bean; Adm. Football Operations: Jack Faulkner; Dir. Marketing: Les Marshall; Dir. Player Personnel: John Math; Dir. Pub. Rel.: Pete Donovan; Head Coach: John Robinson. Home field: Anaheim Stadium (69,007). Colors: Royal blue, gold and white.

All is forgiven since Vince Ferragamo is a born-again Ram.

SCOUTING REPORT

OFFENSE: It's easy to explain the Rams' demise by pointing to front-office chaos and its effect on team morale. Maybe all that is true or maybe this is an overrated bunch. We'll find out when new coach John Robinson, who seems to have some rapport with ownership, takes over this season.

Robinson is an offensive specialist who usually devised effective offenses at Southern California. He certainly won't be lacking in good players with the Rams. Quarterback Vince Ferragamo came back after a year in the CFL and finished strongly, taking over when Bert Jones got hurt. With Jones now retired, there won't be any quarterback controversy this season. Rookie Eric Dickerson's speed will help the offense and players like linemen Dennis Harrah and Irv Pankey have plenty of talent.

Because the Ram receivers were hardly a factor last season, too many passes had to go to backs coming out of the backfield. Robinson has to have his quarterback pass downfield more often.

DEFENSE: The Rams had a pattern last season. They would jump off to a nice, fat halftime lead and think things were going their way. Then, in the second half, the offense would stall and the defense would fall apart. And the lead would turn into a deficit and, finally, a defeat. That is one way to carve out a 2-7 record.

The good news is the Rams had a lot of key players on the injured list near the end of the year. It's tough for them to win without Carl Ekern, Jim Youngblood, Jim Collins and Mel Owens. But even with those players out, the Rams managed to upset San Francisco in the season finale.

If they come back strongly and if players like former Giant Gary Jeter and Nolan Cromwell have big seasons, then it is likely the defense can be much more representative. You just wonder how long Jack Youngblood can continue to play and provide what little pass rush the Rams can muster.

KICKING GAME: Robinson will be happy to have Leroy Irvin as his primary return man, but he might seek a replacement for kicker Mike Lansford, who was 9-of-15 on field goals and didn't even try one from outside the 40 last year. Lansford will be pushed by rookie Chuck Nelson. John Misko did a decent job of punting, posting a 43.6-yard average.

THE ROOKIES: The Rams maneuvered to be in a position to draft Dickerson as the second player chosen in the first round. He

RAMS VETERAN ROSTER

HEAD COACH—John Robinson. Assistant Coaches—Bob Baker, Marv Goux, Gil Haskel, Hudson Houck, Jimmy Raye, Steve Shafer, Fritz Shurmur, Bruce Snyder, Fred Whittingham.

No.	Name	Pos.	Ht.	Wt.	NFL Exp.	College
35	Alexander, Robert	RB-KR	6-0	185	2	West Virginia
52	Andrews, George	LB	6-3	221	5	Nebraska
62	Bain, Bill	G	6-4	285	9	Southern California
86	#Barber, Mike	TE	6-3	237	8	Louisiana Tech
96	Barnett, Doug	DE-C	6-3	250	2	Azusa Pacific
81	Battle, Ron	TE	6-3	225	3	North Texas State
—	Bolinger, Russ	G	6-5	260	7	Long Beach State
90	Brooks, Larry	DT	6-3	255	12	Virginia St.-Petersburg
54	Carson, Howard	LB	6-2	230	3	Howard Payne
50	Collins, Jim	LB	6-2	230	3	Syracuse
42	Collins, Kirk	S	5-11	183	3	Baylor
21	Cromwell, Nolan	S	6-1	197	7	Kansas
70	DeJurnett, Charles	DT	6-4	260	7	San Jose State
88	Dennard, Preston	WR	6-1	183	6	New Mexico
71	Doss, Reggie	DE	6-4	263	6	Hampton Institute
55	Ekern, Carl	LB	6-3	222	7	San Jose State
79	Fanning, Mike	DT	6-6	255	9	Notre Dame
84	Farmer, George	WR	5-10	175	2	Southern University
15	Ferragamo, Vince	QB	6-3	212	6	Nebraska
44	Guman, Mike	FB	6-2	218	4	Penn State
60	Harrah, Dennis	G	6-5	250	9	Miami
87	Hill, Drew	WR	5-9	170	5	Georgia Tech
72	Hill, Kent	G	6-5	260	5	Georgia Tech
47	Irvin, LeRoy	CB-PR	5-11	184	4	Kansas
—	Jeter, Gary	DE	6-4	260	7	Southern California
20	Johnson, Johnnie	S	6-1	185	4	Texas
24	Jones, A.J.	RB	6-1	202	2	Texas
9	Kemp, Jeff	QB	6-0	201	3	Dartmouth
68	Kersten, Wally	T	6-5	270	2	Minnesota
4	Lansford, Mike	K	6-0	183	2	Washington
67	Lapka, Myron	DT	6-4	260	3	Southern California
59	Lilja, George	C	6-4	250	2	Michigan
83	Locklin, Kerry	TE	6-3	217	2	New Mexico State
69	Meisner, Greg	DE	6-3	253	3	Pittsburgh
6	Misko, John	P	6-5	207	2	Oregon State
58	Owens, Mel	LB	6-2	224	3	Michigan
75	Pankey, Irv	T	6-4	267	4	Penn State
49	Perry, Rod	CB	5-9	185	9	Colorado
30	Redden, Barry	FB	5-10	205	2	Richmond
57	Reilly, Mike	LB	6-4	217	2	Oklahoma
78	Slater, Jackie	T	6-4	271	8	Jackson State
56	Smith, Doug	C	6-3	253	6	Bowling Green
23	Smith, Lucious	CB	5-10	190	4	Cal State-Fullerton
37	Sully, Ivory	S	6-0	201	5	Delaware
33	Thomas, Jewerl	RB	5-10	228	4	San Jose State
27	Thomas, Pat	CB	5-9	190	8	Texas A&M
66	Williams, Eric	LB	6-2	235	7	Southern California
85	Youngblood, Jack	DE	6-4	245	13	Florida
53	Youngblood, Jim	LB	6-3	231	11	Tennessee Tech

#Unsigned at press time

TOP FIVE DRAFT CHOICES

Rd.	Name	Sel. No.	Pos.	Ht.	Wt.	College
1	Dickerson, Eric	2	RB	6-3	218	Southern Methodist
2	Ellard, Henry	32	WR	5-11	170	Fresno State
2	Wilcher, Mike	36	LB	6-3	235	North Carolina
4	Nelson, Chuck	87	K	5-11	178	Washington
4	Newsome, Vince	97	DB	6-1	179	Washington

LOS ANGELES RAMS

should take over for the traded Wendell Tyler in fine style. And Fresno State receiver Henry Ellard and Washington kicker Nelson could prove almost as valuable over the long run.

OUTLOOK: If the front office will leave him alone, Robinson might be able to correct the slippage in this franchise, which should be one of the league's best. But don't expect miracles the first year. It will take time to repair the damage that has been done since the team's Super Bowl appearance four years ago.

RAM PROFILES

VINCE FERRAGAMO 29 6-3 212   Quarterback

The return of the prodigal quarterback... Came back after exile in Canada and wound up as the starter when Bert Jones was hurt... Finished with 1,609 passing yards and a 77.7 rating, sixth in the NFC... Had nine interceptions and nine touchdowns... Ranks sixth on the Rams' all-time passing yardage list and his NFL career completion percentage of 56.4 is best in the club's history... Happy to be back and a lot richer, although his CFL experience in Montreal was a rocky one... Born April 24, 1954, in Torrance, Cal.... Attended Nebraska... Rams' fifth-round pick in 1977—and their starting quarterback in the 1979 Super Bowl.

IRV PANKEY 25 6-4 267   Offensive Tackle

The Rams used a second-round draft choice in 1980 to pick this former Penn State standout... And with good reason... They wanted a young replacement when some of their linemen started aging... When Doug France retired because of injuries, his replacement was ready... His coaches says he is the dominant force now in the offensive line... His teammates call him "Spanky"... Born Feb. 15, 1958, in Aberdeen, Md.... Started his college career as a linebacker, then switched to tight end before becoming a tackle his senior season.

NOLAN CROMWELL 28 6-1 197 — Safety

Status in the league is such that when you mention safety, you think of Cromwell almost immediately... Made the Pro Bowl for the third straight time last year... Had three interceptions and now has 22 for his career... Plays with so much intelligence along with gifted natural ability, of course... His 47 tackles were second-best total on the team and he deflected an impressive 11 passes... Born Jan. 30, 1955, in Smith Center, Kan.... Like Redskins' John Riggins, he returns to a Kansas farm in the offseason for privacy.

JACK YOUNGBLOOD 33 6-4 245 — Defensive End

Keeps going on and on, though he talks about retiring... Opponents probably wish he would give it up, so they wouldn't have to worry about his pass rush... Not the player he once was, but he hasn't given way to the years quite yet... Finished the 1982 season with 28 tackles and four sacks... Only Mike Fanning had more sacks... Also tipped away three passes... Born Jan. 26, 1950, in Jacksonville, Fla.... Tennessee Tech grad is country all the way, even in the city lights of Southern California... Owns a western clothing store called "The Wild Bunch," plus a ranch and a sports club in Huntington Beach, Cal.

JOHNNIE JOHNSON 26 6-1 185 — Safety

Has silenced all his critics in Los Angeles with his consistent play since a controversial rookie season of 1980... Was given a big contract as a rookie and that angered many Ram veterans... Last year, he led the team in tackles and had one interception... A standout on a beleaguered Ram defense... Also deflected six passes and recovered two fumbles... Has been a starter almost from the day he was made the Rams' No. 1 1980 choice after a stunning career at Texas... Had 13 interceptions in college... Born Oct. 8, 1956, in La Grange, Tex.... Studying for an accounting degree.

LOS ANGELES RAMS 97

PAT THOMAS 29 5-9 190 — Cornerback

A nifty comeback for the little cornerback in 1982... Had not done much the previous season, as he was hampered by hamstring injury that kept him out of four games and out of the starting lineup for another three... Last season, he intercepted three passes to give him 26 for his career... Only two years ago, he ranked among the very best in the league... Injuries have hurt his progress throughout his NFL career... Born Sept. 1, 1954, in Plano, Tex.... All-American at Texas A&M... Vice president of a communications services company.

LeROY IRVIN 26 5-11 184 — Kick Returner

He was one of the most highly regarded defensive backs in the 1980 draft, good enough to be taken on the third round by the Rams... But no one expected him to become such an outstanding kick returner... Now is staging an annual battle with Washington's Mike Nelms for top honors in the NFC... Averaged 11 yards on 22 punt returns this past season, after compiling 13.4-yard average in 1981... Brought one back 63 yards for a touchdown in 1982... Called just one fair catch... Has wonderful quickness and eventually should break into the secondary... Born Sept. 15, 1957, in Fort Dix, N.J.... Attended University of Kansas.

DENNIS HARRAH 30 6-5 250 — Guard

Another of the Rams who may have hit the down period of his career... Wasn't long ago he was considered one of the premier guards in the league... Still can hold his own, reflecting the ability that, in 1980, led him to be selected to the Pro Bowl although he didn't start until the ninth week... Has been hindered by injuries and contract disputes during his career... Miami (Fla.) alumnus is strong and determined and a lover of contact... Born March 9, 1953, in Charleston, W.Va.... Has such a wonderful build, molded from weightlifting, that his teammates call him "Herk," short for Hercules.

98 THE COMPLETE HANDBOOK OF PRO FOOTBALL

COACH JOHN ROBINSON: He was going to get out of football for good when he retired from his head coaching job at USC... But three months later he took the Rams' hot spot... To do that, he gave up position as USC's vice president of university relations... "I thought I wanted to be out of coaching, but I think the environment with the Rams is something I wanted to be involved in," he said... Compiled a 67-14-2 record at USC, winning a national championship, and his Trojans were among the nation's best teams... Had been courted for other pro jobs and turned down an offer from New England the previous year... Known for his fine offensive mind and his ability to get along with players... Has a wonderful personality and a good sense of humor... Former assistant at Oregon and backfield coach with the Oakland Raiders.

GREATEST QUARTERBACK

Bob Waterfield. The very mention of his name denotes a glamorous image. Handsome, athletic, a quarterback. Married a high school sweetheart, who became a movie queen named Jane Russell. And he played in just the right place, the bright lights of Los Angeles, where a guy with his flair could be fully appreciated.

Waterfield was molded in the image of Sammy Baugh. They didn't cater to quarterbacks in those days. They had to earn a full day's pay, just like the most remote lineman. The Rams—Cleveland in his first year, 1945, and Los Angeles through 1952—got a bargain in Waterfield. The UCLA alumnus averaged 42 yards for his career as a punter, and he scored 498 points as a placekicker. When he retired, his 573 points were third on the all-time list. And for four seasons, he also was a defensive back who intercepted 20 passes.

How about this as a rookie? With the Cleveland Rams, he outdueled Sammy Baugh for the league title to cap the 1945 season in which he was named league MVP.

INDIVIDUAL RAM RECORDS

Rushing

Most Yards Game:	247	Willie Ellison, vs New Orleans, 1971
Season:	1,238	Lawrence McCutcheon, 1977
Career:	6,186	Lawrence McCutcheon, 1973-79

Passing

Most TD Passes Game:	5	Bob Waterfield, vs N.Y. Bulldogs, 1949
	5	Norm Van Brocklin, vs Detroit, 1950
	5	Norm Van Brocklin, vs N.Y. Yanks, 1951
	5	Roman Gabriel, vs Cleveland, 1965
	5	Vince Ferragamo, vs New Orleans, 1980
Season:	30	Vince Ferragamo, 1980
Career:	154	Roman Gabriel, 1962-72

Receiving

Most TD Passes Game:	4	Bob Shaw, vs Washington, 1949
	4	Elroy Hirsch, vs N.Y. Yanks, 1951
	4	Harold Jackson, vs Dallas, 1973
Season:	17	Elroy Hirsch, 1951
Career:	53	Elroy Hirsch, 1949-57

Scoring

Most Points Game:	24	Elroy Hirsch, vs N.Y. Yanks, 1951
	24	Bob Shaw, vs Washington, 1949
	24	Harold Jackson, vs Dallas, 1973
Season:	130	David Ray, 1973
Career:	573	Bob Waterfield, 1945-52
Most TDs Game:	4	Elroy Hirsch, vs N.Y. Yanks, 1951
	4	Bob Shaw, vs Washington, 1949
	4	Harold Jackson, vs Dallas, 1973
Season:	17	Elroy Hirsch, 1951
	17	Wendell Tyler, 1981
Career:	55	Elroy Hirsch, 1949-57

MINNESOTA VIKINGS

TEAM DIRECTORY: Pres.: Max Winter; VP/GM: Mike Lynn; Dir. Administration: Harley Peterson; Dir. FB Oper.: Jerry Reichow; Dir. Pub. Rel.: Merrill Swanson; Head Coach: Bud Grant. Home field: Hubert H. Humphrey Metrodome (62,212). Colors: Purple, white and gold.

SCOUTING REPORT

OFFENSE: The season really began for Minnesota with the 1982 draft, when the Vikings picked Darrin Nelson instead of Marcus Allen. Nelson said he didn't really want to live in the cold North, then went on to gain a mere 136 yards. Allen became the league's best rookie with Oakland, picking up plaudits every yard of the way.

Coach Bud Grant sticks by that choice, but Nelson will have to do a lot more this year to justify Grant's faith. The way the Viking offense goes, there isn't room for more than one back most of the time, anyway—and that back has been Ted Brown. That leaves Nelson out in the cold.

Brown had a fine season, gaining 515 yards and catching 31 passes. That's a plus for the Vikings. Another plus was quarterback Tommy Kramer's health. Kramer's knees held up well and he passed for 2,037 yards and 15 touchdowns. He won't have the retired Ahmad Rashad around as a receiver in 1983, but Sam McCullum isn't a bad fill-in. The line is solid, if not sensational, and tight end Joe Senser is one of the league's best receivers at his position.

DEFENSE: Doug Martin was Mr. Defense for the Vikings last year. He cast off some non-productive seasons to emerge as the league's premier pass-rusher, with 11½ sacks. Shades of the old Purple People Eaters. That's the kind of production Grant needs from him every year, if the Viking defense is to get better.

Until Washington center Jeff Bostic handled him superbly in the playoffs, middle guard Charlie Johnson had also enjoyed a fine season. He was a key acquisition for the Vikings, who got him from Philadelphia after Johnson said he was tired of Dick Vermeil's high-intensity operation. Johnson brought leadership and stability to the middle of the defense, which uses both three- and four-man lines.

Still, the Vikings aren't nearly as quick as they should be on defense, especially at linebacker. Matt Blair remains one of the best, but how long can one man hold up for everyone else?

MINNESOTA VIKINGS 101

Prospect Darrin Nelson had best talk less and run more.

KICKING GAME: Here's a switch. The Vikings, usually the best at blocking kicks, had two blocked that were turned into touchdowns by opponents last year. Punter Greg Coleman enjoyed a fine year (41.1-yard average), but Rich Danmeier still doesn't have the kind of range most teams want from their placekickers.

VIKINGS VETERAN ROSTER

HEAD COACH—Bud Grant. Assistant Coaches—Jerry Burns, Bob Hollway, John Michels, Bus Mertes, Les Steckel, Jed Hughes, Tom Cecchini, Floyd Reese.

No.	Name	Pos.	Ht.	Wt.	NFL Exp.	College
21	Bess, Rufus	CB	5-9	185	5	South Carolina State
59	Blair, Matt	LB	6-5	230	10	Iowa State
62	#Boyd, Brent	G	6-3	260	4	UCLA
23	Brown, Ted	RB	5-10	198	5	North Carolina State
82	#Bruer, Bob	TE	6-5	235	5	Mankato State
8	Coleman, Greg	P	6-0	178	7	Florida A&M
7	Danmeier, Rick	K	6-0	200	6	Sioux Falls
12	Dils, Steve	QB	6-1	190	5	Stanford
73	Elshire, Neil	DE	6-6	260	3	Oregon
32	Galbreath, Tony	RB	6-0	228	8	Missouri
61	#Hamilton, Wes	G	6-3	268	8	Tulsa
45	Hannon, Tom	S	5-11	190	7	Michigan State
36	Harrell, Sam	RB	6-2	225	3	East Carolina
75	Holloway, Randy	DE	6-5	250	6	Pittsburgh
51	Hough, Jim	G	6-2	267	6	Utah State
24	Howard, Bryan	S	6-0	200	2	Tennessee State
56	Huffman, David	C-G	6-6	255	5	Notre Dame
76	Irwin, Tim	T	6-6	275	3	Tennessee
65	Johnson, Charlie	DT	6-3	265	7	Colorado
52	Johnson, Dennis	LB	6-3	230	4	Southern California
53	Johnson, Henry	LB	6-2	235	4	Georgia Tech
83	Jordan, Steve	TE	6-4	230	2	Brown
25	Knoff, Kurt	S	6-2	190	8	Kansas
9	Kramer, Tommy	QB	6-2	200	7	Rice
80	LeCount, Terry	WR	5-10	180	6	Florida
87	Lewis, Leo	WR	5-8	170	3	Missouri
79	Martin, Doug	DE	6-3	258	4	Washington
84	McCullum, Sam	WR	6-2	190	10	Montana State
88	McDole, Mardye	WR	5-11	195	2	Mississippi State
54	McNeill, Fred	LB	6-2	230	10	UCLA
77	Mullaney, Mark	DE	6-6	245	9	Colorado State
20	Nelson, Darrin	RB	5-9	185	2	Stanford
49	Nord, Keith	S	6-0	195	5	St. Cloud State
22	Redwine, Jarvis	RB	5-10	195	3	Nebraska
78	Riley, Steve	T	6-6	255	10	Southern California
68	Rouse, Curtis	G	6-3	290	2	Chattanooga
57	Sendlein, Robin	LB	6-3	225	3	Texas
81	Senser, Joe	TE	6-4	238	4	West Chester State
50	#Siemon, Jeff	LB	6-3	235	12	Stanford
55	Studwell, Scott	LB	6-2	225	7	Illinois
29	Swain, John	CB	6-1	195	3	Miami
67	#Swilley, Dennis	C	6-3	241	7	Texas A&M
66	Tausch, Terry	T	6-5	275	2	Texas
7	Teal, Willie	CB	5-10	195	4	Louisiana State
27	Turner, John	CB	6-0	199	6	Miami
72	White, James	DT	6-3	270	8	Oklahoma State
85	White, Sammy	WR	5-11	190	8	Grambling
11	Wilson, Wade	QB	6-3	210	3	East Texas State
91	Yakavonis, Ray	DT	6-4	250	4	East Stroudsburg State
34	#Young, Rickey	RB	6-2	195	9	Jackson State

#Unsigned at press time

TOP FIVE DRAFT CHOICES

Rd.	Name	Sel. No.	Pos.	Ht.	Wt.	College
1	Browner, Joey	19	DB	6-3	205	Southern California
3	Ashley, Walker Lee	73	LB	6-0	225	Penn State
4	Rush, Mark	100	RB	6-3	215	Miami
5	Stewart, Mark	127	LB	6-3	227	Washington
6	Jones, Mike	159	WR	5-11	176	Tennessee State

THE ROOKIES: Can Joey Browner of USC and Walker Lee Ashley of Penn State find spots in the pros? That's the question surrounding the Vikings' top two picks, both of whom were outstanding college athletes who may not blend into the pro life. If they don't, Minnesota could be deprived of a much-needed quick fix.

OUTLOOK: Grant thought his team, which moved into the playoffs again last year and won a playoff game for the first time since 1977, improved nicely. But the Vikings remain just good enough to be a nuisance, but not good enough to overwhelm anyone. That's a tough way to win a Super Bowl.

VIKING PROFILES

TOMMY KRAMER 28 6-2 200　　　　　　Quarterback

When he was good, he was very good, but when he was erratic, the Vikings had trouble... Not the kind of season he expected, or wanted, but good enough to get Minnesota into the playoffs... Finished with 2,037 passing yards, completed 57.1 percent, threw for 15 touchdowns and suffered 12 interceptions in first season after being treated for alcoholism... Got married and gave up the wild night life for quiet ways at home... Says he has never enjoyed himself more than he does now... Relishes his privacy, which isn't that hard to maintain in Viking land... Rice graduate is one of 11 children... Born March 7, 1955, in San Antonio... Father coached at Texas Lutheran for six years.

TED BROWN 26 5-10 198　　　　　　Running Back

Accidentally shot himself in an offseason incident, but came back and had a fine all-around season... Maturing into the quality back the Vikings thought they had drafted on the first round in 1979... Ran for 515 yards (on 120 carries) and caught 31 passes, both Viking highs last season... Fits in well with coach Bud Grant's offense, which concentrates on short passes and quick opening runs... Born Feb. 2, 1957, in High Point, N.C. ...

104 THE COMPLETE HANDBOOK OF PRO FOOTBALL

Plays basketball and fishes in the offseason, and also concentrates on lifting weights... All-American his senior year at N.C. State.

SAMMY WHITE 29 5-11 189   Wide Receiver

Production was cut by short season and late injuries... Had a dreadful playoff game against Washington, dropping passes, including a sure touchdown toss... Had 29 receptions for 503 yards and five touchdowns... Two more catches and he'll rank second on the Vikings' career receiving list, passing George Foreman (366)... Nice person with a pleasing personality who cares about people... Has a degree in education and has done some teaching... Born March 16, 1954, in Winnsboro, La.... Was a wingback at Grambling... His high school team averaged 64 points per game his senior season.

DARRIN NELSON 24 5-9 185   Running Back

First running back and seventh player overall taken in 1982 draft... A somewhat surprising choice, since the Vikings already seemed deep in running backs... Rushed only 44 times for 136 yards as a rookie and didn't score a touchdown... Also had a mere nine catches... Certainly, he'll become a bigger part of the Vikings' plans in the future... Didn't endear himself to the Minnesota fans by making some wisecracks about the team and the state when he was drafted... Later he said he was "only kidding"... Born Jan. 2, 1959, in Sacramento, Cal. ...Cleveland's Ozzie Newsome and Cincinnati's Charles Alexander are his cousins... Attended Stanford.

MATT BLAIR 32 6-5 230   Linebacker

Mr. Steady and Mr. Reliable... Always gives you a top-notch performance... Always an all-star candidate... Has that long-lasting reputation that comes after years of standout performances... Holds Viking career record for most blocked kicks, an honor on a team that blocks kicks regularly... Carrying on winning Viking tradition as one of the lone holdovers from the team's glory years... Born Sept. 20, 1950, in Honolulu... Played at Iowa State... A free-lance photographer who owns a trucking

MINNESOTA VIKINGS 105

company... Likes golf, basketball, chess and antique cars and runs a camp every summer for disadvantaged kids.

DOUG MARTIN 26 6-3 258 — Defensive End

Led the NFL in sacks last season, fulfilling the promise that prompted the Vikings to pick him on the first round of the 1980 draft after a standout career at the University of Washington... Actually had lost his starting position for most of 1981, but came back very strong in the Vikings' 3-4 alignment last season... At times, the Vikings wondered about trading him, but now they are glad they held onto him... Communications major in college, where he was second-team All-American... Born May 22, 1957, in Fairfield, Conn.... Brother George plays with the Giants.

JOE SENSER 27 6-4 238 — Tight End

Had 29 catches for 261 yards last season to add to his reputation as one of the better pass-receiving tight ends in the business... Made-to-order talent for the Vikings' short-passing game... Fine athletic ability and great hands... Holds NFC record for most receptions by a tight end (79 in 1981)... Two more touchdowns and he'll be Viking record holder for tight ends, surpassing Stu Voigt (17)... Four-year starter in both football and basketball at West Chester State... Majored in criminal justice... Born Aug. 8, 1956, in Philadelphia... Star player on Vikings' basketball team in offseason.

RICKEY YOUNG 29 6-2 195 — Running Back

Every time it seems he is going to be written out of the Viking offense with the arrival of some new draft choice, he hangs on and turns in some key plays... This past season was no different... Didn't play a lot, but produced near the end of the year, when the Vikings were making a playoff bid... Still, it's probably now just a matter of time before he is phased out... Too bad, because he has had some wonderful years, catching 88, 72 and 64 passes in consecutive seasons from 1978–80... Born Dec. 7, 1953, in Mobile, Ala.... Attended Jackson State, where he blocked for Walter Payton.

106 THE COMPLETE HANDBOOK OF PRO FOOTBALL
GREG COLEMAN 28 6-0 178   Punter

All of a sudden, after six years in the league, he is starting to punt like a young colt... Followed up a 41.4-yard average in 1981 with a 41.1 mark last year, the two best averages of his career... Ranked fourth among NFC punters... Came close to producing the longest kick of his career, too... Hit a 67-yarder, which was topped only by the 73-yard bomb he kicked in 1981... Vikings always have liked his dependability and accuracy... Already the Viking leader in career punts (368) and punt yardage (14,761)... Born Sept. 9, 1954, in Jacksonville, Fla. ... Attended Florida A&M, where he was standout in track.

COACH BUD GRANT: Becoming more outspoken the longer he stays in the league... Loves to take shots at the league establishment and at officiating... League tolerates it, because he is so respected—and because lots of times he is telling it like it really is... Seems like the last guy to be outspoken, but he always has been blunt and honest... Has adapted well to changing rules... Old Vikings have given way to new look: a 3-4 defense, a short-passing game, a de-emphasized running game... And once again he took Minnesota to the playoffs... This may not be the powerhouse of years gone by, but while other teams have stumbled, he has kept the Vikings on an even keel for years... Born May 20, 1927, in Superior, Wash.... Attended University of Minnesota... Played two seasons for the NBA Lakers before signing with Philadelphia Eagles, who converted him from defensive end to wide receiver... Won 122 games as coach of Winnipeg in CFL, then took Vikings' job in 1967... Ranks third in victories among active NFL coaches with 16-year NFL mark of 143-79-5 and has led Vikes to four Super Bowls.

GREATEST QUARTERBACK

Now you see him, now you don't.

That's how you have to remember Fran Tarkenton, who brought back the scramble to pro football after it had disappeared with the dominance of the pro set formations. Passers were supposed to

Tommy Kramer makes Bud Grant's short-passing game work.

108 THE COMPLETE HANDBOOK OF PRO FOOTBALL

stay in the pocket and rely on linemen for protection. Move from that pocket and it was their body and future at stake. But Tarkenton never looked at it that way.

Of course, Tarkenton really had no choice. As a rookie from Georgia playing for an expansion team in 1961, he didn't have a whole lot of help in front of him. If he didn't use his running ability, he might have had one of the world's shortest careers. So he took off, and he didn't stop running during an 18-year career that included two stretches with the Vikings (1961-66, 1972-78) and the five years in-between with the Giants.

By the time he was finished he had led the Vikings to three Super Bowl appearances, had played more games (257) at his position than anyone else and had set many of the league's all-time passing records.

He was always the scrambler. Just ask those defensive linemen who tried to tackle him once, twice, three times—on the same play.

INDIVIDUAL VIKING RECORDS

Rushing

Most Yards Game:	200	Chuck Foreman, vs Philadelphia, 1976
Season:	1,155	Chuck Foreman, 1976
Career:	5,879	Chuck Foreman, 1973-79

Passing

Most TD Passes Game:	7	Joe Kapp, vs Baltimore, 1969
Season:	26	Tommy Kramer, 1981
Career	239	Francis Tarkenton, 1961-66, 1972-78

Receiving

Most TD Passes Game:	4	Ahmad Rashad, vs San Francisco, 1979
Season:	11	Jerry Reichow, 1961
Career:	45	Sammy White, 1976-82

Scoring

Most Points Game:	24	Chuck Foreman, vs Buffalo, 1975
	24	Ahmad Rashad, vs San Francisco, 1979
Season:	132	Chuck Foreman, 1975
Career:	1,365	Fred Cox, 1963-77
Most TDs Game:	4	Chuck Foreman, vs Buffalo, 1975
	4	Ahmad Rashad, vs San Francisco, 1979
Season:	22	Chuck Foreman, 1975
Career:	76	Bill Brown, 1962-74

NEW ORLEANS SAINTS

TEAM DIRECTORY: Owner: John Mecom Jr.; Pres.: Eddie Jones; VP-Administration: Fred Williams; Dir. FB Oper.: Pat Peppler; GM/Head Coach: Bum Phillips; Controller: Bob Landry; Dir. Pub. Rel.: Greg Suit. Home field: Superdome (71,330). Colors: Old gold, black and white.

George Rogers has Saints marching to respectability.

SCOUTING REPORT

OFFENSE: Coach Bum Phillips thought last year's Saints made a 50 percent improvement over the way they played in 1981. Much of that progress came on offense, where New Orleans crawled in 1981 and walked last year. Now, if they can only start running.

Not that George Rogers can't run. He is one of the best backs around, but he was plagued last year by injuries. He can't sit out so much or this unit will bog down every week. One thing is for sure: Phillips needs to get more depth in the backfield. There is a dropoff the length of the Empire State Building when Rogers isn't playing.

It's probable that Ken Stabler will be the quarterback, although it makes more sense for David Wilson to take over the job, despite his inexperience. Stabler may be the most confident player Phillips has ever seen, but Wilson represents the franchise's future. And the future should be now.

Phillips has made some moves to younger players along the line and they have paid off already. And as the years go on, this part of the offense is going to really make some progress.

DEFENSE: Phillips decided to bring the Saints back from the football graveyard—which they had never left, even for a season—by building the defense first and then worrying about the offense. That makes sense, since he got his reputation in coaching for his defensive expertise. Besides, his son is the team's defensive coordinator, so why shouldn't family come first?

In any case, the Saints' defense sometimes plays as well as any in the league. This is a physical, aggressive, strong team that plays in the style of the future. The Saints certainly aren't afraid to come after you with blitzes and knock your head off in the secondary. If they go down, they go down fighting.

The best of this impressive bunch is linebacker Rickey Jackson, a bundle of talent and energy. But look for defensive end Bruce Clark to start to shine. He needed a year to get used to the NFL after a two-year stint in the CFL. But he won't be learning the ropes this season.

KICKING GAME: Let's hear it for Russell Erxleben, the most outspoken punter in the league. He can kick the ball pretty well, too, averaging 43.0 yards per kick last season. Morten Andersen, one of three kickers used by the Saints in '82, made good on 2-of-5 field-goal attempts.

NEW ORLEANS SAINTS 111

SAINTS VETERAN ROSTER

HEAD COACH—O.A. (Bum) Phillips. Assistant Coaches—Andy Everest, King Hill, John Levra, Carl Mauck, Lamar McHan, Russell Paternostro, Wade Phillips, Harold Richardson, Joe Spencer, Lance Van Zandt, John Paul Young, Willie Zapalac.

No.	Name	Pos.	Ht.	Wt.	NFL Exp.	College
7	Andersen, Morten	K	6-2	190	2	Michigan State
50	#Bordelon, Ken	LB	6-4	226	7	Louisiana State
85	#Brenner, Hoby	TE	6-4	240	3	Southern California
67	Brock, Stan	T	6-6	285	4	Colorado
75	Clark, Bruce	DE	6-3	270	2	Penn State
78	#Clark, Kelvin	G	6-3	265	3	Nebraska
83	Duckett, Kenny	WR	6-0	187	2	Wake Forest
63	Edelman, Brad	G	6-6	255	2	Missouri
99	Elliott, Tony	DT	6-2	247	2	North Texas State
14	Erxleben, Russell	P	6-4	218	4	Texas
46	#Gajan, Hokie	FB	5-11	211	2	Louisiana State
20	#Gary, Russell	SS	5-11	195	3	Nebraska
33	Gray, Kevin	S	5-11	179	2	Eastern Illinois
72	Gray, Leon	T	6-3	258	11	Jackson State
86	Groth, Jeff	WR	5-10	172	5	Bowling Green
87	Hardy, Larry	TE	6-3	230	6	Jackson State
62	Hill, John	C	6-2	246	12	Lehigh
28	#Hurley, Bill	SS	5-11	195	2	Syracuse
57	Jackson, Rickey	LB	6-2	230	4	Pittsburgh
52	Kovach, Jim	LB	6-2	230	5	Kentucky
21	Krimm, John	FS	6-2	190	2	Notre Dame
64	Lafary, Dave	T	6-7	275	7	Purdue
98	Lewis, Reggie	DE	6-2	248	2	San Diego State
29	Lewis, Rodney	CB	5-11	190	2	Nebraska
84	#Mauti, Rich	WR	6-0	190	6	Penn State
19	Merkens, Guido	QB	6-1	195	6	Sam Houston State
74	Moore, Derland	DT	6-4	253	11	Oklahoma
37	Myers, Tommy	FS	6-0	180	11	Syracuse
55	#Nairne, Rob	LB	6-4	227	7	Oregon State
66	Oubre, Louis	G	6-4	262	2	Oklahoma
51	Paul, Whitney	LB	6-3	220	8	Colorado
53	Pelluer, Scott	LB	6-2	215	3	Washington State
76	Pietrzak, Jim	C	6-5	260	9	Eastern Michigan
25	Poe, Johnnie	CB	6-1	185	3	Missouri
58	Redd, Glen	LB	6-1	225	2	Brigham Young
38	Rogers, George	RB	6-2	220	3	South Carolina
41	Rogers, Jimmy	RB	5-10	190	4	Oklahoma
80	Scott, Lindsay	WR	6-1	190	2	Georgia
54	#Simonini, Ed	LB	6-0	206	8	Texas A&M
79	Slaughter, Chuck	T	6-5	260	2	South Carolina
16	#Stabler, Ken	QB	6-3	210	14	Alabama
89	Thompson, Aundra	WR	6-1	186	7	East Texas State
42	#Tyler, Toussaint	FB	6-2	220	3	Washington
73	Warren, Frank	DE	6-4	275	3	Auburn
49	Wattelet, Frank	FS	6-0	185	3	Kansas
44	Waymer, Dave	CB	6-1	195	4	Notre Dame
94	Wilks, Jim	DE	6-5	252	3	San Diego State
18	Wilson, Dave	QB	6-3	210	2	Illinois
30	Wilson, Wayne	FB	6-3	208	5	Shepherd
56	Winston, Dennis	LB	6-0	228	7	Arkansas

#Unsigned at press time

TOP FIVE DRAFT CHOICES

Rd.	Name	Sel. No.	Pos.	Ht.	Wt.	College
2	Korte, Steve	38	G	6-2	270	Arkansas
3	Tice, John	65	TE	6-6	240	Maryland
3	Austin, Cliff	66	RB	6-0	190	Clemson
4	Lewis, Gary	98	NT	6-5	250	Oklahoma State
8	Greenwood, David	206	DB	6-3	208	Wisconsin

112 THE COMPLETE HANDBOOK OF PRO FOOTBALL

THE ROOKIES: The Saints didn't have a first-round choice, but Arkansas guard Steve Korte, chosen in the second round, is a good one who should have gone earlier. Maryland tight end John Tice could become a fine blocker on Rogers' end sweeps, but Clemson running back Cliff Austin may never have any playing time.

OUTLOOK: This will be a spoiler team this year and a contender next season. But that's still heady stuff for a franchise that has done nothing but disappoint all these years. A lot will depend on what Phillips does at quarterback.

SAINT PROFILES

GEORGE ROGERS 24 6-2 220   Running Back
His absence in the final weeks of the 1982 season, with a hamstring pull, cost the Saints their first-ever playoff spot... Still finished with 535 rushing yards, eighth in the NFC, on 122 carries... Was leading the pack before he got hurt... Certainly didn't have any problems with sophomore jinx... Put Heisman jinx to rest the year before, when he set NFL rookie rushing record (1,674 yards) and scored 13 TDs... Born Dec. 8, 1958, in Duluth, Ga.... Left South Carolina as the NCAA's fourth-leading rusher of all time (4,958 yards)... Full name is George Washington Rogers Jr.

KEN STABLER 37 6-3 210   Quarterback
As long as Bum Phillips remains in coaching, this fascinating man probably will have a quarterbacking job... Came over from Houston in a shocking trade that saw longtime Saints' star Archie Manning go to the Oilers... The Snake's unique concept of training—he does little, if any—didn't hurt him much as he passed for 1,343 yards and six touchdowns and completed 61.9 percent, despite being hindered by an arm injury... Offensive linemen credit him with bringing leadership and stability to the team... Born Dec. 25, 1945, in Foley, Ala.... One of those players who probably could throw a touchdown pass when he is 65—he's that talented... Led Alabama to NCAA title in 1965

and led Oakland to AFC championship game five times and to Super Bowl crown in 1976.

DAVID WILSON 24 6-3 210   Quarterback

The Saints had hoped he would be their starter last year, but his progress was cut off by season-long injury... Is expected to rebound this season, so Guido Merkens no longer has to be the backup quarterback... Taken by the Saints in the 1981 supplemental draft, created when Wilson lost his college eligibility at Illinois... Started four games as a 1981 rookie, completing 51.8 percent of passes... Set or tied 32 NCAA, Big Ten and school records at Illinois in 1980... Born April 27, 1959, in Anaheim, Cal.... Grew up four blocks from Anaheim Stadium... Played in junior college for two seasons.

RUSSELL ERXLEBEN 26 6-4 218   Punter

Made his biggest impact off the field last season... One of the most outspoken critics of the NFLPA leadership, as the Saints' player representative... Claimed he was threatened physically by NFLPA officials after indicating his disapproval of strike policy... Once the season resumed, he finished with a 43.0-yard average, 2.5 yards better than his previous pro best and more of an indication of what was expected from him after a wonderful career at Texas... Born Jan. 13, 1957, in Seguin, Tex.... A scratch golfer who owns his own investment company.

RICH MAUTI 29 6-0 190   Wide Receiver

Would rather be known for his receiving abilities, but seems destined to be singled out for his play on special teams... Caught only four passes last year after spending 1981 on injured reserve with a broken collarbone... Lost his kickoff returning chores, although he led the NFC in that category (25.7 yards per kick) in 1980... His career has been plagued by injuries, most likely because he knows only one way to play—all-out and recklessly... Born May 25, 1954, in East Meadow, N.Y.... Wide receiver and tailback at Penn State, where he was used mainly as a blocker.

RICKEY JACKSON 25 6-2 230   Linebacker

The Saints have one of the best corps of starting linebackers in the league and he's one reason why... Former University of Pittsburgh star is so active and aggressive he sometimes can't slow down... Maybe he's not as good as former teammate Hugh Green, but there isn't that much difference... Had 47 tackles last season, fourth-best on the team... Also had 4½ sacks, one behind team leader Bruce Clark... And he is only going to get better and better... Born March 20, 1958, in Pahokee, Fla.... Hobbies are checkers and fishing... Played defensive end at Pittsburgh.

BRUCE CLARK 25 6-3 270   Defensive End

The Saints outbid the Washington Redskins for his talents... Showed he will be worth the big bucks, after playing two years in Canada... Was fifth on the Saints in tackles and led in sacks, with 5½... Took a while to adjust to the team's 3-4 defense, but should get better and better with experience... Was a Packers' No. 1 choice in 1980, but opted to go to the CFL for more money... A consensus All-American at Penn State and runnerup for the Outland Trophy his senior year... Born March 31, 1958, in Newcastle, Pa.... Saints had to give No. 1 choice to Packers to get him.

GUIDO MERKENS 28 6-1 195   Quarterback-WR

With injury to Dave Wilson, he became a full-time quarterback last year, even starting one game for sore-armed Ken Stabler... Asserted himself well against the Redskins in that start before lack of experience finally caught up to him... Showed ability to scramble, but his timing with receivers was way off... Ran nine times for 30 yards last season and threw 49 passes, completing 18 for 186 yards and a touchdown... Saints' leading receiver in 1981, with 29 catches, but didn't have one last

NEW ORLEANS SAINTS 115

year... Born Aug. 8, 1955, in San Antonio... Played at Sam Houston State, where he was a triple threat.

JIM KOVACH 27 6-2 230   Linebacker

Tied with Frank Wattelet for team high in tackles last season... Had two sacks to accompany his 59 tackles... Remains one of the league's brightest and most versatile players... Attends University of Kentucky medical school in the offseason and played his senior season at Kentucky while in med school... Try that for degree of difficulty—how about 8.5?... Born May 1, 1956, in Parma Heights, Ohio... Instinctive player who flows into play to plug holes... His hobby is golf, when he can find time.

FRANK WATTELET 24 6-0 185   Safety

Had to be one of the best trivia question answers in the league last year... Led the Saints in tackles with 59, tying Jim Kovach, in his first year as a starter... Came out of nowhere to fill the free safety spot... Free agent in 1981 after making second-team All-Big Eight at Kansas... Started three games in 1981 and had an interception... Former pre-med student at Kansas who wants to be a dentist... But that goal has been postponed thanks to his unexpected success in the NFL... Born Oct. 25, 1958, in Paola, Kan.

COACH BUM PHILLIPS: Showing he can build a team through the draft... That was a question after the way he traded draft choices for veterans at Houston... He thought he could win a title with the Oilers with a few personnel maneuvers. With the Saints, he knows it will take him longer, so he is being more patient... His work already is starting to pay off... The Saints' defense improved last year and the offense moved away from being a one-dimensional, run-oriented attack... Key now is good drafts for a number of years to come... Even though he

It's time for New Orleans to "Win One for The Bum-mer."

hasn't got the Saints into the playoffs yet, he still has become a popular figure in New Orleans, where his informal ways have won over the populace... Still one of the funniest men in sports... Born Sept. 29, 1923, in Orange, Tex.... Noted defensive coaching genius... Led Houston to AFC championship games in 1978 and 1979... Has posted record of 63-50 in eight years as an NFL head coach... Real name is Oail.

GREATEST QUARTERBACK

It was like trading away Johnny Unitas or Jimmy Brown. You don't mess with The Franchise. You don't mess with history and tradition. You have to be more considerate than that.

But New Orleans did the unthinkable. Last year, the Saints discarded Archie Manning like so much excess baggage and sent him packing to Houston. It still is tough to see Manning in baby blue, and not the Saints' black and gold. He was the Saints for so many years, when the team was so dreadful and only his talents stood between them and total embarrassment.

NEW ORLEANS SAINTS

Those were tough, frustrating years for him. He was an All-American at Mississippi, used to winning, used to success. For 11 years (1971-81), he took a beating while losing with the Saints. Never a winning season, never a playoff berth, no matter how hard he tried and how much he survived. He gave himself to the community, making charity appearances and spreading good will.

Then they sent him to Houston. Such thanks.

INDIVIDUAL SAINT RECORDS

Rushing

Most Yards Game:	166	George Rogers, vs Dallas 1982
Season:	1,674	George Rogers, 1981
Career:	3,218	Chuck Muncie, 1976-79

Passing

Most TD Passes Game:	6	Billy Kilmer, vs St. Louis, 1969
Season:	23	Archie Manning, 1980
Career:	155	Archie Manning, 1971-81

Receiving

Most TD Passes Game:	3	Dan Abramowicz, vs San Francisco, 1971
Season:	9	Henry Childs, 1977
Career:	37	Dan Abramowicz, 1967-72

Scoring

Most Points Game:	18	Walt Roberts, vs Philadelphia, 1967
	18	Dan Abramowicz, vs San Francisco, 1971
	18	Archie Manning, vs Chicago, 1977
	18	Chuck Muncie, vs San Francisco, 1979
	18	George Rogers, vs Los Angeles, 1981
	18	Wayne Wilson, vs Atlanta, 1982
Season:	99	Tom Dempsey, 1969
Career:	243	Charlie Durkee, 1967-68, 1971-72
Most TDs Game:	3	Walt Roberts, vs Philadelphia, 1967
	3	Dan Abramowicz, vs San Francisco, 1971
	3	Archie Manning, vs Chicago, 1977
	3	Chuck Muncie, vs San Francisco, 1979
	3	George Rogers, vs Los Angeles, 1981
	3	Wayne Wilson, vs Atlanta, 1982
Season:	13	George Rogers, 1981
Career:	37	Dan Abramowicz, 1967-72

NEW YORK GIANTS

TEAM DIRECTORY: Pres.: Wellington Mara; VP/Treasurer: Timothy Mara; VP/GM: George Young; Dir. Pro Personnel: Tom Boisture; Dir. Pub. Rel.: Ed Croke; Head Coach: Bill Parcells. Home field: Giants Stadium (76,500). Colors: Blue, red and white.

SCOUTING REPORT

OFFENSE: The best thing that could happen to the Giant offense is nothing. No holdouts, no injuries, no slumps. Just let new coach Bill Parcells start off with a full deck and let him play his cards over the course of the season.

Certainly, a healthy Giant team has every right to think it can move the ball and play well enough to win. The major weakness, at least compared with the best teams, is the receiving corps. Although it's not pathetic, it just doesn't have the one game-breaking threat the best teams need.

Parcells could help matters by deciding on a starting quarterback quickly. Phil Simms was No. 1 before getting hurt last year. Scott Brunner played adequately at times, but not well enough to take away all hope from Simms that he can be No. 1 again. One thing the Giants don't need is a quarterback controversy.

Another thing they don't need is another so-so effort from Rob Carpenter. He's got to have a good year for them to have one.

DEFENSE: The major reason Parcells got the head coaching job—and was able to buck the trend in the league to hire offensive coordinators as head coaches—was that he had built the Giant defense into something of a mini-legend. The unit has a reputation for standing in there and battling with the best of them and often bailing out the Giant offense when it messes up. Now the defense can't let Parcells down.

The key still is the linebacking. Harry Carson is menacing, Brad Van Pelt eats up enemy runners and Lawrence Taylor is the Magic Johnson of the NFL. He creates fun with his free-lance antics and amazing quickness. He's worth the price of admission, no question. He also generates most of the Giant pass rush, but the team would be in better shape if more of that rush came from the front line.

Cornerback Mark Haynes is one of the league's best, but the secondary could use a new starter or two. Rookie Terry Kinard, a real talent, could be an immediate help.

NEW YORK GIANTS 119

KICKING GAME: Not much to say about Dave Jennings, except what a punter. He doesn't talk badly, either. Joe Danelo is in that pack of adequate-to-fair kickers who lack the range to pull out the big games. Leon Bright, if he can survive, can be a dangerous return man.

THE ROOKIES: The Giants wanted to add some toughness to their secondary, which wasn't that bad before. Now, with Kinard, a No. 1 pick from Clemson, an already good defense will be better. Defensive tackle Leonard Marshall of LSU adds depth and tight end Jamie Williams of Nebraska could be the blocker the Giants have needed at that position.

Giants' Lawrence Taylor plays defense like he invented it.

GIANTS VETERAN ROSTER

HEAD COACH—Bill Parcells. Assistant Coaches—Bill Belichick, Tom Bresnahan, Romeo Crennell, Ron Erhardt, Len Fontes, Pat Hodgson, Lamar Leachman, Bob Ledbetter, Mike Pope.

No.	Name	Pos.	Ht.	Wt.	NFL Exp.	College
67	Ard, Billy	G	6-3	250	3	Wake Forest
74	Baldinger, Rich	T	6-4	270	2	Wake Forest
60	Benson, Brad	T	6-3	258	6	Penn State
45	Bright, Leon	RB	5-9	192	3	Florida State
12	Brunner, Scott	QB	6-5	200	4	Delaware
64	Burt, Jim	T	6-1	255	3	Miami
22	Carpenter, Brian	CB-S	5-10	167	2	Michigan
26	Carpenter, Rob	RB	6-1	230	7	Miami (Ohio)
53	Carson, Harry	LB	6-2	235	8	South Carolina State
31	Chatman, Cliff	RB	6-2	225	2	Central State (Okla.)
29	Currier, Bill	S	6-0	202	7	South Carolina
18	Danelo, Joe	K	5-9	166	9	Washington State
46	Dennis, Mike	CB	5-10	190	4	Wyoming
88	Eddings, Floyd	WR	5-11	177	2	Berkeley
37	Flowers, Larry	S	6-1	190	3	Texas Tech
66	Foote, Chris	C	6-3	250	4	Southern California
83	Gray, Earnest	WR	6-3	195	5	Memphis State
—	Green, David	RB	5-10	208	2	Edinboro State
79	Hardison, Dee	DE	6-4	269	6	North Carolina
36	Haynes, Mark	CB	5-11	185	4	Colorado
27	Heater, Larry	RB	5-11	205	4	Arizona
61	Hughes, Ernie	C	6-3	265	5	Notre Dame
57	Hunt, Byron	LB	6-5	230	3	Southern Methodist
24	Jackson, Terry	CB	5-11	197	6	San Diego State
13	Jennings, Dave	P	6-4	205	10	St. Lawrence
55	Kelley, Brian	LB	6-3	222	11	California Lutheran
63	Kimball, Bruce	G	6-2	260	2	Miami
72	King, Gordon	T	6-6	275	6	Stanford
51	Marion, Frank	LB	6-3	223	7	Florida A&M
75	Martin, George	DE	6-4	245	9	Oregon
54	Matthews, Bill	LB	6-2	235	4	South Dakota State
39	Mayock, Mike	S	6-2	195	2	Boston College
76	McGriff, Curtis	DE	6-5	265	4	Alabama
52	McLaughlin, Joe	LB	6-1	235	4	Massachusetts
85	Mistler, John	WR	6-2	186	3	Arizona State
20	Morris, Joe	RB	5-7	190	3	Syracuse
81	Mullady, Tom	TE	6-3	232	5	Southwest Memphis
77	Neill, Bill	T	6-4	255	3	Pittsburgh
86	Perkins, Johnny	WR	6-2	205	7	Abilene Christian
82	Pittman, Danny	WR	6-2	205	4	Wyoming
28	Reece, Beasley	S	6-1	195	8	North Texas State
8	Reed, Mark	QB	6-3	195	2	Moorhead
17	Rutledge, Jeff	QB	6-1	190	5	Alabama
78	Sally, Jerome	DT	6-3	260	2	Missouri
44	Shaw, Pete	S	5-10	183	7	Northwestern
87	Shirk, Gary	TE	6-1	220	8	Morehead State
69	Simmons, Roy	G	6-3	264	5	Georgia Tech
11	Simms, Phil	QB	6-3	216	4	Morehead State
80	Tabor, Phil	DE	6-4	255	5	Oklahoma
65	Tautolo, John	G	6-3	260	2	UCLA
56	Taylor, Lawrence	LB	6-3	242	3	North Carolina
68	Turner, J.T.	G	6-3	250	7	Duke
59	Umphrey, Rich	C	6-3	255	2	Colorado
10	Van Pelt, Brad	LB	6-5	235	11	Michigan State
73	Weston, Jeff	T	6-5	280	5	Notre Dame
58	Whittington, Mike	LB	6-2	220	4	Notre Dame
25	Woolfolk, Butch	RB	6-2	207	2	Michigan

TOP FIVE DRAFT CHOICES

Rd.	Name	Sel. No.	Pos.	Ht.	Wt.	College
1	Kinard, Terry	10	DB	6-1	190	Clemson
2	Marshall, Leonard	37	DT	6-2	272	Louisiana State
3	Williams, Jamie	63	TE	6-5	230	Nebraska
3	Nelson, Karl	70	T	6-6	271	Iowa State
5	Scott, Malcolm	124	TE	6-4	238	Louisiana State

NEW YORK GIANTS 121

OUTLOOK: They'll make a run for the title, if the pieces hold together. You don't have to be spectacular to go far in the playoffs, just consistent. And you better win the close ones, something the Giants couldn't do consistently last year.

GIANT PROFILES

HARRY CARSON 29 6-2 235   Linebacker

Mean and lean... An all-pro who plays up to high standards every season... Should always be rated among the best inside linebackers in the business... Has knack of plugging gaps and making big plays... Has been in the Pro Bowl four times now... Led the team in tackles once again, with 107, and had his best game ever against Green Bay, when he made 25 tackles, 20 of them solo... Also had three quarterback sacks... Born Nov. 23, 1953, in Florence, S.C.... Former South Carolina State star loves music, fishing, target shooting and soap operas.

MARK HAYNES 24 5-11 185   Cornerback

Made the Pro Bowl for the first time, cementing his status as one of the best young cornerbacks in the league... Had 50 tackles to lead the secondary—a goodly number for a cornerback—and one interception... Normally shut down opponent's receivers... It's getting so teams are starting to throw away from him, which cuts down on his interception chances... Had a disappointing rookie year two seasons ago, but that is all but forgotten now in wake of the progress he has made... Born Nov. 6, 1958, in Kansas City... Attended Colorado, where he switched from running back to cornerback.

LAWRENCE TAYLOR 24 6-3 242   Linebacker

What is so fascinating about him is that, although last year was only his second pro season, he was so good that teams gave him the ultimate defensive honor—devising special offensive blocking schemes to stop him... "You just can't expect a running back to block him one on one," Washington coach Joe Gibbs said... Had 55 tackles, a club-high 7½ sacks

122 THE COMPLETE HANDBOOK OF PRO FOOTBALL

and a blocked kick... Against Detroit on Thanksgiving Day, he caused an interception, caused a fumble, had a one-handed sack and then returned an interception 97 yards for a touchdown... Born Feb. 4, 1959, in Williamsburg, Va.... Didn't play football until his junior year in high school, then starred at North Carolina.

DAVE JENNINGS 31 6-4 205　　　　　　　　　　Punter

Played a controversial role during the players' strike... Spoke out frequently against the union, and he was quoted widely by representatives of management... Don't get Ed Garvey and him together if you want a comfortable evening... Fourth in NFC in punting last season with a 42.8-yard average, but was still selected to the Pro Bowl because of his consistency and accuracy... He had 16 punts inside the 20, by far the most in the NFL... Born June 8, 1952, in New York... Attended St. Lawrence and is a professional radio and television announcer.

BRIAN KELLEY 32 6-3 222　　　　　　　　　　Linebacker

Had perhaps his best season as a Giant, even if it was shortened by the strike... His 83 tackles were second-best on the team, behind fellow linebacker Harry Carson... Also had three interceptions... Enjoyed a standout game against the Redskins, registering 17 tackles, two interceptions and five tackles for losses... One of the finest athletes in California Lutheran history... Lettered in three sports... Born Sept. 1, 1951, in Dallas... Worked summers at the Cowboys' training camp... Owns restaurants in California.

BUTCH WOOLFOLK 23 6-2 207　　　　　　　　Running Back

Giants were hoping that either he or Joe Morris would contribute as rookies last year... Using a No. 1 draft choice to get this former Michigan star proved to be a wise choice... Rob Carpenter was a holdout, so if not for Woolfolk, Giants would have been left without a quality back to open the season... Now that position is one of the deepest on the team... Learned how to be tough under Bo Schembechler at Michigan, but he learned how to be a receiver coming out of the backfield with the

Giants... Caught 23 passes for 224 yards, probably the most surprising aspect of his first-year showing... Gained 439 yards rushing on 112 carries... Born March 1, 1960, in Milwaukee.

ROB CARPENTER 28 6-1 230 — Running Back

Serves as symbol of athlete who finally gets a chance to play and then decides he won't play unless he is paid more... His absence early in the season because of contract holdout didn't help the Giants' playoff chances one bit... When he is playing, the Giants are a different team... Gained 207 yards, second on team, behind Butch Woolfolk... But that certainly was not the production the team wanted from the man responsible for getting the Giants into the 1981 playoffs... Born April 20, 1955, in Lancaster, Ohio... Came from the Houston Oilers, where he backed up Earl Campbell most of his career... Attended Miami of Ohio.

SCOTT BRUNNER 26 6-5 200 — Quarterback

With Phil Simms hurt all season, this Delaware grad had the starting quarterback chores all to himself... Injury ruined what would have been an interesting year-long duel between the two for the starting role... Wound up completing 54 percent of his passes for 2,017 yards and 10 touchdowns... Was sacked 17 times... His 74 rating put him in the lower echelon of NFC quarterbacks and leaves him open to a challenge from Simms this summer... Wasn't as steady or as spectacular as the Giants would have liked... Born March 24, 1957, in Lawrence, N.J.... Father, John, is backfield coach with the Packers... Former participant in the Pass, Punt and Kick contest.

JOE DANELO 29 5-9 166 — Kicker

Giants' leading scorer again, with 54 points, half of what he managed the year before in a full-length season... Made 12-of-21 field goals, and the Giants would like better accuracy than that... Was especially weak outside the 39, from where he missed 6-of-8 attempts... Also failed to convert his only try over 50... If he can't improve range, it takes away from team's chances of winning in last seconds... Loves to run waist-

124 THE COMPLETE HANDBOOK OF PRO FOOTBALL

deep in water, remodel apartments, build patios and furniture and work as a stevedore... Born Sept. 2, 1953, in Spokane, Wash.... Played at Washington State.

BRAD VAN PELT 32 6-5 235   Linebacker

Many teams rate him as the toughest linebacker in the league to run against... Strong and aggressive and, after all these years, he is very intelligent... Uses his experience to break down blocking on sweeps and open up routes for others to make tackles... Finished sixth in tackles last season... With all these good Giant linebackers, there aren't enough tackles to go around... Recovered two fumbles and had two sacks... Born April 5, 1951, in Owosso, Mich.... Turned down $100,000 bonus from St. Louis Cardinals' baseball team... No. 1 pick out of Michigan State.

COACH BILL PARCELLS: The Giants are going against the tide in the NFL by naming their defensive coordinator as Ray Perkins' successor... Trend now is to turn to offensive-minded assistants, usually offensive coordinators... Just look at the other people who became head coaches in the league this year... But it was hard for the Giants to pass up the man who had built their defense into such a respected unit... Besides, the players like him and it made for a very smooth transition after Perkins suddenly bolted for Alabama... A contrast in personalities with Perkins, who was far more introverted... Only head-coaching experience was at the Air Force Academy, and that lasted for one year... Born Aug. 22, 1941, in Englewood, N.J.... Attended Wichita State... College assistant at Hastings, Wichita State, Army, Florida State, Vanderbilt and Texas Tech and had been a pro assistant with New England.

GREATEST QUARTERBACK

There is going to be an argument here. For Giant fans who worship the very mention of Charlie Conerly's name, it is a pure sin to say that New York's all-time best quarterback is Y.A. Tittle.

Granted, Tittle had a short stay (1961-64) in New York and a longer one before that in San Francisco (1951-60). But Tittle is in the Hall of Fame; Conerly is not. And Tittle had a special talent for brilliance that Conerly, as good as he was, lacked.

Who can forget the heart and skills of the balding Louisiana State grad? In three of his years with the Giants (1961-63), he guided them to the title game. He led the league in passing in 1963 and he had two years in which he passed for more than 3,000 yards, something Conerly never achieved. Against Washington in 1962, Tittle put on the greatest one-man display in Giant history, throwing for 505 yards.

As for Conerly, he mellowed wonderfully with time. From 1948 to 1961, this Ole Miss grad was a Giant. He quarterbacked them to the NFL title in 1956, but he never could match the pure magic of Y.A. Tittle.

INDIVIDUAL GIANT RECORDS

Rushing

Most Yards Game:	218	Gene Roberts, vs Chi. Cardinals, 1950
Season:	1,182	Ron Johnson, 1972
Career:	4,638	Alex Webster, 1955-64

Passing

Most TD Passes Game:	7	Y.A. Tittle, vs Washington, 1962
Season:	36	Y.A. Tittle, 1963
Career:	173	Charlie Conerly, 1948-61

Receiving

Most TD Passes Game:	4	Earnest Gray, vs St. Louis, 1980
Season:	13	Homer Jones, 1967
Career:	48	Kyle Rote, 1951-61

Scoring

Most Points Game:	24	Ron Johnson, vs Philadelphia, 1972
	24	Earnest Gray, vs St. Louis, 1980
Season:	107	Pete Gogolak, 1970
Career:	646	Pete Gogolak, 1966-74
Most TDs Game:	4	Ron Johnson, vs Philadelphia, 1972
	4	Earnest Gray, vs St. Louis, 1980
Season:	17	Gene Roberts, 1949
Career:	78	Frank Gifford, 1952-60, 1962-64

126 THE COMPLETE HANDBOOK OF PRO FOOTBALL
PHILADELPHIA EAGLES

TEAM DIRECTORY: Pres.: Leonard Tose; VP/Legal Counsel: Susan Fletcher; Dir. Player Personnel: Lynn Stiles; Dir. Pub. Rel.: Jim Gallagher; Head Coach: Marion Campbell. Home field: Veterans Stadium (72,200). Colors: Kelly green, white and silver.

Ron Jaworski hopes he can turn those boos into cheers.

SCOUTING REPORT

OFFENSE: Marion Campbell is a defensive whiz, which means he won't be much help reconstructing or redirecting the Eagles' offense, once the domain of Dick Vermeil. Like the ex-coach, the offense looked like it was burnt-out last year.

Only after the Eagles went back to a basic, run-oriented approach did the offense show some strength. That may not be a bad route to take—after all, Washington certainly used the run to its advantage in the palyoffs. But even with the help of since-retired Sid Gillman, Vermeil's offense never seemed that imaginative or difficult to stop.

Quarterback Ron Jaworski will have to put up with critics and booing fans once again this year. It's doubtful things will change no matter how well he plays. Getting a fullback to go with Wilbert Montgomery—or moving to a one-back offense—would help, and the growth of young Mike Quick as a receiver is necessary for the passing attack to develop. Vermeil called the offensive line the best he has had, but it's showing some age.

DEFENSE: The Eagles should have realized they were in trouble when they gave up 37 points in their opener last year. They sometimes didn't give up that many in a month in past seasons. But Campbell's insistence on staying with zone defenses finally caught up to him. Teams began picking apart his pride and joy, and suddenly Philadelphia was far from being the league's No. 1-ranked unit.

Things got better by the year's end, so Campbell isn't quite as discouraged as he might have been. Still, the Eagles need a pass-rusher to replace Claude Humphrey (will he show up in the USFL one day?) and maybe Campbell will regret releasing linebacker John Bunting. Cornerback Roynell Young is still a gem and he'll get better, but maybe Herman Edwards can't stay with the faster receivers anymore. The mystique that surrounded the Philly defense is gone. It will be hard to get it back.

KICKING GAME: Punter Max Runager didn't make the big kicks when the Eagles needed them the most. Coverage teams broke down near the end of the season, embarrassing former special teams coach Vermeil. Only placekicker Tony Franklin had a decent season, probably much to Vermeil's surprise.

THE ROOKIES: Running back Michael Haddix, a No. 1 pick from Mississippi State, could supply the speed the Eagles have been lacking. Ditto for Mississippi State's Glen Young at wide

EAGLES VETERAN ROSTER

HEAD COACH—Marion Campbell. Assistant Coaches—John Becker, Fred Bruney, Chuck Clausen, Harry Gamble, Frank Gansz, George Hill, Ken Iman, Billie Matthews, Jerry Wampfler, Dick Wood.

No.	Name	Pos.	Ht.	Wt.	NFL Exp.	College
96	Armstrong, Harvey	G	6-2	255	2	Southern Methodist
63	Baker, Ron	G	6-4	250	6	Oklahoma State
27	Blackmore, Richard	CB	5-10	174	5	Mississippi State
98	Brown, Gregory	DE	6-5	240	3	Kansas State
30	Calhoun, Don	RB	6-0	213	10	Kansas State
37	Campfield, Billy	RB	6-0	205	6	Kansas
17	#Carmichael, Harold	WR	6-8	225	13	Southern
71	#Clarke, Ken	G	6-2	255	6	Syracuse
57	Curcio, Mike	LB	6-1	237	3	Temple
25	DeVaughn, Dennis	CB-S	5-10	175	2	Bishop
46	Edwards, Herman	CB	6-0	194	7	San Diego State
24	Ellis, Ray	S	6-1	192	3	Ohio State
1	Franklin, Tony	K	5-8	182	5	Texas A&M
79	Giddens, Frank	T	6-7	300	3	New Mexico
58	Griggs, Anthony	LB	6-3	220	2	Ohio State
78	Hairston, Carl	DE	6-3	260	8	Maryland State
35	Harrington, Perry	FB	5-11	210	4	Jackson State
68	Harrison, Dennis	DE	6-8	280	6	Vanderbilt
85	Hoover, Melvin	WR	6-0	185	2	Arizona State
7	Jaworski, Ron	QB	6-2	185	9	Youngstown State
97	Johnson, Charles	G	6-1	262	3	Maryland
84	Kab, Vyto	TE	6-5	255	2	Penn State
73	Kenney, Steve	G	6-4	262	4	Clemson
55	LeMaster, Frank	LB	6-2	238	10	Kentucky
41	Logan, Randy	S	6-1	195	11	Michigan
45	Mansfield, Von	CB-S	5-11	185	2	Wisconsin
—	McGlasson, Ed	C	6-4	250	4	Youngstown State
64	Miraldi, Dean	G	6-5	254	3	Utah
99	Mitchell, Leonard	DE	6-7	272	3	Houston
31	Montgomery, Wilbert	RB	5-10	195	7	Abilene Christian
50	#Morriss, Guy	C	6-4	255	11	Texas Christian
34	Oliver, Hubie	FB	5-10	212	3	Arizona
6	Pastorini, Dan	QB	6-2	205	13	Santa Clara
62	Perot, Pete	G	6-2	261	5	Northwest Louisiana
9	Pisarcik, Joe	QB	6-4	220	7	New Mexico State
82	Quick, Mike	WR	6-2	190	2	North Carolina State
56	Robinson, Jerry	LB	6-2	216	5	UCLA
4	Runager, Max	P	6-1	189	5	South Carolina
87	Sampleton, Lawrence	TE	6-5	233	2	Texas
21	#Sciarra, John	S	5-11	185	6	UCLA
76	Sisemore, Jerry	T	6-4	265	11	Texas
61	Slater, Mark	C	6-2	257	6	Minnesota
81	Smith, Ron	WR	6-1	185	6	San Diego State
88	Spagnola, John	TE	6-4	240	5	Yale
54	Valentine, Zack	LB	6-2	220	5	East Carolina
75	#Walters, Stan	T	6-6	275	12	Syracuse
51	Wilkes, Reggie	LB	6-4	230	6	Georgia Tech
22	Wilson, Brenard	FS	6-0	175	5	Vanderbilt
83	Woodruff, Tony	WR	6-0	175	2	Fresno State
43	Young, Roynell	CB	6-1	181	4	Alcorn State

#Unsigned at press time

TOP FIVE DRAFT CHOICES

Rd.	Name	Sel. No.	Pos.	Ht.	Wt.	College
1	Haddix, Michael	8	RB	6-3	215	Mississippi State
2	Hopkins, Wes	35	DB	6-1	205	Southern Methodist
2	Schulz, Jody	46	LB	6-4	235	East Carolina
3	Young, Glen	62	WR	6-3	205	Mississippi State
4	Williams, Michael	89	RB	6-2	209	Mississippi College

receiver. East Carolina's Jody Schultz will be asked to supply depth at linebacker.

OUTLOOK: It may be too easy, and unwise, to write off the Eagles until the effect of Vermeil's departure can be measured. Campbell, who failed as a head coach in Atlanta, is receiving a rare second chance in the NFL. He has a difficult morale-boosting task ahead of him.

EAGLE PROFILES

RON JAWORSKI 32 6-2 185   **Quarterback**

Even ex-coach Dick Vermeil suggested it might be better for him to play somewhere else in the future... But that's easier said than done, when you are talking about getting equal value for a premier starting quarterback... But things have gotten so difficult for him that, even on his good days, he is being booed by Philadelphia fans... After throwing for 2,076 yards last season, he is the Eagles' all-time leader in passes attempted (2,320) and completed (1,236), yardage (16,039) and touchdowns (114)... Born March 23, 1951, in Lackawanna, N.Y.... Former Youngstown State star whose nickname is "Jaws."

WILBERT MONTGOMERY 28 5-10 195 Running Back

Sometime this season, he'll become the Eagles' career record holder for rushing yards and attempts, breaking the all-time marks of 5,860 yards and 1,320 carries held by Steve Van Buren... Didn't have one of his usual standout seasons last year, as he suffered from the Eagles' offensive breakdowns... Wound up with 515 yards, seventh in the NFC, on 114 carries... Ran for seven touchdowns... Would be helped if the Eagles could resolve question mark at fullback... Played at Abilene Christian, where there now is $60,000 Wilbert Montgomery scholarship fund... Born Sept. 16, 1954, in Greenville, Miss.... Named Mississippi's Pro Athlete of the Year in 1980... Has reached 1,000-yard mark in a season three times.

HAROLD CARMICHAEL 33 6-8 225   Wide Receiver

Sometimes, it doesn't seem that the Eagles use him enough... With the height advantage he has over cornerbacks, he should be nearly unstoppable... Yet frequently he all but disappears during games... Tied for eighth in receptions last year in the NFC with 35, for 540 yards... Has played in 151 consecutive games and ranks seventh on the NFL's all-time receiving list, with 551 catches... Born Sept. 22, 1949, in Jacksonville, Fla.... Was selected NFL Man of the Year in 1980 for his numerous community activities... Seventh-round draft choice out of Southern University in 1971, he had thought he would be pro basketball player.

JERRY ROBINSON 26 6-2 216   Linebacker

Made a successful switch from outside to inside linebacker last season... Eagles wanted to take advantage of his quickness and aggressiveness and it paid off... Led the team in tackles with 95, including 67 initial hits... Had only 13 tackles in the first two games, playing on the outside... On the inside, he averaged 11 per game... Dick Vermeil made him his initial first-round draft choice after coaching him at UCLA... Eagles have never regretted that Vermeil wanted him so badly... Born Dec. 18, 1956, in San Francisco... Running back in high school who hopes for broadcasting position after he retires.

ROYNELL YOUNG 25 6-1 181   Cornerback

With four interceptions last year, he has 12 in just three NFL years... A quality first-round 1980 pick who has lived up to every expectation... Had 21 tackles and knocked away 11 passes... Could probably remain effective if the Eagles ever decide to move away from strict zone coverages and start mixing in more man-to-man... Born Dec. 1, 1957, in New Orleans... Received only one firm scholarship offer and attended Alcorn State.

PHILADELPHIA EAGLES 131

TONY FRANKLIN 26 5-8 182   Kicker

Now that Dick Vermeil is gone, maybe he'll be able to relax and kick more consistently...Has a withdrawn personality that makes it difficult to know him well...Even though he kicks barefoot, he still has one of the league's strongest legs...When he's so moved, he can be a devastating kicker...But his critics like to point out that he rarely has won a game in the final seconds...Born Nov. 19, 1956, in Big Springs, Tex....Halfback in high school before switching to kicking...Tried only nine field goals last year, making six, and finished with 41 points...Former Texas A&M standout kicked 59-yarder against Dallas in 1979.

CARL HAIRSTON 30 6-3 260   Defensive End

Has slipped a bit from a few years ago, when ex-Redskin coach Jack Pardee was insisting he was the best defensive end in football...But he's still a quality player who has been part of one of the league's best defenses for years...Watch for this unusual habit: at least once a game, he'll take an injury timeout, come out of the game briefly, and then return quickly...Born Dec. 15, 1952, in Martinsville, Va....Former star at Maryland-Eastern Shore who drove a truck before entering college...A seventh-round 1976 pick.

HERMAN EDWARDS 29 6-0 194   Cornerback

One of the most approachable, talkative players in the league...A good guy...Functions well in the Eagles' zone defenses, but those alignments may be on the way out against the ever-developing passing offenses...Five interceptions last season give him 27 for his career, putting him third on the Eagles' all-time list...Played more minutes last year than any other Eagle...Born April 27, 1954, in Fort Monmouth, N.J....Attended San Diego State, which seems to turn out quality cornerbacks every year....Had 3.5 college grade-point average.

STAN WALTERS 35 6-6 275　　　　　　　Offensive Tackle

One of those classy veteran players who makes the NFL special... Just does his job every year without complaint and does it well... One of the cornerstones of the Philadelphia offensive line... Even in his 11th season, he wound up playing more minutes than any other Eagle offensive player last season... Ninth-round draft choice out of Cincinnati who wound up being a steal for the Eagles... Born May 27, 1948, in Rutherford, N.J., near site of Giants Stadium... Training to be radio sportscaster... Also enjoys boating, especially deep-sea fishing.

DENNIS HARRISON 27 6-8 280　　　　　　　Defensive End

Happy-go-lucky, outgoing type with a winning personality... Quickly maturing into one of the league's best defensive ends after hardly playing his first two seasons with Eagles... Led the team in sacks last season with 10½, a career high... Had only four the year before... Eagles' lone representative in the Pro Bowl last year... A fourth-round 1978 selection out of Vanderbilt... Born July 31, 1956, in Cleveland... State heavyweight wrestling champion in high school... His teammates call him "Bigfoot," in recognition of his size-15 playing shoes.

COACH MARION CAMPBELL: Became the 16th head coach in the Eagles' 50-year history when he replaced Dick Vermeil last January... Vermeil, citing burnout, retired and the Eagles quickly turned the team over to their longtime defensive coordinator and unofficial assistant head coach... Vermeil had always given him complete charge of the defense and never interfered... This will be his second shot at an NFL head-coaching job... Coached the Atlanta Falcons from 1974-76 and had limited success, posting 6-19 record... Some question whether his personality is adaptable to head-coaching responsibilities... No question he is a gifted defensive coach, although the Eagle defense slipped badly this past season after being one of the league's elite... Born May 25, 1929, in Chester,

S.C.... Full name is Francis Marion... Named after Revolutionary War hero... Three-time All-SEC tackle at Georgia went on to distinguished NFL career with San Francisco and Philadelphia from 1954-61... Developed defensive units at Minnesota (1964-66), Los Angeles (1966-68) and Atlanta (1969-76).

GREATEST QUARTERBACK

The Dutchman was great wherever he played. But he was at his best when he put on a Philadelphia uniform and started to snarl at anyone who came near him.

Norm Van Brocklin might win a pure-passers contest, but as Mr. Lovable, forget it. If he liked you, he might not say anything. If he didn't like you, watch out. He could tongue-lash with the best of them, one reason his attempts at coaching met with mixed success. He was just a hard guy to warm up to, even as a winner.

And he was a winner. One of the great mysteries of pro sports

Eagles' 6-8 Harold Carmichael soars over defenders.

is how the Rams, for whom he shared quarterback duties from 1949 through 1957, could have put him in a rotation with, of all people, Billy Wade. Bob Waterfield, okay. But Wade? That was Van Brocklin's last straw in Los Angeles, where his pass to Tom Fears enabled the Rams to beat the Browns in the 1951 title game.

It wasn't until the Dutchman landed in Philadelphia in 1958 that he had fulltime possession of the quarterback post. And he made the most of it, leading the Eagles to victory over the Packers in the 1960 championship game. It was Van Brocklin's valedictory campaign as a player. So he had the last laugh—if he ever laughed—by playing on championship teams with two different franchises.

INDIVIDUAL EAGLE RECORDS

Rushing

Most Yards Game:	205	Steve Van Buren, vs Pittsburgh, 1949
Season:	1,512	Wilbert Montgomery, 1979
Career:	5,680	Steve Van Buren, 1944-51

Passing

Most TD Passes Game:	7	Adrian Burk, vs Washington, 1954
Season:	32	Sonny Jurgensen, 1961
Career:	114	Ron Jaworski, 1977-82

Receiving

Most TD Passes Game:	4	Joe Carter, vs Cincinnati, 1934
	4	Ben Hawkins, vs Pittsburgh, 1969
Season:	13	Tommy McDonald, 1960 and 1961
Career:	76	Harold Carmichael, 1971-82

Scoring

Most Points Game:	25	Bobby Walston, vs Washington, 1954
Season:	114	Bobby Walston, 1954
Career:	881	Bobby Walston, 1951-62
Most TDs Game:	4	Joe Carter, vs Cincinnati, 1934
	4	Clarence Peaks, vs St. Louis, 1958
	4	Tommy McDonald, vs N.Y. Giants, 1959
	4	Ben Hawkins, vs Pittsburgh, 1969
	4	Wilbert Montgomery, vs Washington, 1978
	4	Wilbert Montgomery, vs Washington, 1979
Season:	18	Steve Van Buren, 1945
Career:	77	Steve Van Buren, 1944-51

SAN FRANCISCO 49ERS

TEAM DIRECTORY: Pres.: Edward J. DeBartolo, Jr.; GM/Head Coach: Bill Walsh; Administrative VP: John McVay; Dir. Pub. Rel.: George Heddleston. Home field: Candlestick Park (61,185). Colors: 49er gold and scarlet.

The 49ers' hopes for a revival hinge on Joe Montana.

THE COMPLETE HANDBOOK OF PRO FOOTBALL
SCOUTING REPORT

OFFENSE: Where did all the striking power go? Sometimes it was there, just like in 1981, and sometimes it wasn't, just like in all those past bad seasons. Quarterback Joe Montana still was brilliant, even though his supporting cast let him down at times. Now it's up to coach Bill Walsh to mend the problems.

Walsh helped by trading for Wendell Tyler, formerly of the Los Angeles Rams. Tyler, the NFC's sixth-leading rusher last season, will add much-needed speed and receiving ability to the backfield. The 49ers still need stability along the offensive line, which was disrupted when Walsh decided to put a rookie into the lineup at left tackle. That was part of the problem. Walsh chose to mess with his team's chemistry and his gamble failed. Another example was the big contract given to ex-Patriot Russ Francis, who never did beat out Charle Young at tight end.

The 49ers still have Montana and his wonderful favorite target, Dwight Clark, who led the league in catches last year. If Renaldo Nehemiah ever develops at the other end, watch out.

DEFENSE: Injuries really plagued the 49ers throughout 1982, especially on defense. Walsh wasn't able to start the lineup he wanted in most games, and if there are too many defensive changes, it breaks down continuity and consistency. And that leads to problems.

San Francisco needs a big year from pass rusher Fred Dean, who all but disappeared at times last season after a sensational 1981. Without him, the 49ers don't really have much of a rush. They'll welcome newcomer Cody Jones, the ex-Ram, and will benefit from the return of the injured Dwaine Board up front.

Remarkable Jack Reynolds continues to stand out in the middle. He's helped by platooning, which might extend his career into the 21st century. But even with Reynolds, Walsh was unhappy with the lack of imagination displayed by this unit last season and vows that things will be different this time around.

He'll be helped by growth in the secondary. There are all types of talent, especially in the person of Ronnie Lott. Every team in the league would love to have him.

KICKING GAME: Ray Wersching had another steady season, making 12-of-17 field goals and finishing with 59 points. But Jim Miller was next-to-last in punting and the 49ers were dead last in net punting. It's tough to win that way.

SAN FRANCISCO 49ERS

49ERS VETERAN ROSTER

HEAD COACH—Bill Walsh. Assistant Coaches—Jerry Attaway, Paul Hackett, Norb Hecker, Sherman Lewis, Bobb McKittrick, Bill McPherson, Ray Rhodes, George Seifert, Fred von Appen.

No.	Name	Pos.	Ht.	Wt.	NFL Exp.	College
68	Ayers, John	G	6-5	265	7	West Texas State
63	#Beeson, Terry	LB	6-3	233	7	Kansas
7	Benjamin, Guy	QB	6-3	210	6	Stanford
76	Board, Dwaine	DE	6-5	250	4	North Carolina A&T
57	Bunz, Dan	LB	6-4	225	5	Cal State-Long Beach
60	Choma, John	G-C	6-6	261	3	Virginia
15	Clark, Bryan	QB	6-2	196	2	Michigan State
87	Clark, Dwight	WR	6-3	205	5	Clemson
90	Clark, Mike	DE	6-4	250	3	Florida
47	Collier, Tim	CB	6-0	176	8	East Texas State
—	Collins, George	G-T	6-2	270	6	Georgia
49	Cooper, Earl	FB	6-2	227	4	Rice
51	Cross, Randy	G	6-3	250	8	UCLA
74	Dean, Fred	DE	6-2	236	9	Louisiana Tech
62	Downing, Walt	G-C-T	6-3	270	6	Michigan
—	Evans, Chuck	LB	6-3	235	3	Stanford
71	Fahnhorst, Keith	T	6-6	273	10	Minnesota
—	Favron, Calvin	LB	6-1	227	5	SE Louisiana
54	Ferrari, Ron	LB	6-0	212	2	Illinois
81	Francis, Russ	TE	6-6	242	8	Oregon
24	Gervais, Rick	S	5-11	190	3	Stanford
59	Harper, Willie	LB	6-2	215	10	Nebraska
75	Harty, John	DT	6-4	263	3	Iowa
22	Hicks, Dwight	S	6-1	189	5	Michigan
55	Horn, Bob	LB	6-4	230	8	Oregon State
—	Jones, Cody	DT	6-5	255	9	San Jose State
50	Judie, Ed	LB	6-2	231	2	Northern Arizona
66	Kennedy, Allan	T	6-7	275	2	Washington State
67	Kugler, Pete	DT-DE	6-4	255	3	Penn State
20	Lawrence, Amos	RB	5-10	179	3	North Carolina
52	Leopold, Bobby	LB	6-1	215	4	Notre Dame
42	Lott, Ronnie	CB	6-0	199	3	Southern California
78	Mason, Lindsey	T	6-5	275	5	Kansas
53	#McColl, Milt	LB	6-6	220	3	Stanford
43	McLemore, Dana	KR-CB	5-10	183	2	Hawaii
3	Miller, Jim	P	5-11	183	4	Mississippi
16	Montana, Joe	QB	6-2	200	5	Notre Dame
25	Moore, Jeff	RB	6-0	195	4	Jackson State
83	Nehemiah, Renaldo	WR	6-1	177	2	Maryland
—	Perry, Leon	FB	5-11	230	4	Mississippi
65	Pillers, Lawrence	DT-DE	6-4	250	8	Alcorn A&M
56	Quillan, Fred	C	6-5	266	6	Oregon
80	Ramson, Eason	TE	6-2	234	5	Washington State
64	Reynolds, Jack	LB	6-1	232	14	Tennessee
30	Ring, Bill	RB	5-10	215	3	Brigham Young
88	Solomon, Freddie	WR	5-11	181	9	Tampa
72	Stover, Jeff	DE	6-5	275	2	Oregon
79	Stuckey, Jim	DE	6-4	251	4	Clemson
58	Turner, Keena	LB	6-2	219	4	Purdue
—	Tyler, Wendell	RB	5-10	196	6	UCLA
14	#Wersching, Ray	K	5-11	210	11	California
—	Williams, Jeff	G	6-4	260	6	Rhode Island
45	Williams, Newton	RB	5-10	204	2	Arizona State
40	Williams, Vince	FB	6-0	231	2	Oregon
27	Williamson, Carlton	S	6-0	204	3	Pittsburgh
85	Wilson, Mike	WR	6-3	210	3	Washington State
21	Wright, Eric	CB	6-1	180	3	Missouri
86	#Young, Charle	TE	6-4	234	11	Southern California

#Unsigned at press time

TOP FIVE DRAFT CHOICES

Rd.	Name	Sel. No.	Pos.	Ht.	Wt.	College
2	Craig, Roger	49	RB	6-2	220	Nebraska
3	Montgomery, B.	59	LB	6-2	229	UCLA
4	Holmoe, Tom	90	DB	6-2	180	Brigham Young
5	Gray, Riki	117	LB	6-2	220	Southern California
7	Moten, Gary	175	LB	6-1	206	Southern Methodist

THE ROOKIES: After trading for Tyler, the 49ers used their top draft choice to pick Nebraska back Roger Craig on the second round. He may be the only plus out of what appears to be a dismal draft for the 49ers.

OUTLOOK: Will the real 49ers show up? Are they as good as the Super Bowl champs of two years ago or as bad as the team that couldn't make the playoffs last season? This is the year we should find out.

49ER PROFILES

JOE MONTANA 27 6-2 200   Quarterback

Fall from the top was quick, at least in comparison to that unbelievable Super Bowl year he had in 1981... Hard for anyone to play at that level two years in a row... All he was last year was good... Passed for 2,613 yards and 17 touchdowns to rank third in the NFC with an 87.9 rating... Without a running attack to help him out, he was left almost on his own during most of the year... Set an NFL record with five consecutive 300-yard-plus passing games and recorded four of the top 10 passing days in 49ers' history with outputs of 408, 356, 336 and 334 yards... Born June 11, 1956, in Monongahela, Pa.... Only a third-round 1979 draft choice, out of Notre Dame.

DWIGHT CLARK 26 6-3 205   Wide Receiver

Okay, some guys are faster and quicker, but how can you rate this guy anywhere but in the top four receivers in the league after another standout season last year?... Led league with 60 receptions (remember, that's in just nine games) for an impressive 15.2-yard average... No longer surviving just on nickel-and-dime receptions... Has caught a pass in 43 straight games... Had 12 catches against San Diego, tying the team record... A 10th-round 1979 pick, out of Clemson... Considers himself an electronic-game freak... Born Jan. 8, 1957, in Charlotte, N.C.... Who will ever forget his game-winning catch against Dallas in 1981 NFC championship game?

SAN FRANCISCO 49ERS

JACK REYNOLDS 35 6-1 232 — Linebacker

"Hacksaw" is finally making some money out of his nickname, which he got for actually sawing a car in two... Have you seen the TV ad where he says he hates cars and then starts sawing one in half?... Great stuff from one of the league's most colorful characters... Continues to be taken out of the lineup on passing downs, which cuts into his playing time but probably is prolonging his NFL career... This 34-year-old led the team in tackles once again, with 69... Knocked down four passes... Born Nov. 22, 1947, in Cincinnati... Lives in Bahamas in the offseason... Likes to get dressed in hotel room before games and often rides to stadium in a cab with his full uniform on... Rams let this Tennessee grad go after salary dispute in 1981.

RUSS FRANCIS 30 6-6 242 — Tight End

As hard as this might be to believe, this gifted Oregon grad was a major disappointment in 1982... Instead of making the 49ers much better, as expected, he did little to help them... Couldn't beat out Charle Young for starting tight end job, spent time in the hospital with a bad back and wound up with 23 catches for 278 yards... Scored two touchdowns... Cost the 49ers No. 1 and No. 4 picks to get him from New England... Born April 3, 1953, in Seattle... Was an all-pro with New England before he sat out a season after tiring of football.

RENALDO NEHEMIAH 24 6-1 177 — Wide Receiver

Caught eight passes for 161 yards and a touchdown in his inaugural pro season... Not a very spectacular start for this former world-record-holding high hurdler... But no one ever said he would be an instant sensation in the NFL... It takes time to learn how to play on this level after not having been in pads since high school... Was a high school quarterback, but didn't play football at Maryland... Superior athlete who dominates the Superstars competition... Born March 24, 1959, in Newark, N.J.... Was courted by a half-dozen NFL teams before deciding to sign with the 49ers for a lucrative contract.

140 THE COMPLETE HANDBOOK OF PRO FOOTBALL

RONNIE LOTT 24 6-0 199 — Cornerback

Two straight Pro Bowls for this third-year player from USC... Finished second to Jack Reynolds in tackles, with 68, and had two interceptions... Also was second to Reynolds in 1981... Cornerbacks aren't supposed to rank that high in tackles... They're supposed to be too fragile, remember... But he is anything but docile... Hits with a vengeance... Had a 83-yard interception return for a touchdown against Kansas City that was the second-longest in club history... Has already brought back four interceptions for touchdowns... Born May 8, 1959, in Albuquerque, N.M.... All-American at USC.

RANDY CROSS 29 6-3 250 — Guard

Looked like he would miss most of the season after a freak accident in the offseason led to a broken leg... But he was in the starting lineup from the first game on, a remarkable show of courage... One of the league's better guards, a solid player with fine explosion and determination... But his not being at 100 percent for a while hurt the 49ers' offense in the early going... Cross was injured during a charity appearance... Born April 25, 1954, in Encino, Cal.... Second-round pick out of UCLA.

FRED SOLOMON 30 5-11 181 — Wide Receiver

Have to wonder what he has to do to gain respect... Even though he has been a steady, speedy receiver, he found himself faced with challenge of fighting off Renaldo Nehemiah last season... He won, but really didn't figure that much in the 49er offense... Caught only 19 passes, ranking him fifth on the team... Averaged 17.0 yards per catch and scored three touchdowns... Born Jan. 11, 1953, in Sumter, S.C.... A standout quarterback at the University of Tampa... Involved in a commercial film production company.

SAN FRANCISCO 49ERS

RAY WERSCHING 33 5-11 210   Kicker

Sixth in the NFC in scoring with 59 points... Made 12-of-17 field goals and 23-of-25 extra points... The 49ers call him "Mr. Clutch"... He had a string of 59 straight PATs broken when he missed against San Diego... Teammates also refer to him as "Mo"... That's either short for machine or mohair, since he has more hair than anyone on the team... Had 14 points in Super Bowl XVI... Born Aug. 21, 1950, in Mondsee, Austria, and grew up in California... Graduate of University of California and works as CPA in offseason.

JEFF MOORE 27 6-0 195   Running Back

About the last person you would have expected to wind up as the 49ers' leading rusher last season... Hardly got into the team's press brochure, but that didn't stop him from beating out people like Ricky Patton for starting spot... Gave the team what little running support it had... Gained 281 yards on 85 carries, almost twice as many attempts as the No. 2 man, Bill Ring... Spent two years with Seattle after being drafted on the 12th round... Born Aug. 20, 1956, in Kosciusko, Miss.... Had 104 pro rushing yards before last season... Signed as a free agent before 1982 season.

WENDELL TYLER 28 5-10 196   Running Back

Sixth in the NFC in rushing last year with 564 yards on 137 carries, one year after he gained 1,074 yards... Still one of the bright spots in an otherwise dismal year for the Rams... Will benefit from new coaching and a new offense that might give him more room to run... Remains a prolific scorer... Had nine more rushing TDs and four as a receiver, tying Washington's Mark Moseley in the NFC scoring race, with 78 points... Has 30 touchdowns in short career... Born May 20, 1955, in Shreveport, La.

COACH BILL WALSH: Probably was the first to see the humor of this past season, when he suddenly wasn't being looked upon as a genius...And that's just one year after he wore the tag for leading the 49ers to the Super Bowl title...Same coach, but he probably made some poor personnel moves. By trying to make his machine better, he instead disrupted some of its chemistry ...Needs to boost the running game and get his defense straightened out...Thought long and hard about giving up the coaching part of his general manager-coach position, but couldn't find anyone he liked to take over for him...Had mentioned retirement even before winning the Super Bowl...Born Nov. 30, 1931, in Los Angeles...Was an end at San Jose State and a longtime assistant in the NFL before being named head coach at Stanford...Four-year record with San Francisco is 24-33.

GREATEST QUARTERBACK

John Brodie, you were great in your time. All those passes, all those yards, all those individual achievements. But nary an NFL championship.

Y.A. Tittle, you were terrific, too. For 10 years, your bald head was a San Francisco attraction. But nary an NFL championship.

Joe Montana, you're our man. So what if you have only played four years. Longevity shouldn't be the only factor in picking the best. How about achievement? And can any quarterback, even Brodie or Tittle, match your heroics in 1981? Certainly those two don't have a Super Bowl ring to compare with yours.

You appeared on more covers than Brooke Shields. You brought the 49ers back in the NFC title game against Dallas, you guided them to the Super Bowl win over Cincinnati. You were unflappable, consistent, almost unerring. The more the pressure mounted, the better you played. You were something, Joe Montana. Just think how good you'll be in three or four years. Then even 49er fans might be saying, "John Who? Y.A. Who?"

INDIVIDUAL 49ER RECORDS

Rushing

Most Yards Game:	194	Delvin Williams, vs St. Louis, 1976
Season:	1,203	Delvin Williams, 1976
Career:	8,689	Joe Perry, 1948-60, 1963

Passing

Most TD Passes Game:	5	Frank Albert, vs Cleveland (AAC), 1949
	5	John Brodie, vs Minnesota, 1965
	5	Steve Spurrier, vs Chicago, 1972
Season:	30	John Brodie, 1965
Career:	214	John Brodie, 1957-73

Receiving

Most TD Passes Game:	3	Alyn Beals, vs Brooklyn (AAC), 1948
	3	Alyn Beals, vs Chicago (AAC), 1949
	3	Gordy Soltau, vs Los Angeles, 1951
	3	Bernie Casey, vs Minnesota, 1962
	3	Dave Parks, vs Baltimore, 1965
	3	Gene Washington, vs San Diego, 1972
Season:	14	Alyn Beals (AAC), 1948
Career:	54	Gene Washington, 1969–76

Scoring

Most Points Game:	26	Gordy Soltau, vs Los Angeles, 1951
Season:	114	Gordy Soltau, 1953
Career:	738	Tommy Davis, 1959-69
Most TDs Game:	4	Bill Kilmer, vs Minnesota, 1961
Season:	14	Alyn Beals (AAC), 1948
Career:	80	Joe Perry, 1948-60

ST. LOUIS CARDINALS

TEAM DIRECTORY: Chairman: William Bidwell; Pres.: Bing Devine; Dir. Pro. Personnel: Larry Wilson; Dir. Pub. Rel.: Marty Igel; Head Coach: Jim Hanifan. Home field: Busch Stadium (51,392). Colors: Cardinal red, white and black.

SCOUTING REPORT

OFFENSE: Jim Hanifan is no dummy. He brought in Floyd Peters last year to doctor an ailing defense and Peters did a respectable job. So this year Hanifan went out and hired an offensive coordinator with fine credentials, Rod Dowhower, who had toiled for Denver the past three seasons.

Hanifan liked the way Dowhower has developed young quarterbacks. He's hoping he can work the same magic with Neil Lomax, finding the best ways to utilize Lomax's many gifts. Many believe Lomax is ready to become a top-flight quarterback and lacks only consistent guidance and well-conceived play-calling.

St. Louis, as usual, should have a good offensive line, now that tackles Luis Sharpe and Tootie Robbins have their rookie years behind them and Dan Dierdorf is more comfortable at center. Who can manhandle that 290-pounder in the middle?

And who can handle Ottis Anderson when he is moved to play well? But he isn't the most consistent runner in the league yet.

DEFENSE: Peters did a wonderful job getting the most out of limited talent and disguising weaknesses for most of the season. Until the Redskins scored 28 points on them the last week of the season, the Cardinals hadn't given up more than 20 points in five straight weeks—not bad for what used to be a pop-gun defense.

There might be some personnel changes within the unit by the start of the season. Middle linebacker is a problem, with Craig Puki, the former 49er, getting a chance to beat out Dave Ahrens. Peters probably got the cornerback he needed to go along with Jeff Griffin when the Cards drafted Leonard Smith in the first round. Benny Perrin proved himself as a rookie safety during Ken Greene's contract holdout, and Greene was traded to the Chargers.

Where's the pass rush? In the hands of Curtis Greer and Elois Grooms, the former Saint. It needs to get better, but that's the lament of almost every team in the league.

KICKING GAME: St. Louis has one of the best special-team operations in the NFC. That's partly because Stump Mitchell can

ST. LOUIS CARDINALS 145

be so dangerous, but the Cardinals also cover kicks aggressively. Carl Birdsong had the NFC's best punting average, but Neil O'Donoghue is no better than an average kicker, at best.

THE ROOKIES: If Green Bay pick Tim Lewis wasn't the best cornerback in the draft, then Smith of McNeese State was, so the Cardinals should add much-needed secondary strength. The Cardinals also picked up Baylor cornerback Cedric Mack and two

Ottis Anderson is already Cards' all-time leading rusher.

CARDINALS VETERAN ROSTER

HEAD COACH—Jim Hanifan. Assistant Coaches—Floyd Peters, Tom Bettis, Dick Jamieson, Rudy Feldman, Rod Dowhower, Tom Lovat, Emmitt Thomas, Chuck Banker, Don Brown, Leon McLaughlin.

No.	Name	Pos.	Ht.	Wt.	NFL Exp.	College
58	Ahrens, Dave	LB	6-3	228	3	Wisconsin
51	Allerman, Kurt	LB	6-2	222	7	Penn State
32	Anderson, Ottis	RB	6-2	220	5	Miami
—	Audick, Dan	G-T	6-3	253	6	Hawaii
52	Baker, Charlie	LB	6-2	218	4	New Mexico
41	Bedford, Vance	CB	5-11	170	2	Texas
46	Bessillieu, Don	CB-S	6-1	200	5	Georgia Tech
18	Birdsong, Carl	P	6-0	192	3	SW Oklahoma State
71	Bostic, Joe	G	6-3	265	5	Clemson
69	Brown, Rush	DT	6-2	260	4	Ball State
64	Clark, Randy	C	6-3	254	4	Northern Illinois
60	Cotton, Barney	G	6-5	265	4	Nebraska
73	Dawson, Mike	DT	6-4	270	8	Arizona
72	#Dierdorf, Dan	C	6-3	280	12	Michigan
31	Ferrell, Earl	RB	6-0	215	2	East Tennessee State
65	Galloway, David	DT	6-3	277	2	Florida
57	Gillen, John	LB	6-3	228	3	Illinois
81	Green, Roy	WR	6-0	195	5	Henderson State
75	Greer, Curtis	DE	6-4	252	4	Michigan
35	Griffin, Jeff	CB	6-4	252	3	Utah
78	Grooms, Elois	DE	6-4	250	8	Tennessee Tech
39	Harrell, Willard	RB	5-8	182	9	Pacific
17	Hart, Jim	QB	6-0	210	18	Southern Illinois
54	Junior, E. J.	LB	6-3	235	3	Alabama
89	LaFleur, Greg	TE	6-4	236	3	Louisiana State
16	Lisch, Rusty	QB	6-3	213	4	Notre Dame
15	Lomax, Neil	QB	6-3	215	3	Portland State
40	Love, Randy	RB	6-1	205	5	Houston
80	Marsh, Doug	TE	6-3	240	4	Michigan
76	Mays, Stafford	DE	6-2	250	4	Washington
87	McGill, Eddie	TE	6-6	225	2	Western Carolina
30	Mitchell, Stump	RB-KR	5-9	188	3	The Citadel
24	Morris, Wayne	RB	6-0	210	8	Southern Methodist
38	Nelson, Lee	S	5-10	185	8	Florida State
11	O'Donoghue, Neil	K	6-6	210	7	Auburn
23	Perrin, Benny	S	6-2	178	2	Alabama
70	Plunkett, Art	T	6-7	270	3	Nevada-Las Vegas
50	Puki, Craig	LB	6-1	231	4	Tennessee
63	Robbins, Tootie	T	6-4	270	2	East Carolina
74	Sebro, Bob	G	6-4	255	2	Colorado
53	Shaffer, Craig	LB	6-0	230	2	Indiana State
67	Sharpe, Luis	T	6-4	260	2	UCLA
84	#Shumann, Mike	WR	6-1	185	6	Florida State
44	Smith, Wayne	CB	6-0	175	4	Purdue
21	#Stief, Dave	CB-S	6-3	195	6	Portland State
68	Stieve, Terry	G	6-2	265	7	Wisconsin
79	Thornton, Bruce	DT	6-5	263	5	Illinois
83	Tilley, Pat	WR	5-10	171	8	Louisiana Tech
42	Williams, Herb	CB-S	6-0	200	4	Southern University

#Unsigned at press time

TOP FIVE DRAFT CHOICES

Rd.	Name	Sel. No.	Pos.	Ht.	Wt.	College
1	Smith, Leonard	17	DB	6-0	196	McNeese State
2	Mack, Cedric	44	DB	5-10	180	Baylor
3	Dardar, Ramsey	71	DT	6-2	248	Louisiana State
4	Duda, Mark	96	DT	6-3	263	Maryland
4	Washington, Lionel	103	DB	6-0	184	Tulane

ST. LOUIS CARDINALS 147

defensive tackles, Ramsey Dardar of LSU and Mark Duda of Maryland.

OUTLOOK: Hanifan has improved the Cardinals steadily, and there is no reason that improvement shouldn't continue. He has proven to be a good administrator, hiring excellent assistants. If Lomax develops and Anderson gains consistency, this could be a surprise team.

CARDINAL PROFILES

OTTIS ANDERSON 26 6-2 220   Running Back

Despite assorted injuries, he finished in the top four in NFC rushing, behind Dallas' Tony Dorsett, Detroit's Billy Sims and Chicago's Walter Payton... Picked up 587 yards, averaging a nifty 4.0 per carry... One of those rare players who can be used as the starting point of any offensive rebuilding program... Strong and fast, he can go outside as well as inside—a tough combination to stop... Already holds club all-time rushing records (4,920 yards) after four seasons... Only back to gain 100 or more yards vs. Washington last season... Born Jan. 19, 1957, in West Palm Beach, Fla.... Appeared as extra in the movie "Black Sunday"... First name was misspelled by doctor on birth certificate... Attended Miami.

NEIL LOMAX 24 6-3 215   Quarterback

Made significant progress in his first full season as starter for the Cardinals... Still needed to be bailed out by Jim Hart in the fourth period of some games, but near the season's end, coach Jim Hanifan stuck with him exclusively... Given the name "Gateway Gunner" in nickname contest by a local radio station... Very mobile and the Cardinal offense is starting to take advantage of his rollout ability... Held an amazing 90 NCAA Division 1-AA records when he left Portland State... Born Feb. 17, 1959, in Lake Oswego, Ore.... Passed last season for 1,367 yards and five touchdowns, with 53.2 percent accuracy... Needs to increase touchdown total substantially in future.

JIM HART 39 6-0 210   Quarterback

One of classiest men in the league... And showed it again near end of last season, when coach Jim Hanifan wanted to send him in because Neil Lomax was struggling late in the fourth period... Hart said no, he wasn't warmed up and, besides, it might hurt Lomax's confidence... After years of fulltime duty, he settled into a new role last season... Became a rarely used backup who threw only 33 passes... There was a question whether he could ever adapt to this role, but he handled it very well... Born April 29, 1944, in Evanston, Ill.... A long time ago, he was a star at Southern Illinois before signing as a free agent with St. Louis in 1966... Has thrown for 34,047 yards and 205 TDs, both Cardinal records.

DAN DIERDORF 34 6-3 280   Center

Center... That's right... After years as one of the best tackles in the business, he made an orderly switch to center... Well, orderly most of the time... There were some snapping mix-ups that probably should have been expected from someone who previously had used his hands to ward off pass-rushing defensive ends... Move was made to compensate for his advancing age and make room for new group of tackles... Born June 29, 1949, in Canton, Ohio... Probably better than some of the tackles already in the Hall of Fame in that city... Michigan grad was voted to NFL Team of the Decade for the 1970s.

LUIS SHARPE 23 6-4 260   Offensive Tackle

Made one of the most difficult adjustments in pro football... And one of the most overlooked... Came out of college and immediately started at left tackle... Think about that... Had to face almost every great NFC pass-rusher in his first season, because those rushers are almost exclusively right defensive ends who take advantage of coming in on the quarterback's blind side... Had excellent first season... Born June 16, 1960, in Havana, Cuba... Came to the United States when he was six... The only active Cuban-born player in NFL... Was All-American at UCLA... Might have future in politics.

ST. LOUIS CARDINALS 149

ROY GREEN 26 6-0 195 — Wide Receiver

Settled into fulltime role as a wide receiver last season after an amazingly versatile 1981 season in which he was a wide receiver, defensive back and special-teams star... Caught 32 passes for 454 yards, placing second, behind Pat Tilley, in both categories... Had 33 receptions in 1981, although he started just two games... Fourth-round pick out of Henderson State... A defensive back in college... Born June 30, 1957, in Magnolia, Ark.... Was on the field for 99 plays vs. Washington in 1981... "I've never been around a player like him who has the mental makeup and the physical stamina to play both ways," says coach Jim Hanifan.

TOOTIE ROBBINS 25 6-4 270 — Offensive Tackle

Probably the Cardinals' most pleasant surprise in 1982... Wasn't looked on as an instant starter, but that's what he became... Stepped into right tackle spot, joining fellow rookie Luis Sharpe on offensive line, and more than held his own... Not many teams that could survive, much less make a run for the playoffs, with two rookie tackles... A product of East Carolina, where he was a second-team All-American, the highest national recognition any player had received at East Carolina... Born June 2, 1958, in Merry Hill, N.C.... Runs the 40 in 4.85... Seventh tackle drafted in 1982.

CHARLIE BAKER 25 6-2 218 — Linebacker

After losing a starting position in 1981 because of an ankle sprain, he came back strongly in 1982... How strongly? Only good enough to lead the team in tackles under new defensive coordinator Floyd Peters... Had 67 tackles, one more than fellow linebacker Dave Ahrens... Former star at New Mexico... Ironically, he was benched when he couldn't fit into 4-3 alignment, but that's the formation out of which he was a standout last season... Has a promising future since last year was only his third in the league... Born Sept. 16, 1957, in Odessa, Tex.... Was first-team all-conference in college.

150 THE COMPLETE HANDBOOK OF PRO FOOTBALL

STUMP MITCHELL 24 5-9 188　　　　Kick Returner

One of the most dangerous return men in the business... Natural running back who probably would have success as a starter, if he wasn't playing behind Ottis Anderson... Toughness and durability serve him well in the rugged world of special teams... Sixth in NFC kickoff returns last year, averaging 22.8 yards per kick... Averaged 6.1 in punt returns... Mainstay of the Cardinals' highly regarded special teams... Born March 15, 1959, in St. Mary's, Ga.... Standout running back at The Citadel... First name is Lyvonia.

PAT TILLEY 30 5-10 171　　　　Wide Receiver

It's nice to have this kind of success story to write about... In an era when there is so much concentration on speed and size, he manages to do quite well, thank you, by relying on intelligence and experience... Was sixth in receiving in the NFC last year, with 36 catches for 465 yards... Among wide receivers, he was second, behind only San Francisco's Dwight Clark... Gifted with wonderful concentration and soft hands... Born Feb. 15, 1953, in Marshall, Tex.... Played at Louisiana Tech and still lives in Shreveport, La.

COACH JIM HANIFAN: Big, burly man who appears tough enough to line up with his players right now... A "tell-it-like-it-is" coach who sometimes much too frank with his players... Doing a good job of bringing back the Cardinals, despite a stingy payroll and an owner who rarely courts his players' happiness... Not afraid to make the tough decision... Showed that ability by benching Jim Hart and putting Neil Lomax at quarterback... It was a move that had to be made, but not every coach would have had the courage to do it... Born Sept. 21, 1922, in Compton, Cal.... A Don Coryell protege who coached in high school and was a longtime assistant in college and pros (at St. Louis and San Diego) before getting this opportunity... Still has reputation for being one of the league's premier offensive line coaches, so he'll never be out of a job for long... Three years in St. Louis have produced marks of 5-11, 7-9 and 5-4.

ST. LOUIS CARDINALS 151
GREATEST QUARTERBACK

He sits on the bench now, one of the highest-paid backup quarterbacks in the league. But for so many years he stood out on the field, wearing No. 17, standing up to oncoming linemen and throwing strike after strike downfield. What he lacked in consistency he made up for in streaks. There have been few quarterbacks in NFL history who could get any hotter, and throw better for longer, than Jim Hart.

Only two other players have thrown for 30,000 yards in their careers. Twice he has thrown for 3,000 yards in a season. He holds almost all the club passing records. He is Mr. Cardinal, and this season will set a record for most years with the team (18).

But just as important, he is a terrific person. Conscious of his civic obligations, he is involved in a number of charities and makes numerous public appearances for worthy causes. All this from a former free agent whom the Cardinals happened to sign after a fine college career at Southern Illinois.

INDIVIDUAL CARDINAL RECORDS

Rushing

Most Yards Game:	203	John David Crow, vs Pittsburgh, 1960
Season:	1,605	Ottis Anderson, 1979
Career:	4,920	Ottis Anderson, 1979-82

Passing

Most TD Passes Game:	6	Jim Hardy, vs Baltimore, 1950
	6	Charley Johnson, vs Cleveland, 1965
	6	Charley Johnson, vs New Orleans, 1969
Season:	28	Charley Johnson, 1963
Career:	205	Jim Hart, 1966-82

Receiving

Most TD Passes Game:	5	Bob Shaw, vs Baltimore, 1950
Season:	15	Sonny Randle, 1960
Career:	60	Sonny Randle, 1959-66

Scoring

Most Points Game:	40	Ernie Nevers, vs Chicago, 1929
Season:	117	Jim Bakken, 1967
Career:	1,380	Jim Bakken, 1962-78
Most TDs Game:	6	Ernie Nevers, vs Chicago, 1929
Season:	17	John David Crow, 1962
Career:	60	Sonny Randle, 1959-66

TAMPA BAY BUCCANEERS

TEAM DIRECTORY: Pres.: Hugh Culverhouse; VP/Head Coach: John McKay; VP: Joy Culverhouse; Dir. Administration: Herb Gold; Dir. Player Personnel: Ken Herock; Dir. Pro Personnel: Jack Bushofsky; Dir. Pub. Rel.: Bob Best. Home field: Tampa Stadium (72,128). Colors: Florida orange, white and red.

Hugh Green makes it his business to meet the opposing QB.

SCOUTING REPORT

OFFENSE: If John McKay can figure out some way to get the Bucs off to a quick start every game, this might be a hard-to-handle offense. Tampa Bay seems to always stumble out of the blocks and then has to rally to win. That's not a habit that allows coaches to grow old gracefully.

Tampa Bay should get better, though not everyone enjoyed his best season last year. Doug Williams' quarterback rating fell slightly and he and Kevin House weren't quite the passing item they had been the previous year. But Williams still rates among the league's best athletes. And now the Bucs have Jack Thompson, backup QB from Cincinnati. With speedy James Owens hindered by a sore ankle, free agent Melvin Carter wound up as the starting tailback. With Owens healthy, this could be a strong position. There is no question about fullback James Wilder's strength. He gained 324 yards last year and became a solid part of the offense.

The offensive line protected Williams well and blocked decently on sweeps, but couldn't do much on power runs. A plus was the development of No. 1 pick Sean Farrell, who beat out Greg Roberts for a starting guard spot.

DEFENSE: Under new defensive coordinator Wayne Fontes, the Bucs were more aggressive and gambled more last year, following a trend in the league that says if you sit back and wait, passing teams will pick you apart.

Even though McKay sees a need for better linebacking, there are few better than Hugh Green, who led the team in tackles. Even with the trades that exiled Dewey Selmon and David Lewis last year, the Buc linebacking remained solid and the only reason their 3-4 defense held up. Dave Stalls, with six sacks, was a pleasant surprise at one end and everyone knows how good Lee Roy Selmon is at the other.

This is a good secondary, but it's getting a little old, with everyone 29 or older. That's okay, if age hasn't cut into quickness. Neal Colzie, at strong safety, might have been the unit's most valuable player, even though Green played so well.

KICKING GAME: Both punter Larry Swider and placekicker Bill Capece had good years, with Capece making 18-of-23 field goals and all 14 extra points. But McKay was not very pleased with his coverage teams, so look for some changes for the better there this season.

BUCCANEERS VETERAN ROSTER

HEAD COACH—John McKay. Assistant Coaches—Boyd Dowler, Frank Emanuel, Wayne Fontes, Abe Gibron, Jim Gruden, Kim Helton, Chip Myers, Howard Tippett.

No.	Name	Pos.	Ht.	Wt.	NFL Exp.	College
30	Barrett, Dave	RB	6-0	230	2	Houston
82	Bell, Jerry	TE	6-5	230	2	Arizona State
83	Bell, Theo	WR	6-0	190	7	Arizona
52	Brantley, Scot	LB	6-1	230	4	Florida
34	Brown, Cedric	S	6-2	200	7	Kent State
78	Cannon, John	DE	6-5	250	2	William & Mary
3	#Capece, Bill	K	5-7	170	3	Florida State
87	Carter, Gerald	WR	6-1	190	4	Texas A&M
28	Carver, Melvin	RB	5-11	210	2	Nevada-Las Vegas
20	Colzie, Neal	S	6-2	200	9	Ohio State
33	#Cotney, Mark	S	6-0	200	8	Cameron State
71	Crowder, Randy	DT	6-3	255	6	Penn State
58	Davis, Jeff	LB	6-0	225	2	Clemson
27	Dykes, Donald	CB	5-11	185	4	SE Louisiana
43	Eckwood, Jerry	RB	6-0	200	4	Arkansas
62	Farrell, Sean	G	6-3	260	2	Penn State
88	Giles, Jimmie	TE	6-3	241	7	Alcorn State
11	Golsteyn, Jerry	QB	6-4	200	5	Northern Illinois
53	Green, Hugh	LB	6-2	225	3	Pittsburgh
73	#Hannah, Charley	T	6-6	265	7	Alabama
59	Hawkins, Andy	LB	6-2	230	4	Texas A&I
21	Holt, John	CB-S	5-11	180	3	West Texas State
89	House, Kevin	WR	6-1	175	4	Southern Illinois
56	Johnson, Cecil	LB	6-2	240	7	Pittsburgh
84	Jones, Gordon	WR	6-2	190	5	Pittsburgh
77	Kollar, Bill	DE	6-4	250	9	Montana State
57	Leonard, Jim	C-G	6-3	260	4	Santa Clara
76	Logan, David	NT	6-2	255	5	Pittsburgh
45	Middleton, Terdell	RB	6-0	205	7	Memphis State
24	Morris, Thomas	CB-S	5-11	175	2	Michigan State
1	Morton, Michael	KR-RB	5-8	180	2	Nevada-Las Vegas
35	Moser, Rick	RB	6-0	210	6	Rhode Island
86	#Obradovich, Jim	TE	6-2	225	9	Southern California
44	O'Steen, Dwayne	CB	6-1	195	6	San Jose State
26	Owens, James	RB	5-11	195	4	UCLA
15	Quinn, Jeff	QB	6-3	205	2	Nebraska
75	Reavis, Dave	T	6-5	265	9	Arkansas
66	Reese, Booker	DE	6-3	260	2	Bethune-Cookman
61	Roberts, Greg	G	6-3	265	5	Oklahoma
74	Sanders, Gene	T	6-3	270	5	Texas A&M
63	Selmon, Lee Roy	DE	6-3	260	8	Oklahoma
22	#Smith, Johnny Ray	CB	5-9	180	2	Lamar
72	Snell, Ray	G-T	6-4	265	4	Wisconsin
65	Stalls, Dave	DE	6-5	250	7	Northern Colorado
9	#Swider, Larry	P	6-2	195	5	Pittsburgh
41	Thomas, Norris	CB	6-0	185	7	Southern Mississippi
—	Thompson, Jack	QB	6-3	217	5	Washington State
81	Tyler, Andre	WR	6-0	180	2	Stanford
40	#Washington, Mike	CB	6-2	200	8	Alabama
90	White, Brad	DT	6-2	250	3	Tennessee
32	Wilder, James	RB	6-3	225	2	Missouri
12	Williams, Doug	QB	6-4	214	6	Grambling
50	Wilson, Steve	C	6-4	265	8	Georgia
54	Wood, Richard	LB	6-2	230	9	Southern California
68	Yarno, George	G	6-2	260	5	Washington State

#Unsigned at press time

TOP FIVE DRAFT CHOICES

Rd.	Name	Sel. No.	Pos.	Ht.	Wt.	College
2	Grimes, Randy	45	C	6-4	262	Baylor
3	Castille, Jeremiah	72	DB	5-11	177	Alabama
4	Thomas, Kelly	99	T	6-6	270	Southern California
5	Chickillo, Tony	131	DT	6-3	250	Miami
6	Branton, Rheugene	148	WR	6-4	200	Texas Southern

TAMPA BAY BUCCANEERS   155

THE ROOKIES: The Bucs, without a first-round pick, went for some long-shot players in the draft, including center Randy Grimes of Baylor and tackle Kelly Thomas of USC. The most immediate help could come from cornerback Jeremiah Castille of Alabama. But this was not the best of drafts for the Bucs.

OUTLOOK: According to McKay, this is an improving team that is going to get better this year after making the playoffs last season. He blamed the strike for slowing down the Bucs' progress. This season, there will be no such hurdle.

BUC PROFILES

DOUG WILLIAMS 28 6-4 214   Quarterback

His public disagreements with the NFLPA set up an interesting situation... Here was a team leader saying he would return and play whenever the club gave the word... And Tampa was considered a strong union team... His stand didn't have much apparent effect after the strike was over, but you never know what will happen down the road... Not a year for him to remember on the field, either... Finished next-to-last in NFC passing, throwing more interceptions (11) than touchdown passes (nine)... Completed 53.4 percent for 2,071 yards... And it had a sad aftermath: his wife died following brain surgery last spring... Born Aug. 9, 1955, in Baton Rouge, La.... Wants to be high school coach after he retires... It might help if the Bucs could settle on one offensive coordinator instead of changing almost year to year... Attended Grambling.

LEE ROY SELMON 28 6-3 260   Defensive End

Reached that stage in his career where he is so respected that he can have so-so season and still not have his reputation tarnished... One of the few big-name players who risked career by playing in the NFLPA all-star game... Bucs' player representative... Relies on quickness instead of strength to be effective... One of the first great rushing ends out of a 3-4 formation... Born Nov. 20, 1954, in Eufaula, Okla.... Personable, gracious and intelligent... A legend at Oklahoma.

HUGH GREEN 24 6-2 225 — Linebacker

After spending a season overshadowed by fellow rookie Lawrence Taylor, he's now getting proper recognition... A fine, fine linebacker, one of the league's best... And he's going to get a whole lot better... Made amazing transition from defensive end at Pittsburgh into complete linebacker... Doesn't rush passer as much as Taylor or he probably would have made the same kind of spectacular plays... Better than his Giant rival at covering passes... Won Lombardi Trophy as best lineman in country his senior year... Born July 27, 1959, in Natchez, Miss.... Orphaned at age six and raised by grandparents ... Cooks and sews like expert.

KEVIN HOUSE 25 6-1 175 — Wide Receiver

After spectacular 1981 season, the rest of the league caught up a bit to this splendid sprinter... Led the Tampa Bay wide receivers in catches with 28, for 438 yards, although James Wilder was top receiver on team... His forte is the bomb, made possible by explosive speed that he can use to run past any defensive back... Once ran the 40 in 4.3 seconds while he was at Southern Illinois... Some have compared him to Paul Warfield... Born Dec. 20, 1957, in St. Louis... Drafted by the baseball Cardinals out of college... Owns an aquarium.

JIMMIE GILES 28 6-3 241 — Tight End

Only three other tight ends caught more passes than him in 1982, marking second straight good year after a poor 1980... Perhaps he's not as good as everyone first thought when he came out of Alcorn State, but it's hard to find many who are better athletes within the NFL... His 28 catches were good for 499 yards... Must cope with lack of consistency... Now in his seventh season and sixth with Tampa Bay, he already is the Bucs' all-time leading career receiver (92)... Also is career leader in touchdowns scored (22), passing Ricky Bell last year... Played only two years of football in college after concentrating only on baseball at first... Born Nov. 8, 1954, in Greenville, Miss.... Played pro baseball in 1976 after being drafted by Dodgers.

TAMPA BAY BUCCANEERS 157

JAMES WILDER 25 6-3 225   Running Back

A magnificent 1981 draft choice by the Bucs... Took a year to find a spot and then he took off... Caught 53 passes last season, second in the NFC to San Francisco's Dwight Clark and third in the NFL... Became Doug Williams' much-needed safety valve... As a rookie, he caught 48 passes in 16 games to set team record for backs... Ran for 324 yards on 83 carries in 1982, which came close to exceeding his 370-yard total from rookie season... Strong, powerful, durable runner... Born May 12, 1958, in Sikeston, Mo.... All-time rushing leader at Missouri... Led the Tigers in rushing three straight years.

SCOT BRANTLEY 25 6-1 230   Linebacker

Want a good comeback story to warm your heart in the midst of all this pro sports' money grab?... Here's one for you... Appeared this Florida Gator's football future was ruined after he hurt his head early in his senior season against Georgia Tech... But he was cleared by a group of doctors after the Bucs drafted him as a long shot in the third round... If it hadn't been for the injury, he would have been a certain first-round pick... Now the good news... Wound up starting last season, his third as a pro... During the regular season, he was third on the team in tackles, with nine fewer than leader Hugh Green... Born Feb. 24, 1958, in Chester, S.C.... Avid outdoorsman and good baseball player.

MELVIN CARVER 24 5-11 210   Running Back

Somehow he made it through 12 rounds of the 1982 draft... The computer said no, no, but his ability said yes, yes... Wound up the Bucs' No. 3 rusher (229 yards on 70 carries)... Not bad for a free agent who evidently was considered lacking in talent by the scouts... A junior-college transfer who had two fine seasons at Nevada-Las Vegas... Played fullback in college, but was a speed back for the Bucs last year... A high-school quarterback in California... Born July 14, 1959, in Pensacola, Fla.... Wants to be a coach once his pro career ends.

158 THE COMPLETE HANDBOOK OF PRO FOOTBALL

CECIL JOHNSON 28 6-2 240　　　　　　　　　Linebacker

Teamed with Scot Brantley on the inside of the improved Buc defense... Has become a solid performer who ranks among the best linebackers in the league... Has found a home playing in the middle... No longer has to compensate for quickness problems on the outside... Another free agent who has proven much better than many of the drafted players who came out of college the same season... Was in Tony Dorsett's class at Pittsburgh... Born Aug. 19, 1955, in Miami... Second on the team in tackles last season.

DAVE STALLS 27 6-5 250　　　　　　　　　Defensive End

Even with Lee Roy Selmon as a teammate, he still led the Bucs in sacks with 6½... Even in short season, that was his pro best after six years... Remarkable considering he had plenty of off-field distractions to overcome... Was the team's assistant player rep and public spokesman... Always seemed to be in the middle of some controversy in Tampa... Acquired from Dallas for a pair of draft choices in 1980... Little All-American at Northern Colorado... Born Sept. 19, 1955, in Madison, Wis.... Graduated with degree in zoology.

COACH JOHN McKAY: Despite rumors that he wants to give up coaching and retire to the front office, he keeps going on the front lines... Has turned the Bucs into annual contenders, but also has annual problems with his offense... Can't seem to hang onto offensive coordinators, mainly because he won't give them a free hand to run things as they see fit... How much that hurts quarterback Doug Williams is another question... Remains the wise-cracking coach who gained great notoriety at Southern California, where he posted 127-40-8 record and won four national championships... It's his way or no way... Born July 5, 1924, in Everettsville, W. Va.... Has one of the more relaxed approaches in the league... Doesn't believe in burning the midnight oil, especially in the offseason... Since a 2-26 start in first two years at Tampa Bay, he has compiled 34-38-1 record in his last four seasons.

TAMPA BAY BUCCANEERS 159
GREATEST QUARTERBACK

There have been other quarterbacks at Tampa Bay, even a Heisman Trophy winner by the name of Steve Spurrier. But there is only one quarterback that anyone remembers, Doug Williams. He's good, and he's controversial. That's always an entertaining combination.

Williams is a magnificent athlete: 6-4, 214, strong of arm and body. Cut a mold for a quarterback and he'd be a perfect model. He also is black. That shouldn't be significant, but in the strange world of sports, it is. There never has been a truly successful black pro quarterback—darn few have been given the chance—so when one as good as Williams shows up, there is constant debate over whether he has proven a black can play the spot or not.

The argument should be over. So he has been erratic and in his early years at times lacking. But a more mature Williams, who has carried a franchise now for almost four years, is a bonafide pro quarterback. Maybe he will never be an all-time great, but that can be said about a lot of players. And maybe he will never shake the embarrassment of playing so badly in some nationally televised playoff games the last few years. But a failure? Not Doug Williams.

INDIVIDUAL BUCCANEER RECORDS

Rushing
Most Yards Game:	167	Ricky Bell, vs Green Bay, 1979
Season:	1,263	Ricky Bell, 1979
Career:	3,057	Ricky Bell, 1977-81

Passing
Most TD Passes Games:	4	Doug Williams, vs Minnesota, 1980
	4	Doug Williams, vs Detroit, 1981
Season:	20	Doug Williams, 1980
Career:	73	Doug Williams, 1978-82

Receiving
Most TD Passes Game:	3	Morris Owens, vs Miami, 1976
Season:	9	Kevin House, 1981
Career:	22	Jimmie Giles, 1978-82

Scoring
Most Points Game:	18	Morris Owens, vs Miami, 1976
Season:	79	Garo Yepremian, 1980
Career:	143	Bill Capece, 1981-82
Most TDs Game:	3	Morris Owens, vs Miami, 1976
Season:	9	Ricky Bell, 1979
	9	Kevin House, 1981
Career:	22	Jimmie Giles, 1978-82

WASHINGTON REDSKINS

TEAM DIRECTORY: Chairman: Jack Kent Cooke; Pres.: Edward Bennett Williams; Exec. VP: John Kent Cooke; GM: Bobby Beathard; Dir. Pub. Rel.: Charles Taylor; Head Coach: Joe Gibbs. Home field: Robert F. Kennedy Memorial Stadium (55,045). Colors: Burgundy and gold.

SCOUTING REPORT

OFFENSE: This was going to be the offense of the '80s, with loads of passing under coach Joe Gibbs. Instead, by the end of last year, it had a touch of nostalgia, with John Riggins going right and John Riggins going left. But don't be deceived. Using motion and formation changes, it was an innovative offense that got better as the offensive line matured.

The future also is bright. Riggins has a new, lucrative contract after playing better than ever last season. Joe Washington, coming off two knee operations, should be more effective. The Hogs are the biggest line in the business, made to order for Riggins' runs. And Joe Theismann is coming off the best season in his career after leading the NFC in passing and being selected to the Pro Bowl for the first time. Gibbs also welcomes back receiver Art Monk, who missed the playoffs with an injury. Monk will bolster a strong group of ends that includes Pro Bowler Charlie Brown and tough Alvin Garrett.

Remember, this is an offense that didn't commit turnovers, especially at crucial moments. It was both efficient and productive.

DEFENSE: What began as a question mark last year ended as a major strength. Who would have thought the Redskins would lead the league in fewest points allowed and place fourth in overall defense without making major personnel changes?

This is a defense that lives up to the cliche about the whole being greater than the sum of its parts. Not particularly quick, big or strong, it is well-coordinated, aggressive and imaginative. And it has better depth than in recent years.

Tackle Dave Butz remains the best-known player, but defensive end Dexter Manley came on strong last year and should be a star for years to come. Darryl Grant and Perry Brooks will fight for one tackle spot and Larry Kubin and Neal Olkewicz will vie at middle linebacker. Look for continued improvement from cornerback Vernon Dean, a rookie last year. He seems to lack fear, a good characteristic for his position.

WASHINGTON REDSKINS 161

KICKING GAME: Mark Moseley made NFL history last year by being named MVP by two major organizations. He also set a record for most consecutive field goals. Rookie punter Jeff Hayes struggled and was booed at times by the home fans, but the Redskins think he remains a fine prospect.

THE ROOKIES: With the last pick in most rounds, the Redskins used their choices to go for unknowns, other than first-rounder

The Redskins' most vital weapon is foot of Mark Moseley.

REDSKINS VETERAN ROSTER

HEAD COACH—Joe Gibbs. Assistant Coaches—Don Breaux, Joe Bugel, Bill Hickman, Larry Peccatiello, Richie Petitbon, Jerry Rhome, Dan Riley, Wayne Sevier, Warren Simmons, Charley Taylor, LaVern Torgeson.

No.	Name	Pos.	Ht.	Wt.	NFL Exp.	College
58	Anderson, Stuart	LB	6-1	247	2	Virginia
53	Bostic, Jeff	C	6-2	245	4	Clemson
69	Brooks, Perry	DT	6-3	265	6	Southern
87	Brown, Charlie	WR	5-10	179	2	South Carolina State
65	Butz, Dave	DT	6-7	295	11	Purdue
35	Claitt, Rickey	RB	5-10	206	3	Bethune-Cookman
51	Coleman, Monte	LB	6-2	235	5	Central Arkansas
—	Crissy, Cris	WR	5-11	195	2	Princeton
54	#Cronan, Peter	LB	6-2	238	6	Boston College
32	Dean, Vernon	DB	5-11	178	2	San Diego State
86	Didier, Clint	TE	6-5	240	2	Portland State
89	Garrett, Alvin	WR	5-7	178	4	Angelo State
30	Giaquinto, Nick	RB	5-11	204	4	Connecticut
77	Grant, Darryl	DT	6-1	265	3	Rice
68	Grimm, Russ	G	6-3	270	3	Pittsburgh
38	Harmon, Clarence	RB	5-11	209	7	Mississippi State
5	Hayes, Jeff	P	5-11	175	2	North Carolina
8	Holly, Bob	QB	6-2	205	2	Princeton
40	#Jackson, Wilbur	RB	6-1	219	9	Alabama
66	Jacoby, Joe	T	6-7	295	3	Louisville
22	Jordan, Curtis	CB-S	6-2	205	7	Texas Tech
55	Kaufman, Mel	LB	6-2	218	3	Cal Poly-SLO
50	Kubin, Larry	LB	6-2	234	2	Penn State
62	Laster, Donald	T	6-5	285	2	Tennessee State
79	Liebenstein, Todd	DE	6-6	245	2	Nevada-Las Vegas
56	Lowry, Quentin	LB	6-2	225	3	Youngstown State
72	Manley, Dexter	DE	6-3	253	3	Oklahoma State
73	May, Mark	G	6-6	288	3	Pittsburgh
46	McDaniel, LeCharls	CB	5-9	169	3	Cal Poly-SLO
78	McGee, Tony	DE	6-4	250	13	Bishop
76	Mendenhall, Mat	DE	6-6	255	3	Brigham Young
57	Milot, Rich	LB	6-4	237	5	Penn State
81	Monk, Art	WR	6-3	209	4	Syracuse
3	Moseley, Mark	K	6-0	205	12	Stephen F. Austin
29	#Murphy, Mark	FS	6-4	210	7	Colgate
21	#Nelms, Mike	FS-KR	6-1	185	4	Baylor
79	#Ogrin, Pat	DT	6-5	265	3	Wyoming
52	Olkewicz, Neal	LB	6-0	227	5	Maryland
17	#Owen, Tom	QB	6-1	194	10	Wichita State
23	#Peters, Tony	SS	6-1	177	9	Oklahoma
44	Riggins, John	RB	6-2	235	12	Kansas
80	Seay, Virgil	WR	5-8	175	3	Troy State
—	Smigelsky, Dave	P	5-11	180	2	Virginia Tech
74	Starke, George	T	6-5	260	11	Columbia
7	Theismann, Joe	QB	6-0	195	10	Notre Dame
88	Walker, Rich	TE	6-4	235	7	UCLA
85	Warren, Don	TE	6-4	242	5	San Diego State
25	Washington, Joe	RB	5-10	179	7	Oklahoma
45	#White, Jeris	CB	5-10	188	10	Hawaii
34	#Williams, Clarence	RB	5-10	185	7	South Carolina
47	Williams, Greg	CB-S	5-11	185	2	Mississippi State
84	Williams, Mike	TE	6-4	245	2	Alabama A&M
39	#Wonsley, Otis	RB	5-10	214	3	Alcorn State

#Unsigned at press time

TOP FIVE DRAFT CHOICES

Rd.	Name	Sel. No.	Pos.	Ht.	Wt.	College
1	Green, Darrell	28	DB	5-10	170	Texas A&I
2	Williams, Richard	56	RB	6-0	205	Memphis State
3	Mann, Charles	84	DE	6-6	250	Nevada-Reno
6	Winckler, Bob	166	T	6-2	290	Wisconsin
6	Laufenberg, Babe	168	QB	6-2	190	Indiana

Darrell Green, a speedy Texas A&I cornerback and return man. He could be an immediate plus, but everyone else chosen probably is at least a year or two away.

OUTLOOK: Everything that could have gone right went right for the Redskins last year. They had very few injuries, Riggins played like he was all-world and the defense was better than anyone would have anticipated. But the last three Super Bowl winners have had terrible follow-up seasons, something that could happen to Washington if the injury jinx strikes the wrong positions.

REDSKIN PROFILES

JOE THEISMANN 33 6-0 195   Quarterback

Coming off the season of his life: first-team Pro Bowl, top-rated passer in the NFC, starting quarterback on the Super Bowl champions ... "I'm the happiest man in the world," he said after both the NFC title game and Super Bowl ... Has learned to be patient and not force the big plays. "The big plays will come in our offense, if I just let them happen," he says ... Born Sept. 9, 1949, in New Brunswick, N.J. ... In strike-shortened season, he passed for 2,033 yards and 13 touchdowns and had only nine interceptions. Had strings of 96 and 84 passes without an interception ... Most active of all Redskin players in off-the-field activities ... Owns two restaurants and does frequent television ads ... Attended Notre Dame.

JOHN RIGGINS 34 6-2 235   Running Back

Two years ago, it appeared he might finish out his career as a fringe, fill-in player ... Now he is coming off one of the most electrifying seasons ever enjoyed by a running back ... For a month, during the playoffs, he captured the nation's fancy with his old-fashioned, power running ... Wound up gaining more yards in four postseason games (610) than he did in eight regular-season games (553) ... Put together NFL-record three straight 100-yard playoff games ... Then set Super Bowl records with 166

164 THE COMPLETE HANDBOOK OF PRO FOOTBALL

yards on 38 carries and 43-yard, game-winning TD ramble...Born Aug. 4, 1949, in Lawrence, Kan....One of the league's free spirits, he showed up at the Redskins' pre-Super Bowl party wearing top hat and tails...Sat out 1980 season over contract dispute...Redskins, bidding against USFL Michigan Panthers at end of last year, gave him contract that will net him at least $1.5 million in next two years...Broke all of Gale Sayers' records at Kansas and was drafted by Jets in first round in 1971.

MARK MOSELEY 35 6-0 205   Kicker

Talk about your Hollywood believe-it-or-not story...Came close to losing his kicking job to rookie Dan Miller in training camp...Then proceeded to become the first kicker in league history to be named Most Valuable Player...Already is the top-paid kicker in the NFL..."If I thought a kicker could be the MVP, I would have put an incentive clause in my contract," said a stunned Moseley...Set NFL season record for field-goal percentage by making 20-of-21 (95.2 percent)...Established league mark for consecutive field goals with 23 in a row...Credited new offseason weight program and being unburdened by kickoff chores as factors in his 1982 success...Born March 12, 1948, in Laneville, Tex....Attended Texas A&M before finishing at Stephen F. Austin...His 943 points rank him 13th on NFL's all-time scoring list.

RUSS GRIMM 24 6-3 270   Guard

King Hog, the best of the Redskins' talented offensive linemen...Teamed with tackle Joe Jacoby on the left side to become mainstay on the Redskins' key running plays...Played last part of the season with two stress fractures in left leg...Played three different positions in one game because of injuries to others...Down-to-earth, good-humored, candid...Says that if he wasn't playing football, he would be a construction worker or something that "would keep me outside. I'm not an office worker type."...Born May 2, 1959, in Pittsburgh, and attended the University of Pittsburgh...Was a quarterback in high school.

WASHINGTON REDSKINS 165

DAVE BUTZ 33 6-7 295 — Defensive Tackle

Enjoyed the best season of his long career last year, but still didn't make any all-star teams... Pouted about the oversight... Probably deserved some recognition, since the Redskins were about the toughest in the league to run against and his strength is stopping the run... Has been plagued in the past by inconsistency... When he was good, he was very good, but when he was bad, ouch... "Don't wake me up, I'm enjoying this too much," he said after the Super Bowl win... Born June 23, 1950, in Lafayette, Ala., and attended Purdue... Wears size 12½ shoes, 7EEEEEE in width... The Redskins would like to see him provide a better pass rush at times.

MIKE NELMS 28 6-1 185 — Kick Returner

Made the Pro Bowl for the third straight year, although teams kicked away from him consistently the last half of the season... Didn't have the statistics of the past two years (24.2-yard average on kickoff returns, 7.9-yard average on punt returns), but he hurts his average on punt returns by never calling for a fair catch... "I don't want to and I don't want to pass up a chance to handle the ball," he says... Almost broke a kickoff for a touchdown in the NFC title game... Born April 8, 1955, in Ft. Worth, Tex.... Attended Baylor... Became hit of the Super Bowl media conferences when he showed proficiency at his hobby, doing bird calls.

TONY PETERS 30 6-1 177 — Safety

After eight years in the league, he finally achieved all-star status... Selected to the Pro Bowl for the first time and made some all-league teams... The man who replaced Ken Houston in the Redskin secondary... Was disappointed in his 1981 play, because he thought he was too tentative... Came out last season determined to play like he did at Oklahoma—hitting anything that moved... His aggressiveness helped transform a passive secondary... Was fourth on the team in tackles and had one interception... Born April 28, 1953, in Oklahoma City, Okla.... Began his career with Cleveland before being traded to Washington in 1979.

166 THE COMPLETE HANDBOOK OF PRO FOOTBALL
CHARLIE BROWN 24 5-10 179　　　　　　Wide Receiver

Came out of obscurity to make the Pro Bowl in what was really his first pro season... Spent his rookie year on injured reserve with a bad knee... Became the Redskins' big-play man, catching a handful of long touchdown passes, starting with a 78-yarder in the season opener against Philadelphia... An eighth-round draft pick out of South Carolina State, where he was overshadowed by a run-oriented offense... Has a sliding running style that makes it difficult for cornerbacks to judge his speed... Born Oct. 10, 1958, in Charleston, S.C.... Long, long arms and great leaping ability make him a pick-up basketball standout.

MARK MURPHY 28 6-4 210　　　　　　　　　　Safety

Emerged as one of the top spokesmen for the players' union during the eight-week strike against the NFL... Intelligent and articulate, he was willing to patiently explain the union's position time and time again... One of the chief supporters of union head Ed Garvey... Member of the NFLPA's Executive Board... But didn't let his union activities hurt his overall performance... Led the Redskins in tackles for the fourth straight year, with 100 in nine games... Has 18 interceptions in four years as a starter... Born July 14, 1955, in Fulton, N.Y.... Relies more on heady play and film study than quickness... Colgate grad is one course shy of master's degree in business.

DEXTER MANLEY 24 6-3 240　　　　　　　Defensive End

One of the most talkative, most open players in the league... But backs up his big talk with quickly improving play... Has made great strides in his two pro seasons... Teams ran on him constantly in his rookie year, but not last season... Has made Dallas his personal rival, picking up where Diron Talbert and friends left off... "Tell Dallas to come right to me," he said before the NFC title game... Wound up sacking Danny White, who had to leave the game, and then deflecting a Gary Hogeboom pass that Darryl Grant returned for a touchdown... Led the team with 6½ sacks... Born July 2, 1959, in Houston... Was a stand-up linebacker at Oklahoma State.

COACH JOE GIBBS: Completed a dramatic rise to the top of the coaching profession by guiding the Redskins to the Super Bowl title in only his second year with the team... Never had been a head coach prior to accepting the Redskin job in 1981... Lost the first five games of that 8-8 inaugural season... "I'm honored to be Coach of the Year, but it will mean more if I'm Coach of the Year 10 years from now. That'll mean I've been a success over a long period of time," he says... Has gained a reputation for being a player's coach... He enjoys the company of his athletes, has an open-door policy, and runs an informal ship... But he also has a quick temper and lack of patience with those who don't care... Born Nov. 25, 1943, in Mocksville, N.C.... Taught Bible studies to teenage juvenile delinquents during the players' strike.

GREATEST QUARTERBACK

Maybe Sonny Jurgensen is the most popular Washington Redskin in town, even after retiring a half-decade ago. And after winning the Super Bowl, who would dare say a word against Joe Theismann?

But there is only one Redskin who can be named their all-time best quarterback. George Allen says he was the best of all time, which is a pretty nice accolade. All Sammy Baugh ever said was aw shucks, t'aint nothing.

Slingin' Sam made pro football in Washington. He was owner George Preston Marshall's prize player, the superstar that the Redskins needed when they came to Washington in 1937. Sammy didn't mind the spotlight; it captured him just right, smiling in the 10-gallon hat he brought from Texas Christian University.

In his rookie year, Sammy guided the Redskins to an Eastern Division crown and he threw three touchdown passes to beat the Chicago Bears for the championship. He helped the Redskins win four more divisional titles and another championship while setting all sorts of records. Among other things, he threw 186 touchdown passes and set a mark by playing 16 seasons.

He played defensive back for much of the time as well—11 interceptions to lead the league in 1943—and was the NFL's leading punter for four years.

INDIVIDUAL REDSKIN RECORDS

Rushing

Most Yards Game:	195	Mike Thomas, vs St. Louis, 1976
Season:	1,216	Larry Brown, 1972
Career:	5,875	Larry Brown, 1969-76

Passing

Most TD Passes Game:	6	Sam Baugh, vs Brooklyn, 1943
	6	Sam Baugh, vs St. Louis, 1947
Season:	31	Sonny Jurgensen, 1967
Career:	187	Sammy Baugh, 1937-52

Receiving

Most TD Passes Game:	3	Hugh Taylor (5 times)
	3	Jerry Smith, vs Los Angeles, 1967
	3	Jerry Smith, vs Dallas, 1969
	3	Hal Crisler (once)
	3	Joe Walton (once)
	3	Pat Richter, vs Chicago, 1968
	3	Larry Brown, vs Philadelphia, 1973
	3	Jean Fugett, vs San Francisco, 1976
Season:	12	Hugh Taylor, 1952
	12	Charley Taylor, 1966
	12	Jerry Smith, 1967
Career:	79	Charley Taylor, 1964-77

Scoring

Most Points Game:	24	Dick James, vs Dallas, 1961
	24	Larry Brown, vs Philadelphia, 1973
Season:	114	Curt Knight, 1971
	114	Mark Moseley, 1979
Career:	798	Mark Moseley, 1974-82
Most TDs Game:	4	Dick James, vs Dallas, 1961
Season:	15	Charley Taylor, 1966
Career:	90	Charley Taylor, 1964-77

WASHINGTON REDSKINS 169

On Super Sunday, Joe Theismann was super on defense, too.

INSIDE THE AFC

By DAVE NEWHOUSE

PREDICTED ORDER OF FINISH

EAST	CENTRAL	WEST
New York Jets	Cincinnati	L.A. Raiders
Miami	Pittsburgh	San Diego
Buffalo	Cleveland	Kansas City
New England	Houston	Seattle
Baltimore		Denver

AFC Champion: New York Jets

Please, gypsy woman, gaze into your crystal ball and tell me what you see in the American Football Conference.

Well, my son, the picture is murky. Or is that Cleveland? But, wait, things are growing clearer. I see the East Coast. New York City.

Someone is making a clicking sound. Click...click... kleck...Klecko. Joe Klecko. The crystal ball tells me that if Klecko's knee stops clicking, the Jets will win their division. They have everything else necessary to win, including a head coach who doesn't hear phantom phone calls from Al Davis.

Ah, there is Miami, New Yorkers surrounded by palm trees. Trees...wood...Woodley. Miami made the Super Bowl with David Woodley, lost it because of Woodley. The Dolphins have Killer Bees on defense, but no sting on offense. Gypsy humor.

Buffalo. New England. Baltimore. I have a clear picture of all three: unproven NFL coaches having to win with incomplete rosters, inconsistent quarterbacking. I see a coach, Kush, fighting with an owner, Irsay, for trading away the rights to John Elway for three Baltimore crab cakes and a ticket to the Preakness. I see

---

Dave Newhouse is sports columnist and seer of the Oakland Tribune.

Bengal Pete Johnson blasts and blocks to the playoffs.

Kush with a suitcase in his hand. Where is he going? The crystal ball has grown cloudy.

Wait, it's clearing again. I see Cincinnati and Pittsburgh. Even crystal balls have double exposures, my son. But the Bengals and Steelers are fighting each other for the playoffs. This could be the Steelers' last hurrah. Chuck Noll's, too. Cleveland. It has that nice coach, Rutigliano. Does he have gypsy blood? But the Browns have shaky quarterbacking. I see problems in Houston. Fast living. Old players, young players, a big gap in between. Houston will finish in the soup. Campbell's. You like gypsy humor? You don't like and I shut off the ball.

The scene is shifting again, west. I also see Al Davis winning his division. Who can beat him? San Diego has all that offense, but a defense only a gypsy mother could love. And the frustration of trying for the Super Bowl year after year and falling short now has the Chargers thinking they will never make it.

New coach in Kansas City, same old quarterback problem. Chuck Knox will make Seattle a winner, next year. Not even Elway can lift Denver out of last place.

AFC champion? Let me look deeper into the ball, my son. What is this I see? Jets. Jets of all sizes, flying this way and that...

BALTIMORE COLTS

TEAM DIRECTORY: Pres./Treas.: Robert Irsay; VP: Harriet Irsay; VP/Gen. Counsel: Michael Chernoff; GM: Ernie Accorsi; Dir. Player Personnel: Fred Schubach; Dir. Pro Personnel: Bob Terpening; Dir. Pub. Rel.: Walt Gutowski; Head Coach: Frank Kush. Home field: Memorial Stadium (60,763). Colors: Royal blue and white.

SCOUTING REPORT

OFFENSE: One step from the bottom. The Colts ranked 27th out of 28 in NFL offense, which wasn't surprising, considering coach Frank Kush turned over 64 percent of his roster from the year before. The Colts won't rank 27th again—if they do, Kush will have them running laps around Maryland—but how much better they do depends on the offensive line.

John Sinnott and Nat Hudson, starters on the left side, total three years of experience. The left side will be even younger if rookie Chris Hinton gets to start. Center Ray Donaldson and the right-side starters, Ken Huff and Jeff Hart, have a combined 17 years of experience. So guess which way Curtis Dickey and Randy McMillan will be running this fall?

How far the Colts progress will depend on the protection that line gives quarterback Mike Pagel, who couldn't have been happier that John Elway wound up in Denver. It's doubtful that Mark Hermann, obtained in the Elway deal, will beat out Pagel, who has a deep threat in Raymond Butler, a possession receiver in Matt Bouza and adequate tight ends. But he needs time to find them.

It looks like the Colts' offense is a year away from really scaring folks, but it's going to have some big games this fall. Like maybe once a month.

DEFENSE: The Colts couldn't stop the run last year if you told them what was coming beforehand. Baltimore was last in the league with a yield of 163.7 yards per game. But, once again, the culprit was as much inexperience as anything else.

Two rookies—Leo Wisniewski and Fletcher Jenkins—and second-year player Donnell Thompson manned the defensive line. The Colts have a little more experience at linebacker and in the secondary, but not much. In fact, there isn't a defensive starter with more than five years time in the NFL.

Barry Krauss finally has found a home at inside linebacker, teaming with the promising Johnie Cooks.

BALTIMORE COLTS 173

Donnell Thompson: One of Frank Kush's new breed of Colts.

COLTS VETERAN ROSTER

HEAD COACH—Frank Kush. Assistant Coaches—Zeke Bratkowski, Gunther Cunningham, Hal Hunter, Richard Mann, Roger Theder, Bob Valasente, Rick Venturi, Mike Westhoff.

No.	Name	Pos.	Ht.	Wt.	NFL Exp.	College
26	Anderson, Kim	CB	5-10	182	4	Arizona State
30	#Anderson, Larry	S	5-11	188	6	Louisiana Tech
87	Bailey, Elmer	WR	6-0	195	4	Minnesota
81	Beach, Pat	TE	6-4	243	2	Washington State
85	Bouza, Matt	WR	6-3	211	2	California
52	#Bracelin, Greg	LB	6-1	210	4	California
45	Burroughs, James	CB	6-1	192	2	Michigan State
80	Butler, Ray	WR	6-2	195	4	Southern California
98	Cooks, Johnie	LB	6-4	243	2	Mississippi State
73	Crosby, Cleveland	DE	6-5	250	2	Arizona
75	Crouch, Terry	G	6-2	278	2	Oklahoma
34	#Delaney, Jeff	S	6-1	197	4	Pittsburgh
33	Dickey, Curtis	RB	6-0	209	4	Texas A&M
31	Dixon, Zachary	RB	6-1	204	5	Temple
53	Donaldson, Ray	C	6-4	260	4	Georgia
72	Durham, Steve	DE	6-5	256	2	Clemson
78	Foley, Tim	T	6-6	275	2	Notre Dame
28	Franklin, Cleveland	FB	6-2	216	6	Baylor
25	Glasgow, Nesby	S	5-10	180	5	Washington
91	Green, Bubba	DT	6-4	278	2	North Carolina State
—	Griffin, Wade	T	6-5	278	6	Mississippi
68	#Hart, Jeff	T	6-5	272	7	Oregon State
42	Hatchett, Derrick	CB	5-11	183	4	Texas
27	Hemphill, Darryl	S	6-0	195	2	West Texas State
88	Henry, Bernard	WR	6-0	185	2	Arizona State
—	Herrmann, Mark	QB	6-4	195	3	Purdue
63	Hudson, Nat	G	6-3	265	3	Georgia
62	Huff, Ken	G	6-4	259	9	North Carolina
57	#Humiston, Mike	LB	6-3	238	2	Weber State
11	Humm, David	QB	6-2	194	9	Nebraska
92	Hunter, James	NT	6-5	251	2	Southern California
94	Jenkins, Fletcher	DE	6-2	258	2	Washington
51	Jones, Ricky	LB	6-2	222	7	Tuskegee
55	Krauss, Barry	LB	6-3	232	5	Alabama
86	McCall, Reese	TE	6-6	238	6	Auburn
32	McMillan, Randy	FB	6-0	220	3	Pittsburgh
1	Miller, Dan	K	5-10	172	2	Miami
65	Moore, Jimmy	G	6-5	268	3	Ohio State
49	Odom, Cliff	LB	6-2	225	3	Texas
60	Padjen, Gary	LB	6-2	246	2	Arizona State
18	Pagel, Mike	QB	6-2	201	2	Arizona State
10	##Schlichter, Art	QB	6-2	210	2	Ohio State
83	Sherwin, Tim	TE	6-6	237	3	Boston College
54	Shiver, Sanders	LB	6-2	227	8	Carson-Newman
96	Simmons, Dave	LB	6-5	219	3	North Carolina
79	Sinnott, John	T	6-4	275	3	Brown
84	Smith, Holden	WR	6-1	191	3	California
3	Stark, Rohn	P	6-3	195	2	Florida State
90	Taylor, Hosea	DE	6-5	260	2	Houston
99	Thompson, Donnell	DE	6-4	254	3	North Carolina
64	Utt, Ben	G	6-4	255	2	Georgia Tech
69	Wisniewski, Leo	NT	6-2	263	2	Penn State
38	Wright, Johnnie	RB	6-0	210	2	S. Carolina-Columbus

#Unsigned at press time
##Suspended by the NFL

TOP FIVE DRAFT CHOICES

Rd.	Name	Sel. No.	Pos.	Ht.	Wt.	College
1	*Hinton, Chris	4	G	6-4	265	Northwestern
2	Maxwell, Vernon	29	LB	6-2	225	Arizona State
3	Achica, George	57	DT	6-5	260	Southern California
4	Smith, Phil	85	WR	6-3	190	San Diego State
5	Abramowitz, Sid	113	T	6-5	280	Tulsa

*Acquired from Denver Broncos after draft

The secondary has two good prospects in corner James Burroughs and free safety Nesby Glasgow, though the Colts are thinking of making Glasgow a strong safety. Burroughs tied a club record with a 94-yard interception for a touchdown.

The Colts' comeback player of the year could be defensive end Hosea Taylor, inactive last year but now 25 pounds stronger and ready to challenge Jenkins, who should be a nose tackle, anyway.

KICKING GAME: It's in good hands, er, feet. Rookie Rohn Stark was the NFL runnerup in punting, with a 44.4-yard average. Kicker Dan Miller, who won the job in midseason, is a long-range boomer. He kicked 3-of-4 field goals beyond the 40, including a club-record 58-yarder.

THE ROOKIES: Would have been a great crop with John Elway, but not bad without him. Start with guard Hinton, the fourth overall pick from Northwestern who became a Colt in the Elway deal, and linebacker Vernon Maxwell of Arizona State, the Colts' No. 2 pick, a great blitzer. But, No. 3, George Achica of USC, a nose tackle, signed with the USFL's L.A. Express.

OUTLOOK: Somehow, Kush is going to get this team out of the AFC East cellar. The young Colts will be upstarts this year, knocking off two or three big teams, then make their big move next year. Don't forget one thing: Kush is a winner, and he'll win in the NFL, too. Eventually.

COLT PROFILES

MIKE PAGEL 22 6-2 201   Quarterback

That's Pagel as in bagel... There seems to have been a hole in his scouting report, since the Colts got him in the fourth round of the 1982 draft... But he wrested the starting quarterback job away from Art Schlichter, who was drafted 80 players ahead of him... Whatever he did to turn off the scouts who watched him play at Arizona State, he turned them back on last year by completing 50.2 percent of his passes for 1,281 yards and suffering only seven interceptions in 221 attempts. Not-too-shabby statistics for a rookie playing in a strike-shortened season... Born Sept. 13, 1960, in Douglas, Ariz.... Reserve outfielder on Arizona State's 1981 national baseball champions... Threw for 466 yards and seven touchdowns in one game against Stanford... ASU MVP as a senior.

MARK HERRMANN 24 6-4 195　　　　　　　　Quarterback

Does he have the arm?... This has been the question all along... Had a good enough arm at Purdue to pass for an NCAA-record 9,946 yards, but the pros require a stronger arm and he is no Steve Bartkowski... That's why he was still around when Denver grabbed him in the fourth round of the '81 draft and that's why he was sent to the Colts as part of package for John Elway... Didn't throw a pass as a rookie, then connected on 32-of-60 (53.3 percent) for 421 yards and a touchdown with Denver last year... Also threw four interceptions... Born Jan. 8, 1959, in Cincinnati... Played high school football in Carmel, Ind., before rewriting the record book at Purdue.

CURTIS DICKEY 26 6-0 209　　　　　　　　Running Back

Curtis hurt us... That could be the cry uttered by Colts' opponents in '83, if the young Colts can give him the blocking required to spring his tremendous talent loose... In coaching jargon, he has it all: speed, strength, all-pro potential. If the Colts ever get it together, so will Dickey... He had an off year in '82, but so did the league... Rushed for 232 yards, but for only 3.5 per carry as Colts rebuilt half the offensive line... It's going to come for Dickey, who's only in his fourth year, if he doesn't get killed first... Born Nov. 27, 1956, in Madisonville, Tex.... Career rushing leader at Texas A&M... Blazing sprinter (9.2 at 100 yards, 10.05 at 100 meters) who won three NCAA 60-yard indoor titles.

RANDY McMILLAN 24 6-0 220　　　　　　　　Running Back

The Baltimore Freight... He's a load, a squat body and thunderous thighs coming at you all at once... Coach Frank Kush said McMillan did an "exceptional job" running and blocking last year in only his second season as a Colt... An instant starter as a first-round pick out of Pitt, he led the Colts with 50 receptions, a team record for rookies... Punishing blocker who gives Curtis Dickey much of his running room... A coach's player who works hard and complains rarely... Born Dec. 17, 1958, in Havre de Grace, Md.... Was a winner in college: his teams at Harford (Md.) Community College were 20-0 and his Pitt teams were 22-2... Rushed for 141 yards in Pitt debut and scored twice in '81 Gator Bowl.

RAYMOND BUTLER 27 6-2 195   Wide Receiver

A Butler who gives exceptional service... The Colts' best receiver and one of the NFL's most unsung players... Caught only 17 passes last year, but two were for touchdowns, including a 53-yard bomb... A draft-day steal back in '80, when the Colts found him hiding in the fourth round... Two seasons and 80 receptions later, the Colts knew they had a star. Now if he can convince the rest of football... Those 80 receptions were 52 more than he caught in two years at USC, after leaving Wharton County (Tex.) JC... Born June 28, 1956, in Port Larace, Tex. ... Colts may shift him from flanker to split end this year... On either side, he's dangerous.

MATT BOUZA 25 6-3 211   Wide Receiver

There's one on every team... You know the kind: he looks too short or too slow, somehow incomplete as an athlete. But put him in a game and you get results... Was a 1981 free agent with the 49ers, who cut him that summer ... Received a second chance last year in Baltimore because Colts' running-back coach, Roger Theder, was Bouza's head coach at California... Not fast, but he's in the Dwight Clark mold—a big receiver with good hands who knows how to get open... Led the Colts with 22 catches, scoring twice... Born April 8, 1958, in San Jose, Cal.... Third all-time leading receiver at Cal... Best college year was '79: 52 receptions, plus seven more in the Garden State Bowl.

JEFF HART 29 6-5 272   Offensive Tackle

Hart has heart... If he didn't, he wouldn't be playing in the NFL today... Originally with the 49ers, he was drafted third in 1975... Spent the next year in New Orleans, then washed out of the NFL... After two seasons with the Winnipeg Blue Bombers, he was given a look by the Colts in '79. He stuck and eventually became a starter at tackle... Good pass blocker who plays hard, but must work on run blocking... Answer to the trivia question: Who replaced George Kunz in Baltimore in 1980?... His other claim to fame? He is the only NFL tackle to return a kickoff before and after playing in Winnipeg... Born Sept. 10, 1953, in Portland... Three-year starter at Oregon State.

RAY DONALDSON 25 6-4 260   Center

One of two black centers in the NFL, along with Miami's Dwight Stephenson... In his fourth year with Colts, his third as a starter... Second center and fourth offensive lineman taken in the '80 draft. Baltimore grabbed him in the second round... A dynamite special-teams player as a rookie while backing up at center and guard... All-American at Georgia, where he switched from linebacker to center as a sophomore and left the year before Herschel Walker arrived... Born May 18, 1958, in Rome. Not Italy, Georgia... Still lives in Rome, doing what the Romans do in Georgia, whatever that is. Smelling magnolias?... The flower of the Colts' offensive line, an orchid among weeds.

JOHNIE COOKS 24 6-4 243   Inside Linebacker

Oh, Johnie, oh... Can he play linebacker!... It's easier to spell Johnie than to block him... A moose who can move... Once he learns about offenses, he may be the second coming of Lawrence Taylor... Cooks was the second player taken in the '82 NFL draft... Colts tried him at outside linebacker, obviously thinking of Taylor, before switching him back to his natural inside position, where he is a destroyer... All-American at Mississippi State, where he led the squad in tackles each year and played on two intramural basketball championship teams... Born Nov. 23, 1958, in Leland, Miss.... Had eight tackles in Hula Bowl, 10 in Olympia Gold Bowl... In other words, he's a hitter.

DONNELL THOMPSON 24 6-4 254   Defensive End

Do tell, it's Donnell... The best defensive lineman in Baltimore and getting better... In only his third year in the pros, he has the size, quick feet and strength to be a great one... He would be a standout on many NFL teams, but must be content to grow into stardom with the young, growing Colts... Led Baltimore linemen last year in tackles. He has a natural instinct for finding the football...Born Oct. 27, 1958, in Lumberton, N.C....The pride of Lumberton High, then North Carolina, where he started three years, but only received third-team All-American honors...Not fooled, the Colts drafted him in the first round in '81 as the 18th player chosen...Started 12 games as a rookie.

ROHN STARK 24 6-3 195   Punter

Up, up and away...An amateur pilot who likes to get away from football by taking off to where the air is rare...His punts have a tendency to take flight, too...Hang time is 5.1-5.2 seconds...Last year, the Colts' rookie averaged 44.4 yards, the second-best mark in the NFL ...Baltimore was expecting big things from him, otherwise they wouldn't have made him the 34th player chosen in the draft (the highest-drafted punter since Russell Erxleben was taken in the first round in '79)...Averaged 46 yards in his senior year at Florida State, second-best in nation...Gets the ball off quickly, too...Has never had a punt blocked...Born June 4, 1959, in Minneapolis.

COACH FRANK KUSH: The Desert Pox, now The Baltimore Crab...Like him or loathe him, Kush knows how to win. And he's going to make the Colts a winner, if they don't wilt from exhaustion or criticism, both parts of his coaching philosophy...Those who played for him at Arizona State won't soon forget Camp Kush, where he weeded out the hitters from the quitters... The formula worked: the Sun Devils had a 176-54-1 record in Kush's 22 years in the desert. His .764 winning percentage ranked him second among active college coaches...Kush forced himself out at ASU after one of his players said Kush slapped him during a game...Later was acquitted of charge in court...Coached the CFL Hamilton Tiger-Cats to an 11-4-1 record before getting the Baltimore job last year...Born Jan. 20, 1929, in Windber, Pa....One of 15 children...Played defensive guard at Michigan State, earning All-American honors even though he weighed 175 pounds...Spent three years as an assistant at Arizona State before getting the head job in 1958...Insulted the Colts many times last year; it should pay off with wins this year.

180 THE COMPLETE HANDBOOK OF PRO FOOTBALL

Randy McMillan's style is simple: He runs over people.

GREATEST QUARTERBACK

George Shaw.

C'mon, has Baltimore—or football—ever had a better quarterback than Johnny Unitas? In 18 years, he set more records and broke more barriers than any passer the game has ever known.

He was the first to throw for more than 40,000 yards. He was football's Joe DiMaggio, throwing touchdown passes in 47 consecutive games. Other career records he set were for most passes attempted and completed, most passing yards, most seasons with 3,000 or more yards passing (3) and most touchdown passes (290).

Johnny U. was a legend—an unsung quarterback from Louisville who failed a tryout with the Pittsburgh Steelers before the Colts picked him off the equivalent of football's sandlots, the semipro ranks.

What followed was three NFL championships for the Colts, including the overtime win over the Giants in 1958 that "made" pro football; 10 Pro Bowl appearances, five all-pro selections, three NFL Most Valuable Player awards and induction in the Hall of Fame.

George Shaw, indeed.

INDIVIDUAL COLT RECORDS

Rushing

Most Yards Game:	198	Norm Bulaich, vs N.Y. Jets, 1971
Season:	1,200	Lydell Mitchell, 1976
Career:	5,487	Lydell Mitchell, 1972-77

Passing

Most TD Passes Game:	5	Gary Cuozzo, vs Minnesota, 1965
Season:	32	John Unitas, 1959
Career:	287	John Unitas, 1956-72

Receiving

Most TD Passes Game:	3	Jim Mutscheller, vs Green Bay, 1957
	3	Raymond Berry, vs Dallas, 1960
	3	Raymond Berry, vs Green Bay, 1960
	3	Jimmy Orr, vs Washington, 1962
	3	Jimmy Orr, vs Los Angeles, 1964
	3	Roger Carr, vs Cincinnati, 1976
Season:	14	Raymond Berry, 1959
Career:	68	Raymond Berry, 1955-67

Scoring

Most Points Game:	24	Lenny Moore, vs Chicago, 1958
	24	Lenny Moore, vs Los Angeles, 1960
	24	Lenny Moore, vs Minnesota, 1961
	24	Lydell Mitchell, vs Buffalo, 1975
Season:	120	Lenny Moore, 1964
Career:	678	Lenny Moore, 1956-67
Most TDs Game:	4	Lenny Moore, vs Chicago, 1958
	4	Lenny Moore, vs Los Angeles, 1960
	4	Lenny Moore, vs Minnesota, 1961
	4	Lydell Mitchell, vs Buffalo, 1975
Season:	20	Lenny Moore, 1964
Career:	113	Lenny Moore, 1956-67

BUFFALO BILLS

TEAM DIRECTORY: Pres.: Ralph Wilson; Exec. VP: Patrick J. McGroder; VP/Player Personnel: Norm Pollom; VP/Pub. Rel.: L. Budd Thalman; Head Coach: Kay Stephenson. Home field: Rich Stadium (80,020). Colors: Scarlet red, royal blue and white.

SCOUTING REPORT

OFFENSE: Was there ever a time that Buffalo couldn't run the football? From Cookie Gilchrist to O.J. Simpson to Joe Cribbs, nothing changes. The Bills led the NFL last year with an average of 152.3 yards rushing.

Cribbs, Roosevelt Leaks, Curtis Brown, Roland Hooks... Buffalo sends them at defenses in shifts. The Bills have added Ted McKnight from Kansas City. Throw in Van Williams, a preseason standout a year ago before suffering a knee injury, and Booker Moore, a No. 1 draft pick two years ago whose rookie year was ruined by a rare nerve disorder, and the Bills may have to use the T-formation to get all their backs playing time.

The Bills have an outstanding offensive line in Ken Jones, Reggie McKenzie, Will Grant, Jon Borchardt, Joe Devlin and tight end Mark Brammer. They permitted only 12 sacks, the second-best mark in the league.

Even with good protection, Joe Ferguson had a terrible year in '82. He must have thought he was King Corcoran, because Ferguson couldn't have hit the Great Wall of China from 20 yards away. And he has talented receivers in Jerry Butler, Frank Lewis and young Perry Tuttle.

DEFENSE: Outside linebacker Isiah Robertson announced his retirement and defensive end Sherman White was pondering life after football as well. If they're both gone, new coach Kay Stephenson will have some formidable holes to patch in a defense that ranked second in the AFC a year ago.

Waiting in line for Robertson's job has been Lucius Sanford, while either Ken Johnson or Darrel Irvin is likely to replace White if he calls it quits.

Inside linebacker Shane Nelson is coming off knee surgery with visions of starting again. Who would he replace, Jim Haslett or Eugene Marve, who had a great rookie year? If Nelson is healthy, he'll play somewhere. The other outside linebacker is Ervin Parker, who really came around last year after two years on special teams.

Joe Cribbs' 633 yards ranked sixth among NFL's rushers.

The secondary is solid with Mario Clark, Charles Romes and Steve Freeman, although the retired Bill Simpson will be missed. With Pro Bowlers Fred Smerlas and Ben Williams back on the defensive line and with White and Nelson in the lineup, the Bills' defense will be tough.

KICKING GAME: Is Greg Cater related to Bills' owner Ralph Wilson? In three years, Cater's punting averages have been 38.7, 39.7 and 37.9 yards. His job has to be in danger. Efren Herrera hit only 8-of-14 field-goal attempts as he adjusted to the outdoors after kicking in the Kingdome for Seattle. He should rebound.

THE ROOKIES: Top pick Tony Hunter of Notre Dame is compared to Kellen Winslow coming out of college, and will provide

BILLS VETERAN ROSTER

HEAD COACH—Kay Stephenson. Assistant Coaches—Jerry Glanville, Milt Jackson, Don Lawrence, Miller McCalmon, Perry Moss, Jim Niblack, Al Sandahl, Bob Zeman.

No.	Name	Pos.	Ht.	Wt.	NFL Exp.	College
84	Barnett, Buster	TE	6-5	225	3	Jackson State
73	Borchardt, Jon	T	6-5	255	5	Montana State
86	Brammer, Mark	TE	6-3	235	4	Michigan State
47	Brown, Curtis	RB	5-10	203	7	Missouri
80	Butler, Jerry	WR	6-0	178	5	Clemson
7	Cater, Greg	P	6-0	191	4	Tenn.-Chattanooga
29	Clark, Mario	CB	6-2	195	8	Oregon
20	Cribbs, Joe	RB	5-11	190	4	Auburn
78	Cross, Justin	T	6-6	257	2	Western State (Colo.)
70	Devlin, Joe	T	6-5	250	8	Iowa
12	Ferguson, Joe	QB	6-1	195	11	Arkansas
85	Franklin, Byron	WR	6-1	179	2	Auburn
22	Freeman, Steve	S	5-11	185	9	Mississippi State
53	Grant, Will	C	6-4	248	6	Kentucky
55	Haslett, Jim	LB	6-3	232	5	Indiana, Pa.
1	#Herrera, Efren	K	5-9	190	2	UCLA
87	Holt, Robert	WR	6-1	182	2	Baylor
25	Hooks, Roland	RB	6-0	195	8	North Carolina State
97	Irvin, Darrell	DE	6-4	255	4	Oklahoma
91	#Johnson, Ken	DE	6-5	253	2	Knoxville
72	Jones, Ken	T	6-5	250	8	Arkansas State
52	Keating, Chris	LB	6-2	223	5	Maine
10	Kofler, Matt	QB	6-3	192	2	San Diego State
42	Kush, Rod	S	6-0	188	4	Nebraska-Omaha
48	Leaks, Roosevelt	RB	5-10	225	9	Texas
82	#Lewis, Frank	WR	6-1	196	13	Grambling
60	Lumpkin, Joey	LB	6-2	230	2	Arizona State
61	Lynch, Tom	G	6-5	250	7	Boston College
—	Mahfour, Robbie	QB	6-1	195	2	SE Louisiana
54	Marve, Eugene	LB	6-2	230	2	Saginaw Valley State
67	McKenzie, Reggie	G	6-5	242	12	Michigan
33	#McKnight, Ted	RB	6-1	212	7	Minnesota-Duluth
34	Moore, Booker	FB	5-11	224	2	Penn State
88	Mosley, Mike	WR	6-2	192	2	Texas A&M
59	Nelson, Shane	LB	6-1	225	6	Baylor
38	Nixon, Jeff	S	6-3	190	5	Richmond
62	Parker, Ervin	LB	6-5	240	4	South Carolina State
89	Piccone, Lou	WR	5-9	175	10	West Liberty State
40	Riddick, Robb	RB	6-0	195	2	Millersville State (Pa.)
51	Ritcher, Jim	C-G	6-3	251	4	North Carolina State
26	Romes, Charles	CB	6-1	190	7	North Carolina Central
99	Roopenian, Mark	NT	6-5	254	2	Boston College
57	Sanford, Lucius	LB	6-2	216	7	Georgia Tech
76	Smerlas, Fred	NT	6-3	270	5	Boston College
81	Tuttle, Perry	WR	6-0	178	2	Clemson
41	#Villapiano, Phil	LB	6-2	225	12	Bowling Green
65	Vogler, Tim	C	6-3	245	5	Ohio State
83	#White, Sherman	DE	6-5	250	12	California
77	Williams, Ben	DE	6-3	245	8	Mississippi
27	Williams, Chris	CB	6-0	197	3	Louisiana State

#Unsigned at press time

TOP FIVE DRAFT CHOICES

Rd.	Name	Sel. No.	Pos.	Ht.	Wt.	College
1	Hunter, Tony	12	TE	6-5	226	Notre Dame
1	Kelly, Jim	14	QB	6-3	215	Miami
2	Talley, Darryl	39	LB	6-4	210	West Virginia
3	Junkin, Trey	93	LB	6-1	225	Louisiana Tech
4	Payne, Jimmy	112	DE	6-4	243	Georgia

BUFFALO BILLS 185

a deep threat at tight end. Jim Kelly of Miami should, in time, succeed Joe Ferguson at quarterback. West Virginia linebacker Darryl Talley is a fast, active, sure tackler. Sleeper could be No. 5 Jimmy Payne of Georgia, a fine pass-rusher if healthy.

OUTLOOK: In the AFC East's annual dogfight, who can possibly distinguish the frontrunners from the stragglers? The Bills look like a middle-of-the-pack team unless Stephenson proves he can motivate and coach like Chuck Knox. If the Bills start slowly, they're in trouble.

BILL PROFILES

JOE FERGUSON 33 6-1 195   Quarterback

Thrown for a loss... In fact, he would like to throw the 1982 season back to wherever it came from... Threw 16 interceptions, more than any other quarterback, in only nine games... Passed for 1,597 yards, but had only seven touchdown passes... Well, every quarterback is entitled to a bad season, and this one has never had two in a row... If he gets off slowly this year, first-round pick Jim Kelly will be there to challenge him... Born April 23, 1950, in Alvin, Tex.... Went to Arkansas, a depository for NFL-directed quarterbacks... Emerged to the delight of Buffalo, which drafted him No. 3 in 1973.

FRANK LEWIS 36 6-1 196   Wide Receiver

How long has this been going on?... It's been 12 years, to be exact, since he first confounded an NFL secondary... He's 36 now, but don't say phooey. Looie led the Bills in receptions last year with 28, averaging 15.8 yards a catch and scoring twice, the 36th and 37th regular-season touchdowns of his career... "He's a clutch player, a man for the big games," said admirer and teammate Reggie McKenzie... And, apparently, he's not yet long in the tooth. He had his best year in '81, catching 70 passes. If not for the strike, he likely would have caught 50 in '82... Born July 4, 1947, in Houma, La., where he is a deputy sheriff in the offseason... Another in the long line of great players from Grambling.

JOE CRIBBS 25 5-11 190   Running Back

In search of happiness... Felt unloved by Bills' management until coming to terms on new pact during offseason... They had a contract squabble last year, but it goes deeper than that... Selected to the Pro Bowl, but an injury kept him from playing. The Bills refused to pay his plane fare to the game. That's cold... It shouldn't have been that way, because he is the franchise, plain and simple... Has done everything the Bills could possibly ask of him and more. He runs, receives, makes big plays, wins games. Without him, the Bills are counterfeit... Born Jan. 5, 1958, in Sulligent, Ala.... Played at the USC of the south, Auburn, with James Brooks, William Andrews and all those other running backs... Second-round pick in '80.

JERRY BUTLER 25 6-0 178   Wide Receiver

No buts about Butler... This cat can play!... Fast as a cat, he once beat world-class sprinter Harvey Glance... That was when Butler was running the dashes for Clemson in the spring and dashing under passes in the fall. He set single-season and career receiving records for Tigers... Buffalo drafted him in the first round in 1979 and it has been bombs away ever since. He caught 26 passes last year, four for touchdowns... Born Oct. 10, 1957, in Greenwood, S.C.... Quarterback in Ware Shoals, S.C., before getting a track scholarship to Clemson... The only Buffalo receiver to catch four touchdown passes in a single game... Loves to fish, hike and camp when he isn't camping out in someone's end zone.

REGGIE McKENZIE 33 6-5 242   Guard

The Juice speaks... "Reggie McKenzie is the finest teammate a man could have," O.J. Simpson said... Years ago, they were quite a team, The Juice and Reggie, generating most of the yardage Simpson gained in that memorable 2,000-yard season... The Juice is gone, preparing his induction speech for Canton next year, but McKenzie goes on, throwing blocks for Roosevelt Leaks and Joe Cribbs with the same fervor as ever... How much longer can this old lion protect his territory from the younger lions? Until his growl is not so fierce, which may not be for a year or two... Born July 27, 1950, in Detroit... All-American at Michigan, all-pro once in Buffalo.

BUFFALO BILLS 187

BEN WILLIAMS 29 6-3 245 — Defensive End

Hawaii calls. Finally... It took seven seasons, but he finally made it to the Pro Bowl in Honolulu... Buffalo fans wonder why it took that long, because he had 12 sacks in '80 and 10½ in '81, forcing four fumbles over that two-year span... Recognized as Pro Bowl caliber after the '82 mini-season, during which he gave a maxi-performance... Not big as defensive ends go, but, then, neither is Fred Dean... Both are extremely quick, and Williams is stronger that he looks; he is a dedicated iron pumper... Born Sept. 1, 1954, in Yazoo City, Miss.... Played nose guard at Mississippi... Drafted third by Bills in '76... Loves to play chess... Works in a bank in Jackson, Miss., during off-season.

FRED SMERLAS 26 6-3 270 — Nose Tackle

Smerlas on Smerlas: "I just like to play. I like to hit. I like the feeling of self-accomplishment. When you come in on Mondays and see the films, you want them to be enjoyable."... Has turned in some Academy Award-quality performances... Doesn't have many bad games. In four years with Buffalo, he has been to three Pro Bowls... Many consider him the premier nose tackle in the game... He's quick off the ball, despite his immenseness. Not only is he powerful, but he plays with great intensity... No NFL center in his right mind wants to play him. Few NFL centers are in their right mind after they play him... Born April 8, 1957, in Waltham, Mass.... Boston College product... Bills' No. 2 pick in '79.

SHANE NELSON 28 6-1 225 — Inside Linebacker

Come back, Shane! The Bermuda Triangle needs you... Knee injuries have all but taken away the last two seasons for Nelson, who is trying another comeback, perhaps his last shot at reviving his football career... Together with linebacker Jim Haslett and nose tackle Fred Smerlas, Nelson formed The Bermuda Triangle—the middle of the Bills' defense, which was nearly impossible to run against... Buffalo is a better football team with a healthy Nelson... And to think the Bills signed him as a free agent out of Baylor in 1977... Born May 25, 1955, in

188 THE COMPLETE HANDBOOK OF PRO FOOTBALL

Mathis, Tex., he played at Blinn (Tex.) JC for two years before going to Baylor... Turned down a contract with Dallas to sign with Buffalo.

PERRY TUTTLE 24 6-0 180　　　　　　　　Wide Receiver

Waiting his turn... Tuttle is the logical successor to Frank Lewis, if and when Lewis ever gets old... Realistically, he could put pressure on Lewis this year... Tuttle was a backup to Buffalo's other wide receiver, Jerry Butler, as a Clemson freshman, then erased many of Butler's pass-receiving records... Tuttle has great speed and is an outstanding one-on-one receiver... Bills broke him in slowly last year, with seven receptions for a 15.3 average... Buffalo's No. 1 pick in '82 after helping Clemson win the national championship... All-American as a senior... Born Aug. 2, 1959, in Lexington, N.C.... Youngest of seven children... Hobby is photography... The Ansel Adams of wide receivers.

MARIO CLARK 29 6-2 195　　　　　　　　Cornerback

Want a fast receiver covered? Call Mario... Want a sofa recovered? Call Mario... Want Mario's story covered? Call Mario's wife, Lisa, who has a journalism degree... Has been a fine cornerback for the Bills for seven years... Has worked for his father in the upholstering business and is a talented decorator. Not only that, he majored in architecture and real estate in college... Born March 29, 1954, in Pasadena, Cal., where he still lives... Played football at Oregon, and was the first freshman honored as Player of the Week in the then-Pacific-8 Conference... Bills' No. 1 pick in '76.

COACH KAY STEPHENSON: A boy named Kay... Became the youngest head coach in the NFL (38) when Chuck Knox shuffled out of Buffalo in protest against the penuriousness of the Bills' front office... Knox went 3,000 miles, to Seattle, to get away from Buffalo owner Ralph Wilson and the tight-fisted spending that Knox claimed cost the Bills Tom Cousineau, their No. 1 draft pick who went to Canada and then to Cleveland

BUFFALO BILLS 189

...Knox believed the Bills weren't committed to building a Super Bowl team, so he split. Following his successful act in Buffalo is a coach named Kay...Stephenson spent one year under Knox in Los Angeles in 1977, then came to Buffalo with Knox in '78...Coached the Bills' quarterbacks until opportunity knocked...Said he will have a good working relationship with management or he wouldn't have taken the job. We'll see...Born Dec. 17, 1944, in DeFuniak Springs, Fla....Played quarterback at Florida, San Diego ('67), Buffalo ('68) and with the Jacksonville Sharks ('74) before becoming the WFL team's director of player personnel and offensive coordinator in '75...His only other head-coaching experience: Baker County (Fla.) High School in '73.

No QB has filled the Bill better than Joe Ferguson.

GREATEST QUARTERBACK

It is hoped the handsome Congressman from the state of New York won't take offense with this selection, but Joe Ferguson is a better quarterback than was Jack Kemp during his days with the Buffalo Bills.

Ferguson may not have the political style of Kemp, but if Ferguson ever gets the Bills to the Super Bowl, that could change.

Ferguson holds every important Buffalo passing record and a few that are not so important, such as the most interceptions. But all that comes with longevity. Ferguson has worn a Buffalo uniform for 10 seasons; Kemp lasted eight years.

Shreveport Joe attended the same high school (Woodlawn) as did Terry Bradshaw. Though no one rates Ferguson in the "greatest" categories (greatest arm, greatest release, greatest touch, etc.), he is the kind of quarterback whose accomplishments creep up on you. By the time he is finished playing, Ferguson, who is 33, may rank statistically among the top five quarterbacks in history.

Then, even Jack Kemp would have to cast his vote for Ferguson.

INDIVIDUAL BILL RECORDS

Rushing
Most Yards Game:	273	O. J. Simpson, vs Detroit, 1976
Season:	2,003	O. J. Simpson, 1973
Career:	10,183	O. J. Simpson, 1969-77

Passing
Most TD Passes Game:	5	Joe Ferguson, vs N.Y. Jets, 1979
Season:	25	Joe Ferguson, 1975
Career:	143	Joe Ferguson, 1973-82

Receiving
Most TD Passes Game:	4	Jerry Butler, vs N.Y. Jets, 1979
Season:	10	Elbert Dubenion, 1964
Career:	35	Elbert Dubenion, 1960-67

Scoring
Most Points Game:	30	Cookie Gilchrist, vs New York, 1963
Season:	138	O. J. Simpson, 1975
Career:	420	O. J. Simpson, 1969-77
Most TDs Game:	5	Cookie Gilchrist, vs New York, 1963
Season:	23	O. J. Simpson, 1975
Career:	70	O. J. Simpson, 1969-1977

CINCINNATI BENGALS

TEAM DIRECTORY: Chairman: Austin E. Knowlton; Pres.: John Sawyer; VP/GM: Paul Brown; Asst. GM: Michael Brown; Dir. Player Personnel: Pete Brown; Dir. Pub Rel.: Allan Heim; Bus. Mgr.: John Murdough; Head Coach: Forrest Gregg. Home field: Riverfront Stadium (59,754). Colors: Orange, black and white.

Ken Anderson completed 70.6% of his passes for 2,495 yards.

SCOUTING REPORT

OFFENSE: The Bengals need a breakaway halfback. They've waited on Charles Alexander for four years and he hasn't done the job, putting more pressure on quarterback Ken Anderson and fullback Pete Johnson. The Bengals finished 20th in NFL rushing, as Alexander's career average dropped to 3.5 yards per carry.

The Bengals have other problems. Tight end Dan Ross is a USFL-bound lame duck. Will coach Forrest Gregg, a stickler for loyalty, cut down Ross' playing time and use M.L. Harris? This move would create friction as well as a considerable reduction in offensive production.

A breakaway back might also help the offensive line, which was beaten for 27 sacks in nine games. No wonder the Bengals fell off their Super Bowl perch. Anderson still ranked No. 1 among NFL quarterbacks last year, despite the fact that he was running for his life.

Normally, this should be a great year for Cincinnati receivers. Cris Collinsworth had another big year and David Verser is coming on to challenge Isaac Curtis. But the Ross situation can't help the passing game. Anderson will have to be superhuman to get the Bengals' offense back to 1981 levels.

DEFENSE: The Bengals are tigers against the run, pussy cats against the pass.

Cincinnati's defense plays physically. The front three and the four linebackers hit hard, often in groups. But they don't get after the passer with great frequency, and last year the Bengals gave up 227 passing yards per game, ranking them 22nd in the league.

The Bengals have great cornerbacks in Ken Riley and Louis Breeden and average safeties in Bobby Kemp and Bryan Hicks. The first two had a total of seven interceptions in 1982, while the last two had a total of one.

Cincinnati's four linebackers combined for two interceptions, one each by Bo Harris and Jim LeClair. The Bengal foursome, which also includes Reggie Williams and Glenn Cameron, is run-oriented. Opponents have success against the Bengals with medium-deep passes against the linebackers and safeties.

Unless the Bengals get a better pass rush from Ross Browner, Wilson Whitley and Eddie Edwards—heat is difficult to generate with a three-man line—Gregg might be wise to rush 6-6, 260-pound Glen Collins into the defensive line and play four men.

KICKING GAME: Pat McInally went from the NFL's best punter (45.4 yards per game) to nearly the worst (38.7) in the short

BENGALS VETERAN ROSTER

HEAD COACH—Forrest Gregg. Assistant Coaches—Hank Bullough, Bruce Coslet, Lindy Infante, Dick LeBeau, Jim McNally, Dick Modzelewski, George Sefcik, Kim Wood.

No.	Name	Pos.	Ht.	Wt.	NFL Exp.	College
40	Alexander, Charles	RB	6-1	220	5	Louisiana State
14	Anderson, Ken	QB	6-3	212	13	Augustana (Ill.)
61	Boyarsky, Jerry	NT	6-3	212	13	Pittsburgh
10	Breech, Jim	K	5-6	155	5	California
34	Breeden, Louis	CB	5-11	185	6	North Carolina Central
79	Browner, Ross	DE	6-3	261	6	Notre Dame
74	Bujnoch, Glenn	G	6-6	265	8	Texas A&M
67	Burley, Gary	DE	6-3	274	8	Pittsburgh
58	Bush, Blair	C	6-3	252	6	Washington
50	Cameron, Glenn	LB	6-2	228	9	Florida
76	Collins, Glen	DE	6-6	260	2	Mississippi State
80	Collinsworth, Cris	WR	6-5	192	2	Florida
85	Curtis, Isaac	WR	6-1	192	11	San Diego State
52	#Dinkel, Tom	LB	6-3	237	6	Kansas
73	Edwards, Eddie	DE	6-5	256	7	Miami
49	Frazier, Guy	LB	6-2	215	3	Wyoming
42	Fuller, Mike	PR-S	5-10	182	9	Auburn
45	Griffin, Archie	RB	5-9	184	6	Ohio State
44	Griffin, Ray	CB	5-10	186	6	Ohio State
53	Harris, Bo	LB	6-3	226	9	Louisiana State
83	Harris, M. L.	TE	6-5	238	4	Kansas State
27	Hicks, Bryan	S	6-0	192	4	McNeese
82	Holman, Rodney	TE	6-3	230	2	Tulane
37	Jackson, Robert	S	5-10	184	2	Central Michigan
46	Johnson, Pete	RB	6-0	250	7	Ohio State
26	Kemp, Bobby	S	6-0	186	3	California State
86	Kreider, Steve	WR	6-3	192	5	Lehigh
62	Lapham, Dave	G	6-4	262	10	Syracuse
55	LeClair, Jim	LB	6-3	234	12	North Dakota
87	McNally, Pat	P	6-6	212	8	Harvard
65	Montoya, Max	G	6-5	275	5	UCLA
60	Moore, Blake	C	6-5	267	4	Wooster
78	Munoz, Anthony	T	6-6	278	4	Southern California
68	Obrovac, Mike	T	6-6	275	3	Bowling Green
51	Razzano, Rick	LB	5-11	227	4	Virginia Tech
13	#Riley, Ken	CB	6-0	183	15	Florida A&M
89	Ross, Dan	TE	6-4	235	5	Northeastern
72	St. Clair, Mike	DE	6-5	254	8	Grambling
15	Schonert, Turk	QB	6-1	185	4	Stanford
59	Schuh, Jeff	LB	6-2	228	3	Minnesota
25	Simmons, John	CB	5-11	192	3	Southern Methodist
56	Simpkins, Ron	LB	6-1	235	3	Michigan
23	Tate, Rodney	RB-KR	5-11	190	2	Texas
81	#Verser, David	WR-KR	6-1	200	3	Kansas
63	Wagner, Ray	T	6-3	290	2	Kent State
70	Weaver, Emanuel	NT	6-4	260	2	South Carolina
75	Whitley, Wilson	NT	6-5	265	7	Houston
57	Williams, Reggie	LB	6-0	228	8	Dartmouth
77	Wilson, Mike	T	6-5	271	6	Georgia

#Unsigned at press time

TOP FIVE DRAFT CHOICES

Rd.	Name	Sel. No.	Pos.	Ht.	Wt.	College
1	Rimington, Dave	25	C	6-3	290	Nebraska
2	Horton, Ray	53	DB	5-11	188	Washington
3	Turner, Jim	81	DB	5-11	180	UCLA
4	Maidlow, Steve	109	LB	6-2	235	Michigan State
5	Christensen, Jeff	137	QB	6-3	200	Eastern Illinois

194 THE COMPLETE HANDBOOK OF PRO FOOTBALL

space of a year. McInally will correct that this year—he never has back-to-back bad seasons. Placekicker Jimmy Breech may be the NFL's chip-shot champion. He hits everything under 40, but nothing much from outside of there.

THE ROOKIES: Dave Rimington of Nebraska is as promising a center as John Elway is a quarterback. Rimington will be the next Mike Webster, or better. Cornerback Ray Horton of Washington, a great leaper, could be Ken Riley's heir apparent. Horton's also a fine punt-returner. Strong safety Jimmy Turner of UCLA, the No. 3 selection, could start by next year.

OUTLOOK: The AFC Central is tailor-made for a Bengal resurgence. Outside of Pittsburgh, no one else has a shot at Cincinnati. The Bengals were fat-headed last year, but they still have talent. Whether they can get it all rolling together, like in 1981, is debatable. Prediction: down-to-the-wire fight with the Steelers.

BENGAL PROFILES

KEN ANDERSON 34 6-3 212   Quarterback

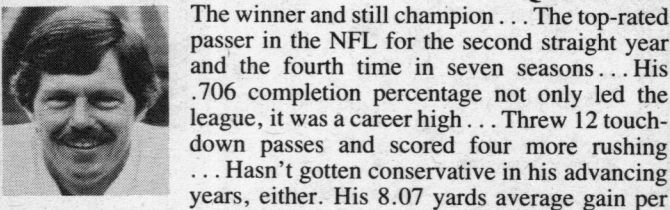

The winner and still champion... The top-rated passer in the NFL for the second straight year and the fourth time in seven seasons... His .706 completion percentage not only led the league, it was a career high... Threw 12 touchdown passes and scored four more rushing ... Hasn't gotten conservative in his advancing years, either. His 8.07 yards average gain per completion tied him for third in the league, proving that he isn't dumping off passes and throwing screens to pad that completion mark... His accuracy still amazes... Was the only NFL quarterback to throw more than 300 passes and keep his interceptions under 10 last year. He had nine... Born Feb. 15, 1949, in Batavia, Ill., and attended Augustana.

CINCINNATI BENGALS

PETE JOHNSON 29 6-0 250 — Running Back

Concrete Pete... Built like the side of a building and almost as difficult to knock down... The best running back in football from a yard out... Scored seven touchdowns last year, mainly from short distance... Though he is used a great deal in short-yardage situations, his career rushing average is right around 4.0 yards per carry... Can do other things besides run. His blocking is fun to watch if you're not the one being blocked and he has sure hands (31 receptions in nine games last year)... Born March 2, 1954, in Peach County, Ga.... Set Ohio State and Big Ten career records with 58 touchdowns... Bengals drafted him in the second round in '77... Only weakness is eating—his weight sometimes hits 275.

CRIS COLLINSWORTH 24 6-5 192 — Wide Receiver

Still riding high... Caught 67 passes as a rookie and likely would have surpassed that figure a year ago if not for the strike. As it was, he caught 49 passes, second-best mark in the AFC... So skinny that if he turned sideways at an intersection, drivers would stare at him waiting for the light to change... But there is an athlete inside that bony body... Before he changed to receiver at Florida, he threw a 99-yard touchdown pass to tie an NCAA record... Might be the best interview in the NFL... Veteran journalists already have compared him to O. J. Simpson, a Hall of Famer in the interview department... Born, talking, Jan. 27, 1959, in Dayton, Ohio.

DAVID VERSER 25 6-1 200 — Wide Receiver

The apprentice... This could be his chance to supplant veteran Isaac Curtis at wide receiver... Curtis is a 10-year starter, but is no longer the deep threat he was as a young burner... Verser caught only four passes last year, but averaged 24.5 yards per catch. One of his receptions was for 56 yards and a touchdown... Has been biding his time mainly as a return man, waiting for Curtis to purchase a rocker... Ol' Isaac

196 THE COMPLETE HANDBOOK OF PRO FOOTBALL

won't give up his position easily; Verser will have to take it away from him... "He flashes class when he runs," said Bengal assistant Lindy Infante of Verser... Born March 1, 1958, in Kansas City, Kan.... No. 1 pick of Bengals in '81 after starring at Kansas.

DAN ROSS 26 6-4 235   Tight End

Long-distance operator? Put this guy through to Ted Kwalick, will you? They've got something in common... Prior to the 1974 season, Kwalick, then a tight end with the 49ers, signed a WFL contract with the Hawaiians for '75. He might as well have been a ghost in '74, because the 49ers wouldn't play him... Ross, the Bengals' tight end, has signed a contract to play for Boston of the USFL, starting in '84... Don't be surprised, Dan ol' boy, if the Bengals make you disappear this fall... Well, at least you'll get to see M.L. Harris' career take off... Sorry, but life can be cruel sometimes... Born Feb. 9, 1957, in Malden, Mass.... Played at Northeastern... Bengals' second-round pick in '79.

ANTHONY MUNOZ 25 6-6 278   Offensive Tackle

Anthony Averse... He's averse to being beaten on the pass rush, so, he seldom is... Became an all-pro his second year and repeated last autumn... Forrest Gregg, his coach and one of the best offensive tackles ever to play the game, says Munoz "moves better than any big man I've ever seen."... Moves like a butterfly, stings like a brakeless diesel... Scatters bodies like a hurricane, too... Born Aug. 19, 1958, in Ontario, Cal., grabbed the doctor and spanked him... An All-American at USC when he was healthy, he sat out his senior season and came back to play in the Rose Bowl... Knee problems throughout college scared some scouts, but not the Bengals, who drafted him No. 1 in '80... He's been healthy ever since.

CINCINNATI BENGALS 197

MIKE WILSON 28 6-5 271 — Offensive Tackle

The bookend... There are folks in the NFL who will argue that the best tackle other than Munoz is the tackle on the other side of the Bengals' offensive line... He's more than just a bookend to Munoz... "He was a big reason we got where we were," Bengals' offensive line coach, Jim McNally, said of Wilson after the Bengals reached Super Bowl XVI... Tremendous strength, equally effective at blocking for the pass or run... Fourth-round draft choice of Bengals in '77, but that's misleading... Signed to play in Canada before the draft. Otherwise, he would have been taken earlier... Born May 28, 1955, in Norfolk, Va.... Standout at Georgia... Joined Bengals in '78 after the one year in Canada.

JIMMY BREECH 27 5-6 155 — Kicker

Big Little Man... Outside of Washington's Mark Moseley, he had the most automatic foot in the NFL in '82 (15 or more attempts).... Banged home 14-of-18 field goals and 25-of-26 PATs... All of Cincinnati is grateful to the Lions and Raiders for letting Breech pass through their organizations... Detroit drafted little Jimmy eighth in '78, then cut him... Raiders signed him for '79. He made 18-of-27 field goals in Oakland, but missed a "gimme" that cost the Raiders a victory against Kansas City. Al Davis never forgot and cut him the next summer... Bengals picked him up and he has been a clutch performer ever since... Born April 11, 1956, in Sacramento, Cal.... Holds all the placekicking records at California.

KEN RILEY 36 6-0 183 — Cornerback

The Chateau Lafitte of cornerbacks... Aging hasn't hurt him one bit... Intercepted five passes to tie for the AFC lead in '82, returning one 56 yards for a touchdown... Now 36, he is back for his 15th season in Cincinnati... His long, distinguished career has killed the careers of those who have aspired to take his job... There is no reason to believe new challengers will replace him this year... Born Aug. 6, 1947, in Bartow, Fla.... Played at Florida A&M when the rest of us were children... Became a starter his second year in Cincinnati and has been all-pro and a Pro Bowler a number of times since... A great player, a great person.

COACH FORREST GREGG: The Iceman... Been in Green Bay, Cleveland, Toronto and Cincinnati so long, you have to thaw Gregg to find his sense of humor... A tough man to get next to, but he's fair and he's decent... Took the Bengals to their only Super Bowl in his second year as their head coach in 1981... Last year was a bummer, in comparison, but there is no reason to think he won't have Bengals back in the Super Bowl chase again this year... The shadow of Vince Lombardi follows him everywhere he goes... "Forrest Gregg is the finest player I ever coached," Lombardi said... Was all-pro eight times under Lombardi and was later voted into the Hall of Fame, joining his old coach... Coaches the Lombardi way: he's demanding, but firm; stony on the outside, but warm on the inside... Born Oct. 18, 1933, in Birthright, Tex.... Played college ball at SMU back in the days of two-way tackles... May be the only NFL player ever to make all-pro at guard and tackle in the same year... Played 14 years for the Packers and one season in Dallas... Coached Cleveland from 1975-77 (3-11, 9-5, 6-7)... Spent a year coaching Toronto of the CFL before taking Bengals' job... Has recorded 25-16 mark in Cincinnati.

GREATEST QUARTERBACK

Who else, but the guy with the tiger stripes on his helmet? Has anyone else ever played quarterback for Cincinnati other than Ken Anderson? There are rumors that, back in the Pleistocene era, Bengal quarterbacks named John Stofa, Greg Cook, Virgil Carter and Sam Wyche existed. Their playbooks were found in hieroglyphic form in stone buried beneath what is now Sleepout Louie's saloon in Cincinnati.

But, when you're talking quarterbacking in Bengaltown, you're talking Anderson. Not only is he the best quarterback in Cincinnati history, he's one of the most accurate passers in pro football history. He reached his zenith in 1981, when was voted NFL Player of the Year by seven different organizations and Comeback Player of the Year by one other. He also led Cincinnati to the Super Bowl.

Anderson is a tremendous all-around athlete. Not only does he have the arm, he also has the legs to remain, at 34, one of the best running quarterbacks in the league. And he has the mind, too, having graduated from Chase College of Law, Northern Kentucky University.

Of course, everyone in Sleepout Louie's knows all that.

INDIVIDUAL BENGAL RECORDS

Rushing
Most Yards Game:	160	Pete Johnson, vs Cleveland, 1978
Season:	1,077	Pete Johnson, 1981
Career:	4656	Pete Johnson, 1977-82

Passing
Most TD Passes Game:	4	Greg Cook, vs Houston, 1969
	4	Ken Anderson, vs Cleveland, 1976
Season:	29	Ken Anderson, 1981
Career:	172	Ken Anderson, 1971-82

Receiving
Most TD Passes Game:	3	Bob Trumpy, vs Houston, 1969
	3	Isaac Curtis, vs Cleveland, 1973
	3	Isaac Curtis, vs Baltimore, 1979
Season:	10	Isaac Curtis, 1974
Career:	51	Isaac Curtis, 1973-82

Scoring
Most Points Game:	19	Horst Muhlmann, vs Buffalo, 1970
	19	Horst Muhlmann, vs Houston, 1972
Season:	115	Jim Breech, 1981
Most TDs Game:	3	Paul Robinson, vs Miami, 1968
	3	Bob Trumpy, vs Houston, 1969
	3	Doug Dressler, vs Houston, 1972
	3	Isaac Curtis, vs Cleveland, 1973
Season:	16	Pete Johnson, 1981
Career:	51	Isaac Curtis, 1973-82

200 THE COMPLETE HANDBOOK OF PRO FOOTBALL
CLEVELAND BROWNS

TEAM DIRECTORY: Pres.: Art Modell; VP/Gen. Counsel: James Bailey; Dir. Player Relations: Paul Warfield; Dir. Player Personnel: Bill Davis; Dir. Operations: Dennis Lynch; VP/Consultant: Nathan Wallack; Dir. Publicity: Kevin Byrne; Head Coach: Sam Rutigliano. Home field: Cleveland Stadium (80,098). Colors: Seal brown, orange and white.

SCOUTING REPORT

OFFENSE: The envelope, please. The Cleveland quarterback is... Brian Sipe or Paul McDonald? It's obvious that one or the

Newsome is Cleveland's pass-catching Wizard of Oz.

other will have to win the job decisively and hold it just as decisively if the Browns are to avoid a divided camp and make something out of the '83 season.

Sipe, to put it bluntly, fell apart last year. McDonald was Jim Dandy to the rescue, lifting the Browns into the playoffs despite a losing record. That travesty won't happen again now that the NFL is back to 16 games. The Browns, like everyone else, will have to get in on merit.

Cleveland is a team crying for leadership. But the No. 1 quarterback had better like having his plays brought in from the sideline, because coach Sam Rutigliano will adopt that format this year.

Injuries to Doug Dieken and Tom DeLeone hurt the offensive line a year ago and Rutigliano doesn't expect Dieken to play the full 16. Hmmmmmm.

The receivers are adequate at best, outside of Ozzie Newsome. The running game is fine with Mike Pruitt, but could be something special if Charles White climbs off his Heisman high horse and plays some football.

DEFENSE: Quick, when is the last time the Browns played defense? Probably 15 years ago.

Cleveland ranked 23rd among NFL defenses a year ago and probably wasn't even that good. Why do you think The Cardiac Kids won all those last-second games three years ago? They had to score more points than their defense could allow.

Rutigliano has to find three guys up front who can stop the run. Rutigliano is so impressed by defensive end Marshall Harris that he's trying him on offense. The Browns' coach is hoping Mike Robinson and Keith Baldwin, both helped by weight training, will man the ends. Ex-Patriot linebacker Bob Golic and a rehabilitated Henry Bradley are the nose tackles.

If that line comes together, the Browns could have a super front seven. The linebackers—Chip Banks, Tom Cousineau, Dick Ambrose and Clay Matthews—will be one of the best foursomes in the league before this season is over.

However, the secondary—Larry Braziel, Clarence Scott, Clinton Burrell and Hanford Dixon—is not a championship mix.

It looks like the Browns will need lots of points again.

KICKING GAME: The Browns don't get much on returns. Steve Cox's 39.1-yard punting average isn't Pro Bowl caliber, either. Kicker Matt Bahr had an average season in '82. There is talk of Cox, who already kicks off, trying long-range field goals, too, because of Bahr's limited range. Too many question marks.

BROWNS VETERAN ROSTER

HEAD COACH—Sam Rutigliano. Assistant Coaches—Dave Adolph, Joe Daniels, Jim Garrett, Howard Mudd, John Petercuskie, Tom Pratt, Dave Redding, Joe Scannella, Marty Schottenheimer, Larrye Weaver.

No.	Name	Pos.	Ht.	Wt.	NFL Exp.	College
80	Adams, Willis	WR	6-2	194	4	Houston
52	Ambrose, Dick	LB	6-0	228	9	Virginia
61	Baab, Mike	C	6-4	270	2	Texas
9	Bahr, Matt	K	5-10	165	5	Penn State
99	Baldwin, Keith	DE	6-4	245	2	Texas A&M
56	Banks, Chip	LB	6-4	233	2	Southern California
91	Bradley, Henry	NT	6-2	260	5	Alcorn State
47	#Braziel, Larry	CB	6-0	184	5	Southern California
49	Burrell, Clinton	S	6-1	192	4	Louisiana State
50	Cousineau, Tom	LB	6-3	225	2	Ohio State
53	Cowher, Bill	LB	6-3	225	3	North Carolina State
15	Cox, Steve	P-K	6-4	195	3	Arkansas
38	Davis, Johnny	FB	6-1	235	6	Alabama
64	DeLamielleure, Joe	G	6-3	245	11	Michigan State
54	DeLeone, Tom	C	6-2	248	12	Ohio State
73	Dieken, Doug	T	6-5	252	13	Illinois
29	Dixon, Hanford	CB	5-11	182	3	Southern Mississippi
83	Feacher, Ricky	WR	5-10	174	8	Mississippi Valley
20	Flint, Judson	S	6-0	201	4	Memphis State
94	Franks, Elvis	DE	6-4	238	4	Morgan State
86	Fulton, Dan	WR	6-2	186	4	Nebraska-Omaha
79	Golic, Bob	NT	6-2	248	4	Notre Dame
26	#Hall, Dino	RB-KR	5-7	196	5	Glassboro State
90	Harris, Marshall	DE	6-6	261	4	Texas Christian
36	Jackson, Bill	S	6-1	202	2	North Carolina
68	Jackson, Robert	G	6-5	260	9	Duke
51	Johnson, Eddie	LB	6-1	210	3	Louisville
48	#Johnson, Lawrence	CB	5-11	204	4	Wisconsin
23	Kafentzis, Mark	S	5-10	185	2	Hawaii
85	Logan, Dave	WR	6-4	216	8	Colorado
57	Matthews, Clay	LB	6-2	230	5	Southern California
16	McDonald, Paul	QB	6-2	185	4	Southern California
71	Miller, Matt	T	6-6	270	4	Colorado
—	Miller, William	RB	5-10	185	1*	Ouachita Baptist
82	Newsome, Ozzie	TE	6-2	232	6	Alabama
58	Nicolas, Scott	LB	6-3	226	2	Miami
43	Pruitt, Mike	RB	6-0	225	8	Purdue
63	Risien, Cody	T	6-7	255	5	Texas A&M
92	Robinson, Mike	DE	6-4	270	3	Arizona
22	Scott, Clarence	S	6-0	190	13	Kansas State
17	Sipe, Brian	QB	6-1	195	10	San Diego State
12	Trocano, Rick	QB-S	6-0	188	3	Pittsburgh
59	Turner, Kevin	LB	6-2	223	4	University of Pacific
42	Walker, Dwight	RB-WR	5-10	185	2	Nicholls State
55	Weathers, Cutis	LB	6-5	220	5	Mississippi
25	White, Charles	RB	5-10	183	4	Southern California
81	Whitwell, Mike	WR	6-0	175	2	Texas A&M

#Unsigned at press time
*Played in CFL in 1982

TOP FIVE DRAFT COICES

Rd.	Name.	Sel. No.	Pos.	Ht.	Wt.	College
2	Brown, Ron	41	WR	5-11	181	Arizona State
3	Camp, Reggie	68	DE	6-5	255	California
5	Contz, Bill	122	T	6-6	252	Penn State
5	Stracka, Tim	145	TE	6-4	220	Wisconsin
6	Puzzuoli, Dave	149	DT	6-3	242	Pittsburgh

THE ROOKIES: Brown for the Browns. Ron Brown of Arizona State, Cleveland's first pick (in round two), is a converted cornerback who can fly at wide receiver. Browns are praying he isn't another Steve Holden. Third-round choice Reggie Camp of California makes the big play, but needs to improve at the point of attack on running plays.

OUTLOOK: A great year out of the quarterback—whoever he is—would make the Browns a representative team. The only way Cleveland could make the playoffs would be to jump out quickly, make believe it is better than it really is and get all the lucky breaks. Otherwise, the Browns are an 8-8 team.

BROWN PROFILES

BRIAN SIPE 34 6-1 195   Quarterback

What happened?... Was it a slump?... Is he over the hill?... Whatever it was, the NFL saw Brian Sipe turn into Brian Yipes a year ago... Formerly the main artery that pumped life into The Cardiac Kids, but last year he threw four TD passes and eight interceptions and lost his starting job to Paul McDonald... "I can't explain why and neither can Brian as to why he slumped after the strike," said coach Sam Rutigliano. "I don't think it will happen to him again. Sometimes it does a player good to get a look from the sideline."... Sipe, 2-4 as a starter, will learn for himself if that sideline seat was beneficial or a sign of the future... Born Aug. 8, 1949, in San Diego... The 13th-round 1972 draft selection of Cleveland, out of San Diego State.

PAUL McDONALD 25 6-2 185   Quarterback

The heir apparent or apparent backup?... Lanky lefthander was 2-1 as a starter and quarterbacked the Browns during their 27-10 playoff loss to the Raiders, when he completed 18-of-37 passes for 281 yards, including a 43-yard touchdown toss to Ricky Feacher... Will have to ward off a fierce comeback bid by Brian Sipe, but—who knows?—the youngster might just win the fight... A tremendous leader at USC, he lasted until the fourth round of the '80 draft before the Browns grabbed him... Why wasn't he drafted earlier? His arm isn't the strongest. But it has gotten stronger... Born Feb. 23, 1958, in Montebello,

204 THE COMPLETE HANDBOOK OF PRO FOOTBALL

Cal.... Led USC to two Rose Bowl victories and a national championship... Academic All-American.

CHARLES WHITE 25 5-10 183 Running Back

Admitted he had a drug problem when he won the Heisman Trophy at USC and then later with the Browns. Says it's over now... His contributions to the Browns increased last year, his third in Cleveland. Perhaps they will increase again this year... Ranked third among AFC running backs with 34 receptions in '82... Lack of size makes him a better receiver than runner, but the Browns plan to run him out of the I-formation at times this fall... That's the same formation that made him a Heisman hero for the Trojans... Born Jan. 22, 1958, in Los Angeles... Set Rose Bowl records with 39 carries for 247 yards in USC's comeback victory over Ohio State as a senior.

MIKE PRUITT 29 6-0 225 Running Back

Nag, nag, nag... That's what 1982 was like for him—one nagging injury after another... The most serious was a groin pull... Averaged only 3.6 yards per carry on his way to a disappointing 516-yard season... The Browns expect him to be in better shape this year and to return to 1,000-yard form... Pruitt had three straight 1,000-yard seasons prior to '82... "We expect another 1,000-yard season, plus he can catch over 60 passes, like he did in 1980 and '81," Rutigliano said... Plays best with a heavy workload... A two-time Pro Bowler, he has tremendous speed (4.4) when his body is sound... Born April 3, 1954, in Chicago... Had modest stats at Purdue, but he was Browns' first pick in '76.

JOE DeLAMIELLEURE 32 6-3 245 Guard

Joe DePendable... "Joe is the same as ever—rough, tough, talented and a one-hundred percenter," coach Sam Rutigliano said... If medals were awarded to offensive linemen, Joe D. would be one of the most decorated blockers in recent memory... Six straight Pro Bowl appearances from 1975-80, all-pro from 1975-79... Still a fine football player who doesn't make many mistakes... Blocks well against the run and pass, and blocks well against the best defensive tackles—the mark of a top-notch lineman... Born April 3, 1951, in Detroit ... Three-time All-Big Ten selection and a 1972 All-American at Michigan State... Originally drafted by Buffalo, then traded to Browns before the '80 season.

CHIP BANKS 23 6-4 233 Outside Linebacker

Win one for The Chipper?... Well, The Chipper won one for himself when he was the only Cleveland player selected to the Pro Bowl last year... "And he's just scratched the surface," said Rutigliano... Was the third player taken in the '82 draft and didn't disappoint the Browns, as have so many other top picks. Where have you gone, Mike Phipps, Steve Holden and Mack Mitchell?... Led the Browns with 5½ sacks and forced two fumbles... Even played some defensive end, as the Browns took advantage of his quickness... Born Sept. 18, 1959, in Lawton, Okla., but was reared in Augusta, Ga.... First name is William... USC fans won't soon forget his great game against Notre Dame as a junior.

TOM COUSINEAU 26 6-3 225 Inside Linebacker

Tommy Wonderful... But his eagerly anticipated NFL debut was anything but wonderful, as he had trouble fighting off blockers in 1982... Played the run better in pursuit than he played the run straight at him... Even so, he led the Browns in tackles with 72... "Tom had adjustment problems he didn't anticipate," Rutigliano said, "but he's ready now to be a great player."... Buffalo had the same idea when the Bills made Cousineau the first player taken in the entire 1979 draft, but he opted for three years in Montreal... Browns traded a No. 1 in '83 and unannounced future draft choices to the Bills for the rights to Cousineau upon his return from CFL... Born May 6, 1957, in Bloomington, Ind.... All-world at Ohio State.

206 THE COMPLETE HANDBOOK OF PRO FOOTBALL

OZZIE NEWSOME 27 6-2 232　　　　　　　　　Tight End

In the future, Browns' fans may remember the name Newsome with the same fondness that they recall Lavelli, Speedie, Warfield and Collins... Has caught 118 passes in his last two seasons... He and Warfield are the only Browns to catch passes for more than 1,000 yards in a season... "There's not a receiver in the NFL who goes after a ball better than Oz," Rutigliano said. "If the ball is close, he'll get it."... Oz would love to follow the yellow-brick road back to Tuscaloosa and coach at Alabama, just like the late Bear Bryant, who was his coach and idol... Born March 15, 1956, in Muscle Shoals, Ala.... Bear Bryant called him the finest receiver ever to play for 'Bama.

MATT BAHR 27 5-10 165　　　　　　　　　Kicker

Prefers snapper DeLeone... That's not a fish entree, it's a center named Tom DeLeone. When he snaps the ball, Bahr is fine. When DeLeone doesn't snap, Bahr is wide left or right... Proving that kickers are a finicky bunch, he made 7-of-15 field goals last year, but 7-of-11 with DeLeone snapping... Rutigliano promises to have DeLeone snapping all year, although an ankle injury has bothered him the last two seasons... Rutigliano also plans to have punter Steve Cox try some long field goals since Bahr hasn't got great range (his longest field goal last year was 46 yards). Cox already kicks off... Born July 6, 1956, in Philadelphia... Kicked for Penn State... Brother Chris kicks for Raiders.

HENRY BRADLEY 29 6-2 260　　　　　　　　　Nose Tackle

Oh, Henry, look at this... You get injured and the Browns find themselves another nose tackle... Nothing like job security in the NFL... Needed knee surgery a year ago. The knee reportedly is sound again, but fighting him for a starting job is Bob Golic, who didn't pan out as a linebacker in New England, but didn't look bad as a nose tackle in Cleveland...

CLEVELAND BROWNS 207

"You need two strong nose tackles," Rutigliano said. "One can't be strong at the end of the season if he never gets spelled."... Born Sept. 4, 1953, in St. Joseph, La.... Played at Alcorn State... Drafted and cut by San Diego in '78... Browns got him, cut him, brought him back... "Best I've faced," said Steelers' Mike Webster.

COACH SAM RUTIGLIANO: "I expect the Browns to contend again. We expect to be there at the end of December and then we can have the opportunity to be the Redskins and 49ers of 1983."... These are the best-laid plans of Rutigliano for the upcoming season. Realistic? Perhaps, with better pass protection and a deep receiving threat ... Under him, the Browns have been a playoff contender more often than not... The gentleman-coach... Unless things go rock bottom, he may have a lifetime job in Cleveland, if he wants it... Owner Art Modell is enamored with this man—and who isn't?... Cleveland made it to the playoffs in '83 in spite of a 4-5 record during the strike-butchered season... "We made it after the dirt already had been delivered to Cleveland Stadium to bury us," he said in his inimitable fashion... Born July 1, 1932, in Brooklyn, he played college ball at Tennessee and Tulsa... Paid his dues as an NFL assistant with Denver, New Orleans, New England and the New York Jets before the Browns made him their fifth head coach in 1977... Was voted AFC Coach of the Year in 1979 and '80... His title with the Browns is vice-president and head coach... Has record of 37-36 with Cleveland.

GREATEST QUARTERBACK

There have been many good quarterbacks in Cleveland, but only one great one—Otto Graham. Milt Plum, Frank Ryan, Bill Nelsen and Brian Sipe, the good ones, would all agree that Graham was a cut above, something special.

Graham doesn't hold many Browns' passing records, but Cleveland didn't keep statistics from the All-America Football

Conference years, 1946-49. But the statistic that counts the most is championships won. In that category, Graham had no rival.

The Browns won all four AAFC championships with Graham at quarterback. Cleveland joined the National Football League in 1950 and played in every NFL championship game through 1955, when Graham retired. So in Graham's 10 years in professional football, Cleveland reached the title game 10 times, winning seven.

Graham had that kind of influence on a team. Paul Brown may have called the plays, but Graham made them work. He was a great athlete, a runner as well as passer. He was an All-American basketball player at Northwestern. Baseball great Bill Dickey once said Graham would have been a tremendous catcher, though Graham never played baseball.

INDIVIDUAL BROWN RECORDS

Rushing

Most Yards Game: 237   Jim Brown, vs Los Angeles, 1957
                                237   Jim Brown, vs Philadelphia, 1961
Season: 1,863   Jim Brown, 1963
Career: 12,312   Jim Brown, 1957-65

Passing

Most TD Passes Game: 5   Frank Ryan, vs N.Y. Giants, 1964
                                5   Bill Nelsen, vs Dallas, 1969
                                5   Brian Sipe, vs Pittsburgh, 1979
Season: 30   Brian Sipe, 1980
Career: 134   Frank Ryan, 1962-68

Receiving

Most TD Passes Game: 3   Mac Speedie, vs Chicago, 1951
                                3   Darrell Brewster, vs N.Y. Giants, 1953
                                3   Ray Renfro, vs Pittsburgh, 1959
                                3   Gary Collins, vs Philadelphia, 1963
                                3   Reggie Rucker, vs N.Y. Jets, 1976
                                3   Larry Poole, vs Pittsburgh, 1977
                                3   Calvin Hill, vs Baltimore, 1978
Season: 13   Gary Collins, 1963
Career: 70   Gary Collins, 1962-71

Scoring

Most Points Game: 36   Dub Jones, vs Chicago Bears, 1951
Season: 126   Jim Brown, 1965
Career: 1,349   Lou Groza, 1950-59, 1961-67
Most TDs Game: 6   Dub Jones, vs Chicago Bears, 1951
Season: 21   Jim Brown, 1965
Career: 126   Jim Brown, 1957-65

DENVER BRONCOS

DENVER BRONCOS 209

TEAM DIRECTORY: Chairman: Edgar F. Kaiser, Jr.; GM: Hein Poulus; Dir. Player Personnel: John Beake; Dir. Pub. Rel.: Charlie Lee; Dir. Publicity: Jim Saccomano; Head Coach: Dan Reeves. Home field: Mile High Stadium (75,103). Colors: Orange, blue and white.

John Elway: Baseball's loss is Broncos' gain.

SCOUTING REPORT

OFFENSE: The Broncos' offense was average at best—until Denver swung the deal with the Colts for the rights to the top draft pick, Stanford quarterback John Elway, who was wrested from the grasp of George Steinbrenner.

Because Denver doesn't play defense like it did three years ago, its offense no longer gets as many gift scoring opportunities. But, as Elway works his way into the starting lineup in place of the inconsistent Steve DeBerg—which should be around midseason—the offense won't need as much assistance to get on the board.

Tight end Riley Odoms, Steve Watson and Rick Upchurch are suitable receivers, that is if Odoms' weight is 230. If it isn't, he'll be gone, replaced by Jim Wright. The Bronco offensive line, built around underrated center Billy Bryan, isn't awesome, but gets the job done.

Unfortunately, the lack of a quality running back—a problem since the departure of Otis Armstrong—is a deficiency that remains. Gerald Willhite has the potential, but it's doubtful that he's big enough, 5-10, 200 pounds, to stand the pounding week after week.

DEFENSE: The names are mostly the same, but their games aren't. It wasn't so long ago that the Broncos' defense ranked first or second in the league several years running. Last year, it was 24th, bringing the real dementia to frustrated Broncomaniacs.

You remember the defensive line—Barney Chavous, Rubin Carter, Don Latimer and Rulon Jones. It hasn't changed much in several years. The linebackers—Bob Swenson, Tom Jackson, Randy Gradishar and Larry Evans—look about the same as always. But their play has gone downhill as a front seven, and only Gradishar made the Pro Bowl last year. Reeves may have waited too long to make changes.

The secondary is going through a transition. Cornerback Louis Wright and strong safety Dennis Smith are set, but free safety Steve Foley may find himself back at cornerback if Steve Wilson doesn't work out there. If Mike Harden works out better at free safety than Foley, the latter will find himself at corner, anyway.

The Bronco defense has lost its magic, which means the magic has gone out of the Broncos.

KICKING GAME: When you've got Rick Upchurch, you've got a kick-return game. Upchurch returned punts 78 and 67 yards for touchdowns last year. Luke Prestridge (45.0 yards per

BRONCOS VETERAN ROSTER

HEAD COACH—Dan Reeves. Assistant Coaches—Marvin Bass, Joe Collier, John Hadl, Stan Jones, Myrel Moore, Nick Nicolau, Fran Polsfoot, Dan Radakovich, Charlie West.

No.	Name	Pos.	Ht.	Wt.	NFL Exp.	College
54	Bishop, Keith	C-G	6-3	260	3	Baylor
77	Boyd, Greg	DE	606	280	6	San Diego State
64	Bryan, Bill	C	6-2	258	6	Duke
58	Busick, Steve	LB	6-4	227	3	Southern California
68	Carter, Rubin	NT	6-0	256	9	Miami
79	Chavous, Barney	DE	6-3	258	11	South Carolina State
78	Clark, Brian	T	6-6	260	2	Clemson
59	Comeaux, Darren	LB	6-1	227	2	Arizona State
17	DeBerg, Steve	QB	6-3	205	7	San Jose State
55	Dennison, Rick	LB	6-2	215	2	Colorado State
85	Egloff, Ron	TE	6-5	227	7	Wisconsin
56	Evans, Larry	LB	6-2	220	8	Mississippi College
43	Foley, Steve	S	6-2	190	8	Tulane
62	Glassic, Tom	G	6-3	260	8	Virginia
53	Gradishar, Randy	LB	6-2	231	10	Ohio State
31	Harden, Mike	S	6-1	192	4	Michigan
60	Howard, Paul	G	6-3	260	10	Brigham Young
28	Jackson, Roger	CB-S	6-0	186	2	Bethune-Cookman
57	Jackson, Tom	LB	5-11	220	11	Louisville
75	Jones, Rulon	DE	6-6	260	4	Utah State
3	Karlis, Rich	K	6-0	180	2	Cincinnati
76	Lanier, Ken	T	6-3	269	3	Florida State
72	Latimer, Don	NT	6-2	265	6	Miami
41	Lytle, Rob	RB	5-11	195	7	Michigan
83	Manning, Wade	WR	5-11	190	4	Ohio State
66	Manor, Brison	DE	6-4	248	7	Arkansas
82	McDaniel, Orlando	WR	6-0	180	2	Louisiana State
71	Minor, Claudie	T	6-4	278	10	San Diego State
88	Odoms, Riley	TE	6-4	235	12	Houston
24	Parros, Rick	RB	5-11	200	3	Utah State
34	Poole, Nathan	RB	5-9	212	4	Louisville
46	Preston, Dave	RB	5-11	195	6	Bowling Green
11	#Prestridge, Luke	P	6-5	235	5	Baylor
50	Ryan, Jim	LB	6-1	215	5	William & Mary
49	Smith, Dennis	S	6-3	200	3	Southern California
70	Studdard, Dave	T	6-4	260	5	Texas
51	Swenson, Bob	LB	6-3	225	8	California
26	Thomas, J.T.	S	6-2	196	10	Florida State
37	Trimble, Steve	CB	5-10	181	3	Maryland
67	Uecker, Keith	T	6-5	260	2	Auburn
80	Upchurch, Rick	WR	5-10	180	9	Minnesota
81	Watson, Steve	WR	6-4	195	5	Temple
47	Willhite, Gerald	RB	5-10	200	2	San Jose State
45	Wilson, Steve	CB	5-10	195	2	Howard
23	Winder, Sammy	RB	5-11	203	2	Southern Mississippi
52	Woodard, Ken	LB	6-1	218	2	Tuskegee Institute
87	Wright, Jim	TE	6-3	240	4	Texas Christian
20	#Wright, Louis	CB	6-2	200	9	San Jose State

#Unsigned at press time

TOP FIVE DRAFT CHOICES

Rd.	Name	Sel. No.	Pos.	Ht.	Wt.	College
1	*Elway, John	1	QB	6-4	202	Stanford
2	Cooper, Mark	31	T	6-5	250	Miami
3	Sampson, Clinton	60	WR	5-11	185	San Diego State
5	Harris, George	116	LB	6-2	215	Houston
5	Baldwin, Bruce	125	DB	6-0	200	Harding (Ark.)

*Acquired from Baltimore Colts after draft

212 THE COMPLETE HANDBOOK OF PRO FOOTBALL

kick) led NFL punters. Rookie Rich Karlis hammered through 11-of-13 field-goal attempts. Special teams are the Broncos' strength.

THE ROOKIES: The Broncos start at the top with Elway at quarterback. Second-round choice Mark Cooper of Miami blocks better against the pass than run. Wide receiver Clinton Sampson of San Diego State, a third-rounder, must curb inconsistency.

OUTLOOK: The cellar, unless Elway has a magical rookie year, which is possible. The Broncos have grown long of tooth and Elway's arrival is the refreshing infusion of talent and youth that the franchise sorely needs. Rookie quarterbacks are supposed to have growing pains, but there aren't many like Elway. Unfairly or not, he holds the Broncos' season in his young hands.

BRONCO PROFILES

STEVE DeBERG 29 6-3 205   Quarterback

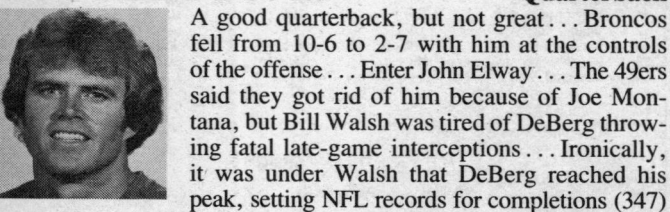

A good quarterback, but not great... Broncos fell from 10-6 to 2-7 with him at the controls of the offense... Enter John Elway... The 49ers said they got rid of him because of Joe Montana, but Bill Walsh was tired of DeBerg throwing fatal late-game interceptions... Ironically, it was under Walsh that DeBerg reached his peak, setting NFL records for completions (347) and attempts (578) in 1979... Has yet to have a season with more touchdown passes than interceptions... Last year it was 7 TDs and 11 INTs, though he completed 58.7 percent for 1,405 yards... Born Jan. 19, 1954, in Oakland... Set nine passing records at San Jose State... Drafted 10th by Dallas in '77, then cut.

DENVER BRONCOS 213

LUKE PRESTRIDGE 26 6-5 235   Punter

Boomer of the Rockies... Won his first NFL punting title last year with a 45.0-yard average, plus his first invitation to the Pro Bowl... Cool Foot Luke also topped the AFC with 14 punts inside the 20... Big year after his punting average had fallen to 40.4 the year before... Of course, the Broncos were 10-6 in '81... Generally, punters do better when their teams are losing, because the offense isn't moving and there is plenty of green area up ahead... Denver was 2-7 last year and its offense ranked 15th in the NFL... Born Sept. 17, 1956, in Houston... Record-setting punter and twice an all-conference first baseman at Baylor... Broncos' No. 7 pick in '79.

RICK UPCHURCH 31 5-10 180   Receiver-Punt Returner

Identity crisis... Would like to be known as a wide receiver, but is recognized mainly as a return man... May be bridging the gap at last... In 1982, he caught 26 passes, three for touchdowns, including a 51-yard bomb... Also led the NFL in punt returns with a 16.1-yard average and two touchdowns, including a 78-yard scamper... Selected to the Pro Bowl as a return man for the fourth time in six years, amazing longevity for a returner... The NFL's all-time leading punt returner has led the league three times in his specialty, scoring eight touchdowns ... Born May 20, 1952, in Toledo... Played at University of Minnesota.

STEVE WATSON 26 6-4 195   Wide Receiver

Human one-iron... Candidate to play the Scarecrow if they remake "The Wizard of Oz."... Gets the job done, however. Does he ever!... Caught 60 passes for 1,244 yards and 13 touchdowns two years ago before the NFL even learned his name... Instead of falling on his face as a one-year flash, he caught 36 passes and two touchdowns in a nine-game season in

'82...Not bad for an ectomorph playing among endomorphs...Came out of nowhere in '81 after catching six passes in each of his first two NFL seasons...An All-East selection at Temple, where he also won two conference championships as a long jumper...Born May 28, 1957, in Baltimore...Denver signed him as a free agent in '79.

BOB SWENSON 30 6-3 225　　　　　Outside Linebacker

One of the best there is...Gives no ground to the great tight ends, who don't look that great against him...Ask the tight ends which outside linebacker they'd rather not face, and most of them would choose him...Not only is he strong, aggressive and quick, he's clever...Getting off the line against him is an all-day chore...Had some memorable battles with Dave Casper before The Ghost was traded from Oakland to Houston. He was probably glad to go, because it meant not having to face Swenson twice a year anymore...Born July 1, 1953, in Stockton, Cal., Swenson played with moderate success at California...Broncos signed him as a free agent in '75...Became a starter his rookie year.

TOM JACKSON 32 5-11 220　　　　　Outside Linebacker

Is the old fire gone?...Was beaten a number of times on passes to running backs, which seldom happened in the past...Has he lost a step? Two steps? Three steps and he's out...Or was it just the one-year blahs?...Denver didn't play well as a team and there might have been a carryover...For most of his 10 years in Denver, he has been a big-play performer, with three career touchdowns...Had an interception last year, his first in three seasons, but it wasn't a typical Jackson season...At his best, he is difficult to sweep against and tough to get behind on a pass...As a younger player, he had 4.5 speed...Born April 4, 1951, in Cleveland...No. 4 pick, out of Louisville, in '73.

DENVER BRONCOS 215

DENNIS SMITH 24 6-3 200 — Strong Safety

Not just any Smith...He's a star on the rise...Had one interception last year after replacing the great Bill Thompson as strong safety...Now with a year's experience, his career should take off...A tremendous athlete, he high-jumped 7-3 at USC, where he earned three letters in track and four in football...While waiting for Thompson to retire, he started three games as cornerback as a rookie in '81...Born Feb. 3, 1959, in Santa Monica, Cal....Lettered in football, track and basketball at Santa Monica High School...Played in the same USC secondary as Ronnie Lott...Intercepted 16 passes in college...Denver's No. 1 pick two years ago.

STEVE FOLEY 29 6-2 190 — Free Safety

Pete Rose of football...Need a position filled, call him...A college quarterback at Tulane, he was shifted to the secondary by the WFL's Jacksonville franchise...After the WFL folded, he joined the Broncos, who had drafted him eighth in 1975...Denver needed a cornerback, so that's where they placed him...Was voted All-AFC in 1978...The Broncos needed a free safety halfway through the '80 season, so he shifted over with no fuss, getting on-the-job training as an instant starter...Has 28 career interceptions, third-highest on Broncos, behind Goose Gonsoulin (43) and Bill Thompson (40)...Born Nov. 11, 1953, in New Orleans and still lives there...Calls it N'awlins.

BARNEY CHAVOUS 32 6-3 258 — Defensive End

Three long-time tourist attractions in the Denver area: Pikes Peak, Vail and Barney Chavous...It seems as if he has been playing defensive end in Denver forever, though this is only his 11th season. Only?...A steady player, taking care of business with little publicity and attention, with no sign yet that he is in need of a replacement...Who knows? He might just

216 THE COMPLETE HANDBOOK OF PRO FOOTBALL

go on forever... Denver drafted him second in 1973, out of South Carolina State, the school of Deacon Jones... Born March 22, 1951, in Aiken, S.C.... Earned only one football letter in high school as a linebacker... Was mainly a weightman in track... Football career took off in college.

COACH DAN REEVES: A coach's moment of truth... Started off with a bang in Denver, nearly leading the Broncos to the playoffs in his head-coaching debut in 1981... Last year, someone let the air out of the balloon, because the Broncos fizzled and flattened out... Now, can he put Denver back on its feet?... This is the true test of a coach, to see if he can fly high again after being knocked down... The NFL will learn a lot about Dan Reeves this year, as will Dan Reeves... Has turned Denver into the Dallas of the Rockies, installing the Cowboys' multiple offense as well as the no-nonsense style of coaching taught by Tom Landry... Sometimes looks as stoic as Landry, and his postgame quotes often show even less life than Landry's... It is easy to see that football consumes him by the bags that appear under his eyes two weeks into the football season... Born Jan. 19, 1944, in Americus, Ga., a hoot and a holler from Plains, and you know who lives there... Played quarterback at South Carolina, then shifted to running back at Dallas, which signed him as a free agent in '65... Became a player-coach, then Landry's offensive coordinator.

GREATEST QUARTERBACK

He never really was given all the credit he deserved, but Craig Morton was a top-notch quarterback. And a courageous one.

He took Dallas to its first Super Bowl, although a sore arm made it difficult for him to shave, let alone throw a football. But he was criticized for throwing the interception (receiver Dan Reeves tipped the pass) that led to the Baltimore field goal that won Super Bowl V.

Morton was voted NFL Player of the Year in 1977, leading Denver to its only Super Bowl. But the Broncos were beaten by a superior Dallas team and Morton was castigated once again.

Morton survived his critics to play 18 distinguished years in the NFL. Having escaped Roger Staubach's shadow in Dallas and a then woebegone New York Giants' franchise, Morton's popularity grew, at last, in Denver.

Slow afoot, because of damage to his knees in college, Morton took vicious shots in the pocket, but stood tall. He completed 17-of-18 passes in one game. He stayed in a hospital, only leaving to attend Denver practices, the week the Broncos beat Oakland to reach the Super Bowl. Morton retired after the 1982 season. He did so with distinction.

INDIVIDUAL BRONCO RECORDS

Rushing

Most Yards Game:	183	Otis Armstrong, vs Houston, 1974
Season:	1,407	Otis Armstrong, 1974
Career:	6,323	Floyd Little, 1967-75

Passing

Most TD Passes Game:	5	Frank Tripucka, vs Buffalo, 1962
Season:	24	Frank Tripucka, 1960
Career:	74	Craig Morton, 1977-82

Receiving

Most TD Passes Game:	3	Lionel Taylor, vs Buffalo, 1960
	3	Bob Scarpitto, vs Buffalo, 1966
	3	Haven Moses, vs Houston, 1973
	3	Steve Watson, vs Baltimore, 1981
Season:	13	Steve Watson, 1981
Career:	44	Lionel Taylor, 1960-66
	44	Haven Moses, 1972-81

Scoring

Most Points Game:	21	Gene Mingo, vs Los Angeles, 1960
Season:	137	Gene Mingo, 1962
Career:	736	Jim Turner, 1971-79
Most TDs Game:	3	Lionel Taylor, vs Buffalo, 1960
	3	Don Stone, vs San Diego, 1962
	3	Bob Scarpitto, vs Buffalo, 1966
	3	Floyd Little, vs Minnesota, 1972
	3	Floyd Little, vs Cincinnati, 1973
	3	Haven Moses, vs Houston, 1973
	3	Otis Armstrong, vs Houston, 1974
	3	Jon Keyworth, vs Kansas City, 1974
	3	Steve Watson, vs Baltimore, 1981
Season:	13	Floyd Little, 1972
	13	Floyd Little, 1973
	13	Steve Watson, 1981
Career:	54	Floyd Little, 1967-75

HOUSTON OILERS

TEAM DIRECTORY: Pres./Owner: K.S. (Bud) Adams Jr.; Exec. VP/GM: Ladd Herzeg; VP/Player Personnel: Mike Holovak; Bus. Mgr.: Lewis Mangum; Dir. Media Rel.: Bob Hyde: Dir. Marketing/Promotions: Rick Nichols; Head Coach: Ed Biles. Home field: Astrodome (50,452). Colors: Scarlet, Columbia blue and white.

SCOUTING REPORT

OFFENSE: Now, ask yourself, can an offense with Earl Campbell finish 26th in the league in rushing? Hard to believe, but it actually happened last year to the Houston Oilers. The once-proud, now woebegone Houston Oilers.

No one likes to attend a funeral. If Campbell is finished as a great running back, do we have to watch? Or are the rumors of his demise greatly exaggerated? We'll know for sure this year when someone named Donnie Craft tries to replace the once superb Campbell.

For two years, coach Ed Biles has been fiddlin' with the Oiler offense. You don't fiddle with that offense unless there is something wrong with Campbell. Donnie Craft, you say? It doesn't sound right, but time has a way of moving on cruelly.

The pressure is on the Oilers' quarterback to perform. But there is a question mark here, too. Archie Manning's days may be over. Is Gifford Nielsen up to the task? Someone has to pick up these Oilers.

Houston has some good players on offense, but without Campbell and a quarterback, there is no life.

DEFENSE: A few bricks shy of a load. Jesse Baker celebrated his first year as a fulltime starter by leading the AFC with 9½ sacks. The big end has other sluggers with him—Ken Kennard, Mike Stensrud, ageless Elvin Bethea and injury-prone Daryle Skaugstad—but this line doesn't have much mobility and can be trapped easily.

The linebacking of Robert Brazile, Gregg Bingham, Daryl Hunt and Avon Riley is more than adequate. In fact, the Oilers don't have a more solid spot.

Houston's pass defense is nonexistent. The Oilers intercepted only three passes last year, the low mark in the NFL. Vernon Perry built a reputation by making four interceptions in one playoff game a few years back, but hasn't done a whole lot since. Mike

HOUSTON OILERS 219

Robert Brazile has been to Pro Bowl seven straight years.

Reinfeldt led the NFL in interceptions four years ago, but his play has fallen off, too.

Biles has promoted all-time great Ken Houston to secondary coach. Working with this group might drive Houston into premature retirement.

KICKING GAME: Florian Kempf is an all-pro name. As for his kicking, well, he made 4-of-6 field goals. We'll know more about Florian this year. Punter John James, the former Falcon, averaged 40.5 yards per kick joining Houston in midseason. Carl Roaches is a standout returner.

THE ROOKIES: The Oilers' first two picks were two big tackles from the West Coast, Bruce Matthews of USC and Harvey Salem of California. They're needed to block for Earl Campbell. Michigan free safety Keith Bostic has all the physical equipment, but

OILERS VETERAN ROSTER

HEAD COACH—Ed Biles. Assistant Coaches—Bill Allerheiligen, Andy Bourgeois, Kay Dalton, Ken Houston, Elijah Pitts, Dick Selcer, Ralph Staub, Chuck Studley, Bill Walsh.

No.	Name	Pos.	Ht.	Wt.	NFL Exp.	College
56	Abraham, Robert	LB	6-1	217	2	North Carolina State
31	Allen, Gary	RB	5-10	183	2	Hawaii
39	#Armstrong, Adger	RB	6-0	225	4	Texas A&M
86	Arnold, Walt	TE	6-3	234	4	New Mexico
80	#Bailey, Harold	WR	6-2	193	3	Oklahoma State
75	#Baker, Jesse	DE	6-5	272	5	Jacksonville State
65	Bethea, Elvin	DE	6-2	252	16	North Carolina A&T
54	Bingham, Gregg	LB	6-1	225	11	Purdue
52	Brazile, Robert	LB	6-4	245	9	Jackson State
81	Bryant, Steve	WR	6-2	194	2	Purdue
00	#Burrough, Ken	WR	6-3	220	12	Texas Southern
34	Campbell, Earl	RB	5-11	240	6	Texas
58	#Carter, David	C	6-2	262	7	Western Kentucky
87	Casper, Dave	TE	6-4	241	10	Notre Dame
40	Craft, Donnie	RB	6-0	209	2	Louisville
66	Davidson, Greg	C	6-2	254	4	North Texas State
35	Edwards, Stan	RB	6-0	215	2	Michigan
60	Fisher, Ed	G	6-3	259	10	Arizona State
36	Hartwig, Carter	CB-S	6-0	205	5	Southern California
84	Holston, Mike	WR	6-3	192	3	Morgan State
50	#Hunt, Daryl	LB	6-3	239	5	Oklahoma
22	Kay, Bill	CB	6-1	190	3	Purdue
4	Kempf, Florian	K	5-9	170	2	Pennsylvania
71	Kennard, Ken	DE	6-2	258	7	Angelo State
72	#Koncar, Mark	T	6-5	270	7	Colorado
10	Luck, Oliver	QB	6-2	198	2	West Virginia
8	Manning, Archie	QB	6-3	211	13	Mississippi
63	Munchak, Mike	G	6-3	263	2	Penn State
14	Nielsen, Gifford	QB	6-4	205	6	Brigham Young
32	Perry, Vernon	S	6-2	210	5	Jackson State
21	Randle, Tate	CB	6-0	202	2	Texas Tech
37	Reinfeldt, Mike	S	6-2	196	9	Wisconsin-Milwaukee
82	Renfro, Mike	WR	6-0	184	6	Texas Christian
53	#Riley, Avon	LB	6-3	219	3	UCLA
85	Roaches, Carl	KR-WR	5-8	170	4	Texas A&M
62	Schuhmacher, John	T	6-3	269	5	Southern California
90	Skaugstad, Daryle	DE	6-5	268	3	California
83	Smith, Tim	WR	6-2	202	4	Nebraska
67	Stensrud, Mike	MG	6-5	290	5	Iowa State
70	Taylor, Malcolm	DE	6-6	288	2	Tennessee State
28	Thomaselli, Rich	RB	6-1	196	3	West Virginia Wesleyan
51	Thompson, Ted	LB	6-1	229	9	Southern Methodist
76	Towns, Morris	T	6-4	261	7	Missouri
20	Tullis, Willie	CB-KR	6-0	190	4	Troy State
68	#Williams, Ralph	T	6-3	276	2	Southern
33	Wilson, J.C.	CB	6-0	178	6	Pittsburgh
89	#Wilson, Tim	TE	6-3	235	7	Maryland

#Unsigned at press time

TOP FIVE DRAFT CHOICES

Rd.	Name	Sel. No.	Pos.	Ht.	Wt.	College
1	Matthews, Bruce	9	T	6-5	265	Southern California
2	Salem, Harvey	30	T	6-7	270	California
2	Bostic, Keith	42	DB	6-1	205	Michigan
3	Joiner, Tim	58	LB	6-3	210	Louisiana State
3	Dressel, Chris	69	TE	6-4	225	Stanford

has difficulty reading plays. Fourth pick Tim Joiner, LSU linebacker, must add weight. Stanford tight end Chris Dressell is a backup for Dave Casper.

OUTLOOK: If the Oilers make it out of the cellar, it will be a miracle. This is a bad football team, and only the most diehard Houston fan would believe otherwise. The only good thing about the Oilers is their fight song—it's easily the best in the NFL.

OILER PROFILES

EARL CAMPBELL 28 5-11 240 **Running Back**

There are whispers: "Is Campbell through?" ... There are denials: "Aw, he's just 28. How can he be through?" ... There are counters to denials: "Yeah, John Brockington was washed up before he was 28." ... We'll know for sure this year whether Campbell's 1982 statistics—538 yards, 3.4-yard average, two touchdowns—are proof that the bloom is off The Tyler Rose ... Oilers switched from a pounding offense—Campbell's specialty—to a balanced attack in 1981 ... Immediately, there were trade rumors ... Now the Oilers say they're looking for a way to use Campbell more. If it's *Earl Campbell*, why would you use him less? ... Born March 25, 1955, in Tyler, Tex. ... Won Heisman Trophy at Texas in 1977.

ARCHIE MANNING 34 6-3 211 **Quarterback**

Time's running out ... Took a physical beating all those years in New Orleans, when the Saints' biggest enemy was the Saints ... The franchise never got better and the sacks and the beatings continued until he hardly had a passing arm (they rebuilt it once) or any confidence left ... After 11 years, the Saints paroled him sending him to Houston, where the situation, as it turned out, was even worse than in New Orleans ... Was only so-so his first year with the Oilers (50.8 percent, 6 TDs, 8 interceptions) ... Maybe it's too late for him now ... One of football's classiest citizens, yet he may never make the playoffs ... Born May 19, 1949, in Drew, Miss ... All-time great at Ole Miss ... Saints' first pick in '71.

222 THE COMPLETE HANDBOOK OF PRO FOOTBALL

GIFFORD NIELSEN 28 6-4 205   Quarterback

Duel in the Dome... Oilers have been grooming him for the quarterback's job for five years. After all that time, all we know about him is that he is well-groomed... Injuries have gotten in the way. But, if his body stays in one piece, he should be No. 1... What a contrast in Houston, which is used to party-lovin' quarterbacks like Dan Pastorini and Ken Stabler, to have Nielsen and Manning dueling each other for No. 1. It's like John The Baptist competing against Saint Thomas Becket... The one lingering doubt about Nielsen is his arm: is it NFL-strong?... Born Oct. 25, 1954, in Provo, Utah... First of a series of great BYU quarterbacks (Marc Wilson, Jim McMahon)... Drafted third by Oilers in '78.

DAVE CASPER 31 6-4 241   Tight End

Still great after all these years... Led the Oilers in receiving and scoring—36 catches and 36 points—conclusive evidence that The Ghost is still the most... One of the best tight ends in the game and has been since 1976... Clutch receiver, tough blocker, gritty performer. Plays every year with a bad back, hardly ever misses a game... Bright, uninhibited free spirit... Honors graduate from Notre Dame, but would rather fish and listen to Willie Nelson than do anything else... Born Feb. 2, 1952, in Bemidji, Minn... Grew up in Chilton, Wis... Made one of the great catches in Sugar Bowl history as Notre Dame beat Alabama... Raiders' No. 2 pick in '74... Needs 46 catches to reach 400.

KEN BURROUGH 35 6-3 220   Wide Receiver

Double-zero to go?... One gets the feeling that Houston is phasing him out... The Oilers are talking of Harold Bailey, Mike Renfro and Mike Holston as their wide receivers... They've forgotten Burrough, who spent all of '82 on injured reserve... But have they forgotten that he has been one of the NFL's best deep threats for 12 years?... Caught a 71-yard touchdown pass in '81... Who's to say he can't still go long two years later?... Caught 421 passes, 49 for touchdowns, during his splendid career, without once receiving all-pro recognition... Born July

MIKE MUNCHAK 23 6-3 263   Guard

Munchak is no Munchkin... Big and getting bigger, he won a starting guard position in training camp... Was injured six plays after the strike was settled and didn't return until late in the season... First offensive lineman taken in the '82 draft, No. 8 pick overall... Selected ahead of his more heralded Penn State teammate, Sean Farrell... Reminds some in Houston of Bob Young, the big, wide, talented Oiler guard now retired... Born May 3, 1960, in Scranton, Pa.... Could have played another year at Penn State after redshirting a season, but decided to graduate on time with his class, with a B average in business administration... A future all-pro.

MIKE RENFRO 28 6-0 184   Wide Receiver

Like father, like son... Father, Ray, was a standout player for the Cleveland Browns... Mike had his most productive year in '82 for the Oilers, catching a career-high three touchdown passes, including a 54-yard bomb... Started off slowly with leg injuries, but coach Ed Biles said he was one of the team's hardest workers during the strike... "The latter part of the season, he was just an outstanding receiver," Biles said. "Mike has the knack for getting open, and he's a competitor."... Born June 19, 1955, in Fort Worth, Tex.... Set school and conference receiving records at Texas Christian... Oilers drafted him fourth in '78.

ROBERT BRAZILE 30 6-4 245   Outside Linebacker

Has been to the Pro Bowl seven straight years, the only Oiler selected last season... Think of Houston's defense and you think of him... Now in his ninth season, Brazile remains a force at outside linebacker, perhaps even more so than a few years ago, when he was content to fall on piles and pick up opponents as a gesture of sportsmanship... Has returned to his active, earlier style, knocking down running backs before helping them back up, tackling from water bucket to water bucket... Born Feb. 7, 1953, in Pineland, Ala.... Moved from tight end to linebacker

224 THE COMPLETE HANDBOOK OF PRO FOOTBALL

at Jackson State, where his teammates were Chicago's Walter Payton and Houston teammate Vernon Perry... Oilers' No. 1 pick in 1975.

AVON RILEY 25 6-3 219   Outside Linebacker

Avon does his calling on running backs, whom he hits often and with enthusiasm—his calling card... Became a regular last year, starting all nine games in his second NFL season ... Replaced long time Oiler Ted Washington on the outside... It may not be until the 1990s before this man gives up his job... And he is a steal for the Oilers—a ninth-round pick two years ago... Houston found out that, though he is small as linebackers go, he is strong for his weight and hits hard... Oilers also found out he was fast when he took a kickoff reverse and raced 51 yards against San Francisco... Born Feb. 10, 1958, in Savannah, Ga.... Led UCLA in tackles in '80 and was named All-Pac 10.

GREGG BINGHAM 32 6-1 225   Inside Linebacker

Hoss and a half... As hard to move out of the middle as a Texas plow horse... Started off the '82 season, uncharacteristically, with injuries, then regained his inside job and nearly led the team in tackles... The nine previous seasons, he was the club leader in tackles nine times... Isn't very tall, but he's strong and likes action... His best year was '80 when he had 212 tackles (112 solo)... Fairly good on pass coverage: 20 interceptions in 10 seasons... Doesn't make many mistakes; a very consistent player... Same thing at Purdue: UPI Lineman of the Week at least once during each of three varsity seasons... Born March 13, 1951, in Evanston, Ill.... Oilers' fourth pick in 1973.

COACH ED BILES: The man on the hot seat... His 8-17 record in two years won't buy coaching longevity, unless there is a drastic turnaround—and soon ... Did a fine job coaching Houston's defense in the 1970s, but it was a pretty talented defense to coach... Anyway, when Bum Phillips was given the ax after leading the Oilers to three straight playoffs, Biles was named to replace him... That's like trying to follow Woody Al-

HOUSTON OILERS 225

len in a comedy competition... He's doing his best and still has a good working relationship with the Houston media... But is his best good enough?... Things got worse last year, not better... Houston was one town that welcomed the strike—it meant the city didn't have to watch the Oilers for two months... Houston was last in the NFL in offense *and* defense... Born Oct. 18, 1931, in Glendale, Ohio... Played for Ara Parseghian at Miami of Ohio, the "Cradle of Coaches"... Coached 13 years at Xavier of Ohio, posting 40-27-3 record in seven years as head coach... Catholic Coach of the Year in '65... An assistant with the New York Jets and New Orleans before joining Houston in '74.

GREATEST QUARTERBACK

George Blanda became a legend in Oakland, but he's still the best quarterback who ever played for the Houston Oilers.

He arrived in the American Football League after having washed

For Oilers to run smoothly, they need more Earl.

out of the National Football League. Washed out, but not a washout, Blanda quickly led the Oilers to back-to-back AFL championships.

As an Oiler, he once threw seven touchdown passes in a game, and threw for 300 or more yards 16 times. He holds most significant Oiler passing records, including touchdown passes, with 165. Dan Pastorini is second with 96. Blanda played seven seasons in Houston, Pastorini nine.

The thing that made Blanda great was his irascibility. He'd throw an interception, then come back and throw the winning touchdown pass. He might miss a field goal, but not with the game on the line. His irascible manner made him impervious to pressure, and it was Blanda's ability to perform under pressure, as much as his longevity, that landed him in the Pro Football Hall of Fame.

INDIVIDUAL OILER RECORDS

Rushing

Most Yards Game:	216	Billy Cannon, vs New York, 1961
Season:	1,934	Earl Campbell, 1980
Career:	6,995	Earl Campbell, 1978-82

Passing

Most TD Passes Game:	7	George Blanda, vs New York, 1961
Season:	36	George Blanda, 1961
Career:	165	George Blanda, 1960-66

Receiving

Most TD Passes Game:	3	Bill Groman, vs New York, 1960
	3	Bill Groman, vs New York, 1961
	3	Billy Cannon, vs New York, 1961
	3	Charlie Hennigan, vs San Diego, 1961
	3	Charlie Hennigan, vs Buffalo, 1963
	3	Charles Frazier, vs Denver, 1966 (twice)
	3	Dave Casper, vs Pittsburgh, 1981
Season:	17	Bill Groman, 1961
Career:	51	Charlie Hennigan, 1960-66

Scoring

Most Points Game:	30	Billy Cannon, vs New York, 1961
Season:	115	George Blanda, 1960
Career:	596	George Blanda, 1960-66
Most TDs Game:	5	Billy Cannon, vs New York, 1961
Season:	19	Earl Campbell, 1979
Career:	57	Earl Campbell, 1978-82

KANSAS CITY CHIEFS

TEAM DIRECTORY: Owner: Lamar Hunt; Pres.: Jack Steadman; VP/GM: Jim Schaaf; Dir. Player Personnel: Les Miller; Dir. Pub. Rel.: Bob Sprenger; Head Coach: John Mackovic. Home field: Arrowhead Stadium (78,094). Colors: Red and gold.

Gary Barbaro swiped three passes as Chief of secondary.

SCOUTING REPORT:

OFFENSE: "Eventually there will be a No. 1 quarterback, as quickly as possible," John Mackovic said. "I believe in one quarterback."

Only Mackovic, the Chiefs' fifth head coach in nine years, has three quarterbacks, Bill Kenney, Steve Fuller and rookie Todd Blackledge. Kenney started the first three games and the final three games of the '82 season. Fuller started the middle three.

One of them has to emerge as the clear-cut No. 1 choice, because the Chiefs face a tough schedule. Mackovic's history, resume and style spell offense. This is what he believes in and what the Chiefs most desperately need. If anyone can find a quarterback in Kansas City, it should be Mackovic.

Kansas City's offensive line is adequate, though guard Brad Budde is a coming star. The running backs and receivers are fine. Halfback Joe Delaney had nagging injuries plus an eye operation last year. This year, he is expected to play like he did in 1981, his rookie season.

One thing's for sure. The Chiefs will scare the NFL more with their offense under Mackovic. As for winning, we'll see.

DEFENSE: Mackovic will stay with the 3-4 alignment. Art Still is one of the best defensive linemen in football and a three-time Pro Bowler. The other defensive end, Mike Bell, has Pro-Bowl potential, but will he ever realize it? He has spent most of his career in the Chiefs' training room.

Kansas City wound up a respectable 10th in the league in defense and would have finished higher with a better performance against the run. Bell would help here, if he can play the full 16 games. Nose tackle Ken Kremer is adequate, because he can rush the passer.

The Chiefs change linebackers faster than Lon Chaney changed faces, but managed to play the entire 1982 season with the same set—Gary Spani, Jerry Blanton, Thomas Howard and Charles Jackson. All are replaceable, other than Spani.

The secondary could be one of the league's best, if Lloyd Burrus continues his improvement at strong safety. He broke up nine passes, had an interception and two blocked kicks last year. Corners Gary Green and Eric Harris and free safety Gary Barbaro rank with the best in the game.

KICKING GAME: Not too bad. Nick Lowery is one of the game's finest placekickers, leading the AFC with 19 field goals last year. The Chiefs have two dangerous return men in J.T. Smith

CHIEFS VETERAN ROSTER

HEAD COACH—John Mackovic. Assistant Coaches—Bud Carson, Walt Corey, Dan Daniel, Doug Graber, J.D. Helm, C.T. Hewgley, Rod Humeniuk, Pete McCulley, Willie Peete, Jim Vechiarella, Richard Williamson.

No.	Name	Pos.	Ht.	Wt.	NFL Exp.	College
76	Acker, Bill	NT-DE	6-3	255	4	Texas
26	#Barbaro, Gary	S	6-4	210	8	Nicholls State
85	Beckman, Ed	TE	6-4	239	7	Florida State
99	Bell, Mike	DE	6-4	260	4	Colorado State
57	Blanton, Jerry	LB	6-1	236	5	Kentucky
45	Bryant, Trent	CB	5-10	178	3	Arkansas
66	Budde, Brad	G	6-4	260	4	Southern California
34	Burruss, Lloyd	S	6-0	202	3	Maryland
88	Carson, Carlos	WR-KR	5-10	174	4	Louisiana State
20	#Cherry, Deron	S	5-11	190	3	Rutgers
41	Christopher, Herb	S	5-10	198	5	Morris Brown
65	Condon, Tom	G	6-3	275	10	Boston College
50	Daniels, Calvin	LB	6-3	236	2	North Carolina
37	Delaney, Joe	RB	5-10	184	3	NW State (La.)
84	#Dixon, Al	TE	6-5	238	7	Iowa State
4	Fuller, Steve	QB	6-4	198	5	Clemson
11	Gagliano, Bob	QB	6-3	195	3	Utah State
21	#Gaines, Clark	RB	6-1	214	7	Wake Forest
77	Getty, Charlie	T	6-4	270	10	Penn State
7	Gossett, Jeff	P	6-2	197	3	Eastern Illinois
24	Green, Gary	CB	5-11	184	7	Baylor
48	Hadnot, James	RB	6-2	245	4	Texas Tech
82	Hancock, Anthony	WR-KR	6-0	187	2	Tennessee
44	Harris, Eric	CB	6-3	202	4	Memphis State
56	Haynes, Louis	LB	6-0	227	2	North Texas State
60	Herkenhoff, Matt	T	6-4	272	8	Minnesota
52	Howard, Thomas	LB	6-2	215	7	Texas Tech
43	Jackson, Billy	RB	5-10	215	3	Alabama
51	Jackson, Charles	LB	6-2	222	6	Washington
9	Kenney, Bill	QB	6-4	211	4	Northern Colorado
55	Klug, Dave	LB	6-4	230	3	Concordia (Minn.)
91	Kremer, Ken	NT	6-4	252	5	Ball State
71	#Lindstrom, Dave	DE	6-6	255	6	Boston University
8	Lowery, Nick	P-K	6-4	189	4	Dartmouth
74	Mangiero, Dino	NT-DE	6-2	264	4	Rutgers
89	#Marshall, Henry	WR	6-2	220	8	Missouri
53	Olenchalk, John	C-LB	6-0	225	2	Stanford
61	Parrish, Don	NT-DE	6-2	255	6	Pittsburgh
38	Roquemore, Durwood	S	6-1	180	2	Texas A&I
70	#Rourke, Jim	T-G	6-5	263	4	Boston College
81	Scott, Willie	TE	6-4	245	3	South Carolina
73	Simmons, Bob	G	6-4	255	7	Texas
86	Smith, J.T.	KR-WR	6-2	185	6	North Texas State
59	Spani, Gary	LB	6-2	228	6	Kansas State
69	Steinfeld, Al	C-T	6-4	26	2	C.W. Post
67	Still, Art	DE	6-7	252	6	Kentucky
64	Studdard, Les	C	6-4	260	2	Texas
39	Thompson, Del	RB	6-0	203	2	Texas El-Paso

#Unsigned at press time

TOP FIVE DRAFT CHOICES

Rd.	Name	Sel. No.	Pos.	Ht.	Wt.	College
1	Blackledge, Todd	7	QB	6-4	219	Penn State
2	Lutz, Dave	34	T	6-7	285	Georgia Tech
3	Lewis, Albert	61	DB	6-4	180	Grambling
4	Wetzel, Ron	92	TE	6-7	235	Arizona State
5	Arnold, Jim	119	P	6-3	205	Vanderbilt

230 THE COMPLETE HANDBOOK OF PRO FOOTBALL

and Anthony Hancock. Punter Jeff Gossett averaged 41.4 yards per kick and his longest punt was 56 yards.

THE ROOKIES: Another quarterback for Chiefs. Top pick Blackledge of Penn State is intelligent, a good leader, but doesn't have the best touch near the goal line. Georgia Tech offensive tackle David Lutz, taken in second round, dominates at the point of attack, and he can run, too. Grambling cornerback Albert Lewis must improve aggressiveness.

OUTLOOK: In the immortal words of Keith Jackson, "Oooh, boy." The Chiefs play Dallas, Miami, Washington, San Diego and the Los Angeles Raiders away, Cincinnati, the New York Giants, Buffalo, the Raiders and the Chargers at home. Out of 16 games on the schedule, 10 look like they'll be murderous. The Chiefs will be lucky to go 8-8.

CHIEF PROFILES

BILL KENNEY 28 6-4 211   **Quarterback**

Musical quarterbacks... Are they playing Kenney's tune?... Took away Steve Fuller's job last year, though there was little separating the two statistically... Kenney was given a 77.0 rating by the NFL, Fuller 77.3... Neither mark is worth bragging about... The Eiffel Tower of quarterbacks—his mobility is nil... But he won the No. 1 job fair and square with his passing arm (56.2 percent, 1,192 yards, 7 TDs, 6 INTs)... Born Jan. 20, 1955, in San Francisco... His father, Charles, was a 49er guard in '47... Started college at Arizona State, moved to a JC, then Northern Colorado... Played tight end as a junior, before subbing at quarterback... Miami drafted him 12th in '78, then traded him to Washington, which cut him before Chiefs picked him up.

KANSAS CITY CHIEFS

STEVE FULLER 26 6-4 198 — Quarterback

Waiting game... Will he ever become a permanent No. 1 quarterback? That is the question... Who knows?... If he doesn't show some promise this year, Kansas City will think seriously of dumping him as a bad investment, though he was a No. 1 pick in '79... Has athletic ability, which might be the problem... Good all-around athlete, but doesn't stand out in any one area—such as throwing a football (52.7 percent, 665 yards, 3 TDs, 2 INTs in '82)... Maybe coach John Mackovic, whose specialty is offense, can make something out of him. Otherwise, look for the Fuller brushoff... Born Jan. 5, 1957, in Enid, Okla.... Had a great career at Clemson... Valedictorian in high school... Gave up chance at Rhodes Scholarship to play in NFL.

JOE DELANEY 24 5-10 184 — Running Back

Little Joe The Rambler... Rushed for 380 yards (4.0 per carry) following his 1,121-yard rookie debut in '81, which, according to Chiefs' watchers, created more excitement in Kansas City than anything since the Super Bowl IV championship of 1970... May have been somewhat tentative last year following May surgery for a detached retina... Should be more confident this fall... An exciting little back who is fun to watch and hard to tackle because of his uncanny ability to duck defenders... Chiefs' scouts did themselves proud in getting him in second round of the '81 draft... Born Oct. 30, 1958, in Henderson, Tex.... Football and track star at Northwest Louisiana.

ANTHONY HANCOCK 23 6-0 187 — Wide Receiver

Stick of dynamite, ready to explode... Exactly what the Chiefs need—a deep threat. I mean a *deeeep* threat... He can flat fly... Runs the 40 in 4.45... Was a 13.88 hurdler at Tennessee and part of the Vols' shuttle hurdle relay team that set a world record... Chiefs took him in the first round last year, trading five spots up to get him... Broke in slowly, but caught seven passes for a 16.6-yard average and a 41-yard touchdown... Expect more from him this year, a whole lot more... Born June 10, 1960, in Cleveland... Caught 11 passes for 196 yards for Tennessee in the Garden State Bowl.

232 THE COMPLETE HANDBOOK OF PRO FOOTBALL
BILLY JACKSON 23 5-10 215   Running Back

Pete Johnson II?...Doesn't have impressive statistics, except under the category "touchdowns"...Scored 10 as a rookie, then three more during last year's mini-season...His rushing averages of 3.6 and 2.8 yards per carry those two years are somewhat misleading ...Chiefs use him mainly to get first downs and touchdowns...Third-and-one, send in Jackson. Third-and-goal, send in Jackson...Runs like a barrel with legs...Longest pro run was 26 yards in '81. It must have felt like a marathon to him, since he isn't used to running more than three yards at a time...Born Sept. 13, 1959, in Phenix City, Ala....Blocked mainly at Alabama, though he rushed for 606 yards as a senior...Chiefs' seventh-round choice in '81.

CARLOS CARSON 24 5-10 174   Wide Receiver

Heeeere's Carlos!...If Carson keeps improving his act, he may get his own late-night TV show in Kansas City...Caught five passes as a rookie in '80, seven in '81, then 27 last year for 18.6 yards per catch and two touchdowns ...And that was in nine games...Imagine what he might do over a 16-game season... Coach John Mackovic is imagining... He's an unknown. How unknown is he? He is so unknown, the Chiefs didn't get wise until the fifth round of the draft...Born Dec. 28, 1958, in Lake Worth, Fla....Played at LSU, where over a two-game span, he caught six consecutive passes for touchdowns, an NCAA record...Even The Mighty Carson Art Players couldn't top that routine.

NICK LOWERY 27 6-4 189   Kicker

Another Jan Stenerud?...Replaced Stenerud in Kansas City and now Chiefs' fans are having a hard time deciding who is better...Kicked a 57-yard field goal two games after he beat out Stenerud in '80, thereby breaking the Norwegian's club record of 55 yards...Two years ago, he was selected to the Pro Bowl...Last year, he led the AFC in field-goal attempts (24) and connections (19) and made all 17 conversion tries...Is 65-for-87 in field goals (.747) as a Chief...Was 0-for-1 as a Patriot back in '78...Stenerud was 279-of-436 in Kansas City

KANSAS CITY CHIEFS 233

(.641)...Born May 27, 1956, in Munich...Father was in U.S. Foreign Service...Went to Dartmouth.

GARY SPANI 27 6-2 228 — Inside Linebacker

One-man demolition derby...Loves collisions, throwing his body around...Especially loves the heavy traffic at inside linebacker, which is like rush hour on the freeway, with cars coming from everywhere...He dents more than he is dented with his reckless play ...Though his publicity file is empty, he is considered the third-best inside linebacker in AFC, behind Steelers' Jack Lambert and Broncos' Randy Gradishar...Born Jan. 9, 1956, in the metropolis of Santanta, Kan....Attended high school in Manhattan, Kan., home of Kansas State, where he majored in personnel management, perhaps to get an idea of how pro football is run...Chiefs drafted him third in '78.

GARY GREEN 27 5-11 184 — Cornerback

Who said, "It's not easy being Green?"...This guy is having no difficulty whatsoever...For the second successive year, he was chosen to play in the Pro Bowl...Regarded as one of the best cornerbacks in the game...Other corners are green with envy...Though he has been bothering wide receivers for six years, he didn't score his first NFL touchdown until last autumn, on a 42-yard interception return...He was so happy he strung four words together to express his joy. You see, he doesn't say much...Born Oct. 22, 1955, in San Antonio, Tex....Went to Baylor, where he majored in physical education and minored in—you guessed it—speech...Chiefs' first draft pick in '77.

GARY BARBARO 29 6-4 210 — Free Safety

Biggest pickpocket in NFL...Now has 39 interceptions in seven seasons...Picked off three last year, running one back 43 yards for his third NFL touchdown...At 6-4, he is the tallest safety in football and the most difficult to throw over...As living proof that good things come in big packages, he has played in last three Pro Bowls...Who's the best free safety in the league? If he isn't first, he's a close second to Rams' Nolan

Cromwell... Born Feb. 11, 1954, in New Orleans, he played college ball at Nicholls State and was the first product of that school to make the NFL... Kansas City took him in the third round in '76, and it has been a life of thievery ever since.

COACH JOHN MACKOVIC: Is there an offense in Kansas City?... We're about to find out, since the fourth Kansas City coach since Hank Stram was forced out in 1974 is totally offensive-minded... Was the quarterback coach for Dallas the last two years and didn't hurt the development of Danny White... If he can develop quarterbacks Bill Kenney and Steve Fuller, he will be the most welcome addition to Missouri since Harry Truman... Arrives in stormy times... Citizens of Kansas City are tired of the Chiefs' front office and its inability to hire/keep quality coaches... Marv Levy improved the Chiefs over four straight years, had one off season and was fired... Even saintly Lamar Hunt's credibility suffered after that... There is pressure on Mackovic from management to restore its damaged respectability... Born Oct. 1, 1943, in Barberton, Ohio, he played quarterback at Wake Forest... Was a college assistant at Army, San Jose State, Arizona and Purdue, then became head coach at Wake Forest, reviving a dead program... Guided the Deacons to an 8-3 record in '79 and a Tangerine Bowl berth.

GREATEST QUARTERBACK

The envelope please. And the winner is... Len Dawson.
Was there ever any doubt that it would be Dawson, considering the Kansas City Chiefs have never been able to successfully replace him?
A better question might be to name someone else who has played quarterback for Kansas City. Mike Livingston, Steve Fuller and Bill Kenney have tried to take Dawson's place, though not very well. The stumper is who played quarterback in K.C. before Dawson? Here's a clue: Oh, I wish I were in the land of....
That's right, Cotton Davidson.
Len Dawson's name is synonymous with quarterbacking in

Kansas City. Little wonder, since he holds all Chiefs' passing records and led Kansas City to two Super Bowls, winning one.

Dawson failed in the National Football League before finding fame in the "other league." He spent 14 seasons in Kansas City, becoming almost as famous as Arthur Bryant's, that city's famous rib emporium.

Dawson led the AFL in passing four times, threw six touchdown passes in one game and five in two other games.

INDIVIDUAL CHIEF RECORDS

Rushing

Most Yards Game:	193	Joe Delaney, vs Houston, 1981
Season:	1,121	Joe Delaney, 1981
Career:	4,451	Ed Podolak, 1969-77

Passing

Most TD Passes Game:	6	Len Dawson, vs Denver, 1964
Season:	30	Len Dawson, 1964
Career:	237	Len Dawson, 1962-75

Receiving

Most TD Passes Game:	4	Frank Jackson, vs San Diego, 1964
Season:	12	Chris Burford, 1962
Career:	57	Otis Taylor, 1965-75

Scoring

Most Points Game:	30	Abner Haynes, vs Oakland, 1961
Season:	129	Jan Stenerud, 1968
Career:	1,231	Jan Stenerud, 1967-79
Most TDs Game:	5	Abner Haynes, vs Oakland, 1961
Season:	19	Abner Haynes, 1962
Career:	60	Otis Taylor, 1965-75

LOS ANGELES RAIDERS

TEAM DIRECTORY: Managing Gen. Partner: Al Davis; Gen. Partner: E.W. McGah; Exec. Asst.: Al LoCasale; Admin. Asst.: Irv Kaze; Bus. Mgr.: Ken LaRue; Dir. Publications: Bill Glazier; Head Coach: Tom Flores. Home field: Los Angeles Memorial Coliseum (94,000). Colors: Silver and black.

SCOUTING REPORT

OFFENSE: Coach Tom Flores is quick to point out that Marc Wilson has improved at quarterback and is showing more signs of leadership in practice. Wilson started two years ago when Jim Plunkett was injured, but as soon as Plunkett was healthy, Flores rushed him back into the lineup.

This would suggest the Raiders are down on Wilson, who played well in Plunkett's absence. Is it Wilson's arm or his play-calling? Anyway, Plunkett, who'll be 36 in December, still is No. 1.

Plunkett had a good year until his final pass of the playoffs. If he can string together two productive seasons, the Raiders are in the Super Bowl hunt again.

Marcus Allen could make any team a Super Bowl contender, if everything else is in order. Kenny King is a fine running mate. Cliff Branch and Malcolm Barnwell are fast receivers. If Bob Chandler can come back from injuries, the pass-catching corps will be that much stronger.

Tight end Todd Christensen is reliable. The offensive line is solid, the only question mark being Mickey Marvin's knee. If he can't make it back, Ed Muransky is his replacement.

DEFENSE: The Raiders were second from the top in the NFL against the run and second from the bottom against the pass. If the Raiders bridge that gap, they can go all the way.

Part of the problem was a young cornerback, Ted Watts. He's through learning the ropes and should have a productive season in '83. Pushing Watts is James Davis, who returned two interceptions for a total of 107 yards and one touchdown. He should have had two, but began waving the ball prematurely and was tackled from behind on one return.

Lester Hayes has had two off years (for him) after his spectacular '80 season. He's still a strong cover man. Free safety Burgess Owens had a superb year. Strong safety Mike Davis led the team in vicious hits and yellow flags.

LOS ANGELES RAIDERS   237

Age is creeping up on Ted Hendricks (35) and Lyle Alzado (34), but they had tremendous autumns a year ago. Matt Millen got his weight down and his performance up and Rod Martin was his typical self: great year, no recognition.

The Raiders are deep in defensive linemen. Howie Long could be the best, even if Alzado matches last year's effort.

KICKING GAME: The biggest question about the Raiders is what happened to Ray Guy? Last year, his punting average dropped to 39.1 yards per kick and his longest kick was 57 yards. Back pains have resulted from all those knee-to-chin follow-throughs. His best years may be over. Chris Bahr made 10-of-16 field goals, a good year for him.

The Stork has been calling on quarterbacks for 14 years.

RAIDERS VETERAN ROSTER

HEAD COACH—Tom Flores. Assistant Coaches—Sam Boghosian, Willie Brown, Chet Franklin, Earl Leggett, Joe Madro, Bob Mishak, Steve Ortmayer, Charlie Sumner, Ray Willsey, Art Shell.

No.	Name	Pos.	Ht.	Wt.	NFL Exp.	College
32	Allen, Marcus	RB	6-2	210	2	Southern California
77	Alzado, Lyle	DE	6-3	250	13	Yankton
10	Bahr, Chris	K	5-10	175	8	Penn State
56	Barnes, Jeff	LB	6-2	225	7	California
80	Barnwell, Malcolm	WR	5-11	185	3	Virginia Union
40	Berns, Rick	RB	6-2	205	4	Nebraska
21	#Branch, Cliff	WR	5-10	170	12	Colorado
73	Browning, Dave	WR	6-5	245	6	Washington
81	Burke, Randy	WR	6-2	195	5	Kentucky
85	Chandler, Bob	WR	6-1	180	12	Southern California
46	#Christensen, Todd	TE	6-3	230	5	Brigham Young
50	Dalby, Dave	C	6-3	250	12	UCLA
79	Davis, Bruce	T	6-6	280	5	UCLA
45	Davis, James	CB	6-0	190	2	Southern
36	Davis, Mike	S	6-3	205	6	Colorado
8	#Guy, Ray	P	6-3	195	11	Southern Mississippi
86	Harvey, Marvin	TE	6-3	220	2	Southern Mississippi
27	Hawkins, Frank	RB	5-9	210	3	Nevada-Reno
61	Hawkins, Mike	LB	6-3	245	6	Texas A&I
37	Hayes, Lester	CB	6-0	200	7	Texas A&M
83	Hendricks, Ted	LB	6-7	235	15	Miami
48	Hill, Kenny	S	6-0	195	3	Yale
42	Jackson, Monte	CB	5-11	195	9	San Diego State
31	Jensen, Derrick	TE	6-1	220	5	Texas-Arlington
90	Jones, Willie	DE	6-4	245	4	Florida State
33	King, Kenny	RB	5-11	205	5	Oklahoma
62	Kinlaw, Reggie	DT	6-2	245	4	Oklahoma
70	Lawrence, Henry	T	6-4	270	10	Florida A&M
75	Long, Howie	DE	6-5	265	3	Villanova
60	Marsh, Curt	G	6-4	275	7	Washington
53	Martin, Rod	LB	6-2	220	7	Southern California
65	Marvin, Mickey	G	6-4	275	7	Tennessee
26	McElroy, Vann	S	6-2	190	2	Baylor
23	McKinney, Odis	S	6-2	190	6	Colorado
55	Millen, Matt	LB	6-2	255	4	Penn State
28	Montgomery, Cleotha	WR	5-8	185	3	Abilene Christian
82	Muhammad, Calvin	WR	5-11	190	1	Texas Southern
76	Muransky, Ed	T	6-7	280	2	Michigan
51	Nelson, Bob	LB	6-4	235	7	Nebraska
44	Owens, Burgess	S	6-2	220	11	Miami
54	Peterson, Calvin	LB	6-3	225	8	UCLA
25	Phillips, Irvin	CB	6-1	190	2	Arkansas Tech
16	Plunkett, Jim	QB	6-2	217	13	Stanford
34	Pruitt, Greg	RB	5-10	195	11	Oklahoma
84	Ramsey, Derrick	TE	6-5	235	6	Kentucky
29	Reed, Tony	RB	5-10	190	6	Colorado
74	Reese, Archie	DT	6-3	275	6	Clemson
68	Robinson, Johnny	DT	6-2	260	3	Louisiana Tech
52	Romano, Jim	C	6-3	260	9	Penn State
58	Squirek, Jack	LB	6-4	225	2	Illinois
66	#Sylvester, Steve	C-G	6-4	260	9	Notre Dame
63	#Upshaw, Gene	G	6-5	255	16	Texas A&I
67	Van Divier, Randy	G	6-5	265	3	Washington
99	Vaughan, Ruben	DE	6-2	240	3	Colorado
20	Watts, Ted	CB	6-0	190	3	Texas Tech
38	Willis, Chester	RB	5-11	195	3	Auburn
6	Wilson, Marc	QB	6-6	205	4	Brigham Young

#Unsigned at press time

TOP FIVE DRAFT CHOICES

Rd.	Name	Sel. No.	Pos.	Ht.	Wt.	College
1	Mosebar, Don	26	T	6-7	270	Southern California
2	Pickel, Bill	54	DT	6-6	275	Rutgers
3	Caldwell, Tony	82	LB	6-2	222	Washington
4	Townsend, Greg	110	DE	6-4	235	Texas Christian
5	Williams, Dokie	138	WR	5-11	175	UCLA

LOS ANGELES RAIDERS 239

THE ROOKIES: A big, strong tackle in the Raider mold, USC's Don Mosebar didn't let the Raiders know he'd had back surgery. If this first-rounder is okay, he could start by his second or third year. Defensive tackle Bill Pickel of Rutgers had back problems they knew about and should be fine. Washington linebacker Tony Caldwell is underrated, while Dokie Williams has blazing speed and is excellent at returning kickoffs.

OUTLOOK: The Raiders practiced in one town, played in another and made the playoffs. This year, it comes down to pass offense and pass defense. If the Raiders get both, they have an excellent chance of reaching the Super Bowl, even if they practice in Poughkeepsie and play in Petaluma.

RAIDER PROFILES

JIM PLUNKETT 35 6-2 217   Quarterback

Roller-coaster man... More ups and downs than anyone in football... Finished '82 season on a down cycle, throwing the interception that cost the Raiders a possible comeback playoff victory over the Jets... Needing only a field goal to send the game into overtime, Plunkett had tight end Todd Christensen open over the middle for a first down, but elected to throw to Cliff Branch in triple coverage and Jet linebacker Lance Mehl intercepted... But, just when you think Plunkett's down for the count, he gets back up... Look for him to be the Raiders' quarterback again this year... Completed 58.2 percent for 2,035 yards, 14 TDs... Born Dec. 5, 1947, in San Francisco... Stanford grad is only quarterback to win the Heisman Trophy, Rose Bowl and Super Bowl... Only active NFL player to run a marathon.

MARCUS ALLEN 23 6-2 210   Running Back

Can he play Hamlet?... Stepped into the NFL with the stage presence of Olivier, leading the NFL in touchdowns (13)... Runs with a dramatic flair... Flew into the end zone like a graceful swan to win one game... Did it all—Pro Bowl, Rookie of the Year, all-pro—in his NFL debut, just like Gale Sayers and Hugh McElhenny in yesteryear... And he did it all

240 THE COMPLETE HANDBOOK OF PRO FOOTBALL

with graciousness—he's a class act all the way around... Right now, 10 other teams are tormented by having passed him up in the first round, so that the Raiders could get him... Born March 26, 1960, in San Diego... Quarterback in high school, then a fullback at USC before becoming the fourth Trojan tailback to win the Heisman... Gained 697 yards (4.4 per carry) as a rookie.

KENNY KING 26 5-11 205   Running Back

King who abdicated... Surrendering his halfback job with the Raiders was like an abdication, at first, because he was giving up something he had worked years to get... Was moved to fullback at Oklahoma, because there was a halfback named Billy Sims... Was moved to the bench in Houston, because there was a back named Earl Campbell... After being traded to the Raiders in '80, King finally reached the throne. He was given the halfback job and made the Pro Bowl that same season... Felt like a king until the Raiders drafted Marcus Allen... Took it nobly, shifting back to fullback with nary a grumble. Why? Because he likes Allen as a person... He's a nice guy himself... Born March 7, 1957, in Clarendon, Tex.

HENRY LAWRENCE 30 6-4 270   Offensive Tackle

The sound of music?... "Baaaaaby! Baaaaaby!" ... Was forever walking around the Raider locker room singing these two words and nothing more... No one on the Raiders seemed to pay much attention, but, then, if you know the Raiders, they aren't bothered by anything... Whether they thought he had a voice or not was never revealed... Someone must have thought so, because he was given a record contract, and his first record was released during offseason... The Marvin Gaye of tackles?... A solid run-blocker who has improved his pass-blocking... Born Sept. 26, 1951, in Danville, Pa., he worked as a migrant as a child, grew up in Florida... Raiders' No. 1 choice out of Florida A&M in '74.

LOS ANGELES RAIDERS 241

MICKEY MARVIN 27 6-4 275   Guard

Storybook romance... Hey, they still exist!... This big, blond Raider guard fell in love with a Raider cheerleader and they married... On game day, he throws blocks on the field and his wife, Lisa, leads cheers on the sideline... But there is suspense even in storybooks... Injured his knee in the fading moments of the playoff loss to the Jets and spent the offseason in rehabilitation... There, mopping his brow and offering encouragement, was Lisa... A team off the field, they hope to be a team on the field again this fall... Born Oct. 2, 1955, in Hendersonville, N.C.... Played his college ball at Tennessee... Raiders' fourth-round pick in '77.

TODD CHRISTENSEN 27 6-3 230   Tight End

Todzilla... That's his nickname, honest!... In-house joke... But he is no longer a household secret as a tight end... Caught 42 passes last year, tying him with Atlanta's William Andrews for eighth in the NFL... Scored four touchdowns and became a clutch third-down performer... Keeps alive the Raiders' great tight-end tradition: Billy Cannon, Raymond Chester, Dave Casper, Ken Herock... Just kidding on the last one, folks... Dallas drafted Christensen as a running back, talked to him about playing tight end, but he resisted... At Oakland, his resistance gave out. It was tight end or nothing, and he worked his way from No. 4 to No. 1... Born Aug. 3, 1956, in Bellefont, Pa.... Went to BYU.

CLIFF BRANCH 35 5-10 170   Wide Receiver

Wonderful whippet... Thirty catches and four touchdowns last year give him 435 and 62 for his career, well up there among active receivers... Though he is now up there in years, too, he hasn't slowed down much and can still get open deep... Secondaries have the same respect for him they always have, although they no longer line up in a sprinter's stance, facing the same way he does when he comes off the ball... Career looked to be in jeopardy two years ago because of drugs, but he said he overcame that problem and his play last year seemed to confirm that... Born Aug. 1, 1948, in Houston... World-class sprinter at

Colorado... Raiders drafted him fourth in '72... Averaged 24.2 yards per catch in '76.

TED HENDRICKS 35 6-7 235   Outside Linebacker

Sears Tower in cleats... Isn't getting older, he's getting better... Well, he certainly isn't getting any worse!... Made the last three Pro Bowls after an absence of six years... A great athlete who makes big tackles, blocks kicks, recovers fumbles and is a holy terror on the blitz... And he has never missed a game in 14 NFL seasons, 199 straight, while playing on three Super Bowl champions—one in Baltimore, two in Oakland... NFL's senior active linebacker, and there is no reason to believe that he won't play for, at least, two more seasons... Born Nov. 1, 1947, in Guatemala City, Guatemala... Reared in Hialeah, Fla.... Three-time All-American at University of Miami... Colts' No. 2 pick in '69... Played with Green Bay in '74.

LYLE ALZADO 34 6-3 250   Defensive End

The Crush is back... The spit and fire of Denver's Orange Crush defense in the '70s... Then the flame burned out when he was traded to Cleveland... Raiders picked him out of the ashes, and the Phoenix flew again, despite weighing 250 pounds... Played last year like he did in '77 and should have been invited to the Pro Bowl, but somehow was left off the AFC team... Against the Jets in the playoffs, it looked like he had performed the first NFL beheading. In a moment of anger, he ripped the helmet off Jet tackle Chris Ward so quickly there was fear that Ward's head still was inside it... Does get excited at times... Born April 3, 1949, in Brooklyn... Played at Yankton (S.D.) College.

HOWIE LONG 23 6-5 265   Defensive End

Raider mean... Plays an intimidating game, much like Alzado, and should someday be as effective... Replaced an injured John Matuszak... Even if Tooz hadn't retired, he might have kept the job... Raider watchers say Long is nearly as strong as the Tooz and is quicker afoot.... Improved loads last year... Jets' all-pro tackle Marvin Powell was caught hold-

LOS ANGELES RAIDERS 243

ing three times against him... The last NFL player to come out of Villanova, which gave up football after he left... Raiders drafted him in the second round of the '81 draft... Born Jan. 12, 1960, in Somerville, Mass.... Boxing champion in college... Haymaker Howie.

COACH TOM FLORES: So near, so far... Raiders had AFC's best record last year (8-1), but were knocked off one game short of the conference championship... It wasn't the head coach's fault, however... In his playing days as a Raider, he never would have forced the pass Jim Plunkett forced that the Jets intercepted to preserve their playoff win... Did a good job picking the team up after a 7-9 season in '81, although Marcus Allen helped, too... Has the good fortune to work under a knowledgeable football owner, but the misfortune of having to put up with Al Davis day after day... Through the good and bad, he has a 35-22 record as a head coach, a 5-1 mark in the playoffs and a Super Bowl championship... He's so emotionless on the sideline, it is sometimes easy to forget the Raiders even have a head coach... His predecessor was John Madden, which is like following Jonathan Winters with Ben Kingsley... He is a thinker, not a screamer (Madden was both) and carries on quietly... Born March 21, 1937, in Fresno, Cal.... Son of Mexican fruit pickers... Played at College of Pacific... Original Raider back in '60... Named head coach in '79.

GREATEST QUARTERBACK

The Raiders are the only team to have three different Super Bowl quarterbacks. But there is only one Snake.

Ken Stabler personifies the gutty, gambling, two-minute quarterback. Find a way to win—that's The Snake's motto. And he found many different ways in Oakland, falling forward and pitching the "sea-of-hands" pass to Clarence Davis to defeat Miami, running to beat New England and—the topper—fumbling the ball into the end zone to stun San Diego.

Stabler throws passes three-quarter, side-arm and under-hand, any angle it takes to complete them. Though his best years are behind him, he remains one of the great medium-distance passers ever to play the game.

He has always lived even harder than he has played. Stabler sees himself as another Bobby Layne, his hero, who also studied a few game plans by the light of the jukebox.

The Raiders have had two other successful quarterbacks, Daryle (The Mad Bomber) Lamonica and Jim Plunkett. But there is only one quarterback whom long-time Raider rooters identify with—and that's Stabler. For years, he made the Oakland Coliseum the "House of Thrills."

INDIVIDUAL RAIDER RECORDS

Rushing

Most Yards Game:	200	Clem Daniels, vs N.Y. Jets, 1963
Season:	1,273	Mark van Eeghen, 1977
Career:	5,907	Mark van Eeghen, 1974-81

Passing

Most TD Passes Game:	6	Tom Flores, vs Houston, 1963
	6	Daryle Lamonica, vs Buffalo, 1969
Season:	34	Daryle Lamonica, 1969
Career:	150	Ken Stabler, 1970-79

Receiving

Most TD Passes Game:	4	Art Powell, vs Houston, 1963
Season:	16	Art Powell, 1963
Career:	76	Fred Biletnikoff, 1965-78

Scoring

Most Points Game:	24	Art Powell, vs Houston, 1963
Season:	117	George Blanda, 1968
Career:	863	George Blanda, 1967-75
Most TDs Game:	4	Art Powell, vs Houston, 1963
Season:	16	Art Powell, 1975
	16	Pete Banaszak, 1975
Career:	77	Fred Biletnikoff, 1965-78

MIAMI DOLPHINS

TEAM DIRECTORY: Pres.: Joseph Robbie; Head Coach: Don Shula; Dir. Pro Scouting: Charley Winner; Dir. Player Personnel: Chuck Connor; Dir. Pub. Rel.: Dick Horning. Home field: Orange Bowl (75,289). Colors: Aqua and orange.

A.J. Duhe helps put sting in Killer Bee defense.

SCOUTING REPORT

OFFENSE: Coach Don Shula has the citizenry of Miami searching the town along with him. Something valuable has been lost by the Dolphins, and Shula might even offer a reward for its recovery. The missing object is the forward pass.

It was last seen in the capable hands of Bob Griese, who turned it over to David Woodley, who misplaced it. If located, please return to Woodley, who's lost without it.

The Dolphins had the second-worst air attack in the conference last year, but made the Super Bowl. Just think what Miami would have done against Washington with a passing game? Shula thought about it all spring and summer.

Otherwise, Miami is strong. Andra Franklin, Tony Nathan, Woody Bennett, Tom Vigorito and CFL refugee David Overstreet blend their versatile talents at running back. Duriel Harris, Nat Moore and Jimmy Cefalo do the same thing at wide receiver, although Moore has slowed down. There isn't one great player among Bruce Hardy, Ronnie Lee and Joe Rose, but, together, they make a pretty good tight end.

Miami's line—when hasn't Miami had a great line?—is rock solid, with Jon Giesler, Bob Kuechenberg, Dwight Stephenson, Jeff Toews and Eric Laakso. But room may be made for veteran guard Ed Newman and, in time, young guard Roy Foster.

DEFENSE: Bzzzzzzzzzz. The Killer Bees are back. Doug Betters, Kim Bokamper, Bob Baumhower, Bob Brudzinski, Glenn Blackwood, Lyle Blackwood and Mr. Bill (Arnsparger), the beekeeper.

The Killer Bees created a sensation last year, ranking No. 1 in the NFL in defense and buzzing off to Pasadena, where their stingers failed to penetrate some tough Hogs from Washington.

However, the Bees are young—their oldest starter is 32-year-old Lyle Blackwood—and will be back for more. If they're lacking anywhere, it's against the run. The Dolphin defense is made up of quick, lean athletes, as opposed to stay-in-the-trenches behemoths. This explains why Miami ranked 24th in rushing defense. But the Dolphins were first in the league against the pass, so they have to give up yardage somewhere.

Gerald Small and Don McNeal are dependable cornerbacks, even if their last names don't begin with B. Linebackers A.J. Duhe, Earnest Rhone and Larry Gordon are Killer Bees in spirit, too.

If the Bees and non-B's stay healthy, the Dolphins will continue to dominate.

MIAMI DOLPHINS 247

DOLPHINS VETERAN ROSTER

HEAD COACH—Don Shula. Assistant Coaches—Bill Arnsparger, Tom Keane, Bob Matheson, John Sandusky, Mike Scarry, David Shula, Carl Taseff, Junior Wade.

No.	Name	Pos.	Ht.	Wt.	NFL Exp.	College
70	Barnett, Bill	DE	6-4	260	4	Nebraska
73	Baumhower, Bob	DT	6-5	260	7	Alabama
34	Bennett, Woody	FB	6-2	222	4	Miami
75	Betters, Doug	DE	6-7	260	6	Nevado-Reno
72	#Bishop, Richard	NT	6-1	265	8	Louisville
47	Blackwood, Glenn	S	6-0	186	5	Texas
42	Blackwood, Lyle	S	6-1	188	11	Texas Christian
58	Bokamper, Kim	DE	6-6	250	7	San Jose State
56	Bowser, Charles	LB	6-3	222	2	Duke
59	Brudzinski, Bob	LB	6-4	230	7	Ohio State
81	Cefalo, Jimmy	WR	5-11	188	6	Penn State
76	Clark, Steve	DT	6-4	255	2	Utah
63	#Dennard, Mark	C	6-1	252	5	Texas A&M
33	Diana, Rich	RB	5-9	220	2	Yale
77	Duhe, A.J.	LB	6-4	245	7	Louisiana State
85	Duper, Mark	WR	5-9	185	2	NW State (La.)
61	Foster, Roy	G-T	6-4	275	2	Southern California
37	Franklin, Andra	FB	5-10	225	3	Nebraska
79	Giesler, Jon	T	6-5	260	5	Michigan
50	Gordon, Larry	LB	6-4	230	8	Arizona State
74	Green, Cleveland	T	6-3	262	5	Southern
84	Hardy, Bruce	TE	6-4	230	6	Arizona State
82	Harris, Duriel	WR	5-11	176	8	New Mexico State
88	Heflin, Vince	WR	6-0	185	2	Central State
53	Hester, Ron	LB	6-1	218	2	Florida State
31	Hill, Eddie	RB	6-2	210	5	Memphis State
11	Jensen, Jim	QB	6-4	212	3	Boston University
49	Judson, William	CB	6-1	181	2	South Carolina State
40	Kozlowski, Mike	S	6-0	198	4	Colorado
67	Kuechenberg, Bob	G	6-2	255	14	Notre Dame
68	Laakso, Eric	T	6-4	265	6	Tulane
44	Lankford, Paul	CB	6-1	178	2	Penn State
86	Lee, Ronnie	TE	6-3	236	5	Baylor
28	McNeal, Don	CB	5-11	192	4	Alabama
89	Moore, Nat	WR	5-9	188	10	Florida
22	Nathan, Tony	RB	6-0	206	5	Alabama
64	Newman, Ed	G	6-2	255	11	Duke
3	Orosz, Tom	P	6-1	204	3	Ohio State
—	Overstreet, David	RB	5-10	204	*	Oklahoma
78	Poole, Ken	DE	6-3	251	3	Northeast Louisiana
54	Potter, Steve	LB	6-3	235	3	Virginia
55	Rhone, Earnest	LB	6-2	224	8	Henderson (Ark.)
80	Rose, Joe	TE	6-3	230	4	California
52	Shull, Steve	LB	6-1	220	4	William & Mary
48	Small, Gerald	CB	5-11	192	6	San Jose State
57	Stephenson, Dwight	C	6-2	255	4	Alabama
10	#Strock, Don	QB	6-5	220	10	Virginia Tech
60	Toews, Jeff	G	6-3	255	5	Washington
32	Vigorito, Tom	RB	5-10	197	3	Virginia
5	#Von Schamann, Uwe	K	6-0	188	5	Oklahoma
41	Walker, Fulton	CB	5-10	193	3	West Virginia
16	Woodley, David	QB	6-2	204	4	Louisiana State

*Played in CFL in 1982
#Unsigned at press time

TOP FIVE DRAFT CHOICES

Rd.	Name	Sel. No.	Pos.	Ht.	Wt.	College
1	Marino, Dan	27	QB	6-4	215	Pittsburgh
2	Charles, Mike	55	DT	6-4	273	Syracuse
3	Benson, Charles	76	DE	6-4	255	Baylor
6	Roby, Reggie	167	P	6-3	230	Iowa
7	Woetzel, Keith	195	LB	6-2	225	Rutgers

KICKING GAME: Fulton Walker set a Super Bowl record with a 98-yard kickoff return. Vigarito returned a regular-season punt 59 yards for a touchdown. Uwe von Schamann nailed 15-of-20 field-goal tries. The only weakness is punter Tom Orosz (38.7 yards per kick). Miami hasn't had a consistent punter since Larry Seiple.

THE ROOKIES: Top pick Dan Marino of Pitt regressed as a senior. If Miami can stop him from throwing interceptions, he might challenge David Woodley in time. Otherwise, Marino's strictly a backup. The Dolphins picked up two pass-rushers in Mike Charles of Syracuse and Charles Benson of Baylor. Iowa punter Reggie Roby averaged 48 yards, but lacks hang time.

OUTLOOK: If Woodley doesn't improve his passing, Miami won't come close to repeating last year's success story. Washington shut down Woodley in the second half of the Super Bowl, and Dolphin opponents will have better success after seeing that. Let's judge Woodley over 16 games, not nine.

DOLPHIN PROFILES

DAVID WOODLEY 24 6-2 204   Quarterback

Steve Ensminger, where are you?... Ensminger split time at quarterback with Woodley at LSU... Woodley is with the Dolphins, but where is Ensminger?... Would Ensminger have gone 0-for-8 in the second half against the Redskins in Super Bowl XVII?... But Woodley has come a long way since those LSU days. In fact, he has done very well in the pros, considering he is the first NFL quarterback in years (ever?) who amassed more touchdowns running than passing in college... But he couldn't match Washington's Joe Theismann in productivity in the Super Bowl and that's why the Dolphins lost... Born Oct. 25, 1958, in Shreveport, La., where Terry Bradshaw and Joe Ferguson got their starts... Drafted eighth by Miami in '80.

MIAMI DOLPHINS 249

ANDRA FRANKLIN 24 5-10 225   Running Back

Mini-Csonka... That's what they're calling him... Bulled for 701 yards (4.0 per carry) for the third-best rushing effort of the NFL mini-season... Scored seven touchdowns... Suffered from Franco Harris Disease in college—he was a blocker first, runner a distant second... Harris opened holes for Lydell Mitchell at Penn State, just as Franklin opened holes for Rick Berns, I.M. Hipp and Jarvis Redwine at Nebraska... Chuck Connor of the Dolphins' scouting office said he was the best blocking back in college football... Coach Don Shula said, "Hmmmmm," then drafted him in the second round two years ago... Has scored 17 touchdowns in pros... Born Aug. 22, 1959, in Anniston, Ala.... One The Bear missed.

TOM VIGORITO 23 5-10 197   All-Purpose

That's right, all-purpose... It's a new position in the NFL, pioneered by this man... Running back, slotback, wide receiver, punt returner, blocker... Don't be surprised if he throws a pass off a double-reverse this year... Can do about anything... Punt? Give him a week... Placekick? Two weeks... Last year, the versatile one returned a punt 59 yards for a touchdown, rushed for 99 yards (5.2 per carry), including a 33-yard touchdown, and caught 24 passes for 186 yards... Has 4.5 speed in the 40 and bench presses 365 pounds, nearly double his weight... Born Oct. 23, 1959, in Passaic, N.J.... Went to the University of Virginia, where he rushed for 2,912 yards and didn't fumble in one stretch of 302 carries... Fifth-round pick in 1981.

JIMMY CEFALO 26 5-11 188   Wide Receiver

Not too big, not too fast, but open most of the time... Started the last Super Bowl off with a bang, faking Redskin defensive backs out of their low-cuts on a 76-yard touchdown pass from David Woodley... Cefalo has a lot of Fred Biletnikoff in him: deceptive speed and an impressive number of ways to get open... His 17 catches during the 1982 regular-season averaged out to 20.9 yards... That amounted to an off year, because he had averaged 21.8 yards the year before and 24.2 as a rookie (six catches) in 1978... His career average is 20.8... Born Oct.

250 THE COMPLETE HANDBOOK OF PRO FOOTBALL

5, 1956, in Pittston, Pa.... Tremendous career at Penn State, though it was a national secret... Third-round Miami pick in '78.

BOB KUECHENBERG 35 6-2 255   Guard

No man is an island?... Lives on Star Island, Miami Beach, where he and wife Marilyn have a mansion they renovated... "Kooch" is the only Dolphin left who has played in all four Super Bowls... "The last of the Mohicans, huh?" he said. "Actually, I'm a little like Napoleon in Moscow—my supply lines have been cut off. I'm an island. There's nobody within four years of me behind me."... Was an island during the strike, too, when he was the only Dolphin who trained at the team's practice facility.... Hit the weights hard and made the Pro Bowl for the first time in four years... Born Oct. 14, 1947, in Gary, Ind.... Played at Notre Dame... Dolphin free-agent signee in 1970.

DWIGHT STEPHENSON 25 6-2 255   Center

Coming all-pro... Played exceptionally well last year, his third NFL season, and received attention not normally accorded a center when Merlin Olsen focused on his blocking during playoff telecasts... That could pay off in all-pro honors this year, although he is capable of earning same without the aid of TV cameras... Gets into his blocks quickly and aggressively... The only knock against him is that he doesn't snap off the shotgun formation. Mark Dennard handles that assignment... Might detract from Stephenson's chances for recognition, though it shouldn't... Born Nov. 20, 1957, in Murfreesboro, N.C.... Played at Alabama.

LYLE BLACKWOOD 28 6-1 188   Free Safety

Fifth time's the charm... Passed through Denver (1973), Cincinnati (1973-75), Seattle (1976) and Baltimore (1977-80) before finding a Super Bowl home in Miami... Reckless tackler, good eye for the football, just like his brother, Glenn... Led the NFL with 10 interceptions in '77, picked off four more in each of the next two seasons, including a 78-yard touchdown return in '78... Picked off three more last year, including one in Super Bowl... Was predominantly a return man his first four years in the league... Broncos drafted him ninth in '73, then waived

MIAMI DOLPHINS 251

him that pre-season... Seattle got him in the expansion draft in '76... Born Sept. 25, 1954, in San Antonio... All-Southwest Conference twice at TCU.

GLENN BLACKWOOD 26 6-0 186   Strong Safety

The younger half... Glenn's rookie year ended because of brother... Lyle was blocking for the Colts' punt returner and Glenn, charging downfield to make the tackle for Miami, dodged his brother and landed awkwardly, tearing knee ligaments... Thanks, brother... Parents of Blackwood brothers, who had driven from New Orleans to Miami to see that game, sent Lyle to bed without supper... Both brothers are very religious, organizing chapel meetings on Dolphin road trips and working for the Campus Crusade for Christ... Born Feb. 23, 1957, in San Antonio... Played in the same Texas secondary as Johnnie Johnson (Rams), Derrick Hatchett (Colts) and Ricky Churchman (49ers).

A.J. DUHE 27 6-4 245   Inside Linebacker

Playoff sensation... Nearly unstoppable during the postseason until he ran into a bunch of Hogs at the Super Bowl... But even in that game, he intercepted a pass and had five solo tackles... His biggest game was against the Jets in the AFC title game, when he intercepted three passes and returned one for a touchdown... In that game, the Jets had trouble blocking him, because they had trouble finding him. He was coming from the inside, outside and over the top... Adam Joseph was a defensive end before the Dolphins moved him to linebacker, but they, at times, use him as both... Big, rangy athlete, making him perfect for the blitz... Born Nov. 27, 1955, in New Orleans ... Dolphins' No. 1 pick in 1977, out of LSU.

BRUCE HARDY 27 6-4 230   Tight End

Flashback!... It is April 29, 1974, and your latest copy of Sports Illustrated has arrived... There on the cover, standing on an otherwise empty highway near Copperton, Utah, is the "Nation's Best High School Athlete"— Bruce Hardy of Bingham High... Twice the state's MVP in both football and basketball, twice all-state in baseball... Update! It is Jan.

30, 1983, Rose Bowl Stadium, Super Bowl Sunday. There at tight end for the Miami Dolphins, Bruce Hardy... Changed from quarterback to tight end at Arizona State... Dolphins' ninth-round pick in '78... Dependable blocker, good receiver, one of three Dolphin tight ends along with Joe Rose, Ronnie Lee... Born June 1, 1956, in Murray, Utah.

COACH DON SHULA: More succinctly, the coach... Returned to the Super Bowl after a nine-year hiatus... "I never thought I would miss having breakfast with you guys," he told the media, with a big grin, during Super Bowl week... As it turned out, he didn't have enough offense to beat Washington, but he lost no respect in losing... The general feeling is that he'll be in contention again. When isn't he?... Respected throughout his profession, by those who report on football and by the fans... Has won 201 games in 19 years. Tom Landry has won 202 in 22 and no other active coach is close. Up ahead are Curly Lambeau (231 wins in 33 years) and George Halas (320 in 40)... He's 53. Will he stay around, say, another 15 years in order to catch Halas? Maybe... Has mellowed over the years... Sips wine, reflectively... Oldest of his five children, David, has joined him as an assistant coach... Will the coach stay in Miami, where his relationship with the owner barely exists?... Had a 17-0 season in 1972. What owner couldn't live with that?... Born Jan. 4, 1930, in Painesville, Ohio... In our minds, he will live forever.

GREATEST QUARTERBACK

Quarterbacks who wear glasses do complete passes.

Bob Griese proved it in his later years as he proved, without a doubt, that he was the finest quarterback ever to put on a Miami Dolphins' sea-green and orange uniform.

Miami had quarterbacks named Dick Wood and Rick Norton before it got wise and drafted Griese in 1967. The late Joe Thomas said he had decided to pick Griese over state hero Steve Spurrier, and was prepared for the ensuing media and fan furor. But the San Francisco 49ers made a deal that allowed them to choose Spurrier just before it was the Dolphins' turn to pick.

Thomas settled on the right choice, because Griese would lead the Dolphins to three straight Super Bowls, including two championships and the memorable 17-0 season of 1973.

Griese was a solid, if not spectacular quarterback, who benefitted from having a tremendous running back in Larry Csonka and a great receiver in Paul Warfield. Griese didn't have to throw often during the Miami glory years, but when he did, he got results. Often overlooked was Griese's ability as a runner. More easily remembered is Griese the leader.

INDIVIDUAL DOLPHIN RECORDS

Rushing

Most Yards Game:	197	Mercury Morris, vs New England, 1973
Season:	1,258	Delvin Williams, 1978
Career:	6,737	Larry Csonka, 1968-74, 1979

Passing

Most TD Passes Game:	6	Bob Griese, vs St. Louis, 1977
Season:	22	Bob Griese, 1977
Career:	192	Bob Griese, 1967-80

Receiving

Most TD Passes Game:	4	Paul Warfield, vs Detroit, 1973
Season:	12	Nat Moore, 1977
Career:	48	Nat Moore, 1974-82

Scoring

Most Points Game:	24	Paul Warfield, vs Detroit, 1973
Season:	117	Garo Yepremian, 1971
Career:	830	Garo Yepremian, 1970-78
Most TDs Game:	4	Paul Warfield, vs Detroit, 1973
Season:	13	Nat Moore, 1977
	13	Larry Csonka, 1979
Career:	57	Larry Csonka, 1968-74, 1979

254 THE COMPLETE HANDBOOK OF PRO FOOTBALL
NEW ENGLAND PATRIOTS

TEAM DIRECTORY: Pres.: William Sullivan Jr.; VP: Bucko Kilroy; GM: Patrick J. Sullivan; Dir. Media Rel.: Tom Hoffman; Head Coach: Ron Meyer. Home field: Sullivan Stadium (61,297). Colors: Red, white and blue.

SCOUTING REPORT

OFFENSE: The team that doesn't want to pass. Ron Meyer must think he's still in the Southwest Conference, where it's run, run, incomplete pass, run, run, incomplete pass, etc.

The Patriots finished second in the league in rushing, while attempting and completing fewer passes than any other club. That's fine and dandy, but balanced attacks win football games, and Meyer won't be able to get away with a disproportionate offense if he expects to reach the playoffs again.

New England has the ability to throw, with quarterback Steve Grogan's strong arm and Stanley Morgan's high-octane speed. Don Hasselbeck (6-7) is a big target at tight end, though he shared time last year with Lin Dawson. The other wide receiver, currently Morris Bradshaw, needs to produce more, according to Meyer.

Tony Collins has led the club in rushing the last two years. Ex-Raider Mark van Eeghen was a pleasant surprise, but now Robert Weathers is ready to play somewhere and Vagas Ferguson is back from an inactive season (hamstring injury).

Meyer felt that Pete Brock, John Hannah, Ron Wooten, Brian Holloway and Shelby Jordan constituted "the best offensive line in the NFL," but now Hannah has retired.

DEFENSE: Growing, without serious growing pains. The Patriots didn't do badly on defense last year, considering they started three rookies and two second-year players among their front seven.

Kenneth Sims and Lester Williams, the club's top two picks last year, started at defensive end and nose tackle, respectively. Inside linebacker Clayton Weishuhn, a third-round selection, started every game. Don Blackmon and Larry McGrew, both second-year linebackers, won starting jobs as well.

Defensive end Julius Adams and linebacker Steve Nelson were the only Patriot veterans to survive this "youth-must-serve" approach, though George Crump and Andre Tippett are pushing Adams and Nelson, respectively.

The Pats finished 25th in the league against the rush, but, with more experience, that yield should come down. New England

NEW ENGLAND PATRIOTS 255

Streaky Steve Grogan can still heave the long one.

PATRIOTS VETERAN ROSTER

HEAD COACH—Ron Meyer. Assistant Coaches—Tommy Brasher, Cleve Bryant, LeBaron Caruthers, Steve Endicott, Lew Erber, Bill Muir, Rod Rust, Dante Scarnecchia, Steve Sidwell, Steve Walters.

No.	Name	Pos.	Ht.	Wt.	NFL Exp.	College
85	Adams, Julius	DE	6-3	270	12	Texas Southern
55	Blackmon, Don	LB	6-3	245	3	Tulsa
88	Bradshaw, Morris	WR	6-1	195	10	Ohio State
58	Brock, Pete	C	6-5	275	8	Colorado
81	Brown, Preston	WR	5-11	187	3	Vanderbilt
3	Camarillo, Rich	P	5-11	191	3	Washington
12	Cavanaugh, Matt	QB	6-2	212	6	Pittsburgh
65	Clark, Steve	T	6-5	270	2	Kansas State
26	Clayborn, Ray	CB	6-0	186	7	Texas
33	Collins, Tony	RB	5-11	203	3	East Carolina
44	Cowan, Larry	RB	5-11	194	2	Jackson State
91	Crump, George	DE	6-4	260	2	East Carolina
75	Cryder, Bob	G	6-4	293	6	Alabama
87	Dawson, Lin	TE	6-3	240	3	North Carolina State
47	Dombroski, Paul	DB	6-0	185	4	Linfield
43	Ferguson, Vagas	RB	6-0	213	3	Notre Dame
10	Flick, Tom	QB	6-1	190	3	Washington
59	Golden, Tim	LB	6-2	220	2	Florida
14	Grogan, Steve	QB	6-4	210	9	Kansas State
68	Haley, Darryl	T	6-4	279	2	Utah
80	#Hasselbeck, Don	TE	6-7	245	7	Colorado
40	#Haynes, Mike	CB	6-2	195	8	Arizona State
70	Henson, Luther	NT	6-0	275	2	Ohio State
76	Holloway, Brian	T	6-7	288	3	Stanford
51	Ingram, Brian	LB	6-4	230	2	Tennessee
38	James, Roland	S	6-2	191	4	Tennessee
83	Jones, Cedric	WR	5-11	184	2	Duke
74	Jordan, Shelby	T	6-7	280	8	Washington (Mo.)
22	Lee, Keith	CB-S	5-11	193	3	Colorado State
31	Marion, Fred	CB-S	6-2	196	2	Miami
50	McGrew, Larry	LB	6-5	233	2	Southern California
86	Morgan, Stanley	WR	5-11	180	7	Tennessee
57	Nelson, Steve	LB	6-2	230	10	North Dakota State
98	Owens, Dennis	NT	6-1	252	2	North Carolina State
25	Sanford, Rick	S	6-1	192	5	South Carolina
77	Sims, Kenneth	DE	6-5	279	2	Texas
1	Smith, John	K	6-0	185	10	Southampton (Eng.)
27	Smith, Ricky	CB-S	6-0	174	2	Alabama State
78	Spears, Ron	DE	6-6	255	2	San Diego State
30	Tatupu, Mosi	FB	6-0	227	6	Southern California
56	Tippett, Andre	LB	6-3	231	2	Iowa
82	Toler, Ken	WR	6-2	191	3	Mississippi
34	#van Eeghen, Mark	FB	6-2	220	10	Colgate
24	Weathers, Robert	RB	6-2	217	2	Arizona State
53	Weishuhn, Clayton	LB	6-2	220	2	Angelo State
62	Wheeler, Dwight	C	6-3	269	5	Tennessee State
72	Williams, Lester	NT	6-3	272	2	Miami
61	Wooten, Ron	G	6-4	280	2	North Carolina
54	Zamberlin, John	LB	6-2	226	5	Pacific Lutheran

#Unsigned at press time

TOP FIVE DRAFT CHOICES

Rd.	Name	Sel. No.	Pos.	Ht.	Wt.	College
1	Eason, Tony	15	QB	6-4	205	Illinois
2	Wilson, Darryal	47	WR	6-0	182	Tennessee
3	Starring, Stephen	74	WR	5-10	174	McNeese State
3	Moore, Steve	80	G	6-5	260	Tennessee State
4	Rembert, Johnny	101	LB	6-2	235	Clemson

does a great job against the pass—the Pats ranked fifth in NFL—thanks to corners Mike Haynes and Raymond Clayborn and safeties Roland James and Rick Sanford, who had the league's longest interception return last year (99 yards).

KICKING GAME: John Smith didn't get much work last year, making 5-of-8 field-goal attempts and 6-of-7 PATs after rejoining the team for the final four games following an injury. Rich Camarillo was a punting surprise (43.7 yards per kick, third in AFC). Ricky Smith had the year's longest kickoff return (98 yards).

THE ROOKIES: Quarterback Tony Eason of Illinois joins the Patriots' quarterback derby. Must develop a deep arm to go with his short game. Wide receivers Darryal Wilson of Tennessee and Stephen Starring of McNeese State are burners, with Starring superb at returning kicks. If Tennessee State guard-center Steve Moore can improve his upper body strength, he could be a find.

OUTLOOK: Settling the quarterback situation will have a settling effect on the offense. However, with Grogan's hot-and-cold streaks, the club won't be consistent enough to challenge Miami and the Jets for the division title.

PATRIOT PROFILES

STEVE GROGAN 30 6-4 210   **Quarterback**

"Steve Grogan is our starter at quarterback," says coach Ron Meyer... There often has been doubt in the past, even last year, during Meyer's coaching debut... But he won back his job early in the season and held it for the duration... For all his recent problems in New England, he holds most of the Patriots' passing records and figures to wrap them all up this season—if he plays all 16 games... No longer dangerous afoot, but he still has the arm to go deep... His only real flaw is accuracy... If there is such a thing as a streak passer, it is he... Born July 24, 1953, in San Antonio... Pats' fifth-round pick in 1975, out of Kansas State.

258 THE COMPLETE HANDBOOK OF PRO FOOTBALL

MATT CAVANAUGH 26 6-2 212   Quarterback

Had golden fleece and lost it... Beat out Steve Grogan for the quarterback job last summer, started the first three regular-season games, then was benched... If he gets a second chance, it may not be soon... His coach is a one-quarterback man and Grogan has the job for now... Cavanaugh had better not look back, because Tom Flick may be gaining on him for the No. 2 job... In fact, when Grogan received a concussion against Pittsburgh, Flick replaced him for three ineffective series before Cavanaugh came on to lead the Pats to a pair of touchdowns... Born Oct. 27, 1956, in Youngstown, Ohio... Big star at Pitt... New England drafted him in the second round in 1978.

MARK van EEGHEN 31 6-2 220   Running Back

He's got those Shirley Temple curls... There is no running back in the NFL who looks so harmless—until he straps on his helmet... Raiders dumped their all-time leading rusher and the Patriots picked him up... Rushed for 386 yards (4.7 per carry), second on the club behind Tony Collins, and scored his one touchdown on a reception... "Mark is a very exceptional player, day in and day out," Meyer said. "He gave a big boost to our club, not only in terms of rushing and blocking, but leadership."... Isn't ready to play unless he, well, upchucks before a game... Had three 1,000-yard seasons in Oakland and won two Super Bowl rings... Born April 19, 1952, in Cambridge, Mass.... Played at Colgate.

MOSI TATUPU 28 6-0 227   Running Back

Pago Pago kid... Standout on special teams, where he plays without fear and sometimes without his senses... Hits with such recklessness, he doesn't know if he's in New England or New Zealand... Tremendous blocker at running back, when he gets the chance to play... Got a rare opportunity in last year's blizzard game against Miami and rushed for 81 yards on 13 carries... Was second-best performer on the field that day, behind the guy who drove the snow plow... Born April 26, 1955, in Pago, Pago, American Samoa and reared in Hawaii... One of the best high-school football players in Hawaii's history... Pats' No.

NEW ENGLAND PATRIOTS

8 draft pick in 1978, out of USC, where he opened holes for All-Americans.

BRIAN HOLLOWAY 24 6-7 288 — Offensive Tackle

Big 'un... Put on 15 pounds in a year... If he gets any bigger, the Patriots may register him as a Hereford... Holloway was the team's No. 1 draft choice two years ago, broke in as a rookie starter and gained experience—and size—last year... His blocking helped the Pats finish second in league rushing... "Brian really excelled at times," Meyer said... If he gets as big as that farm house he's remodeling in upstate New York, he may be impossible to move... Born July 25, 1959, in Omaha, Neb.... Father is a retired Air Force pilot and an executive with the Ford Motor Co.... Graduated from Stanford with a degree in economics... Hobby is photography... Interested in a law career.

STANLEY MORGAN 28 5-11 180 — Wide Receiver

Getting work at last... For five years, the Patriots threw to him on occasion... Consequently, he never caught more than 45 passes a season... But, last year, he caught seven passes in a game twice... "We want Stanley to be able to attain those big results on a more consistent basis," Meyer said... So does Stanley... Though he enters this season with 216 catches, far behind club leader Jim Colclough (283), he needs only 133 yards to pass Colclough as the Pats' all-time reception-yardage leader... Born Feb. 17, 1955, in Easley, S.C.... Played running back, wingback and wide receiver at Tennessee, averaging 9.2 yards each time he touched the ball.

KENNETH SIMS 23 6-5 279 — Defensive End

The No. 1 No. 1... First player taken in the 1982 draft, he started his career indifferently, then caught fire... Led the team in sacks (4½) and quarterback pressures (13) and finished fourth in tackles... "He was the most productive of our defensive linemen," Meyer said. "We have every reason to believe that Kenneth can live up to the high expectations we have for him."... When you're the No. 1 No. 1, you'd better... In fairness to him, he was a defensive tackle in college in a four-man front, then was moved to defensive end in a three-man front... Must have felt a draft on his outside at first... Born Oct. 31, 1959, in Kosse, Tex.... Broke leg his last year at Texas, but it didn't hurt his draft status.

LESTER WILLIAMS 23 6-3 272   Nose Tackle

Another rookie starter on the defensive line, he started every game at nose tackle... Not even a wrist injury, which forced him to wear a cast all year, could keep him out of the lineup... Drafted after Ken Sims in the first round with the pick obtained from San Francisco in the Russ Francis trade... Tremendous strength and good movement... Could be one of NFL's best nose tackles in a year or two... In one game for the University of Miami (Fla.), he had 14 solo tackles, three assists, three sacks, a fumble recovery, a blocked field goal and a blocked PAT... Born Jan. 19, 1959, in Miami... State prep wrestling champion at Carol City High.

JULIUS ADAMS 35 6-3 270   Defensive End

The most famous Adams in Massachusetts since John... This is his 13th year with the Patriots, but apparently not his last... "We hope that Julius can continue to play at his present level for the next few years," Meyer said... Still the starting defensive right end, with no serious challengers... Has become a teacher as well, helping youngsters Kenneth Sims and Lester Williams learn the pro game... "Julius is a pro's pro," Meyer said... Always has been... Born April 26, 1948, in Macon, Ga., where he operates a farm in the offseason... A four-year starter at Texas Southern... Pats' second-round pick behind Jim Plunkett in 1971... The only Patriot left from that year.

MIKE HAYNES 30 6-2 195   Cornerback

Back in style... Returned to the Pro Bowl after a one-year absence, meaning he has been named to the all-star game six years out of seven... Four interceptions in '82 leaves him at 28, one behind the Pats' all-time leader, Ron Hall... Might have made the Pro Bowl in '81, if a collapsed lung hadn't forced him out of eight games... Good cover man; and hard to shake one-on-one... Impressive pro debut in '76, intercepting eight passes

NEW ENGLAND PATRIOTS 261

and returning two punts for touchdowns... Hasn't matched those stats since, but Mike Haynes is a hard act to follow, even for Mike Haynes... Born July 1, 1953, in Dennison, Tex.... Two-year All-American at Arizona State... Patriots' No. 1 pick.

COACH RON MEYER: Is he an innovative coach?... How many other coaches would have thought to send a snow-sweeping machine out on the field to clear an area for a game-winning field goal?... It may not have been kosher, but it worked... Ran a hard camp his first year in New England. The veterans moaned, but it paid off... The Patriots made it to the playoffs with a 5-4 record... Has won big wherever he has gone—Nevada-Las Vegas and Southern Methodist, plus six successful seasons as a Purdue assistant and two years as a Dallas Cowboy talent scout... Knows talent, having recruited Otis Armstrong, Darryl Stingley and Dave Butz at Purdue... "Ron is a real class guy who made me what I am as both a player and a person," Stingley said... Born Feb. 17, 1941, in Westerville, Ohio, Meyer went to Purdue himself, as a walk-on... Led the team in minutes played his last two years and was named to the All-Big Ten Academic Team... Recruited Eric Dickerson and Craig James at SMU, which explains the Mustangs' 10-1 record in '81... That's nothing. His 1974 UNLV team was 12-1.

GREATEST QUARTERBACK

Oooh, this is a toughie.

The problem is that the Patriots have never had a quarterback that stood out for any extended period of time. Maybe their greatest quarterback would be best decided by the process of elimination.

Let's see, their first quarterback was Butch Songin. Next.

Ah, the Kentucky Babe, Vito (Babe) Parilli, who holds most of the Patriots' passing records and led them to their only title game, in 1963.

Then there was Tom Sherman, Mike Taliaferro and Joe Kapp. Next, next, next.

How about Jim Plunkett, whose injuries and frustrations in

262 THE COMPLETE HANDBOOK OF PRO FOOTBALL

New England rubbed the luster off his Heisman Trophy? His biggest success came later in Oakland.

That brings us to Steve Grogan, football's best streak passer. When he's on, he's really on. When he's off, he's way off. And he can be both on the same day.

Now he's fighting for his job with Matt Cavanaugh.

The greatest quarterback? Parilli and Grogan, tie. Sorry, Butch.

INDIVIDUAL PATRIOT RECORDS

Rushing

Most Yards Game:	208	Jim Nance, vs Oakland, 1966
Season:	1,458	Jim Nance, 1966
Career:	5,453	Sam Cunningham, 1973-79, 1981-82

Passing

Most TD Passes Game:	5	Babe Parilli, vs Buffalo, 1964
	5	Babe Parilli, vs Miami, 1967
	5	Steve Grogan, vs N.Y. Jets, 1979
Season:	31	Babe Parilli, 1964
Career:	132	Babe Parilli, 1961-67

Receiving

Most TD Passes Game:	3	Billy Lott, vs Buffalo, 1961
	3	Gino Cappelletti, vs Buffalo, 1964
	3	Jim Whalen, vs Miami, 1967
	3	Harold Jackson, vs N.Y. Jets, 1979
Season:	12	Stanley Morgan, 1979
Career:	42	Gino Cappelletti, 1960-70

Scoring

Most Points Game:	28	Gino Cappelletti, vs Houston, 1965
Season:	155	Gino Cappelletti, 1964
Career:	1,130	Gino Cappelletti, 1960-70
Most TDs Game:	3	Billy Lott, vs Buffalo, 1961
	3	Billy Lott, vs Oakland, 1961
	3	Larry Garron, vs Oakland, 1964
	3	Gino Cappelletti, vs Buffalo, 1964
	3	Larry Garron, vs San Diego, 1966
	3	Jim Whalen, vs Miami, 1967
	3	Sam Cunningham, vs Buffalo, 1974
	3	Mack Herron, vs Buffalo, 1974
	3	Sam Cunningham, vs Buffalo, 1975
	3	Harold Jackson, vs N.Y. Jets, 1979
Season:	13	Steve Grogan, 1976
	13	Stanley Morgan, 1979
Career:	49	Sam Cunningham, 1973-79, 1981-82

NEW YORK JETS

TEAM DIRECTORY: Chairman: Leon Hess; Pres.: Jim Kensil; Dir. Player Personnel: Mike Hickey; Dir. Pro Personnel: Jim Royer; Dir. Pub. Rel.: Frank Ramos; Head Coach: Joe Walton. Home field: Shea Stadium (60,000). Colors: Kelly green and white.

Richard Todd should be even better in the Joe Walton era.

SCOUTING REPORT

OFFENSE: The most balanced attack in pro football. The Jets finished fourth in NFL in rushing, seventh in passing and fourth in overall offense. Joe Walton was largely responsible for those statistics as the Jets' offensive coordinator. Now Walton is the Jets' head coach.

"You win with discipline and basics," he said, "but I like to have some fun with the game, too. I think the players enjoy doing something different once in a while and I think the fans enjoy it."

It will be interesting to see what comes out of Walton's bag of tricks now that he has complete control of the bag. How about the single wing?

The Jets have it all on offense; a line that blocks equally well for the run or pass, a quarterback (Richard Todd) who is good, but can get better, a dangerous running back (Freeman McNeil), dangerous receivers (Wesley Walker and Lam Jones) and an imaginative head coach.

And the Jets are deep in receivers (Derrick Gaffney, Bobby Jones) and running backs (Mike Augustyniak, Scott Dierking, Bruce Harper, Dwayne Crutchfield, Marion Barber).

This offense should score lots of points.

DEFENSE: Where have you gone, Joe Klecko? Nowhere. In fact, Klecko is expected to be fully recovered from the knee injury that caused him to miss almost all of last season and left him a shell of himself in the playoffs.

With Klecko as his old self, the Jets' defensive line will again be the best in football. Mark (The Animal) Gastineau, Marty Lyons and Abdul Salaam complete the foursome. Though Gastineau got most of the attention in Klecko's absence last year, Lyons was a better player. He was awesome in the playoffs.

The linebacking is stable with Greg Buttle and the underrated Lance Mehl. Stan Blinka is best against the run, but Bob Crable may be better overall and could push Blinka for a starting job. It's important that New York have a set lineup here, because the design of its defense is geared to the talents of its linebackers.

The secondary, even without Klecko's pass rush, finished third in the AFC with 17 interceptions. Corners Bobby (Big Play) Jackson and Jerry Holmes, and safeties Darrol Ray and Ken Schroy give the Jets their best secondary in years.

KICKING GAME: Despite those crazy wind currents at Shea Stadium, Pat Leahy made 11-of-17 field-goal attempts, including

NEW YORK JETS 265

JETS VETERAN ROSTER

HEAD COACH—Joe Walton. Assistant Coaches—Bill Baird, Ralph Baker, Ray Callahan, Mike Faulkiner, Joe Gardi, Bobby Hammond, Rich Kotite, Larry Pasquale, Jim Ringo.

No.	Name	Pos.	Ht.	Wt.	NFL Exp.	College
60	Alexander, Dan	G	6-4	260	7	Louisiana State
35	Augustyniak, Mike	RB	6-0	220	3	Purdue
31	Barber, Marion	FB	6-3	224	2	Minnesota
83	Barkum, Jerome	TE	6-4	227	12	Jackson State
78	#Bennett, Barry	DT-DE	6-4	257	6	Concordia
—	Bingham, Guy	C-G-T	6-3	255	4	Montana
54	Blinka, Stan	LB	6-2	230	5	Sam Houston State
51	Buttle, Greg	LB	6-3	232	8	Penn State
88	Coombs, Tom	TE	6-3	236	2	Idaho
50	Crable, Bob	LB	6-3	228	2	Notre Dame
55	Crosby, Ron	LB	6-3	227	6	Penn State
45	Crutchfield, Dwayne	FB	6-0	235	2	Iowa State
25	Dierking, Scott	RB	5-10	220	7	Purdue
65	Fields, Joe	C	6-2	253	9	Widener
81	Gaffney, Derrick	WR	6-1	182	6	Florida
99	Gastineau, Mark	DE	6-5	276	5	E. Central State (Okla.)
94	Guilbeau, Rusty	DE	6-4	250	2	McNeese State
42	Harper, Bruce	RB-KR	5-8	177	7	Kutztown State
47	Holmes, Jerry	CB-S	6-2	175	4	West Virginia
40	Jackson, Bobby	CB	5-10	180	6	Florida State
27	Johnson, Jesse	S-CB	6-3	188	4	Colorado
89	Jones, Bobby	WR	5-11	185	6	None
80	Jones, Johnny	WR	5-11	180	4	Texas
73	Klecko, Joe	DE	6-3	269	7	Temple
5	Leahy, Pat	K	6-0	189	10	St. Louis
71	Luscinski, Jim	T-G	6-5	275	2	Norwich
29	Lynn, Johnny	CB	6-0	198	4	UCLA
93	Lyons, Marty	DT	6-5	269	5	Alabama
24	McNeil, Freeman	RB	5-11	225	3	UCLA
56	Mehl, Lance	LB	6-0	235	4	Penn State
77	Neil, Kenny	DE-DT	6-4	244	2	Iowa State
62	Pellegrini, Joe	C-G	6-4	252	2	Harvard
79	Powell, Marvin	T	6-5	271	7	Southern California
15	#Ramsey, Chuck	P	6-2	189	7	Wake Forest
28	Ray, Darrol	S	6-1	206	4	Oklahoma
61	Roman, John	T	6-4	265	8	Idaho State
76	Rudolph, Ben	DT-DE	6-5	270	3	Cal State-Long Beach
10	Ryan, Pat	QB	6-3	210	6	Tennessee
74	Salaam, Abdul	DT	6-3	269	8	Kent State
48	Schroy, Ken	S	6-2	198	7	Maryland
82	Shuler, Mickey	TE	6-3	236	6	Penn State
87	Sohn, Kurt	WR-KR	5-11	176	3	Fordham
45	Springs, Kirk	S-CB	6-0	192	3	Miami (Ohio)
14	Todd, Richard	QB	6-2	207	8	Alabama
70	Waldemore, Stan	G-C-T	6-4	269	6	Nebraska
85	Walker, Wesley	WR	6-0	179	7	California
72	Ward, Chris	T	6-3	267	6	Ohio State
57	Woodring, John	LB	6-2	232	3	Brown

#Unsigned at press time

TOP FIVE DRAFT CHOICES

Rd.	Name	Sel. No.	Pos.	Ht.	Wt.	College
1	O'Brien, Ken	24	QB	6-4	195	Cal-Davis
2	Hector, Johnny	51	RB	5-11	200	Texas A&M
3	*Townsell, Jojo	78	WR	5-8	180	UCLA
4	Howell, Wes	105	TE	6-3	220	California
5	Walker, John	136	DT	6-5	257	Nebraska-Omaha

*Signed with Los Angeles Express of USFL

266 THE COMPLETE HANDBOOK OF PRO FOOTBALL

10 of his last 13 (4-of-5 in the playoffs). Chuck Ramsey's punting (38.5-yard average) leaves a lot to be desired.

The return game? Bruce Harper. Enough said.

THE ROOKIES: Top choice Ken O'Brien wasn't the best known quarterback in the draft, but the California-Davis product has all the tools. Beating out Richard Todd will take time, however. Texas A&M's Johnny Hector gives the Jets their 435th running back on the roster. Watch tight end Wes Howell of California, a basketball player who played one year of football, superbly, in college.

OUTLOOK: The best team in the AFC or, at the worst, one of the top three. If Klecko is, as the Jets say, 100 percent rehabilitated, there is no reason why the Jets shouldn't reach the Super Bowl. If Klecko is OK, and the Jets *don't* play in the Super Bowl, there ought to be an NFL investigation.

JET PROFILES

RICHARD TODD 29 6-2 207   Quarterback

Wha' happened?...His career reached its zenith last year...Then came the AFC championship game in Miami, when he threw five interceptions, including one where he looked A.J. Duhe in the face before throwing him the interception that became a Dolphin TD...Has the ability to be a Super Bowl quarterback if he can overcome those mental lapses back into rookiedom that occasionally slow his growth...Has the arm and the receivers—he only needs the maturity...Rated sixth among NFL passers last year...Born Nov. 19, 1953, in Birmingham, Ala....Last in a series of great quarterbacks to play for Alabama...Jets' No. 1 draft pick in '76...Has pilot's license.

FREEMAN McNEIL 24 5-11 225 — Running Back

Top of the heap... Led all NFL rushers with 786 yards and a 5.2-yard average (40 or more carries)... Doesn't have burner speed, but knows how to run with the football... Has tremendous acceleration and charges into tacklers... That's what happened against the Raiders in the playoffs: he charged into Burgess Owens, but this time he fumbled... Raiders recovered, but New York saved itself with a game-ending interception... In near-depression afterward... A quiet, modest type... Hardly the big-head type... Born April 22, 1959, in Jackson, Miss.... All-time rushing leader at UCLA... Third player taken in the '81 draft... Loves to work on cars... Calls himself a "Volkswagen fanatic."

JOE FIELDS 29 6-2 253 — Center

Self-made player... Started college at Rutgers-Camden, which didn't have a football team, then was persuaded to transfer to Widener, the school Billy (White Shoes) Johnson made famous... Gained 25 pounds between his junior and senior years, when he decided to play pro football... Even then, it wasn't easy... Was drafted in the 14th round in 1975, when the NFL draft lasted 17 rounds, then showed up at the Jets' rookie camp with baby fat... Lifted weights by night and snapped balls to his wife and father by day... It has all paid off: he is one of the best centers in the NFL and a two-time Pro Bowl pick... Born Nov. 14, 1953, in Woodbury, N.J.

WESLEY WALKER 28 6-0 179 — Wide Receiver

The goodbye guy... When he gets a pass in the open, it's goodbye... One of the fastest receivers in football... Caught six touchdown passes last year, giving him 32 in six seasons... Career average is 20 yards per catch... And he's legally blind in one eye... The pros let him pass through the first round before the Jets grabbed him in the second, back in '77... The reason was a knee operation his senior year at California, where he set an NCAA record with an average of 25.7 yards per reception... Sprinter on the Cal track team... Born May 26, 1955, in San Bernardino, Cal.... Moved around as a kid, never spending more than three years at one school, because his father was in the military... Finished high school in Carson, Calif.

MIKE AUGUSTYNIAK 27 6-0 220　　　　Running Back

Call him "Augie"... Name is pronounced Awe-gus-TIN-E-ack... Before any of the Jets could get it down pat, this free agent from Purdue became a starter as a rookie... How the NFL computers missed the NFL's newest human bowling ball is anyone's guess... Perhaps the computers digested the information on Augie, including his squat build, and projected him as a hod carrier... Purdue guessed wrong on him, too... Was a college walk-on who eventually earned a scholarship at Purdue, but only lettered his last two years... Now he's the pride of Leo, Ind., where he was born July 17, 1956... Tremendous heart, great competitor.

MARK GASTINEAU 26 6-5 276　　　　Defensive End

Sad Sack... Goes into body contortions and gyrations when he sacks the quarterbacks... It causes a negative reaction, especially when the quarterback is lying there hurt, so Gastineau has more critics than admirers in the game... The sad thing about all this is that Gastineau doesn't need to put on a show... Would have made the Pro Bowl the last two years, anyway... Fast, strong and aggressive, he looks like an overgrown wide receiver with his lean build... Born Nov. 20, 1956, in Ardmore, Okla.... Transferred from Arizona State to East Central (Okla.) State... Jets drafted him second in '79... The next year, he ripped the facemask off a lineman's helmet with his bare hands.

LANCE MEHL 25 6-3 235　　　　Outside Linebacker

Lance Who?... Lance (Pell) Mehl, that's who... Received national attention for his two second-half interceptions that saved the Jets' playoff win over the Raiders... But Jet officials felt he was deserving of publicity all along... "Lance should be all-pro," said ex-Jets' head coach Walt Michaels. "He's a very intelligent, complete player who leads by example."... Where else would the Jets find this kind of linebacker other than Penn State?... "Mehl may have been as good as any inside linebacker we've ever had here," Penn State coach Joe Paterno said... If that's so, how did Mehl last to the third round of the '80 draft?... Now he's an outside linebacker... Born Feb. 14, 1958, in Bellaire, Ohio.

JOE KLECKO 29 6-3 269   Defensive End

Oooh, was he missed... His knee injury last year—he missed most of the season and limped through the playoffs—didn't help the Jets... When he's right, well, listen to Miami coach Don Shula talk about him and Mark Gastineau: "One's the best in the league, the other is even better. You can put them in any order you want."... Sports Illustrated picked him as its NFL Player of the Year in 1981, after he set a Jets' record with 20½ sacks... Tremendous force against the pass or run... Might be the strongest player in the league... Born Oct. 15, 1943, in Chester, Pa.... Played one year in high school, passed up college for two years to drive a truck... Then went to Temple and was drafted sixth by Jets in '77.

BOBBY JACKSON 26 5-10 180   Cornerback

The Jackson five... Had five interceptions last year to tie for the conference lead... Saved the best for the last, returning an interception 77 yards for a touchdown and running 80 yards with a fumble for another score in the regular-season finale at Minnesota... Tremendously quick, he had the same time in the 40—4.38—as Lam Jones and Wesley Walker in competition to determine the fastest Jet... Isn't noticed much on defense, because of all those other Jet stars, but he has 15 interceptions in five seasons, despite missing most of 1981 with an Achilles problem, calf injury and broken arm... Born Dec. 23, 1956, in Albany, Ga.... Florida State product... Jets' sixth pick in 1978.

GREG BUTTLE 29 6-3 232   Inside Linebacker

The man in the middle... Does everything well, though not spectacularly... Good against the run, good at dropping back into the passing lanes, good leader... Hey, he played at Penn State... Nittany Lions' coach Joe Paterno rates him, Dave Robinson and Jack Ham as the best linebackers ever to play at the school... Didn't drive the NFL scouts wild, however. The Jets found him available in the third round of the '76 draft... Started as a rookie and has gotten better ever since... Born June 20, 1954, in Atlantic City, N.J.... Owns a restaurant called "Buttle's Ground Floor Cafe"... Player rep on the Jets... Sang in barbershop quartet in college... You ought to hear him do "Sweet Adeline."

COACH JOE WALTON: Jets like to hire longtime NFL assistants as head coaches... Walt Michaels spent 14 years as an apprentice before getting his chance... Michaels lost his job last year, not because New York lost to Miami for the conference championship, but because he accused Al Davis of making a phone call to the Jet locker room at halftime of playoff game vs. Raiders... When Michaels complained the next week about the soggy turf in Miami, Jets' president Jim Kensil had enough and canned him... Walton also spent 14 years as an NFL assistant, the last two as the Jets' offensive coordinator and quarterback coach... Brings tranquility, something the Jets sorely need following Michaels' outbursts... Coached with the Giants and Redskins before joining the Jets... Played for the Redskins and Giants in a seven-year NFL career... Y.A. Tittle called him "the best third-down receiver in the game, bar none."... An All-American receiver at Pitt in 1956... Born Dec. 15, 1935, in Beaver Falls, Pa., which was known as Joe Walton's hometown before it became Joe Willie's... His fine offensive mind should have a stabilizing effect on the erratic Richard Todd.

GREATEST QUARTERBACK

Yeah, I know, this one requires thinking. So, here are a few hints. He hated girls, loathed the limelight, threw the football with a slow release, drank only milk and was a stay-at-home kind of guy.

Just kidding. Can't fool you, can I? You knew it was Joe Willie Namath all along. Al Dorow, did you think it was you?

Namath was the New York Jets, was he not? So, how can he not be the Jets' greatest quarterback? He gave them publicity at a time when no one noticed them. It is said, with some degree of accuracy, that Namath saved not only the franchise, but the league as well.

The AFL was stumbling toward obsolescence when Namath arrived, but it went out in a trail of glory after Namath pulled off the upset of upsets—the Super Bowl III defeat of Baltimore.

Namath was a story wherever he went, on the field and off. There was Bachelors Three. The Fu Manchu mustache. The Super Bowl victory guarantee. The movie motorcyclist. The Oscar presenter.

Now he's L'il Abner, with a new Daisy Mae every night.

INDIVIDUAL JET RECORDS

Rushing

Most Yards Game:	180	Matt Snell, vs Houston, 1964
Season:	1,005	John Riggins, 1975
Career:	5,135	Emerson Boozer, 1966-75

Passing

Most TD Passes Game:	6	Joe Namath, vs Baltimore, 1972
Season:	26	Al Dorow, 1960
	26	Joe Namath, 1967
Career:	170	Joe Namath, 1965-76

Receiving

Most TD Passes Game:	3	Art Powell, vs Denver, 1960
	3	Don Maynard, vs Denver, 1963
	3	Don Maynard, vs San Diego, 1967
	3	Don Maynard, vs Miami, 1968
	3	Rich Caster, vs Baltimore, 1972
	3	Wesley Walker, vs Detroit, 1982
Season:	14	Art Powell, 1960
	14	Don Maynard, 1965
Career:	88	Don Maynard, 1960-72

Scoring

Most Points Game:	19	Jim Turner, vs Buffalo, 1968
Season:	145	Jim Turner, 1968
Career:	697	Jim Turner, 1964-70
Most TDs Game:	3	Art Powell, vs Denver, 1960
	3	Don Maynard, vs Denver, 1963
	3	Emerson Boozer, vs Denver, 1967
	3	Emerson Boozer, vs Miami, 1967
	3	Don Maynard, vs San Diego, 1967
	3	Billy Joe, vs Boston, 1968
	3	Don Maynard, vs Miami, 1968
	3	Emerson Boozer, vs Buffalo, 1972
	3	Rich Caster, vs Baltimore, 1972
	3	Emerson Boozer, vs New England, 1972 (twice)
	3	John Riggins, vs San Diego, 1974
	3	Kevin Long, vs Buffalo, 1978
	3	Kevin Long, vs Detroit, 1979
	3	Wesley Walker, vs Detroit, 1982
Season:	14	Art Powell, 1960
	14	Don Maynard, 1965
	14	Emerson Boozer, 1972
Career:	88	Don Maynard, 1960-72

PITTSBURGH STEELERS

TEAM DIRECTORY: Chairman: Art Rooney; Pres.: Daniel Rooney; VP: John McGinley; VP: Art Rooney Jr.; Dir. Player Personnel: Dick Haley; Dir. Publicity: Joe Gordon; Head Coach: Chuck Noll. Home field: Three Rivers Stadium (59,000). Colors: Black and gold.

SCOUTING REPORT

OFFENSE: As Terry Bradshaw goes, so go... You've heard this said many times about many players, but it's never more applicable than here. When Bradshaw has a big year, so do the Steelers.

He grasped the Steelers' new offense—less Franco Harris, more Bradshaw—late last season and led the team into the playoffs for the first time in three years.

Things looked in order for 1983, then Lynn Swann retired and Jim Smith signed for a million dollars and the city of Mobile to play for the Birmingham Stallions of the USFL. So who does Bradshaw have for wide receivers beside John Stallworth? Backups Calvin Sweeney and—surprise!—Greg Hawthorne, who failed at running back. Bradshaw would rather have Smith.

Harris is running less and blocking and catching more to save his 33-year-old legs for Jim Brown's record. Therefore, the competition at halfback between Frank Pollard, the two-year incumbent (4.4-yard average), and Walter Abercrombie, last year's top pick who missed the entire 1982 season with a knee injury, becomes even more vital.

The line looks great, better than the overall offensive picture.

DEFENSE: Somewhere, Mean Joe Greene is smiling. The Steel Curtain was found in some warehouse and has been draped across the Steeler defensive line again.

Last year, the front four led a charge that resulted in 34 sacks, second-best in the NFL to the Raiders' 38. Steel Curtain II gave up 84 yards per game rushing, the stingiest mark in the league.

Defensive end Tom Beasley and nose tackle Gary Dunn tied for the club lead with six sacks. John Goodman improved against the run, but his sack total dropped to two. Rookies Edmund Nelson and Keith Willis, a free agent, played a lot a year ago. Bob Kohrs will act again as a swingman, though he is most effective as a stand-up linebacker coming on the blitz. End Keith Gary, the Steelers' No. 1 pick in '81, is back from Canada.

Last year's move to the 3-4 was like Thanksgiving dinner to

PITTSBURGH STEELERS 273

Now that Swann's flown, John Stallworth is getting his due.

STEELERS VETERAN ROSTER

HEAD COACH—Chuck Noll. Assistant Coaches—Ron Blackledge, Tony Dungy, Dennis Fitzgerald, Dick Hoak, Jon Kolb, Tom Moore, Woody Widenhofer.

No.	Name	Pos.	Ht.	Wt.	NFL Exp.	College
34	Abercrombie, Walter	RB	5-11	201	2	Baylor
1	Anderson, Gary	K	5-11	156	2	Syracuse
65	Beasley, Tom	DE-NT	6-5	248	6	Virginia Tech
54	Bingham, Craig	LB	6-2	211	2	Syracuse
47	Blount, Mel	CB	6-3	205	14	Southern
23	Bohannon, Fred	S-CB	6-0	201	2	Mississippi Valley State
71	Boures, Emil	C-G	6-1	252	2	Pittsburgh
12	Bradshaw, Terry	QB	6-3	210	14	Louisiana Tech
79	#Brown, Larry	T	6-4	270	13	Kansas
56	Cole, Robin	LB	6-2	220	7	New Mexico
5	Colquitt, Craig	P	6-1	182	5	Tennessee
77	Courson, Steve	G	6-1	260	6	South Carolina
89	Cunningham, Bennie	TE	6-5	260	8	Clemson
45	Davis, Russell	RB	6-1	231	4	Michigan
55	Donnalley, Rick	C-G	6-2	257	2	North Carolina
67	#Dunn, Gary	NT	6-3	260	7	Miami
20	French, Ernest	S	5-11	195	2	Alabama A&M
—	Gary, Keith	DE	6-3	257	1*	Oklahoma
95	Goodman, John	DE	6-6	250	3	Oklahoma
17	Goodson, John	P	6-3	204	2	Texas
32	Harris, Franco	RB	6-2	225	12	Penn State
27	Hawthorne, Greg	RB-WR	6-2	225	5	Baylor
53	Hinkle, Bryan	LB	6-1	214	2	Oregon
62	Ilkin, Tunch	T	6-3	253	4	Indiana State
29	Johnson, Ron	S	5-10	200	6	Eastern Michigan
90	Kohrs, Bob	LB-DE	6-3	245	3	Arizona State
58	Lambert, Jack	LB	6-4	220	10	Kent State
50	Little, David	LB	6-1	220	3	Florida
16	Malone, Mark	QB	6-4	223	4	Arizona State
57	Merriweather, Mike	LB	6-2	215	2	Pacific
64	Nelson, Edmund	NT-DE	6-3	263	2	Auburn
—	Newton, Tom	RB	6-0	220	7	California
66	Peterson, Ted	T	6-5	256	7	Eastern Illinois
44	Pollard, Frank	RB	5-10	210	4	Baylor
87	Rodgers, John	TE	6-2	220	2	Louisiana Tech
36	Ruff, Guy	LB	6-1	215	2	Syracuse
31	#Shell, Donnie	S	5-11	190	10	South Carolina State
82	#Stallworth, John	WR	6-2	191	10	Alabama A&M
18	Stoudt, Cliff	QB	6-4	218	7	Youngstown State
85	Sweeney, Calvin	WR	6-2	190	4	Southern California
83	Sydnor, Willie	WR-KR	5-11	170	2	Syracuse
38	Thornton, Sidney	RB	5-11	230	7	NW State (La.)
51	Toews, Loren	LB	6-3	220	11	California
42	Washington, Anthony	CB	6-1	204	3	Fresno State
41	Washington, Sam	S	5-8	180	2	Mississippi Valley State
52	Webster, Mike	C	6-1	255	10	Wisconsin
93	Willis, Keith	DE	6-1	251	2	Northeastern
37	Wilson, Frank	TE-RB	6-2	233	2	Rice
73	Wolfley, Craig	G	6-1	265	4	Syracuse
49	Woodruff, Dwayne	CB	5-11	198	5	Louisville
22	Woods, Rick	S-KR	6-0	196	2	Boise State

*Played in CFL in 1982
#Unsigned at press time

TOP FIVE DRAFT CHOICES

Rd.	Name	Sel. No.	Pos.	Ht.	Wt.	College
1	Rivera, Gabriel	21	DT	6-3	280	Texas Tech
2	Capers, Wayne	52	WR	6-3	200	Kansas
3	Seabaugh, Todd	79	LB	6-4	220	San Diego State
4	Metcalf, Isaac	106	DB	6-2	193	Baylor
5	Skansi, Paul	133	WR	5-11	190	Washington

linebacker Robin Cole, who got extra helpings of playing time and had his best season yet. Jack Lambert and Loren Toews are set inside, with Bryan Hinkle and Mike Merriweather fighting it out for the other linebacker spot.

With a full season at free safety under his belt, Ron Johnson will make the secondary—Mel Blount, Dwayne Woodruff and Donnie Shell included—even stronger.

KICKING GAME: No more hoops. Punter Craig Colquitt missed last season after tearing his right achilles tendon playing basketball. Reports are that he is coming back, which means his replacement, John Goodson (40.4-yard average) may be gone. Kicker Gary Anderson made 10-of-12 field-goal attempts, including 5-of-6 from outside the 40.

THE ROOKIES: Señor Sack. First-rounder Gabriel Rivera, Texas Tech nose tackle, can chase down quarterbacks or running backs. His only problem is girth; if he can control that, he could be all-pro down the road. Kansas wide receiver Wayne Capers has a chance to start as rookie. A longshot pick, No. 133 in the draft, is Washington receiver Paul Skansi, not fast, but great on patterns.

OUTLOOK: If the Steeler defense keeps coming on, if Hawthorne builds on last season's debut at wide receiver, if Bradshaw hasn't lost the touch, if Harris hasn't lost his legs, the Steelers may win the AFC Central. It just might happen, all you Terrible Towel wavers.

STEELER PROFILES

TERRY BRADSHAW 34 6-3 210   **Quarterback**

A comeback year for Bradshaw?... When has he had a bad year?... Heck, he threw 22 touchdown passes in '81... Yeah, but the Steelers didn't make the playoffs in 1981 and they did in '82, and it's always the quarterback who makes that possible, right?... Bradshaw's 17 touchdown throws last year tied him with San Diego's Dan Fouts and San Francisco's Joe Montana for the NFL lead... Completed 52.9 percent for 1,768 yards and suffered 11 interceptions... If any quarterback can lift a team to the heights by himself, it is Bradshaw... Has great strength and accuracy in his arm even now... When he's on, so

276 THE COMPLETE HANDBOOK OF PRO FOOTBALL

are the Steelers... Born Sept. 2, 1948, in Shreveport, La.... Starting his 14th year... Attended Louisiana Tech.

FRANCO HARRIS 33 6-2 225   Running Back

Francophiles, take note... Your man is closing in on greatness... Needs 294 yards to pass O.J. Simpson and move into second place on the all-time rushing list... The leader, Jim Brown, is 1,469 yards away... With two normal seasons and no injuries, Franco will become the career leader... Already has nearly 250 more carries than Brown, which makes his durability even more remarkable... Or is it Harris' desire to step out of bounds instead of taking a hit that has preserved him?... Now, now, let's not be nasty... If he didn't step out of bounds, maybe he *wouldn't* be here today... Rushing total is 10,943 yards... Born March 7, 1950, in Fort Dix, N.J.... NFL's most famous Army brat... Gained 604 yards last year (4.3 per carry)... Attended Penn State.

JOHN STALLWORTH 31 6-2 191   Wide Receiver

The Shadow knows... The Shadow is this man, who has been following Lynn Swann for years... With Swann retired, he can receive the recognition he so rightfully deserves... Caught seven touchdown passes last year, including a 74-yard bomb... Was selected to the Pro Bowl for the second straight year, catching seven passes to lead both teams... With 38 receptions and 159 yards, he will replace Swann as the all-time club leader... At his best in big games... Caught 73-yard touchdown pass in Super Bowl XIV, then made another remarkable catch to set up clinching score... Born July 15, 1952, in Tuscaloosa, Ala., went to Alabama A&M.

LARRY BROWN 34 6-4 270   Offensive Tackle

Good things don't happen overnight... It took him 12 years to reach the Pro Bowl, even though he wasn't all that bad the previous 11... One of those rare football players who changed from tight end to tackle without leaving the starting lineup... As a tight end, he was used as a receiver about every other eclipse... His main purpose was to block for Franco Harris, and it still is—only now he doesn't have to worry about running out for passes... A dues-paying member of the Steelers' Beautiful Biceps

Club... Pittsburgh is Muscle Beach East, and those bulging biceps on the offensive line have had a lot to do with Harris' success... Born June 16, 1949, in Jacksonville, Fla.... Played at Kansas.

MIKE WEBSTER 31 6-1 255   Center

Webster's dictionary starts off with "a" for all-pro... Voted all-pro for the fifth consecutive year and played in the Pro Bowl for the fifth year running, too... The NFL is teeming with great young centers now, but he still is looked upon as the center's center... Not only is he destructive to defensive linemen, he is indestructible... Has played in 145 straight games. The Steelers' record is 182 straight, held by his predecessor, Ray Mansfield... Played the final four games of the '80 season and the Pro Bowl with cartilage damage in his knee that required surgery later... Born March 18, 1952, in Tomahawk, Wis.... Steelers' fifth-round pick, out of Wisconsin, in 1974.

LOREN TOEWS 31 6-3 220   Inside Linebacker

OK, who can pronounce it?... No, dummy, not Toes. Taves!... But don't feel badly, it took him 10 years to find his identity... For nine years, he played every linebacker position for the Steelers, but never as a starter, unless someone was hurt... Pittsburgh fans began to pronounce Toews "Tough," as in luck... Then the Steelers went to a four-linebacker alignment and he was told he had a chance to start, if he would move from the outside, where he played the majority of the time, to next to Lambert... He did and became a fulltime starter, playing even more physically than before... Born Nov. 3, 1951, in Dinuba, Cal.... Played at California... Steelers' eighth choice in 1973.

JACK LAMBERT 31 6-4 220   Inside Linebacker

Search and destroy... That has been his style of play through nine NFL seasons, though his role changed somewhat when Pittsburgh changed from a 4-3 to 3-4 defense... This restricted his responsibilities somewhat, though it didn't prevent him from making the Pro Bowl for the eighth straight year... If he is selected after this season, he will become the first linebacker to be chosen nine successive times... Any other questions about his greatness?... Had only one interception a year ago, making his career total 26, but now that he has the hang of the 3-4, look out!... Born July 8, 1952, in Mantua, Ohio... Great player at Kent State and even greater with Steelers, who drafted him second in 1974.

DWAYNE WOODRUFF 26 5-11 198   Cornerback

Quiz time... Who was the Steelers' Most Valuable Player last year?... No, not Terry Bradshaw, Franco Harris, Mike Webster or Donnie Shell... Jack Lambert? Guess again... It was this man, of the pass-defense firm of Blount, Shell, Woodruff and Johnson... Picked off five passes to share the conference lead... Three of those happened on clutch situations in close games... Second quiz... Who plays cornerback in Pittsburgh with Mel Blount?... That's right, it's this guy. You're learning... Born Feb. 18, 1957, in Bowling Green, Ky.... Changed from running back and wide receiver to cornerback his junior year at Louisville... Steelers' sixth pick in 1979.

DONNIE SHELL 31 5-11 190   Strong Safety

There is no stronger strong safety in football *or* at least none who hits as strongly... But he isn't just another mountain of muscle... Intercepted five passes last year to tie for the AFC lead and increase his career total to 31... Over the last four years, his interception totals read: five, seven, five, five. The numbers of bruises he has left on NFL tight ends are even more impressive... He's got credentials, too... Named all-pro and went to Pro Bowl the last five years... Has master's degree in guidance and counseling... Manager of commercial properties in Columbia, S.C., in offseason... Born Aug. 26, 1952, in Whitmire, S.C.... South Carolina State graduate... Steelers signed him as a free agent in 1974.

GREG HAWTHORNE 26 6-2 225   Wide Receiver

The great experiment... Hawthorne bombed out as a running back in three seasons... Chuck Noll decided to try him as a wide receiver because of his good hands and speed... He caught 12 passes for a 15.2-yard average and three touchdowns, including a 46-yard reception ... With Jim Smith now with Birmingham of the USFL, Hawthorne has an excellent chance to start and resurrect a sagging NFL career... Born Sept. 5, 1956, in Fort Worth, Tex.... Standout at Baylor, though broken hip ended his senior year after three games, starting a pattern... Steelers drafted him No. 1 in '79 to match with Franco Harris in backfield, but minor injuries and Hawthorne's reluctance to seize the opportunity made him a receiver.

COACH CHUCK NOLL: Look who's back!... After a two-year absence from the playoffs, the Steelers returned to the playoffs, though briefly... San Diego beat Pittsburgh in the first round, 31-28, on a beaut of a comeback... May have the magic again, but it's doubtful that he will weave the same spell he cast over the league in the '70s... Four Super Bowl victories in four appearances may be too much for anyone to duplicate... But the sleeping giant in Pittsburgh is awake, and that's enough to get attention in Cincinnati... Pittsburgh does have a problem: Noll's expertise in the early years has lost its sharpness. That's the primary reason why the Steelers fell on hard times... He's playing with mainly the same bodies, which means the club may be up to a one-year run, but nothing beyond... The younger Steelers can't seem to beat out the older Steelers... His teaching ability—his main strength as a coach—is being tested now as it hasn't been since his early years in Pittsburgh... Born Jan. 5, 1932, in Cleveland... Dayton graduate who played seven years for the Cleveland Browns, then retired to get into coaching... His 14-year career record is 123-75-1 in regular season and 14-5 in postseason play.

GREATEST QUARTERBACK

We all know that Terry Bradshaw is the greatest Pittsburgh quarterback. He has four Super Bowl rings, so who's going to argue?

But the Steelers have played football for 50 years, and Bradshaw has been with them only the last 13. Who were the other Steeler passers, Bradshaw's competition?

Remember Warren Heller? Back in the single-wing days, Heller led the Steelers in passing their first two years, 1934-35. He completed a combined 40 passes in 153 attempts, numbers which wouldn't get ol' Warren into the Continental League these days. However, he also led Pittsburgh in rushing twice.

After Heller came Ed Matesic, Ed Fiske, Frank Filchock, Hugh McCullough, Bill Patterson, Boyd Brumbaugh, Bullet Bill Dudley, Johnny Clement, Joe Geri, Chuck Ortmann, Jim Finks, Ted Marchibroda, Bobby Layne, Rudy Bukich, Kent Nix and Dick Shiner, among others.

Layne is Pittsburgh's best quarterback other than Bradshaw, although Bobby had his best years in Detroit. Bradshaw holds all the Pittsburgh passing records and now he's trying to put them out of sight.

INDIVIDUAL STEELER RECORDS

Rushing

Most Yards Game:	218	John Fuqua, vs Philadelphia, 1970
Season:	1,246	Franco Harris, 1975
Career:	10,943	Franco Harris, 1972-82

Passing

Most TD Passes Game:	5	Terry Bradshaw, vs Atlanta, 1981
Season:	28	Terry Bradshaw, 1978
Career:	210	Terry Bradshaw, 1970-82

Receiving

Most TD Passes Game:	4	Roy Jefferson, vs Atlanta, 1968
Season:	12	Buddy Dial, 1961
Career:	51	Lynn Swann, 1974-82

Scoring

Most Points Game:	24	Ray Mathews, vs Cleveland, 1954
	24	Roy Jefferson, vs Atlanta, 1968
Season:	123	Roy Gerela, 1973
Career:	770	Roy Gerela, 1971-78
Most TDs Game:	4	Ray Mathews, vs Cleveland, 1954
	4	Roy Jefferson, vs Atlanta, 1968
Season:	14	Franco Harris, 1976
Career:	93	Franco Harris, 1972-82

SAN DIEGO CHARGERS

TEAM DIRECTORY: Pres.: Eugene Klein; GM: John Sanders; Asst. to Pres.: Jack Teele; Asst. GM: Tank Younger; Dir. Pub. Rel.: Rick Smith; Head Coach: Don Coryell. Home field: Jack Murphy Stadium (52,675). Colors: Blue, gold and white.

Will Dan Fouts become NFL's first 5,000-yard QB this year?

SCOUTING REPORT

OFFENSE: Take the Thundering Herd, Four Horsemen, Fielding H. "Point-a-Minute" Yost, The Galloping Ghost and Don Hutson, throw them together and what have you got? Half as good an offense as the San Diego Chargers.

Last year, the Chargers averaged 25 first downs, 32 points and 450 yards a game, improving on their 1981 statistics, a feat that no one in the NFL thought possible.

San Diego can throw the football better than anyone. San Francisco threw more passes and Cincinnati completed more than San Diego last year, but the Chargers amassed nearly 50 more passing yards per game (325.2 average) than the runnerup 49ers.

The Chargers just might surpass last year's totals, as Dan Fouts takes aim at the NFL's first 5,000-yard passing season. At his disposal, he has the game's best tight end, Kellen Winslow, and its most exciting receiver, Wes Chandler, along with Charlie Joiner and the unsung Eric Sievers.

Unless Fouts' protection up front grows too old, not many teams will stop him. Oh, we mustn't forget Chuck Muncie and James Brooks—the Chargers' running game finished 11th in the league.

DEFENSE: Take The Little Sisters of the Poor and what have you got? Twice as good a defense as the Chargers. And the Little Sisters fight off more passes than the Chargers.

San Diego ranked 28th in pass defense. Dead last, despite a new defensive coordinator, Tom Bass, and two new safeties, Bruce Laird and Tim Fox. And now they've added Ken Greene from St. Louis.

The Chargers haven't recovered from the loss of pass-rusher Fred Dean two years ago or the weight problem of Louie Kelcher, who may have eaten himself out of football. Without these two, the Charger front four had only 19 sacks last year. Gary Johnson and Leroy Jones, who underwent offseason knee surgery and is doubtful, are all that's left from that once-impressive line.

The linebacking isn't earth-shaking, either. Woody Lowe's a good one, but Linden King, Cliff Thrift and David Lewis don't cut it. Lewis, a one-time Pro Bowler who was brought over from Tampa Bay, was a real flop in 1982.

The secondary, without the aid of a strong rush, is highly vulnerable. The Charger offense averages 32 points per game, sure, but the Charger defense yields 24 per game. San Diego's offense has to score faster than San Diego's defense can give up points and that's no small challenge.

SAN DIEGO CHARGERS 283

CHARGERS VETERAN ROSTER

HEAD COACH—Don Coryell. Assistant Coaches—Tom Bass, Marv Braden, Earnel Durden, Dave Levy, Al Saunders, Jerry Smith, Jim Wagstaff, Chuck Weber, Ernie Zampese.

No.	Name	Pos.	Ht.	Wt.	NFL Exp.	College
91	Ackerman, Richard	DT	6-4	254	2	Memphis State
27	Allen, Jeff	CB	5-11	194	3	California-Davis
37	Bauer, Hank	RB	5-10	200	7	California-Lutheran
42	Bell, Ricky	RB	6-1	216	7	Southern California
6	Benirschke, Rolf	K	6-1	175	7	California-Davis
50	Bradley, Carlos	LB	6-0	226	3	Wake Forest
21	Brooks, James	RB	5-9	177	3	Auburn
7	Buford, Maury	P	6-0	185	2	Texas Tech
25	Cappelletti, John	FB	6-1	215	9	Penn State
89	Chandler, Wes	WR	5-11	183	6	Florida
77	Claphan, Sam	T	6-6	267	3	Oklahoma
82	Duckworth, Bobby	WR	6-3	197	2	Arkansas
76	Ferguson, Keith	DE	6-5	241	3	Ohio State
14	#Fouts, Dan	QB	6-3	210	11	Oregon
48	Fox, Tim	S	6-0	190	8	Ohio State
75	Gissinger, Andrew	T	6-5	279	2	Syracuse
—	Goode, Don	LB	6-2	231	9	Kansas
—	Greene, Ken	S	6-3	205	6	Washington State
43	Gregor, Bob	S	6-2	190	3	Washington State
—	Henderson, Reuben	CB	6-1	200	3	San Diego State
88	Holohan, Pete	TE	6-4	240	3	Notre Dame
40	Jodat, Jim	FB	5-11	208	7	Carthage
79	Johnson, Gary	DT	6-2	252	9	Grambling
18	Joiner, Charlie	WR	5-11	180	15	Grambling
68	#Jones, Leroy	DE	6-8	270	8	Norfolk State
74	Kelcher, Louis	DT	6-5	310	9	Southern Methodist
57	King, Linden	LB	6-5	245	6	Colorado State
30	#Laird, Bruce	S	6-1	195	12	American International
53	Lewis, David	LB	6-4	245	7	Southern California
64	Loewen, Chuck	G-T	6-4	264	4	South Dakota
51	Lowe, Woodrow	LB	6-0	226	8	Alabama
11	Luther, Ed	QB	6-3	202	4	San Jose State
62	Macek, Don	C-G	6-2	260	8	Boston College
60	McKnight, Dennis	C-G	6-3	253	2	Drake
24	McPherson, Miles	S	6-0	175	2	New Haven
—	Moore, Jeff	WR	6-1	188	4	Tennessee
46	Muncie, Chuck	RB	6-3	220	8	California
52	Preston, Ray	LB	6-0	220	4	Syracuse
56	Rush, Bob	C-T	6-5	270	6	Memphis State
87	Scales, Dwight	WR	6-2	182	7	Grambling
66	Shields, Billy	T	6-8	284	9	Georgia
85	Sievers, Eric	TE	6-4	235	3	Maryland
59	#Thrift, Cliff	LB	6-1	230	5	E. Central State (Okla.)
70	#Washington, Russ	T	6-7	295	16	Missouri
67	White, Ed	G	6-2	280	15	California
63	Wilkerson, Doug	G	6-3	262	14	North Carolina Central
29	Williams, Mike	CB	5-10	186	9	Louisiana State
80	Winslow, Kellen	TE	6-6	240	5	Missouri
90	#Woodcock, John	DE	6-3	257	7	Hawaii
49	Young, Andre	S	6-0	203	2	Louisiana Tech
90	Young, Wilbur	DT	6-6	285	13	William Penn (Iowa)

#Unsigned at press time

TOP FIVE DRAFT CHOICES

Rd.	Name	Sel. No.	Pos.	Ht.	Wt.	College
1	Smith, Billy Ray	5	LB	6-3	228	Arkansas
1	*Anderson, Gary	20	WR	6-1	180	Arkansas
1	Byrd, Gill	22	DB	5-1	192	San Jose State
4	Walters, Danny	95	DB	6-2	191	Arkansas
6	**Johnson, Trumaine	141	WR	6-3	185	Grambling

*Signed with Tampa Bay of USFL
**Playing for Chicago Blitz of USFL

284 THE COMPLETE HANDBOOK OF PRO FOOTBALL

KICKING GAME: With Brooks returning kickoffs and punts, the Chargers aren't hurting. With Rolf Benirschke taking the placements (16-of-22 field-goal attempts as the NFL's leading scorer), the Chargers aren't hurting. With Maury Buford punting (41.3-yard average, but two punts blocked), they're hurting a little.

THE ROOKIES: Billy Ray Smith, the fifth overall pick in the draft, is quick, strong and can blitz, but the Arkansas inside linebacker is weak on pass coverage, making him a perfect addition to the team. Arkansas wide receiver Gary Anderson, 20th overall, decided against the Chargers in favor of the USFL's Tampa Bay Bandits. Talented San Jose State cornerback Gill Byrd, the Chargers' third first-round pick, is coming off knee surgery.

OUTLOOK: The Chargers always will be a Super Bowl threat with Air Coryell, but unless something is done about that porous defense, they will never make it. There is too much pressure each week on the offense. It catches up to San Diego in the playoffs, when defense takes over.

CHARGER PROFILES

DAN FOUTS 32 6-3 210   Quarterback

The charge in the Chargers... Became a free agent after the 1982 season... No other NFL team was willing to meet his asking price of $7 million for five years... At press time, he was still negotiating a new contract with the Chargers... Without him as pilot, Air Coryell just wouldn't be the same... Fouts, without a doubt, is the catalyst that makes things happen... Passed for more than 4,000 yards three straight years, then 2,883 during the strike season (61.8 percent, 17 TDs, 11 INTs)... Born June 10, 1951, in San Francisco... Chargers' No. 3 pick in '73 after starring at Oregon.

SAN DIEGO CHARGERS

CHUCK MUNCIE 30 6-3 220   Running Back

Let the trade winds blow... There were rumors he would be traded to the 49ers, though he did nothing in 1982 to suggest the Chargers should get rid of him... Rushed for 569 yards (4.1 per carry), scored eight touchdowns on the ground and a ninth on a reception, caught 25 passes overall... Yet trouble follows him like a rain cloud... Was named as having a drug problem by Don Reese in last year's controversial Sports Illustrated article... Has admitted he underwent treatment for drugs... It's too bad he abused that incredible talent... Most people in football feel he could be one of the all-time greats... Born March 17, 1953, in Uniontown, Pa.... Played at California... Broke into NFL with Saints.

KELLEN WINSLOW 25 6-6 240   Tight End

Killer Kellen... The way he finishes off tacklers—and entire teams—is deadly... Pittsburgh had Chargers beaten in playoff game last year until his touchdown catch buried the Steelers... His playoff performance against Miami in 1981 was a classic... A tight end who caught five touchdown passes in one game... Last year, he led the AFC with 54 receptions. Two years ago, his 88 receptions led the league. Three years ago, his 89 catches were a record for NFL tight ends... No wonder many consider him the most valuable property in the league... Born Nov. 5, 1957, in St. Louis... Good but not great career at Missouri... No. 1 pick in '79.

WES CHANDLER 27 5-11 186   Wide Receiver

From all-flustered to all-pro... Three-plus years in New Orleans is enough to fluster anyone... Traded to San Diego in '81, he exploded a year later for 49 catches, nine touchdowns, and the NFL's only 1,000-yard receiving performance (1,032) during the strike season... Had an amazing year, as well, for the types of catches he made... His acrobatics reminded Charger fans of John Jefferson... And no one in Bordertown thought the Chargers would ever find anyone to compare to Jefferson... A tremendously versatile athlete who ran and caught with elan at Florida... Born Aug. 22, 1956, in New Smyrna Beach, Fla.... Saints' No. 1 pick in '78.

CHARLIE JOINER 35 5-11 183 Wide Receiver

September song... To some, this means the end... To him it means the start of another football season... Turns 36 in October, one month into his 15th NFL season... Chargers are planning a party for him, when he retires at 50... The way he keeps playing, who knows how long he'll go on?... His 36 receptions last year left him with 531, ranking him second behind Philadelphia's Harold Carmichael (551) among active receivers... One thing he didn't do last year that he has done 47 times in his career was get into the end zone... Knowing Joiner, he'll be so embarrassed by that fact that he may score 10 times this year... Born Oct. 14, 1947, in Many, La.... Grambling product... Also played with Houston and Cincinnati in pros.

ROLF BENIRSCHKE 28 6-1 175 Kicker

Kicks for critters... Donates $50 to the San Diego Zoo for every field goal he makes and, combined with matching donations from Charger fans, he raised $160,000 for animals two years ago... Led the NFL in scoring last year with 80 points... His courageous story is well-known by now... Overcame an intestinal ailment that caused him to lose 50 pounds from a thin frame and nearly led to his death... Has had four operations, the last one this winter to fit him with a special "bag" for the disposal of bodily wastes... Goes on with life as if nothing has happened... Tremendous human being... Born Feb. 7, 1955, in Boston... Attended California-Davis... Raiders' 12th pick in 1977.

DOUG WILKERSON 36 6-3 262 Guard

On a roll... Waited 11 years for a Pro Bowl invitation, now has hit it three times in a row... At 36, he could be contented and call it quits... But the Chargers keep getting close to the Super Bowl and he'd love to help the team over the hump... Not that he hasn't been helpful all these years, keeping Dan Fouts on his feet... Isn't playing like an oldtimer... Has a powerful upper body, suited for pass-blocking... Legs are still young, which makes him a good open-field blocker... Was originally drafted No. 1 by Houston in 1970, then was traded to San Diego for Willie Frazier... Born March 27, 1947, in Fayetteville, N.C.... Went to North Carolina Central.

SAN DIEGO CHARGERS 287

ED WHITE 36 6-2 280 — Guard

Moose on the move... One of the strongest players in football... For several years, he was the NFL wrist-wrestling champion. Most of his matches lasted about a second... All-pro a handful of times, a Pro Bowler four times... Perfect for San Diego's style of pass offense, which is designed for Dan Fouts to get rid of the ball in three or four seconds... Simply shoves his man once at the line of scrimmage, knocking him into New Mexico. By the time he recovers, it's the next down... His only problem is his weight. He has played at close to 300 pounds... Born June 4, 1947, in San Diego... All-American defensive tackle at California... Drafted second by Minnesota in 1969, then traded to Chargers in 1978.

GARY JOHNSON 31 6-3 252 — Defensive Tackle

Big hands, bigger talent... Fourth straight Pro Bowl appearance last year by Johnson, one of football's best defensive tackles... Excellent against the run, even better against the pass... Led NFL with 17½ sacks in '80, a Charger record... All-pro several times... Got the nickname "Big Hands" in eighth-grade gym class, when an instructor said, "Keep your big hands off my basketball."... But, the truth is, he first palmed a basketball in nursery school... Born Aug. 31, 1952, in Shreveport, La., he grew up in Bossier City, then went to Grambling... Chargers drafted him No. 1 in 1975... Wife, Alice, is "Little Hands" and son, Gary Jr., is "Tiny Hands"... That's it?... Look, ma, no more hands.

TIM FOX 29 6-0 190 — Free Safety

Still sly as a... Intercepted four passes last year, brought them back a combined 103 yards, third-best INT return-yardage figure in the NFL... There were rumors in New England the year before that he was washed up... But the little guy with the big heart and let-it-all-hang-out tackling style proved his critics wrong... "He's not a good athlete, he's a great athlete," former Charger assistant coach Larrye Weaver said last year... Has little regard for opponents or his own body... "He really gets after people," said Charger assistant Jim Wag-

COACH DON CORYELL: How will his nerves stand another season if the Chargers don't reach the Super Bowl?... His nervous nature is legendary... Not only is he unsure where the game plan is, he begins to lisp... During one Monday night game, Frank Gifford said, "Don Coryell doesn't even know if he is in San Diego."... Chargers have been to the playoffs the last four years, twice reaching the AFC championship game before being eliminated... This must be extremely difficult on their coach, who is tightly wound, as they say... Before each training camp, he disappears into the mountains on a back-packing trip to clear away the cobwebs... One week into camp, he's back to normal, looking like an amnesia victim who can't remember who he is, where he is or how he got there... But don't be fooled: he is a born winner... In 25 years of coaching at the collegiate and professional levels, he has had one losing season... Born Oct. 17, 1924, in Seattle... A defensive back at Washington... Coached at Whittier and San Diego State... Posted 42-27 record with the St. Louis Cardinals (1973-77) before joining the Chargers in 1978... His four-year record in San Diego is 47-22.

GREATEST QUARTERBACK

Want to start an argument at Bully's in San Diego? Stand up and shout, "Dan Fouts is the best quarterback the Chargers have ever had." You can bet some gray-haired fella at the end of the bar will look up from his Scotch and shout back: "Hey, kid, ever heard of Hadl?"

This is the argument that rages among the most ardent Charger fans. Fouts has put together four extraordinary years. No quarterback in football can generate such offensive firepower. By the time he is done, Fouts may rewrite the record book.

At this juncture of his career, Fouts' statistics are comparable to John Hadl's, perhaps a tad better. Hadl could breathe fire, too, although his forte, unlike Fouts' medium-deep throws, was the bomb.

Both men had competition for their jobs. Hadl had to beat out Tobin Rote. Fouts had to beat out Johnny Unitas (in his last hurrah) and Jesse Freitas. Both men had great receivers. Hadl had Lance Alworth and Gary Garrison. Fouts had John Jefferson, Charlie Joiner, Kellen Winslow and Wes Chandler.

So who wins? Fouts, at the wire. But don't say it at Bully's.

INDIVIDUAL CHARGER RECORDS

Rushing

Most Yards Game:	206	Keith Lincoln, vs Boston, 1964
Season:	1,162	Don Woods, 1974
Career:	4,963	Paul Lowe, 1960-67

Passing

Most TD Passes Game:	6	Dan Fouts, vs Oakland, 1981
Season:	33	Dan Fouts, 1981
Career:	201	John Hadl, 1962-72

Receiving

Most TD Passes Game:	5	Kellen Winslow, vs Oakland, 1981
Season:	14	Lance Alworth, 1965
Career:	81	Lance Alworth, 1962-70

Scoring

Most Points Game:	30	Kellen Winslow, vs Oakland, 1981
Season:	118	Rolf Benirschke, 1980
Career:	500	Lance Alworth, 1962-70
Most TDs Game:	5	Kellen Winslow, vs Oakland, 1981
Season:	19	Chuck Muncie, 1981
Career:	83	Lance Alworth, 1962-70

SEATTLE SEAHAWKS

TEAM DIRECTORY: Managing Gen. Partner: Elmer Nordstrom; Dir. Oper.: Mike McCormack; GM: John Thompson; Dir. Player Personnel: Dick Mansperger; Dir. Pub. Rel.: Don Andersen; Dir. Publicity: Gary Wright; Head Coach: Chuck Knox. Home field: Kingdome (64,757). Colors: Blue, green and silver.

SCOUTING REPORT

OFFENSE: The Seahawks aren't going to fly without a standout running back. Without one, they are dead ducks.

Sherman Smith led Seattle in rushing last year, but it was a dubious honor. No team leader in the NFL had as few yards as Smith's 202. The one-time Sherman tank hasn't been the same since knee surgery. Rookie Curt Warner brightens the picture that includes journeyman halfbacks Theotis Brown and Horace Ivory. The fullback scene is uninspiring: Don Doornink, David Hughes and ex-Ram Cullen Bryant.

Jim Zorn likely will be named No. 1 quarterback over Dave Krieg on the basis of experience, but Zorn must prove he can hold the job after two mediocre seasons.

Seattle has the two biggest tight ends on one team in Mike Tice and Pete Metzelaars, who are both 6-7. Tice is the better blocker and Metzelaars the better receiver. Ex-Colt Roger Carr started the last two games at wide receiver, with Steve Largent. Paul Johns and Byron Walker are capable backups.

From left to right in the offensive interior line, it's Ron Essink, Edwin Bailey, John Yarno, ex-Colt Robert Pratt and Steve August. There isn't an all-star in the bunch.

DEFENSE: The Seahawks likely will switch to a 3-4 defense, which was new coach Chuck Knox's alignment in Buffalo. This may be a handicap to Jacob Green, because pass rushers generally do better in a four-man front. But it should be a boon to the other Seahawks.

For instance, Michael Jackson was out of place as a middle linebacker in a 4-3, because he's too small. He'll return to the outside with Bruce Scholtz, the 6-6 second-round pick who started every game as a rookie. Keith Butler moves from the outside to the middle. The other inside linebacker will be Joe Norman or Shelton Robinson.

The odd man out in the front three is Robert Hardy, who'll play in four-man situations. Green and impressive second-year

SEATTLE SEAHAWKS 291

man Jeff Bryant are the ends and Manu Tuiasosopo is the nose tackle, a perfect position for his smallish frame and active style.

The secondary, which permitted a league-low four touchdown passes, returns intact. The corners are Dave Brown and Keith Simpson. Kenny Easley and John Harris were designated as safe-

Jim Zorn must prove there's still life in that left arm.

SEAHAWKS VETERAN ROSTER

HEAD COACH—Chuck Knox. Assistant Coaches—Tom Catlin, George Dyer, Chick Harris, Ralph Hawkins, Ken Meyer, Steve Moore, Ray Prochaska, Rusty Tillman, Joe Vitt.

No.	Name	Pos.	Ht.	Wt.	NFL Exp.	College
12	Adkins, Sam	QB	6-2	214	7	Wichita State
63	#Anderson, Fredell	DE	6-4	245	4	Prairie View
76	August, Steve	T	6-5	254	7	Tulsa
65	Bailey, Edwin	G	6-4	265	3	South Carolina State
82	Bell, Mark	DE	6-4	240	4	Colorado State
68	Boyd, Dennis	T	6-6	255	6	Oregon State
22	Brown, Dave	CB	6-2	190	9	Michigan
30	Brown, Theotis	RB	6-2	225	5	UCLA
31	Bryant, Cullen	FB	6-1	235	11	Colorado
77	Bryant, Jeff	DE	6-5	260	2	Clemson
53	Butler, Keith	LB	6-4	225	6	Memphis State
71	Campbell, Jack	T	6-5	277	2	Utah
87	Carr, Roger	WR	6-2	195	10	Louisiana Tech
33	Doornink, Dan	FB	6-3	210	6	Washington State
25	Dufek, Dan	S	6-0	195	7	Michigan
66	Dugan, Bill	G	6-4	271	3	Penn State
45	Easley, Kenny	S	6-3	206	3	UCLA
64	Essink, Ron	T	6-6	254	4	Grand Valley State
50	Flones, Brian	LB	6-1	228	3	Washington State
56	Gaines, Greg	LB	6-3	220	2	Tennessee
78	Graham, David	DE	6-6	250	2	Morehouse
79	Green, Jacob	DE	6-3	247	4	Texas A&M
75	Hardy, Robert	DT	6-2	250	5	Jackson State
44	Harris, John	S	6-2	200	6	Arizona State
46	Hughes, David	FB	6-0	220	3	Boise State
32	#Ivory, Horace	RB	6-0	198	7	Oklahoma
55	Jackson, Michael	LB	6-1	220	5	Washington
85	Johns, Paul	WR	5-11	170	3	Tulsa
27	Johnson, Greggory	S	6-1	188	3	Oklahoma State
9	Johnson, Norm	K	6-2	193	2	UCLA
26	#Justin, Kerry	CB	5-11	175	6	Oregon State
62	Kauahi, Kani	C	6-2	260	2	Hawaii
17	Krieg, Dave	QB	6-1	185	4	Milton
60	Kuehn, Art	C	6-3	255	8	UCLA
37	Lane, Eric	RB	6-0	195	3	Brigham Young
80	Largent, Steve	WR	5-11	184	8	Tulsa
48	McAlister, Ken	S	6-5	220	2	San Francisco
88	Metzelaars, Pete	TE	6-7	240	2	Wabash
72	Nash, Joe	DT	6-3	250	2	Boston College
52	Norman, Joe	LB	6-1	220	4	Indiana
61	#Pratt, Robert	G	6-4	250	10	North Carolina
57	Robinson, Shelton	LB	6-2	233	2	North Carolina
81	Sawyer, John	TE	6-2	230	8	Southern Mississippi
58	Scholtz, Bruce	LB	6-6	240	2	Texas
42	Simpson, Keith	CB	6-1	195	6	Memphis State
47	Smith, Sherman	RB	6-4	225	8	Miami (Ohio)
59	Thomas, Rodell	LB	6-2	225	3	Alabama State
86	Tice, Mike	TE	6-7	250	3	Maryland
74	Tuiasosopo, Manu	DT	6-3	252	5	UCLA
89	Walker, Byron	WR	6-4	190	2	Citadel
8	West, Jeff	P	6-2	220	8	Cincinnati
70	White, Mike	DT	6-5	266	5	Albany State
54	Williams, Eugene	LB	6-1	220	2	Tulsa
51	Yarno, John	C	6-5	251	7	Idaho
10	Zorn, Jim	QB	6-2	200	8	Cal Poly-Pomona

#Unsigned at press time

TOP FIVE DRAFT PICKS

Rd.	Name	Sel. No.	Pos.	Ht.	Wt.	College
1	Warner, Curt	3	RB	5-11	195	Penn State
5	Castor, Chris	123	WR	6-0	160	Duke
6	Gipson, Reginald	150	RB	6-2	200	Alabama A&M
7	Merriman, Sam	177	LB	6-3	225	Idaho
8	Hernandez, Matt	210	T	6-6	260	Purdue

SEATTLE SEAHAWKS

ties last year, but under Knox, Easley will be "strong" and Harris "free."

KICKING GAME: Jeff West averaged 38.2 yards per punt, barely above his career average, which means his days in Seattle are numbered. Kicker Norm Johnson missed his first three field goals, causing Seattle fans to scream for Efren Herrera, but made 10 of his last 11. Paul Johns was third in AFC punt returns.

THE ROOKIES: The league's worst ground game gets well in a hurry with Warner, the Penn State running back, a tough carrier and fine receiver. Warner was the third player taken in the draft. Seattle didn't draft again until the fifth round, picking up Duke wide receiver Chris Castor, who's slow and built like a broom—a skinny Steve Largent.

OUTLOOK: With the addition of Knox, any outlook is improved. The defense has a lot of talent, but will need a year to learn the 3-4. The offense has less talent, unless Knox has a few trades under his hat. Realistically, Seattle shouldn't be expected to frighten teams for another year.

SEAHAWK PROFILES

JIM ZORN 30 6-2 200   **Quarterback**

Need someone to play the viola in a symphony orchestra? Zorn can do that... Need someone to fill in as a morning disc jockey? Zorn can do that too... Speed-skating, commencement speaker, community service... There is little Zorn can't do... What the Seahawks are looking for from Zorn, however, is solid quarterback play, something he hasn't provided consistently the last two years... Zorn has been in and out of the lineup, looking erratic at best... He dropped from a 59.4 percent completion mark in '81 to 51.4 last year... With a new coach and a new outlook in Seattle, there is hope he can pick up the pieces and start anew himself... Born May 10, 1953, in Whittier, Cal.... Played at Cal Poly-Pomona... Signed as a free agent by Dallas in '75, then released.

DAVE KRIEG 24 6-1 185   Quarterback

Football's Uncle Miltie... Kreig attended Milton College... You know, in the Illini-Badger Conference... Kreig was a four-year starter at Milton, Conference Player of the Year... He lettered three years as a baseball player and served on the Milton student senate... Signed as a free agent by Seattle in '80... Krieg has aspirations to become the Seahawk quarterback... Took over the final three games of the '81 season after Zorn broke an ankle... Played sparingly last year (49-for-78, 62.8 percent)... Has thrown nine career touchdown passes compared to seven interceptions, not bad stats for one who came to the NFL from the NAIA... Born Oct. 20, 1958, in Iola, Wis.... Finished seventh among NAIA passers as a Milton senior.

KENNY EASLEY 24 6-3 206   Safety

Pro Bowl his second year... Greatness his third?... This could be the season when Easley becomes all-pro... The potential is there; boy, is there potential!... Three-year consensus All-American, four-year all-conference at UCLA ... He knows how to "hawk" passes; four interceptions last year in nine games. He can run, he can hit. He passed out concussions like trading stamps in college... OK, we're exaggerating here, but Easley is a punishing hitter... The only Seahawk to make the Pro Bowl last year... Born Jan. 15, 1959, in Chesapeake, Va.... Quarterback and defensive back in high school... Played JV basketball at UCLA... Drafted No. 1 by Seattle in '81, became an instant starter.

JOHN HARRIS 27 6-2 200   Safety

No safety with this safety... Harris intercepted 10 passes two years ago, high in the AFC, then followed with four more last fall, one off the AFC lead... Has 26 interceptions in five-and-a-half seasons... Safer to throw against the Seattle corners than safeties Easley and Harris... The latter has returned two interceptions for touchdowns, yet hasn't received a nod from the Pro Bowl folks... Born June 13, 1956, at Fort Benning, Ga.... Valedictorian of his high school class in Miami... Two-year All-Western Athletic Conference choice at Arizona State, where he intercepted 16 passes and also returned punts... Graduated with political science degree... Seattle found him in the seventh round in '78.

STEVE LARGENT 28 5-11 184 — Wide Receiver

Elmer's Glue... Largent's hands are like glue, but he is also the adhesive that holds the Seattle passing game together... It is amazing what he has accomplished in seven seasons: 399 receptions and 49 touchdowns... If Largent can keep this up for another seven seasons, he might be football's all-time pass-receiving leader... He doesn't look especially fast, but he can outrun many cornerbacks... His forte, though, is putting on moves that will leave the defensive back's head in the Space Needle and his feet in Lake Washington... Bum Phillips hasn't forgiven himself for letting Largent get away from Houston in '76—for an eighth-round pick, at that... Born Sept. 28, 1954, in Tulsa, Okla.... Played at Tulsa.

JACOB GREEN 26 6-3 247 — Defensive End

Sack happy... Green set a club record with 12 quarterback sacks two years ago, but didn't have a chance to break the single-season record last year because of the short season... Watch his smoke this year!... Green plays the run well enough, but he really gets after the quarterback... Many NFL people believe a player's best productivity comes between his fourth and eighth seasons. This is Green's fourth year... Already the club's career leader in sacks, he'll now attempt to run that record out of sight... Born Jan. 21, 1957, in Pasadena, Tex., home of Gilley's... All-American at Texas A&M, where he had 38 career sacks... Seattle picked him first in '80, to bag quarterbacks... He has.

DAN DOORNINK 27 6-3 210 — Running Back

Calling Dr. Doornink!... He has spent the last few offseasons in medical school at the University of Washington... His father and brother are both physicians... Young Dan may become the Seahawks' team doctor someday ... Right now, he's more interested in being their rushing leader... He ran for only 178 yards last year (4.0), but added another 176 yards on

22 receptions. No touchdowns...Not the fastest back in the league, he still had one run of 46 yards and a reception of 44 yards...Born Feb. 1, 1956, in beautiful, downtown Wapato, Wash....Lettered in three sports at Wapato High before picking up four letters in football at Washington State...Spent the '78 season with the Giants, who drafted him seventh, before joining Seattle.

JEFF BRYANT 23 6-5 260   Defensive End

Jeff Who?...When the Seahawks took Bryant early in the first round, that was the reaction...There were questions about the Seahawks' mentality...It was suggested they change their names to the Seattle Condors ...But the Seahawks knew what they were doing...Bryant became a rookie starter and an immediate force on the front four...He is projected as a future star...The folks at Clemson could have told the NFL that...First-team All-Atlantic Coast Conference pick as a senior, when Clemson (12-0) won the national championship...Hey, the Tigers didn't do it with only offense...Born May 22, 1960, in Atlanta...Strongman who bench-presses 425 pounds, dead-lifts 680 pounds.

MICHAEL JACKSON 26 6-1 220   Outside Linebacker

Pac-Man...Don't leave anything around, like an errant pass or a loose football, because Pac-Man will gobble it up...Jackson is Pac-Man...He has a great nose—er, mouth—for the football...He was a quarterback and safety at Pasco (Wash.) High, which meant he had to gobble down some chow to get up to 220 pounds and play linebacker at Washington...He gobbled up an interception late in the Rose Bowl that preserved the Huskies' upset victory over Michigan on New Year's Day, 1978...The Seahawks drafted him in the third round in '79, and he has led the team in tackles most of the time since...Born July 15, 1957, in Pasco...Picked off two passes last year...Dedicated them to Ms. Pac-Man, whoever she is.

SEATTLE SEAHAWKS

KEN McALISTER 23 6-5 220 **Linebacker-Tight End**

May get the NFL's Woody Allen Award: "Sleeper" of the Year...McAlister was a tremendous high-school linebacker in Oakland, but decided to play basketball in college and started four years at the University of San Francisco just before the program caved in...He averaged 12.4 points and 5.4 rebounds as a senior, but the NBA wasn't interested...So McAlister decided to try football again...The Seahawks signed him as a free agent, playing him on special teams as a rookie, while fattening his bones to make him a linebacker or possibly a tight end...McAlister is a great athlete; had he played football instead of basketball in college, he might have been a first-round pick...Born April 15, 1960, in Oakland.

COACH CHUCK KNOX: Where Knox goes, winning follows...The Seahawks are not that far away...They have a young, aggressive defense that might be ready to wreak havoc on the AFC West...The questions are on offense, but Knox is good at finding answers...In nine full seasons as an NFL head coach, he has had seven seasons with 10 or more victories...He took over a disastrous situation in Buffalo and put the Bills in the playoffs twice...Before that, he produced five straight division champions with the Los Angeles Rams ...Expect a revitalized Seahawk team, which disintegrated under Jack Patera's scowl...Mike McCormack replaced Patera in midseason and got the Seahawks back to 4-5. McCormack could have had the coaching job this year if he wanted, but he had had his fill in Philadelphia and Baltimore...He preferred to remain Seattle's general manager and talked Knox into coming west ...Knox couldn't work any more with Buffalo management, so the move back to the West Coast was an easy decision to make...Born April 27, 1932, in Sewickley, Pa....Played tackle for Juniata (Pa.) College...No longer the conservative coach ...NFL record is 91-50-1.

Original Seahawk Steve Largent has caught 49 TD passes.

GREATEST QUARTERBACK

Seattle's greatest quarterback is almost its only quarterback. There is no question Jim Zorn is the best quarterback the Seahawks have produced, because until 1982, he was the only quarterback in the franchise's short history. Then along came Dave Krieg, and the quarterback position became a two-man hunt. Zorn will try to reclaim his job in 1983.

Zorn has been one of the league's most exciting quarterbacks for most of his seven years. His running and passing have thrilled Seahawk fans and thrown opponents out of whack trying to contain him.

At one time, Zorn's versatility was so important to the Seahawks because the threat of his running forced defenses to play loose. Now 30, he isn't as quick anymore, and he'll have to win back the quarterback job with mainly his arm.

Quarterbacks have slumps, so Zorn may come back.

INDIVIDUAL SEAHAWK RECORDS

Rushing

Most Yards Game:	152	Sherman Smith, vs Chicago, 1978
Season:	805	Sherman Smith, 1978
Career:	3,429	Sherman Smith, 1976-82

Passing

Most TD Passes Game:	4	Steve Myer, vs Tampa Bay, 1977
	4	Jim Zorn, vs Buffalo, 1977
	4	Jim Zorn, vs San Diego, 1977
Season:	20	Jim Zorn, 1979
Career:	100	Jim Zorn, 1976-82

Receiving

Most TD Passes Game:	2	Steve Largent (seven times, most recently vs Oakland, 1979)
	2	Sam McCullum, vs St. Louis, 1976
	2	Dan Doornink, vs Green Bay, 1981
Season:	10	Steve Largent, 1977
Career:	49	Steve Largent, 1976-82

Scoring

Most Points Game:	18	David Sims, vs New York Jets, 1978
	18	David Sims, vs Cleveland, 1978
	18	Sherman Smith, vs Cleveland, 1979
Season:	100	Efren Herrera, 1979
Career:	331	Efren Herrera, 1978-81
Most TDs Game:	3	David Sims, vs New York Jets, 1978
	3	David Sims, vs Cleveland, 1978
	3	Sherman Smith, vs Cleveland, 1979
Season:	15	David Sims, 1978
Career:	49	Steve Largent, 1976-82

OFFICIAL 1982 NFL STATISTICS

(Compiled by Elias Sports Bureau)

RUSHING

TOP TEN RUSHERS

	Att	Yards	Avg	Long	TD
McNeil, Freeman, Jets	151	786	5.2	48	6
Dorsett, Tony, Dall.	177	745	4.2	t99	5
Franklin, Andra, Mia.	177	701	4.0	t25	7
Allen, Marcus, Raiders	160	697	4.4	53	11
Sims, Billy, Det.	172	639	3.7	29	4
Cribbs, Joe, Buff.	134	633	4.7	t62	3
Collins, Anthony, N.E.	164	632	3.9	54	1
Johnson, Pete, Cin.	156	622	4.0	21	7
Harris, Franco, Pitt.	140	604	4.3	21	2
Payton, Walter, Chi.	148	596	4.0	26	1

NFC - INDIVIDUAL RUSHERS

	Att	Yards	Avg	Long	TD
Dorsett, Tony, Dall.	177	745	4.2	t99	5
Sims, Billy, Det.	172	639	3.7	29	4
Payton, Walter, Chi.	148	596	4.0	26	1
Anderson, Ottis, St.L.	145	587	4.0	64	3
Andrews, William, Atl.	139	573	4.1	t19	5
Tyler, Wendell, Rams	137	564	4.1	54	9
Riggins, John, Wash.	177	553	3.1	19	3
Rogers, George, N.O.	122	535	4.4	38	3

t = Touchdown
Leader based on most yards gained

NFL STATISTICS 301

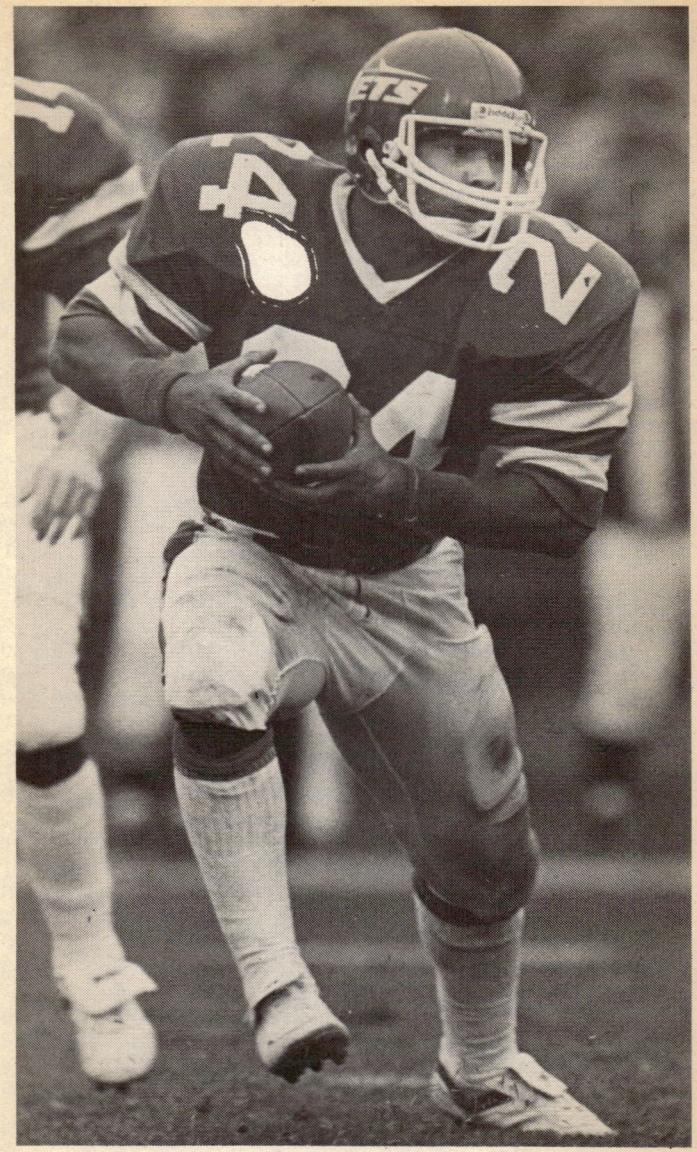

Jet Freeman McNeil led the NFL in rushing last year.

302 THE COMPLETE HANDBOOK OF PRO FOOTBALL

	Att	Yards	Avg	Long	TD
Montgomery, Wilbert, Phil.	114	515	4.5	t90	7
Brown, Ted, Minn.	120	515	4.3	30	1
Ivery, Eddie Lee, G.B.	127	453	3.6	32	9
Woolfolk, Butch, Giants	112	439	3.9	18	2
Wilson, Wayne, N.O.	103	413	4.0	20	3
Wilder, James, T.B.	83	324	3.9	47	3
Riggs, Gerald, Atl.	78	299	3.8	37	5
Moore, Jeff, S.F.	85	281	3.3	19	4
Morris, Wayne, St.L.	84	274	3.3	11	4
Guman, Mike, Rams	69	266	3.9	15	2
Springs, Ron, Dall.	59	243	4.1	t46	2
Owens, James, T.B.	76	238	3.1	14	0
Harrington, Perry, Phil.	56	231	4.1	37	1
Carver, Mel, T.B.	70	229	3.3	t13	1
Ellis, Gerry, G.B.	62	228	3.7	29	1
Suhey, Matt, Chi.	70	206	2.9	15	3
Carpenter, Rob, Giants	67	204	3.0	23	1
Washington, Joe, Wash.	44	190	4.3	40	1
Mitchell, Stump, St.L.	39	189	4.8	t32	1
Ring, Billy, S.F.	48	183	3.8	11	1
Rogers, Jimmy, N.O.	60	178	3.0	32	2
Rodgers, Del, G.B.	46	175	3.8	13	1
Cain, Lynn, Atl.	54	173	3.2	8	1
Harmon, Clarence, Wash.	38	168	4.4	20	1
Williams, Doug, T.B.	35	158	4.5	14	2
Theismann, Joe, Wash.	31	150	4.8	16	0
Nelson, Darrin, Minn.	44	136	3.1	18	0
Bussey, Dexter, Det.	48	136	2.8	10	0
Lomax, Neil, St.L.	28	119	4.3	19	1
Montana, Joe, S.F.	30	118	3.9	21	1
Galbreath, Tony, Minn.	39	116	3.0	12	1
Robinson, Bo, Atl.	19	108	5.7	16	0
McMahon, Jim, Chi.	24	105	4.4	11	1
Lofton, James, G.B.	4	101	25.3	t83	1
Newsome, Tim, Dall.	15	98	6.5	25	1
Danielson, Gary, Det.	23	92	4.0	16	0
White, Danny, Dall.	17	91	5.4	21	0
Thomas, Jewerl, Rams	16	80	5.0	11	0
Chatman, Cliff, Giants	22	80	3.6	13	2
Newhouse, Robert, Dall.	14	79	5.6	27	1
Gajan, Hokie, N.O.	19	77	4.1	12	0
Kramer, Tommy, Minn.	21	77	3.7	t18	3
Cooper, Earl, S.F.	24	77	3.2	9	0
Jones, Bert, Rams	11	73	6.6	17	0
Williams, Vince, S.F.	20	68	3.4	12	0
King, Horace, Det.	18	67	3.7	25	0
Hipple, Eric, Det.	10	57	5.7	20	0

NFL STATISTICS 303

	Att	Yards	Avg	Long	TD
Young, Rickey, Minn.	16	49	3.1	11	1
Morris, Joe, Giants	15	48	3.2	7	1
McClendon, Willie, Chi.	17	47	2.8	13	0
Meade, Mike, G.B.	14	42	3.0	19	0
Harris, Leroy, Phil.	17	39	2.3	14	2
Wonsley, Otis, Wash.	11	36	3.3	7	0
Merkens, Guido, N.O.	9	30	3.3	19	0
Giamonna, Louie, Phil.	11	29	2.6	8	1
Jensen, Jim, G.B.	9	28	3.1	10	0
Brunner, Scott, Giants	19	27	1.4	10	1
Redden, Barry, Rams	8	24	3.0	7	0
Hill, Tony, Dall.	1	22	22.0	22	0
Peoples, George, Dall.	7	22	3.1	7	0
Gentry, Dennis, Chi.	4	21	5.3	9	0
Monk, Art, Wash.	7	21	3.0	14	0
Tyler, Toussaint, N.O.	10	21	2.1	11	0
Huckleby, Harlan, G.B.	4	19	4.8	7	0
Dickey, Lynn, G.B.	13	19	1.5	11	0
Wehrli, Roger, St.L.	1	18	18.0	t18	1
Cromwell, Nolan, Rams	1	17	17.0	t17	1
Kane, Rick, Det.	7	17	2.4	6	0
Jefferson, John, G.B.	2	16	8.0	11	0
Thompson, Leonard, Det.	2	16	8.0	13	0
Coleman, Greg, Minn.	1	15	15.0	15	0
Perry, Leon, Giants	3	14	4.7	15	0
Harrell, Willard, St.L.	4	14	3.5	8	0
Heater, Larry, Giants	3	13	4.3	8	0
Eddings, Floyd, Giants	2	12	6.0	16	0
Hodge, Floyd, Atl.	2	11	5.5	11	0
Walker, Rick, Wash.	2	11	5.5	6	0
Easley, Walt, S.F.	5	11	2.2	5	0
Johnson, Butch, Dall.	1	9	9.0	9	0
Strong, Ray, Atl.	4	9	2.3	4	0
Jaworski, Ron, Phil.	10	9	0.9	6	0
Holmes, Jack, N.O.	2	8	4.0	5	0
Green, Roy, St.L.	6	8	1.3	13	0
Harper, Roland, Chi.	3	7	2.3	8	0
Lawrence, Amos, S.F.	5	7	1.4	4	0
DuPree, Billy Joe, Dall.	1	6	6.0	t6	1
Jackson, Wilbur, Wash.	4	6	1.5	2	0
Bright, Leon, Giants	1	5	5.0	5	0
Dils, Steve, Minn.	1	5	5.0	5	0
Giaquinto, Nick, Wash.	1	5	5.0	5	0
Hoover, Mel, Phil.	1	5	5.0	5	0
Miller, Willie, Rams	1	5	5.0	5	0
Jackson, Alfred, Atl.	1	4	4.0	4	0
Thomas, Calvin, Chi.	5	4	0.8	3	0

304 THE COMPLETE HANDBOOK OF PRO FOOTBALL

	Att	Yards	Avg	Long	TD
Bartkowski, Steve, Atl.	13	4	0.3	10	1
Alexander, Robert, Rams	1	3	3.0	3	0
Nichols, Mark, Det.	1	3	3.0	3	0
Moorehead, Emery, Chi.	2	3	1.5	6	0
Morton, Michael, T.B.	2	3	1.5	2	0
Ferragamo, Vince, Rams	4	3	0.8	2	1
Campfield, Billy, Phil.	1	2	2.0	2	0
Thompson, Aundra, N.O.	1	2	2.0	2	0
Redwine, Jarvis, Minn.	2	2	1.0	2	0
Battle, Ron, Rams	1	1	1.0	1	0
Giles, Jimmy, T.B.	1	1	1.0	1	0
Groth, Jeff, N.O.	1	1	1.0	1	0
Rubick, Rob, Det.	1	1	1.0	t1	1
Evans, Vince, Chi.	2	0	0.0	6	0
Stachowicz, Ray, G.B.	2	0	0.0	0	0
Hogeboom, Gary, Dall.	3	0	0.0	0	0
House, Kevin, T.B.	1	-1	-1.0	-1	0
LeMaster, Frank, Phil.	1	-1	-1.0	-1	0
Nehemiah, Renaldo, S.F.	1	-1	-1.0	-1	0
Watts, Rickey, Chi.	1	-1	-1.0	-1	0
Cosbie, Doug, Dall.	1	-2	-2.0	-2	0
LeCount, Terry, Minn.	1	-3	-3.0	-3	0
Stabler, Ken, N.O.	3	-4	-1.3	0	0
Scott, Lindsey, N.O.	1	-4	-4.0	-4	0
Solomon, Freddie, S.F.	1	-4	-4.0	-4	0
Scott, Fred, Det.	1	-6	-6.0	-6	0
Waddy, Billy, Rams	2	-11	-5.5	5	0

AFC - INDIVIDUAL RUSHERS

	Att	Yards	Avg	Long	TD
McNeil, Freeman, Jets	151	786	5.2	48	6
Franklin, Andra, Mia.	177	701	4.0	t25	7
Allen, Marcus, Raiders	160	697	4.4	53	11
Cribbs, Joe, Buff.	134	633	4.7	t62	3
Collins, Anthony, N.E.	164	632	3.9	54	1
Johnson, Pete, Cin.	156	622	4.0	21	7
Harris, Franco, Pitt.	140	604	4.3	21	2
Muncie, Chuck, S.D.	138	569	4.1	27	8
Campbell, Earl, Hou.	157	538	3.4	22	2
Pruitt, Mike, Clev.	143	516	3.6	17	3
Brooks, James, S.D.	87	430	4.9	t48	6
Leaks, Roosevelt, Buff.	97	405	4.2	17	5

NFL STATISTICS 305

	Att	Yards	Avg	Long	TD
van Eeghen, Mark, N.E.	82	386	4.7	17	0
Delaney, Joe, K.C.	95	380	4.0	36	0
Willhite, Gerald, Den.	70	347	5.0	23	2
McMillan, Randy, Balt.	101	305	3.0	13	1
Parros, Rick, Den.	77	277	3.6	14	1
King, Kenny, Raiders	69	264	3.8	21	2
Winder, Sammy, Den.	67	259	3.9	18	1
White, Charles, Clev.	69	259	3.8	t18	3
Dixon, Zachary, Balt.	58	249	4.3	32	1
Jackson, Billy, K.C.	86	243	2.8	18	3
Pollard, Frank, Pitt.	62	238	3.8	18	2
Nathan, Tony, Mia.	66	233	3.5	15	1
Dickey, Curtis, Balt.	66	232	3.5	25	1
Woodley, David, Mia.	36	207	5.8	29	2
Alexander, Charles, Cin.	64	207	3.2	18	1
Smith, Sherman, Sea.	63	202	3.2	19	0
Brown, Curtis, Buff.	41	187	4.6	19	0
Doornink, Dan, Sea.	45	178	4.0	46	0
Augustyniak, Mike, Jets	50	178	3.6	16	4
Hadnot, James, K.C.	46	172	3.7	25	0
Tatupu, Mosi, N.E.	30	168	5.6	26	0
Franklin, Cleveland, Balt.	43	152	3.5	19	0
Brown, Theotis, Sea.	53	141	2.7	17	2
Dierking, Scott, Jets	38	130	3.4	11	1
Harper, Bruce, Jets	20	125	6.3	40	0
Zorn, Jim, Sea.	15	113	7.5	35	1
Hughes, David, Sea.	30	106	3.5	13	0
Abercrombie, Walter, Pitt.	21	100	4.8	34	2
Vigorito, Tom, Mia.	19	99	5.2	t33	1
Manning, Archie, N.O.-Hou.	13	85	6.5	24	0
Anderson, Ken, Cin.	25	85	3.4	t12	4
Weathers, Robert, N.E.	24	83	3.5	18	1
Pagel, Mike, Balt.	19	82	4.3	32	1
Cappelletti, John, S.D.	22	82	3.7	17	0
Preston, Dave, Den.	19	81	4.3	13	0
Crutchfield, Dwayne, Jets	22	78	3.5	8	1
Davis, Russell, Pitt.	24	72	3.0	9	0
Hawthorne, Greg, Pitt.	15	68	4.5	11	0
Miller, Cleo, Clev.	16	61	3.8	17	0
Edwards, Stan, Hou.	15	58	3.9	8	0
Fuller, Steve, K.C.	10	56	5.6	12	0
Hawkins, Frank, Raiders	27	54	2.0	11	2
Hill, Eddie, Mia.	13	51	3.9	13	0
Ivory, Horace, Sea.	13	51	3.9	27	1
Ferguson, Joe, Buff.	16	46	2.9	13	1
Sipe, Brian, Clev.	13	44	3.4	12	0
Grogan, Steve, N.E.	9	42	4.7	19	1

THE COMPLETE HANDBOOK OF PRO FOOTBALL

	Att	Yards	Avg	Long	TD
Craft, Donald, Hou.	18	42	2.3	10	3
Kenney, Bill, K.C.	13	40	3.1	12	0
Griffin, Archie, Cin.	12	39	3.3	t10	1
Moore, Booker, Buff.	16	38	2.4	9	0
Nielsen, Gifford, Hou.	9	37	4.1	9	0
Poole, Nathan, Den.	7	36	5.1	20	0
Thornton, Sidney, Pitt.	6	33	5.5	13	1
Chandler, Wes, S.D.	5	32	6.4	21	0
Diana, Richard, Mia.	8	31	3.9	7	0
Stoudt, Cliff, Pitt.	11	28	2.5	8	0
DeBerg, Steve, Den.	8	27	3.4	t6	1
Swann, Lynn, Pitt.	1	25	25.0	25	0
Marshall, Henry, K.C.	3	25	8.3	16	0
Barber, Marion, Jets	8	24	3.0	4	0
Hooks, Roland, Buff.	5	23	4.6	9	0
Pruitt, Greg, Raiders	4	22	5.5	13	0
Kofler, Matt, Buff.	2	21	10.5	12	0
Cunningham, Sam, N.E.	9	21	2.3	4	0
Bledsoe, Curtis, K.C.	10	20	2.0	5	0
Barnwell, Malcolm, Raiders	2	18	9.0	14	0
Curtis, Isaac, Cin.	3	15	5.0	8	0
Willis, Chester, Raiders	6	15	2.5	5	0
Whittington, Arthur, Buff.	7	15	2.1	4	0
Armstrong, Adger, Hou.	8	15	1.9	5	0
Bennett, Woody, Mia.	9	15	1.7	5	0
Hall, Dino, Clev.	2	14	7.0	13	0
Bailey, Harold, Hou.	1	13	13.0	13	0
Harris, Duriel, Mia.	1	13	13.0	13	0
Branch, Cliff, Raiders	2	10	5.0	7	0
Butler, Raymond, Balt.	3	10	3.3	10	0
Bradshaw, Terry, Pitt.	8	10	1.3	6	0
Stallworth, John, Pitt.	1	9	9.0	9	0
Casper, Dave, Hou.	2	9	4.5	8	0
Largent, Steve, Sea.	1	8	8.0	8	0
Stark, Rohn, Balt.	1	8	8.0	8	0
Fouts, Dan, S.D.	9	8	0.9	9	1
Herrmann, Mark, Den.	3	7	2.3	t6	1
Jodat, Jim, S.D.	3	7	2.3	3	0
Thompson, Delbert, K.C.	4	7	1.8	4	0
Bell, Ricky, S.D.	2	6	3.0	4	0
Plunkett, Jim, Raiders	15	6	0.4	10	0
Ferguson, Vagas, N.E.	1	5	5.0	5	0
Toler, Ken, N.E.	1	4	4.0	4	0
Cowan, Larry, Mia.-N.E.	1	3	3.0	3	0
Holt, Robert, Buff.	1	3	3.0	3	0
Schlichter, Art, Balt.	1	3	3.0	3	0
Wright, Johnnie, Balt.	1	3	3.0	3	0

NFL STATISTICS

	Att	Yards	Avg	Long	TD
Cavanaugh, Matt, N.E.	2	3	1.5	3	0
Morgan, Stanley, N.E.	2	3	1.5	3	0
Davis, Johnny, Clev.	4	3	0.8	2	1
Taylor, Billy, Raiders	4	3	0.8	2	0
Jones, Johnny, Jets	1	2	2.0	2	0
Allen, Gary, Hou.	2	2	1.0	9	0
Lytle, Rob, Den.	2	2	1.0	2	0
Tate, Rodney, Cin.	2	2	1.0	2	0
Verser, David, Cin.	1	1	1.0	1	0
Gaines, Clark, K.C.	1	0	0.0	0	0
Studdard, Les, K.C.	1	0	0.0	0	0
Johns, Paul, Sea.	1	-1	-1.0	-1	0
Ryan, Pat, Jets	1	-1	-1.0	-1	0
Krieg, Dave, Sea.	6	-3	-0.5	4	0
Guy, Ray, Raiders	2	-3	-1.5	7	0
Harris, M.L., Cin.	2	-3	-1.5	5	0
Watson, Steve, Den.	1	-4	-4.0	-4	0
Wright, James, Den.	1	-4	-4.0	-4	0
Todd, Richard, Jets	13	-5	-0.4	t7	1
Christensen, Todd, Raiders	1	-6	-6.0	-6	0
Schonert, Turk, Cin.	3	-8	-2.7	-3	0
Strock, Don, Mia.	3	-9	-3.0	0	0
Upchurch, Rick, Den.	2	-10	-5.0	-3	0
Cox, Steve, Clev.	2	-11	-5.5	0	0
Collinsworth, Cris, Cin.	1	-11	-11.0	-11	0
McDonald, Paul, Clev.	7	-13	-1.9	10	0
Luther, Ed, S.D.	1	-13	-13.0	-13	0

308   THE COMPLETE HANDBOOK OF PRO FOOTBALL

Wendell Tyler, now a 49er, Rammed for nine TDs in '82.

TOP TEN SCORERS - KICKERS

	XP	XPA	FG	FGA	PTS
Benirschke, Rolf, S.D.	32	34	16	22	80
Moseley, Mark, Wash.	16	19	20	21	76
Lowery, Nick, K.C.	17	17	19	24	74
Capece, Bill, T.B.	14	14	18	23	68
Breech, Jim, Cin.	25	26	14	18	67
von Schamann, Uwe, Mia.	21	22	15	20	66
Stenerud, Jan, G.B.	25	27	13	18	64
Bahr, Chris, Raiders	32	33	10	16	62
Leahy, Pat, Jets	26	31	11	17	59
Wersching, Ray, S.F.	23	25	12	17	59

TOP TEN SCORERS - NON-KICKERS

	TD	R	P	M	PTS
Allen, Marcus, Raiders	14	11	3	0	84
Tyler, Wendell, Rams	13	9	4	0	78
Ivery, Eddie Lee, G.B.	10	9	1	0	60
Chandler, Wes, S.D.	9	0	9	0	54
Montgomery, Wilbert, Phil.	9	7	2	0	54
Muncie, Chuck, S.D.	9	8	1	0	54
Brown, Charlie, Wash.	8	0	8	0	48
Moore, Jeff, S.F.	8	4	4	0	48
Andrews, William, Atl.	7	5	2	0	42
Franklin, Andra, Mia.	7	7	0	0	42
Johnson, Pete, Cin.	7	7	0	0	42
McNeil, Freeman, Jets	7	6	1	0	42
Stallworth, John, Pitt.	7	0	7	0	42

TOP TEN PASS RECEIVERS

	No	Yards	Avg	Long	TD
Clark, Dwight, S.F.	60	913	15.2	51	5
Winslow, Kellen, S.D.	54	721	13.4	40	6
Wilder, James, T.B.	53	466	8.8	32	1
Chandler, Wes, S.D.	49	1032	21.1	t66	9
Collinsworth, Cris, Cin.	49	700	14.3	50	1
Newsome, Ozzie, Clev.	49	633	12.9	54	3
Ross, Dan, Cin.	47	508	10.8	28	3
Christensen, Todd, Raiders	42	510	12.1	50	4
Andrews, William, Atl.	42	503	12.0	t86	2
Marshall, Henry, K.C.	40	549	13.7	t44	3

PASSING

NFC INDIVIDUAL QUALIFIERS

	Att	Comp	Pct Comp	Yards	Avg Gain
Theismann, Joe, Wash.	252	161	63.9	2033	8.07
White, Danny, Dall.	247	156	63.2	2079	8.42
Montana, Joe, S.F.	346	213	61.6	2613	7.55
McMahon, Jim, Chi.	210	120	57.1	1501	7.15
Bartkowski, Steve, Atl.	262	166	63.4	1905	7.27
Ferragamo, Vince, Rams	209	118	56.5	1609	7.70
Jaworski, Ron, Phil.	286	167	58.4	2076	7.26
Kramer, Tommy, Minn.	308	176	57.1	2037	6.61
Dickey, Lynn, G.B.	218	124	56.9	1790	8.21
Brunner, Scott, Giants	298	161	54.0	2017	6.77
Stabler, Ken, N.O.	189	117	61.9	1343	7.11
Lomax, Neil, St.L.	205	109	53.2	1367	6.67
Williams, Doug, T.B.	307	164	53.4	2071	6.75
Danielson, Gary, Det.	197	100	50.8	1343	6.82

AFC INDIVIDUAL QUALIFIERS

	Att	Comp	Pct Comp	Yards	Avg Gain
Anderson, Ken, Cin.	309	218	70.6	2495	8.07
Fouts, Dan, S.D.	330	204	61.8	2883	8.74
Todd, Richard, Jets	261	153	58.6	1961	7.51
Grogan, Steve, N.E.	122	66	54.1	930	7.62
Bradshaw, Terry, Pitt.	240	127	52.9	1768	7.37
Plunkett, Jim, Raiders	261	152	58.2	2035	7.80
Kenney, Bill, K.C.	169	95	56.2	1192	7.05
DeBerg, Steve, Den.	223	131	58.7	1405	6.30
Nielsen, Gifford, Hou.	161	87	54.0	1005	6.24
Woodley, David, Mia.	179	98	54.7	1080	6.03
Pagel, Mike, Balt.	221	111	50.2	1281	5.80
Zorn, Jim, Sea.	245	126	51.4	1540	6.29
Manning, Archie, N.O.-Hou.	132	67	50.8	880	6.67
Sipe, Brian, Clev.	185	101	54.6	1064	5.75
McDonald, Paul, Clev.	149	73	49.0	993	6.66
Ferguson, Joe, Buff.	264	144	54.5	1597	6.05

TOP TEN PUNTERS

	No	Yds	Long	Avg
Prestridge, Luke, Den.	45	2026	65	45.0
Stark, Rohn, Balt.	46	2044	60	44.4
Birdsong, Carl, St.L.	54	2365	65	43.8
Camarillo, Rich, N.E.	49	2140	76	43.7
Misko, John, Rams	45	1961	59	43.6
Erxleben, Russell, N.O.	46	1976	60	43.0
Jennings, Dave, Giants	49	2096	73	42.8
White, Danny, Dall.	37	1542	56	41.7
Swider, Larry, T.B.	39	1620	59	41.5
Gossett, Jeff, K.C.	33	1366	56	41.4

NFL STATISTICS

TD	Pct TD	Long	Int	Pct Int	Rating Points
13	5.2	78	9	3.6	91.3
16	6.5	49	12	4.9	91.1
17	4.9	55	11	3.2	87.9
9	4.3	t50	7	3.3	80.1
8	3.1	t86	11	4.2	78.1
9	4.3	t85	9	4.3	77.7
12	4.2	57	12	4.2	77.5
15	4.9	65	12	3.9	77.3
12	5.5	t80	14	6.4	75.4
10	3.4	47	9	3.0	74.1
6	3.2	48	10	5.3	71.9
5	2.4	42	6	2.9	70.1
9	2.9	t62	11	3.6	69.4
10	5.1	t70	14	7.1	60.3

TD	Pct TD	Long	Int	Pct Int	Rating Points
12	3.9	t56	9	2.9	95.5
17	5.2	t44	11	3.3	93.6
14	5.4	t56	8	3.1	87.3
7	5.7	t62	4	3.3	84.2
17	7.1	t74	11	4.6	81.4
14	5.4	52	15	5.7	77.3
7	4.1	51	6	3.6	77.0
7	3.1	t51	11	4.9	67.2
6	3.7	46	8	5.0	64.6
5	2.8	46	8	4.5	63.4
5	2.3	t53	7	3.2	62.4
7	2.9	50	11	4.5	62.1
6	4.5	t54	8	6.1	61.8
4	2.2	t40	8	4.3	61.0
5	3.4	t56	8	5.4	59.5
7	2.7	47	16	6.1	56.3

Total Punts	TB	Blk	Opp Ret	Ret Yds	In 20	Net Avg
45	5	0	25	227	14	37.8
46	12	0	26	226	8	34.3
54	6	0	36	288	8	36.2
49	5	0	26	191	10	37.7
46	2	1	31	401	10	33.0
46	6	0	29	239	6	35.2
49	3	0	25	207	16	37.3
37	2	0	21	118	6	37.4
40	6	1	23	192	6	32.7
33	5	0	20	247	6	30.9

TOP TEN INTERCEPTORS

	No	Yards	Avg	Long	TD
Walls, Everson, Dall.	7	61	8.7	37	0
Riley, Ken, Cin.	5	88	17.6	t56	1
Jackson, Bobby, Jets	5	84	16.8	t77	1
Woodruff, Dwayne, Pitt.	5	53	10.6	30	0
Shell, Donnie, Pitt.	5	27	5.4	18	0
Watkins, Bobby, Det.	5	22	4.4	20	0
Edwards, Herman, Phil.	5	3	0.6	3	0

13 tied with 4

TOP TEN KICKOFF RETURNERS

	No	Yards	Avg	Long	TD
Mosley, Mike, Buff.	18	487	27.1	66	0
Hall, Alvin, Det.	16	426	26.6	t96	1
Pruitt, Greg, Raiders	14	371	26.5	55	0
Nelms, Mike, Wash.	23	557	24.2	58	0
Redwine, Jarvis, Minn.	12	286	23.8	76	0
Smith, Ricky, N.E.	24	567	23.6	t98	1
Watts, Rickey, Chi.	14	330	23.6	36	0
Bohannon, Fred, Pitt.	14	329	23.5	57	0
Manning, Wade, Den.	15	346	23.1	34	0
Redden, Barry, Rams	22	502	22.8	85	0
Mitchell, Stump, St.L.	16	364	22.8	33	0

TOP TEN PUNT RETURNERS

	No	FC	Yards	Avg	Long	TD
Upchurch, Rick, Den.	15	3	242	16.1	t78	2
Brooks, James, S.D.	12	4	138	11.5	29	0
Johnson, Billy, Atl.	24	4	273	11.4	71	0
Johns, Paul, Sea.	19	10	210	11.1	37	0
Irvin, LeRoy, Rams	22	1	242	11.0	t63	1
Woods, Rick, Pitt.	13	2	142	10.9	20	0
Martin, Robbie, Det.	26	5	275	10.6	58	0
Vigorito, Tom, Mia.	20	5	192	9.6	t59	1
Solomon, Freddie, S.F.	13	1	122	9.4	27	0
Bright, Leon, Giants	37	0	325	8.8	33	0

NFL STANDINGS 1921–1982

1921

	W	L	T	Pct.
Chicago Staleys	10	1	1	.909
Buffalo All-Americans	9	1	2	.900
Akron, Ohio, Pros	7	2	1	.778
Green Bay Packers	6	2	2	.750
Canton, Ohio, Bulldogs	4	3	3	.571
Dayton Triangles	4	3	1	.571
Rock Island Independents	5	4	1	.556
Chicago Cardinals	2	3	2	.400
Cleveland Indians	2	6	0	.250
Rochester Jeffersons	2	6	0	.250
Detroit Heralds	1	7	1	.125
Columbus Panhandles	0	6	0	.000
Cincinnati Celts	0	8	0	.000

1922

	W	L	T	Pct.
Canton, Ohio, Bulldogs	10	0	2	1.000
Chicago Bears	9	3	0	.750
Chicago Cardinals	8	3	0	.727
Toledo Maroons	5	2	2	.714
Rock Island Independents	4	2	1	.667
Dayton Triangles	4	3	1	.571
Green Bay Packers	4	3	3	.571
Racine, Wis., Legion	5	4	1	.556
Akron, Ohio, Pros	3	4	2	.429
Buffalo All-Americans	3	4	1	.429
Milwaukee Badgers	2	4	3	.333
Marion, O., Oorang Indians	2	6	0	.250
Minneapolis Marines	1	3	0	.250
Evansville Crimson Giants	0	2	0	.000
Louisville Brecks	0	3	0	.000
Rochester Jeffersons	0	3	1	.000
Hammond, Ind., Pros	0	4	1	.000
Columbus Panhandles	0	7	0	.000

1923

	W	L	T	Pct.
Canton, Ohio, Bulldogs	11	0	1	1.000
Chicago Bears	9	2	1	.818
Green Bay Packers	7	2	1	.778
Milwaukee Badgers	7	2	3	.778
Cleveland Indians	3	1	3	.750
Chicago Cardinals	8	4	0	.667
Duluth Kelleys	4	3	0	.571
Buffalo All-Americans	5	4	3	.556
Columbus Tigers	5	4	1	.556
Racine, Wis., Legion	4	4	2	.500
Toledo Maroons	2	3	2	.400
Rock Island Independents	2	3	3	.400
Minneapolis Marines	2	5	2	.286
St. Louis All-Stars	1	4	2	.200
Hammond, Ind., Pros	1	5	1	.167
Dayton Triangles	1	6	1	.143
Akron, Ohio, Indians	1	6	0	.143
Marion, O., Oorang Indians	1	10	0	.091
Rochester Jeffersons	0	2	0	.000
Louisville Brecks	0	3	0	.000

1924

	W	L	T	Pct.
Cleveland Bulldogs	7	1	1	.875
Chicago Bears	6	1	4	.857
Frankford Yellowjackets	11	2	1	.846
Duluth Kelleys	5	1	0	.833
Rock Island Independents	6	2	2	.750
Green Bay Packers	8	4	0	.667
Buffalo Bisons	6	4	0	.600
Racine, Wis., Legion	4	3	3	.571
Chicago Cardinals	5	4	1	.556
Columbus Tigers	4	4	0	.500
Hammond, Ind., Pros	2	2	1	.500
Milwaukee Badgers	5	8	0	.385
Dayton Triangles	2	7	0	.222
Kansas City Cowboys	2	7	0	.222
Akron, Ohio, Indians	1	6	0	.143
Kenosha, Wis., Maroons	0	5	1	.000
Minneapolis Marines	0	6	0	.000
Rochester Jeffersons	0	7	0	.000

1925

	W	L	T	Pct.
Chicago Cardinals	11	2	1	.846
Pottsville, Pa., Maroons	10	2	0	.833
Detroit Panthers	8	2	2	.800
New York Giants	8	4	0	.667
Akron, Ohio, Indians	4	2	2	.667
Frankford Yellowjackets	13	7	0	.650
Chicago Bears	9	5	3	.643
Rock Island Independents	5	3	3	.625
Green Bay Packers	8	5	0	.615
Providence Steamroller	6	5	1	.545
Canton, Ohio, Bulldogs	4	4	0	.500
Cleveland Bulldogs	5	8	1	.385
Kansas City Cowboys	2	5	1	.286
Hammond, Ind., Pros	1	3	0	.250
Buffalo Bisons	1	6	2	.143
Duluth Kelleys	0	3	0	.000
Rochester Jeffersons	0	6	1	.000
Milwaukee Badgers	0	6	0	.000
Dayton Triangles	0	7	1	.000
Columbus Tigers	0	9	0	.000

1926

	W	L	T	Pct.
Frankford Yellowjackets	14	1	1	.933
Chicago Bears	12	1	3	.923
Pottsville, Pa., Maroons	10	2	1	.833
Kansas City Cowboys	8	3	1	.727
Green Bay Packers	7	3	3	.700
Los Angeles Buccaneers	6	3	1	.667
New York Giants	8	4	1	.667
Duluth Eskimos	6	5	2	.545
Buffalo Rangers	4	4	2	.500
Chicago Cardinals	5	6	1	.455
Providence Steamroller	5	7	0	.417
Detroit Panthers	4	6	2	.400
Hartford Blues	3	7	0	.300
Brooklyn Lions	3	8	0	.273
Milwaukee Badgers	2	7	0	.222
Akron, Ohio, Indians	1	4	3	.200
Dayton Triangles	1	4	1	.200
Racine, Wis., Legion	1	4	0	.200
Columbus Tigers	1	6	0	.143
Canton, Ohio, Bulldogs	1	9	3	.100
Hammond, Ind., Pros	0	4	0	.000
Louisville Colonels	0	4	0	.000

1927

	W	L	T	Pct.
New York Giants	11	1	1	.917
Green Bay Packers	7	2	1	.778
Chicago Bears	9	3	2	.750
Cleveland Bulldogs	8	4	1	.667
Providence Steamroller	8	5	1	.615
New York Yankees	7	8	1	.467
Frankford Yellowjackets	6	9	3	.400
Pottsville, Pa., Maroons	5	8	0	.385
Chicago Cardinals	3	7	1	.300
Dayton Triangles	1	6	1	.143
Duluth Eskimos	1	8	0	.111
Buffalo Bisons	0	5	0	.000

1928

	W	L	T	Pct.
Providence Steamroller	8	1	2	.889
Frankford Yellowjackets	11	3	2	.786
Detroit Wolverines	7	2	1	.778
Green Bay Packers	6	4	3	.600
Chicago Bears	7	5	1	.583
New York Giants	4	7	2	.364
New York Yankees	4	8	1	.333
Pottsville, Pa., Maroons	2	8	0	.200
Chicago Cardinals	1	5	0	.167
Dayton Triangles	0	7	0	.000

1929

	W	L	T	Pct.
Green Bay Packers	12	0	1	1.000
New York Giants	13	1	1	.929
Frankford Yellowjackets	9	4	5	.692
Chicago Cardinals	6	6	1	.500
Boston Bulldogs	4	4	0	.500
Orange, N.J., Tornadoes	3	4	4	.429
Stapleton Stapes	3	4	3	.429
Providence Steamroller	4	6	2	.400
Chicago Bears	4	9	2	.308
Buffalo Bisons	1	7	1	.125
Minneapolis Red Jackets	1	9	0	.100
Dayton Triangles	0	6	0	.000

1930

	W	L	T	Pct.
Green Bay Packers	10	3	1	.769
New York Giants	13	4	0	.765
Chicago Bears	9	4	1	.692
Brooklyn Dodgers	7	4	1	.636
Providence Steamroller	6	4	1	.600
Stapleton Stapes	5	5	2	.500
Chicago Cardinals	5	6	2	.455
Portsmouth, O., Spartans	5	6	3	.455
Frankford Yellowjackets	4	14	1	.222
Minneapolis Red Jackets	1	7	1	.125
Newark Tornadoes	1	10	1	.091

1931

	W	L	T	Pct.
Green Bay Packers	12	2	0	.857
Portsmouth, O., Spartans	11	3	0	.786
Chicago Bears	8	5	0	.615
Chicago Cardinals	5	4	0	.556
New York Giants	7	6	1	.538
Providence Steamroller	4	4	3	.500
Stapleton Stapes	4	6	1	.400
Cleveland Indians	2	8	0	.200
Brooklyn Dodgers	2	12	0	.143
Frankford Yellowjackets	1	6	1	.143

1932

	W	L	T	Pct.
Chicago Bears	7	1	6	.875
Green Bay Packers	10	3	1	.769
Portsmouth, O., Spartans	6	2	4	.750
Boston Braves	4	4	2	.500
New York Giants	4	6	2	.400
Brooklyn Dodgers	3	9	0	.250
Chicago Cardinals	2	6	2	.250
Stapleton Stapes	2	7	3	.222

1933

EASTERN DIVISION

	W	L	T	Pct.	Pts.	OP
N.Y. Giants	11	3	0	.786	244	101
Brooklyn	5	4	1	.556	93	54
Boston	5	5	2	.500	103	97
Philadelphia	3	5	1	.375	77	158
Pittsburgh	3	6	2	.333	67	208

WESTERN DIVISION

	W	L	T	Pct.	Pts.	OP
Chi. Bears	10	2	1	.833	133	82
Portsmouth	6	5	0	.545	128	87
Green Bay	5	7	1	.417	170	107
Cincinnati	3	6	1	.333	38	110
Chi. Cardinals	1	9	1	.100	52	101

NFL Championship: Chicago Bears 23, N.Y. Giants 21

NFL STANDINGS

1934

EASTERN DIVISION
	W	L	T	Pct.	Pts.	OP
N.Y. Giants	8	5	0	.615	147	107
Boston	6	6	0	.500	107	94
Brooklyn	4	7	0	.364	61	153
Philadelphia	4	7	0	.364	127	85
Pittsburgh	2	10	0	.167	51	206

WESTERN DIVISION
	W	L	T	Pct.	Pts.	OP
Chi. Bears	13	0	0	1.000	286	86
Detroit	10	3	0	.769	238	59
Green Bay	7	6	0	.538	156	112
Chi. Cardinals	5	6	0	.455	80	84
St. Louis	1	2	0	.333	27	61
Cincinnati	0	8	0	.000	10	243

NFL Championship: N.Y. Giants 30, Chicago Bears 13

1935

EASTERN DIVISION
	W	L	T	Pct.	Pts.	OP
N.Y. Giants	9	3	0	.750	180	96
Brooklyn	5	6	1	.455	90	141
Pittsburgh	4	8	0	.333	100	209
Boston	2	8	1	.200	65	123
Philadelphia	2	9	0	.182	60	179

WESTERN DIVISION
	W	L	T	Pct.	Pts.	OP
Detroit	7	3	2	.700	191	111
Green Bay	8	4	0	.667	181	96
Chi. Bears	6	4	2	.600	192	106
Chi. Cardinals	6	4	2	.600	99	97

NFL Championship: Detroit 26, N.Y. Giants 7
One game between Boston and Philadelphia was canceled.

1936

EASTERN DIVISION
	W	L	T	Pct.	Pts.	OP
Boston	7	5	0	.583	149	110
Pittsburgh	6	6	0	.500	98	187
N.Y. Giants	5	6	1	.455	115	163
Brooklyn	3	8	1	.273	92	161
Philadelphia	1	11	0	.083	51	206

WESTERN DIVISION
	W	L	T	Pct.	Pts.	OP
Green Bay	10	1	1	.909	248	118
Chi. Bears	9	3	0	.750	222	94
Detroit	8	4	0	.667	235	102
Chi. Cardinals	3	8	1	.273	74	143

NFL Championship: Green Bay 21, Boston 6

1937

EASTERN DIVISION
	W	L	T	Pct.	Pts.	OP
Washington	8	3	0	.727	195	120
N.Y. Giants	6	3	2	.667	128	109
Pittsburgh	4	7	0	.364	122	145
Brooklyn	3	7	1	.300	82	174
Philadelphia	2	8	1	.200	86	177

WESTERN DIVISION
	W	L	T	Pct.	Pts.	OP
Chi. Bears	9	1	1	.900	201	100
Green Bay	7	4	0	.636	220	122
Detroit	7	4	0	.636	180	105
Chi. Cardinals	5	5	1	.500	135	165
Cleveland	1	10	0	.091	75	207

NFL Championship: Washington 28, Chicago Bears 21

1938

EASTERN DIVISION
	W	L	T	Pct.	Pts.	OP
N.Y. Giants	8	2	1	.800	194	79
Washington	6	3	2	.667	148	154
Brooklyn	4	4	3	.500	131	161
Philadelphia	5	6	0	.455	154	164
Pittsburgh	2	9	0	.182	79	169

WESTERN DIVISION
	W	L	T	Pct.	Pts.	OP
Green Bay	8	3	0	.727	223	118
Detroit	7	4	0	.636	119	108
Chi. Bears	6	5	0	.545	194	148
Cleveland	4	7	0	.364	131	215
Chi. Cardinals	2	9	0	.182	111	168

NFL Championship: N.Y. Giants 23, Green Bay 17

1939

EASTERN DIVISION
	W	L	T	Pct.	Pts.	OP
N.Y. Giants	9	1	1	.900	168	85
Washington	8	2	1	.800	242	94
Brooklyn	4	6	1	.400	108	219
Philadelphia	1	9	1	.100	105	200
Pittsburgh	1	9	1	.100	114	216

WESTERN DIVISION
	W	L	T	Pct.	Pts.	OP
Green Bay	9	2	0	.818	233	153
Chi. Bears	8	3	0	.727	298	157
Detroit	6	5	0	.545	145	150
Cleveland	5	5	1	.500	195	164
Chi. Cardinals	1	10	0	.091	84	254

NFL Championship: Green Bay 27, N.Y. Giants 0

1940

EASTERN DIVISION
	W	L	T	Pct.	Pts.	OP
Washington	9	2	0	.818	245	142
Brooklyn	8	3	0	.727	186	120
N.Y. Giants	6	4	1	.600	131	133
Pittsburgh	2	7	2	.222	60	178
Philadelphia	1	10	0	.091	111	211

WESTERN DIVISION
	W	L	T	Pct.	Pts.	OP
Chi. Bears	8	3	0	.727	238	152
Green Bay	6	4	1	.600	238	155
Detroit	5	5	1	.500	138	153
Cleveland	4	6	1	.400	171	191
Chi. Cardinals	2	7	2	.222	139	222

NFL Championship: Chicago Bears 73, Washington 0

1941

EASTERN DIVISION
	W	L	T	Pct.	Pts.	OP
N.Y. Giants	8	3	0	.727	238	114
Brooklyn	7	4	0	.636	158	127
Washington	6	5	0	.545	176	174
Philadelphia	2	8	1	.200	119	218
Pittsburgh	1	9	1	.100	103	276

WESTERN DIVISION
	W	L	T	Pct.	Pts.	OP
Chi. Bears	10	1	0	.909	396	147
Green Bay	10	1	0	.909	258	120
Detroit	4	6	1	.400	121	195
Chi. Cardinals	3	7	1	.300	127	197
Cleveland	2	9	0	.182	116	244

Western Division playoff: Chicago Bears 33, Green Bay 14
NFL Championship: Chicago Bears 37, N.Y. Giants 9

1942

EASTERN DIVISION
	W	L	T	Pct.	Pts.	OP
Washington	10	1	0	.909	227	102
Pittsburgh	7	4	0	.636	167	119
N.Y. Giants	5	5	1	.500	155	139
Brooklyn	3	8	0	.273	100	168
Philadelphia	2	9	0	.182	134	239

WESTERN DIVISION
	W	L	T	Pct.	Pts.	OP
Chi. Bears	11	0	0	1.000	376	84
Green Bay	8	2	1	.800	300	215
Cleveland	5	6	0	.455	150	207
Chi. Cardinals	3	8	0	.273	98	209
Detroit	0	11	0	.000	38	263

NFL Championship: Washington 14, Chicago Bears 6

1943

EASTERN DIVISION
	W	L	T	Pct.	Pts.	OP
Washington	6	3	1	.667	229	137
N.Y. Giants	6	3	1	.667	197	170
Phil-Pitt	5	4	1	.556	225	230
Brooklyn	2	8	0	.200	65	234

WESTERN DIVISION
	W	L	T	Pct.	Pts.	OP
Chi. Bears	8	1	1	.889	303	157
Green Bay	7	2	1	.778	264	172
Detroit	3	6	1	.333	178	218
Chi. Cardinals	0	10	0	.000	95	238

Eastern Division playoff: Washington 28, N.Y. Giants 0
NFL Championship: Chicago Bears 41, Washington 21

1944

EASTERN DIVISION
	W	L	T	Pct.	Pts.	OP
N.Y. Giants	8	1	1	.889	206	75
Philadelphia	7	1	2	.875	267	131
Washington	6	3	1	.667	169	180
Boston	2	8	0	.200	82	233
Brooklyn	0	10	0	.000	69	166

WESTERN DIVISION
	W	L	T	Pct.	Pts.	OP
Green Bay	8	2	0	.800	238	141
Chi. Bears	6	3	1	.667	258	172
Detroit	6	3	1	.667	216	151
Cleveland	4	6	0	.400	188	224
Card-Pitt	0	10	0	.000	108	328

NFL Championship: Green Bay 14, N.Y. Giants 7

1945

EASTERN DIVISION
	W	L	T	Pct.	Pts.	OP
Washington	8	2	0	.800	209	121
Philadelphia	7	3	0	.700	272	133
N.Y. Giants	3	6	1	.333	179	198
Boston	3	6	1	.333	123	211
Pittsburgh	2	8	0	.200	79	220

WESTERN DIVISION
	W	L	T	Pct.	Pts.	OP
Cleveland	9	1	0	.900	244	136
Detroit	7	3	0	.700	195	194
Green Bay	6	4	0	.600	258	173
Chi. Bears	3	7	0	.300	192	235
Chi. Cardinals	1	9	0	.100	98	228

NFL Championship: Cleveland 15, Washington 14

NFL STANDINGS 317

1946

EASTERN DIVISION
	W	L	T	Pct.	Pts.	OP
N.Y. Giants	7	3	1	.700	236	162
Philadelphia	6	5	0	.545	231	220
Washington	5	5	1	.500	171	191
Pittsburgh	5	5	1	.500	136	117
Boston	2	8	1	.200	189	273

WESTERN DIVISION
	W	L	T	Pct.	Pts.	OP
Chi. Bears	8	2	1	.800	289	193
Los Angeles	6	4	1	.600	277	257
Green Bay	6	5	0	.545	148	158
Chi. Cardinals	6	5	0	.545	260	198
Detroit	1	10	0	.091	142	310

NFL Championship: Chicago Bears 24, N.Y. Giants 14

1947

EASTERN DIVISION
	W	L	T	Pct.	Pts.	OP
Philadelphia	8	4	0	.667	308	242
Pittsburgh	8	4	0	.667	240	259
Boston	4	7	1	.364	168	256
Washington	4	8	0	.333	295	367
N.Y. Giants	2	8	2	.200	190	309

WESTERN DIVISION
	W	L	T	Pct.	Pts.	OP
Chi. Cardinals	9	3	0	.750	306	231
Chi. Bears	8	4	0	.667	363	241
Green Bay	6	5	1	.545	274	210
Los Angeles	6	6	0	.500	259	214
Detroit	3	9	0	.250	231	305

Eastern Division playoff: Philadelphia 21, Pittsburgh 0
NFL Championship: Chicago Cardinals 28, Philadelphia 21

1948

EASTERN DIVISION
	W	L	T	Pct.	Pts.	OP
Philadelphia	9	2	1	.818	376	156
Washington	7	5	0	.583	291	287
N.Y. Giants	4	8	0	.333	297	388
Pittsburgh	4	8	0	.333	200	243
Boston	3	9	0	.250	174	372

WESTERN DIVISION
	W	L	T	Pct.	Pts.	OP
Chi. Cardinals	11	1	0	.917	395	226
Chi. Bears	10	2	0	.833	375	151
Los Angeles	6	5	1	.545	327	269
Green Bay	3	9	0	.250	154	290
Detroit	2	10	0	.167	200	407

NFL Championship: Philadelphia 7, Chicago Cardinals 0

1949

EASTERN DIVISION
	W	L	T	Pct.	Pts.	OP
Philadelphia	11	1	0	.917	364	134
Pittsburgh	6	5	1	.545	224	214
N.Y. Giants	6	6	0	.500	287	298
Washington	4	7	1	.364	268	339
N.Y. Bulldogs	1	10	1	.091	153	368

WESTERN DIVISION
	W	L	T	Pct.	Pts.	OP
Los Angeles	8	2	2	.800	360	239
Chi. Bears	9	3	0	.750	332	218
Chi. Cardinals	6	5	1	.545	360	301
Detroit	4	8	0	.333	237	259
Green Bay	2	10	0	.167	114	329

NFL Championship: Philadelphia 14, Los Angeles 0

1950

AMERICAN CONFERENCE
	W	L	T	Pct.	Pts.	OP
Cleveland	10	2	0	.833	310	144
N.Y. Giants	10	2	0	.833	268	150
Philadelphia	6	6	0	.500	254	141
Pittsburgh	6	6	0	.500	180	195
Chi. Cardinals	5	7	0	.417	233	287
Washington	3	9	0	.250	232	326

NATIONAL CONFERENCE
	W	L	T	Pct.	Pts.	OP
Los Angeles	9	3	0	.750	466	309
Chi. Bears	9	3	0	.750	279	207
N.Y. Yanks	7	5	0	.583	366	367
Detroit	6	6	0	.500	321	285
Green Bay	3	9	0	.250	244	406
San Francisco	3	9	0	.250	213	300
Baltimore	1	11	0	.083	213	462

American Conference playoff: Cleveland 8, N.Y. Giants 3
National Conference playoff: Los Angeles 24, Chicago Bears 14
NFL Championship: Cleveland 30, Los Angeles 28

1951

AMERICAN CONFERENCE
	W	L	T	Pct.	Pts.	OP
Cleveland	11	1	0	.917	331	152
N.Y. Giants	9	2	1	.818	254	161
Washington	5	7	0	.417	183	296
Pittsburgh	4	7	1	.364	183	235
Philadelphia	4	8	0	.333	234	264
Chi. Cardinals	3	9	0	.250	210	287

NATIONAL CONFERENCE
	W	L	T	Pct.	Pts.	OP
Los Angeles	8	4	0	.667	392	261
Detroit	7	4	1	.636	336	259
San Francisco	7	4	1	.636	255	205
Chi. Bears	7	5	0	.583	286	282
Green Bay	3	9	0	.250	254	375
N.Y. Yanks	1	9	2	.100	241	382

NFL Championship: Los Angeles 24, Cleveland 17

THE COMPLETE HANDBOOK OF PRO FOOTBALL

1952

AMERICAN CONFERENCE

	W	L	T	Pct.	Pts.	OP
Cleveland	8	4	0	.667	310	213
N.Y. Giants	7	5	0	.583	234	231
Philadelphia	7	5	0	.583	252	271
Pittsburgh	5	7	0	.417	300	273
Chi. Cardinals	4	8	0	.333	172	221
Washington	4	8	0	.333	240	287

NATIONAL CONFERENCE

	W	L	T	Pct.	Pts.	OP
Detroit	9	3	0	.750	344	192
Los Angeles	9	3	0	.750	349	234
San Francisco	7	5	0	.583	285	221
Green Bay	6	6	0	.500	295	312
Chi. Bears	5	7	0	.417	245	326
Dallas	1	11	0	.083	182	427

National Conference playoff: Detroit 31, Los Angeles 21
NFL Championship: Detroit 17, Cleveland 7

1953

EASTERN CONFERENCE

	W	L	T	Pct.	Pts.	OP
Cleveland	11	1	0	.917	348	162
Philadelphia	7	4	1	.636	352	215
Washington	6	5	1	.545	208	215
Pittsburgh	6	6	0	.500	211	263
N.Y. Giants	3	9	0	.250	179	277
Chi. Cardinals	1	10	1	.091	190	337

WESTERN CONFERENCE

	W	L	T	Pct.	Pts.	OP
Detroit	10	2	0	.833	271	205
San Francisco	9	3	0	.750	372	237
Los Angeles	8	3	1	.727	366	236
Chi. Bears	3	8	1	.273	218	262
Baltimore	3	9	0	.250	182	350
Green Bay	2	9	1	.182	200	338

NFL Championship: Detroit 17, Cleveland 16

1954

EASTERN CONFERENCE

	W	L	T	Pct.	Pts.	OP
Cleveland	9	3	0	.750	336	162
Philadelphia	7	4	1	.636	284	230
N.Y. Giants	7	5	0	.583	293	184
Pittsburgh	5	7	0	.417	219	263
Washington	3	9	0	.250	207	432
Chi. Cardinals	2	10	0	.167	183	347

WESTERN CONFERENCE

	W	L	T	Pct.	Pts.	OP
Detroit	9	2	1	.818	337	189
Chi. Bears	8	4	0	.667	301	279
San Francisco	7	4	1	.636	313	251
Los Angeles	6	5	1	.545	314	285
Green Bay	4	8	0	.333	234	251
Baltimore	3	9	0	.250	131	279

NFL Championship: Cleveland 56, Detroit 10

1955

EASTERN CONFERENCE

	W	L	T	Pct.	Pts.	OP
Cleveland	9	2	1	.818	349	218
Washington	8	4	0	.667	246	222
N.Y. Giants	6	5	1	.545	267	223
Chi. Cardinals	4	7	1	.364	224	252
Philadelphia	4	7	1	.364	248	231
Pittsburgh	4	8	0	.333	195	285

WESTERN CONFERENCE

	W	L	T	Pct.	Pts.	OP
Los Angeles	8	3	1	.727	260	231
Chi. Bears	8	4	0	.667	294	251
Green Bay	6	6	0	.500	258	276
Baltimore	5	6	1	.455	214	239
San Francisco	4	8	0	.333	216	298
Detroit	3	9	0	.250	230	275

NFL Championship: Cleveland 38, Los Angeles 14

1956

EASTERN CONFERENCE

	W	L	T	Pct.	Pts.	OP
N.Y. Giants	8	3	1	.727	264	197
Chi. Cardinals	7	5	0	.583	240	182
Washington	6	6	0	.500	183	225
Cleveland	5	7	0	.417	167	177
Pittsburgh	5	7	0	.417	217	250
Philadelphia	3	8	1	.273	143	215

WESTERN CONFERENCE

	W	L	T	Pct.	Pts.	OP
Chi. Bears	9	2	1	.818	363	246
Detroit	9	3	0	.750	300	188
San Francisco	5	6	1	.455	233	284
Baltimore	5	7	0	.417	270	322
Green Bay	4	8	0	.333	264	342
Los Angeles	4	8	0	.333	291	307

NFL Championship: N.Y. Giants 47, Chicago Bears 7

NFL STANDINGS 319

1957

EASTERN CONFERENCE
	W	L	T	Pct.	Pts.	OP
Cleveland	9	2	1	.818	269	172
N.Y. Giants	7	5	0	.583	254	211
Pittsburgh	6	6	0	.500	161	178
Washington	5	6	1	.455	251	230
Philadelphia	4	8	0	.333	173	230
Chi. Cardinals	3	9	0	.250	200	299

WESTERN CONFERENCE
	W	L	T	Pct.	Pts.	OP
Detroit	8	4	0	.667	251	231
San Francisco	8	4	0	.667	260	264
Baltimore	7	5	0	.583	303	235
Los Angeles	6	6	0	.500	307	278
Chi. Bears	5	7	0	.417	203	211
Green Bay	3	9	0	.250	218	311

Western Conference playoff: Detroit 31, San Francisco 27
NFL Championship: Detroit 59, Cleveland 14

1958

EASTERN CONFERENCE
	W	L	T	Pct.	Pts.	OP
N.Y. Giants	9	3	0	.750	246	183
Cleveland	9	3	0	.750	302	217
Pittsburgh	7	4	1	.636	261	230
Washington	4	7	1	.364	214	268
Chi. Cardinals	2	9	1	.182	261	356
Philadelphia	2	9	1	.182	235	306

WESTERN CONFERENCE
	W	L	T	Pct.	Pts.	OP
Baltimore	9	3	0	.750	381	203
Chi. Bears	8	4	0	.667	298	230
Los Angeles	8	4	0	.667	344	278
San Francisco	6	6	0	.500	257	324
Detroit	4	7	1	.364	261	276
Green Bay	1	10	1	.091	193	382

Eastern Conference playoff: N.Y. Giants 10, Cleveland 0
NFL Championship: Baltimore 23, N.Y. Giants 17, sudden-death overtime

1959

EASTERN CONFERENCE
	W	L	T	Pct.	Pts.	OP
N.Y. Giants	10	2	0	.833	284	170
Cleveland	7	5	0	.583	270	214
Philadelphia	7	5	0	.583	268	278
Pittsburgh	6	5	1	.545	257	216
Washington	3	9	0	.250	185	350
Chi. Cardinals	2	10	0	.167	234	324

WESTERN CONFERENCE
	W	L	T	Pct.	Pts.	OP
Baltimore	9	3	0	.750	374	251
Chi. Bears	8	4	0	.667	252	196
Green Bay	7	5	0	.583	248	246
San Francisco	7	5	0	.583	255	237
Detroit	3	8	1	.273	203	275
Los Angeles	2	10	0	.167	242	315

NFL Championship: Baltimore 31, N.Y. Giants 16

1960 AFL

EASTERN DIVISION
	W	L	T	Pct.	Pts.	OP
Houston	10	4	0	.714	379	285
N.Y. Titans	7	7	0	.500	382	399
Buffalo	5	8	1	.385	296	303
Boston	5	9	0	.357	286	349

WESTERN DIVISION
	W	L	T	Pct.	Pts.	OP
L.A. Chargers	10	4	0	.714	373	336
Dall. Texans	8	6	0	.571	362	253
Oakland	6	8	0	.429	319	388
Denver	4	9	1	.308	309	393

AFL Championship: Houston 24, L.A. Chargers 16

1960 NFL

EASTERN CONFERENCE
	W	L	T	Pct.	Pts.	OP
Philadelphia	10	2	0	.833	321	246
Cleveland	8	3	1	.727	362	217
N.Y. Giants	6	4	2	.600	271	261
St. Louis	6	5	1	.545	288	230
Pittsburgh	5	6	1	.455	240	275
Washington	1	9	2	.100	178	309

WESTERN CONFERENCE
	W	L	T	Pct.	Pts.	OP
Green Bay	8	4	0	.667	332	209
Detroit	7	5	0	.583	239	212
San Francisco	7	5	0	.583	208	205
Baltimore	6	6	0	.500	288	234
Chicago	5	6	1	.455	194	299
L.A. Rams	4	7	1	.364	265	297
Dall. Cowboys	0	11	1	.000	177	369

NFL Championship: Philadelphia 17, Green Bay 13

1961 AFL

EASTERN DIVISION
	W	L	T	Pct.	Pts.	OP
Houston	10	3	1	.769	513	242
Boston	9	4	1	.692	413	313
N.Y. Titans	7	7	0	.500	301	390
Buffalo	6	8	0	.429	294	342

WESTERN DIVISION
	W	L	T	Pct.	Pts.	OP
San Diego	12	2	0	.857	396	219
Dall. Texans	6	8	0	.429	334	343
Denver	3	11	0	.214	251	432
Oakland	2	12	0	.143	237	458

AFL Championship: Houston 10, San Diego 3

1961 NFL

EASTERN CONFERENCE
	W	L	T	Pct.	Pts.	OP
N.Y. Giants	10	3	1	.769	368	220
Philadelphia	10	4	0	.714	361	297
Cleveland	8	5	1	.615	319	270
St. Louis	7	7	0	.500	279	267
Pittsburgh	6	8	0	.429	295	287
Dall. Cowboys	4	9	1	.308	236	380
Washington	1	12	1	.077	174	392

WESTERN CONFERENCE
	W	L	T	Pct.	Pts.	OP
Green Bay	11	3	0	.786	391	223
Detroit	8	5	1	.615	270	258
Baltimore	8	6	0	.571	302	307
Chicago	8	6	0	.571	326	302
San Francisco	7	6	1	.538	346	272
Los Angeles	4	10	0	.286	263	333
Minnesota	3	11	0	.214	285	407

NFL Championship: Green Bay 37, N.Y. Giants 0

1962 AFL

EASTERN DIVISION
	W	L	T	Pct.	Pts.	OP
Houston	11	3	0	.786	387	270
Boston	9	4	1	.692	346	295
Buffalo	7	6	1	.538	309	272
N.Y. Titans	5	9	0	.357	278	423

WESTERN DIVISION
	W	L	T	Pct.	Pts.	OP
Dall. Texans	11	3	0	.786	389	233
Denver	7	7	0	.500	353	334
San Diego	4	10	0	.286	314	392
Oakland	1	13	0	.071	213	370

AFL Championship: Dallas Texans 20, Houston 17, sudden-death overtime

1962 NFL

EASTERN CONFERENCE
	W	L	T	Pct.	Pts.	OP
N.Y. Giants	12	2	0	.857	398	283
Pittsburgh	9	5	0	.643	312	363
Cleveland	7	6	1	.538	291	257
Washington	5	7	2	.417	305	376
Dall. Cowboys	5	8	1	.385	398	402
St. Louis	4	9	1	.308	287	361
Philadelphia	3	10	1	.231	282	356

WESTERN CONFERENCE
	W	L	T	Pct.	Pts.	OP
Green Bay	13	1	0	.929	415	148
Detroit	11	3	0	.786	315	177
Chicago	9	5	0	.643	321	287
Baltimore	7	7	0	.500	293	288
San Francisco	6	8	0	.429	282	331
Minnesota	2	11	1	.154	254	410
Los Angeles	1	12	1	.077	220	334

NFL Championship: Green Bay 16, N.Y. Giants 7

1963 AFL

EASTERN DIVISION
	W	L	T	Pct.	Pts.	OP
Boston	7	6	1	.538	317	257
Buffalo	7	6	1	.538	304	291
Houston	6	8	0	.429	302	372
N.Y. Jets	5	8	1	.385	249	399

WESTERN DIVISION
	W	L	T	Pct.	Pts.	OP
San Diego	11	3	0	.786	399	255
Oakland	10	4	0	.714	363	282
Kansas City	5	7	2	.417	347	263
Denver	2	11	1	.154	301	473

Eastern Division playoff: Boston 26, Buffalo 8
AFL Championship: San Diego 51, Boston 10

1963 NFL

EASTERN CONFERENCE
	W	L	T	Pct.	Pts.	OP
N.Y. Giants	11	3	0	.786	448	280
Cleveland	10	4	0	.714	343	262
St. Louis	9	5	0	.643	341	283
Pittsburgh	7	4	3	.636	321	295
Dallas	4	10	0	.286	305	378
Washington	3	11	0	.214	279	398
Philadelphia	2	10	2	.167	242	381

WESTERN CONFERENCE
	W	L	T	Pct.	Pts.	OP
Chicago	11	1	2	.917	301	144
Green Bay	11	2	1	.846	369	206
Baltimore	8	6	0	.571	316	285
Detroit	5	8	1	.385	326	265
Minnesota	5	8	1	.385	309	390
Los Angeles	5	9	0	.357	210	350
San Francisco	2	12	0	.143	198	391

NFL Championship: Chicago 14, N.Y. Giants 10

NFL STANDINGS

1964 AFL

EASTERN DIVISION
	W	L	T	Pct.	Pts.	OP
Buffalo	12	2	0	.857	400	242
Boston	10	3	1	.769	365	297
N.Y. Jets	5	8	1	.385	278	315
Houston	4	10	0	.286	310	355

WESTERN DIVISION
	W	L	T	Pct.	Pts.	OP
San Diego	8	5	1	.615	341	300
Kansas City	7	7	0	.500	366	306
Oakland	5	7	2	.417	303	350
Denver	2	11	1	.154	240	438

AFL Championship: Buffalo 20, San Diego 7

1964 NFL

EASTERN CONFERENCE
	W	L	T	Pct.	Pts.	OP
Cleveland	10	3	1	.769	415	293
St. Louis	9	3	2	.750	357	331
Philadelphia	6	8	0	.429	312	313
Washington	6	8	0	.429	307	305
Dallas	5	8	1	.385	250	289
Pittsburgh	5	9	0	.357	253	315
N.Y. Giants	2	10	2	.167	241	399

WESTERN CONFERENCE
	W	L	T	Pct.	Pts.	OP
Baltimore	12	2	0	.857	428	225
Green Bay	8	5	1	.615	342	245
Minnesota	8	5	1	.615	355	296
Detroit	7	5	2	.583	280	260
Los Angeles	5	7	2	.417	283	339
Chicago	5	9	0	.357	260	379
San Francisco	4	10	0	.286	236	330

NFL Championship: Cleveland 27, Baltimore 0

1965 AFL

EASTERN DIVISION
	W	L	T	Pct.	Pts.	OP
Buffalo	10	3	1	.769	313	226
N.Y. Jets	5	8	1	.385	285	303
Boston	4	8	2	.333	244	302
Houston	4	10	0	.286	298	429

WESTERN DIVISION
	W	L	T	Pct.	Pts.	OP
San Diego	9	2	3	.818	340	227
Oakland	8	5	1	.615	298	239
Kansas City	7	5	2	.583	322	285
Denver	4	10	0	.286	303	392

AFL Championship: Buffalo 23, San Diego 0

1965 NFL

EASTERN CONFERENCE
	W	L	T	Pct.	Pts.	OP
Cleveland	11	3	0	.786	363	325
Dallas	7	7	0	.500	325	280
N.Y. Giants	7	7	0	.500	270	338
Washington	6	8	0	.429	257	301
Philadelphia	5	9	0	.357	363	359
St. Louis	5	9	0	.357	296	309
Pittsburgh	2	12	0	.143	202	397

WESTERN CONFERENCE
	W	L	T	Pct.	Pts.	OP
Green Bay	10	3	1	.769	316	224
Baltimore	10	3	1	.769	389	284
Chicago	9	5	0	.643	409	275
San Francisco	7	6	1	.538	421	402
Minnesota	7	7	0	.500	383	403
Detroit	6	7	1	.462	257	295
Los Angeles	4	10	0	.286	269	328

Western Conference playoff: Green Bay 13, Baltimore 10, sudden-death overtime
NFL Championship: Green Bay 23, Cleveland 12

1966 AFL

EASTERN DIVISION
	W	L	T	Pct.	Pts.	OP
Buffalo	9	4	1	.692	358	255
Boston	8	4	2	.667	315	283
N.Y. Jets	6	6	2	.500	322	312
Houston	3	11	0	.214	335	396
Miami	3	11	0	.214	213	362

WESTERN DIVISION
	W	L	T	Pct.	Pts.	OP
Kansas City	11	2	1	.846	448	276
Oakland	8	5	1	.615	315	288
San Diego	7	6	1	.538	335	284
Denver	4	10	0	.286	196	381

AFL Championship: Kansas City 31, Buffalo 7

1966 NFL

EASTERN CONFERENCE
	W	L	T	Pct.	Pts.	OP
Dallas	10	3	1	.769	445	239
Cleveland	9	5	0	.643	403	259
Philadelphia	9	5	0	.643	326	340
St. Louis	8	5	1	.615	264	265
Washington	7	7	0	.500	351	355
Pittsburgh	5	8	1	.385	316	347
Atlanta	3	11	0	.214	204	437
N.Y. Giants	1	12	1	.077	263	501

WESTERN CONFERENCE
	W	L	T	Pct.	Pts.	OP
Green Bay	12	2	0	.857	335	163
Baltimore	9	5	0	.643	314	226
Los Angeles	8	6	0	.571	289	212
San Francisco	6	6	2	.500	320	325
Chicago	5	7	2	.417	234	272
Detroit	4	9	1	.308	206	317
Minnesota	4	9	1	.308	292	304

NFL Championship: Green Bay 34, Dallas 27
Super Bowl I: Green Bay (NFL) 35, Kansas City (AFL) 10

322 THE COMPLETE HANDBOOK OF PRO FOOTBALL

1967 AFL

EASTERN DIVISION

	W	L	T	Pct.	Pts.	OP
Houston	9	4	1	.692	258	199
N.Y. Jets	8	5	1	.615	371	329
Buffalo	4	10	0	.286	237	285
Miami	4	10	0	.286	219	407
Boston	3	10	1	.231	280	389

WESTERN DIVISION

	W	L	T	Pct.	Pts.	OP
Oakland	13	1	0	.929	468	238
Kansas City	9	5	0	.643	408	254
San Diego	8	5	1	.615	360	352
Denver	3	11	0	.214	256	409

AFL Championship: Oakland 40, Houston 7

1967 NFL

EASTERN CONFERENCE

Capitol Division

	W	L	T	Pct.	Pts.	OP
Dallas	9	5	0	.643	342	268
Philadelphia	6	7	1	.462	351	409
Washington	5	6	3	.455	347	353
New Orleans	3	11	0	.214	233	379

Century Division

	W	L	T	Pct.	Pts.	OP
Cleveland	9	5	0	.643	334	297
N.Y. Giants	7	7	0	.500	369	379
St. Louis	6	7	1	.462	333	356
Pittsburgh	4	9	1	.308	281	320

WESTERN CONFERENCE

Coastal Division

	W	L	T	Pct.	Pts.	OP
Los Angeles	11	1	2	.917	398	196
Baltimore	11	1	2	.917	394	198
San Francisco	7	7	0	.500	273	337
Atlanta	1	12	1	.077	175	422

Central Division

	W	L	T	Pct.	Pts.	OP
Green Bay	9	4	1	.692	332	209
Chicago	7	6	1	.538	239	218
Detroit	5	7	2	.417	260	259
Minnesota	3	8	3	.273	233	294

Conference Championships: Dallas 52, Cleveland 14; Green Bay 28, Los Angeles 7
NFL Championship: Green Bay 21, Dallas 17
Super Bowl II: Green Bay (NFL) 33, Oakland (AFL) 14

1968 AFL

EASTERN DIVISION

	W	L	T	Pct.	Pts.	OP
N.Y. Jets	11	3	0	.786	419	280
Houston	7	7	0	.500	303	248
Miami	5	8	1	.385	276	355
Boston	4	10	0	.286	229	406
Buffalo	1	12	1	.077	199	367

WESTERN DIVISION

	W	L	T	Pct.	Pts.	OP
Oakland	12	2	0	.857	453	233
Kansas City	12	2	0	.857	371	170
San Diego	9	5	0	.643	382	310
Denver	5	9	0	.357	255	404
Cincinnati	3	11	0	.214	215	329

Western Division playoff: Oakland 41, Kansas City 6
AFL Championship: N.Y. Jets 27, Oakland 23

1968 NFL

EASTERN CONFERENCE

Capitol Division

	W	L	T	Pct.	Pts.	OP
Dallas	12	2	0	.857	431	186
N.Y. Giants	7	7	0	.500	294	325
Washington	5	9	0	.357	249	358
Philadelphia	2	12	0	.143	202	351

Century Division

	W	L	T	Pct.	Pts.	OP
Cleveland	10	4	0	.714	394	273
St. Louis	9	4	1	.692	325	289
New Orleans	4	9	1	.308	246	327
Pittsburgh	2	11	1	.154	244	397

WESTERN CONFERENCE

Coastal Division

	W	L	T	Pct.	Pts.	OP
Baltimore	13	1	0	.929	402	144
Los Angeles	10	3	1	.769	312	200
San Francisco	7	6	1	.538	303	310
Atlanta	2	12	0	.143	170	389

Central Division

	W	L	T	Pct.	Pts.	OP
Minnesota	8	6	0	.571	282	242
Chicago	7	7	0	.500	250	333
Green Bay	6	7	1	.462	281	227
Detroit	4	8	2	.333	207	241

Conference Championships: Cleveland 31, Dallas 20; Baltimore 24, Minnesota 14
NFL Championship: Baltimore 34, Cleveland 0
Super Bowl III: N.Y. Jets (AFL) 16, Baltimore (NFL) 7

NFL STANDINGS

1969 AFL

EASTERN DIVISION

	W	L	T	Pct.	Pts.	OP
N.Y. Jets	10	4	0	.714	353	269
Houston	6	6	2	.500	278	279
Boston	4	10	0	.286	266	316
Buffalo	4	10	0	.286	230	359
Miami	3	10	1	.231	233	332

WESTERN DIVISION

	W	L	T	Pct.	Pts.	OP
Oakland	12	1	1	.923	377	242
Kansas City	11	3	0	.786	359	177
San Diego	8	6	0	.571	288	276
Denver	5	8	1	.385	297	344
Cincinnati	4	9	1	.308	280	367

Divisional playoffs: Kansas City 13, N.Y. Jets 6; Oakland 56, Houston 7
AFL Championship: Kansas City 17, Oakland 7

1969 NFL

EASTERN CONFERENCE

Capitol Division

	W	L	T	Pct.	Pts.	OP
Dallas	11	2	1	.846	369	223
Washington	7	5	2	.583	307	319
New Orleans	5	9	0	.357	311	393
Philadelphia	4	9	1	.308	279	377

Century Division

	W	L	T	Pct.	Pts.	OP
Cleveland	10	3	1	.769	351	300
N.Y. Giants	6	8	0	.429	264	298
St. Louis	4	9	1	.308	314	389
Pittsburgh	1	13	0	.071	218	404

WESTERN CONFERENCE

Coastal Division

	W	L	T	Pct.	Pts.	OP
Los Angeles	11	3	0	.786	320	243
Baltimore	8	5	1	.615	279	268
Atlanta	6	8	0	.429	276	268
San Francisco	4	8	2	.333	277	319

Central Division

	W	L	T	Pct.	Pts.	OP
Minnesota	12	2	0	.857	379	133
Detroit	9	4	1	.692	259	188
Green Bay	8	6	0	.571	269	221
Chicago	1	13	0	.071	210	339

Conference Championships: Cleveland 38, Dallas 14; Minnesota 23, Los Angeles 20
NFL Championship: Minnesota 27, Cleveland 7
Super Bowl IV: Kansas City (AFL) 23, Minnesota (NFL) 7

1970

AMERICAN CONFERENCE

Eastern Division

	W	L	T	Pct.	Pts.	OP
Baltimore	11	2	1	.846	321	234
Miami*	10	4	0	.714	297	228
N.Y. Jets	4	10	0	.286	255	286
Buffalo	3	10	1	.231	204	337
Boston	2	12	0	.143	149	361

Central Division

	W	L	T	Pct.	Pts.	OP
Cincinnati	8	6	0	.571	312	255
Cleveland	7	7	0	.500	286	265
Pittsburgh	5	9	0	.357	210	272
Houston	3	10	1	.231	217	352

Western Division

	W	L	T	Pct.	Pts.	OP
Oakland	8	4	2	.667	300	293
Kansas City	7	5	2	.583	272	244
San Diego	5	6	3	.455	282	278
Denver	5	8	1	.385	253	264

NATIONAL CONFERENCE

Eastern Division

	W	L	T	Pct.	Pts.	OP
Dallas	10	4	0	.714	299	221
N.Y. Giants	9	5	0	.643	301	270
St. Louis	8	5	1	.615	325	228
Washington	6	8	0	.429	297	314
Philadelphia	3	10	1	.231	241	332

Central Division

	W	L	T	Pct.	Pts.	OP
Minnesota	12	2	0	.857	335	143
Detroit*	10	4	0	.714	347	202
Chicago	6	8	0	.429	256	261
Green Bay	6	8	0	.429	196	293

Western Division

	W	L	T	Pct.	Pts.	OP
San Francisco	10	3	1	.769	352	267
Los Angeles	9	4	1	.692	325	202
Atlanta	4	8	2	.333	206	261
New Orleans	2	11	1	.154	172	347

Wild Card qualifier for playoffs
Divisional playoffs: Baltimore 17, Cincinnati 0; Oakland 21, Miami 14
AFC Championship: Baltimore 27, Oakland 17
Divisional playoffs: Dallas 5, Detroit 0; San Francisco 17, Minnesota 14
NFC Championship: Dallas 17, San Francisco 10
Super Bowl V: Baltimore (AFC) 16, Dallas (NFC) 13

1971

AMERICAN CONFERENCE
Eastern Division

	W	L	T	Pct.	Pts.	OP
Miami	10	3	1	.769	315	174
Baltimore*	10	4	0	.714	313	140
New England	6	8	0	.429	238	325
N.Y. Jets	6	8	0	.429	212	299
Buffalo	1	13	0	.071	184	394

Central Division

	W	L	T	Pct.	Pts.	OP
Cleveland	9	5	0	.643	285	273
Pittsburgh	6	8	0	.429	246	292
Houston	4	9	1	.308	251	330
Cincinnati	4	10	0	.286	284	265

Western Division

	W	L	T	Pct.	Pts.	OP
Kansas City	10	3	1	.769	302	208
Oakland	8	4	2	.667	344	278
San Diego	6	8	0	.429	311	341
Denver	4	9	1	.308	203	275

NATIONAL CONFERENCE
Eastern Division

	W	L	T	Pct.	Pts.	OP
Dallas	11	3	0	.786	406	222
Washington*	9	4	1	.692	276	190
Philadelphia	6	7	1	.462	221	302
St. Louis	4	9	1	.308	231	279
N.Y. Giants	4	10	0	.286	228	362

Central Division

	W	L	T	Pct.	Pts.	OP
Minnesota	11	3	0	.786	245	139
Detroit	7	6	1	.538	341	286
Chicago	6	8	0	.429	185	276
Green Bay	4	8	2	.333	274	298

Western Division

	W	L	T	Pct.	Pts.	OP
San Francisco	9	5	0	.643	300	216
Los Angeles	8	5	1	.615	313	260
Atlanta	7	6	1	.538	274	277
New Orleans	4	8	2	.333	266	347

*Wild Card qualifier for playoffs

Divisional playoffs: Miami 27, Kansas City 24, sudden-death overtime; Baltimore 20, Cleveland 3
AFC Championship: Miami 21, Baltimore 0
Divisional playoffs: Dallas 20, Minnesota 12; San Francisco 24, Washington 20
NFC Championship: Dallas 14, San Francisco 3
Super Bowl VI: Dallas (NFC) 24, Miami (AFC) 3

1972

AMERICAN CONFERENCE
Eastern Division

	W	L	T	Pct.	Pts.	OP
Miami	14	0	0	1.000	385	171
N.Y. Jets	7	7	0	.500	367	324
Baltimore	5	9	0	.357	235	252
Buffalo	4	9	1	.321	257	377
New England	3	11	0	.214	192	446

Central Division

	W	L	T	Pct.	Pts.	OP
Pittsburgh	11	3	0	.786	343	175
Cleveland*	10	4	0	.714	268	249
Cincinnati	8	6	0	.571	299	229
Houston	1	13	0	.071	164	380

Western Division

	W	L	T	Pct.	Pts.	OP
Oakland	10	3	1	.750	365	248
Kansas City	8	6	0	.571	287	254
Denver	5	9	0	.357	325	350
San Diego	4	9	1	.321	264	344

NATIONAL CONFERENCE
Eastern Division

	W	L	T	Pct.	Pts.	OP
Washington	11	3	0	.786	336	218
Dallas*	10	4	0	.714	319	240
N.Y. Giants	8	6	0	.571	331	247
St. Louis	4	9	1	.321	193	303
Philadelphia	2	11	1	.179	145	352

Central Division

	W	L	T	Pct.	Pts.	OP
Green Bay	10	4	0	.714	304	226
Detroit	8	5	1	.607	339	290
Minnesota	7	7	0	.500	301	252
Chicago	4	9	1	.321	225	275

Western Division

	W	L	T	Pct.	Pts.	OP
San Francisco	8	5	1	.607	353	249
Atlanta	7	7	0	.500	269	274
Los Angeles	6	7	1	.464	291	286
New Orleans	2	11	1	.179	215	361

*Wild Card qualifier for playoffs

Divisional playoffs: Pittsburgh 13, Oakland 7; Miami 20, Cleveland 14
AFC Championship: Miami 21, Pittsburgh 17
Divisional playoffs: Dallas 30, San Francisco 28; Washington 16, Green Bay 3
NFC Championship: Washington 26, Dallas 3
Super Bowl VII: Miami (AFC) 14, Washington (NFC) 7

NFL STANDINGS 325

1973

AMERICAN CONFERENCE

Eastern Division
	W	L	T	Pct.	Pts.	OP
Miami	12	2	0	.857	343	150
Buffalo	9	5	0	.643	259	230
New England	5	9	0	.357	258	300
Baltimore	4	10	0	.286	226	341
N.Y. Jets	4	10	0	.286	240	306

Central Division
	W	L	T	Pct.	Pts.	OP
Cincinnati	10	4	0	.714	286	231
Pittsburgh*	10	4	0	.714	347	210
Cleveland	7	5	2	.571	234	255
Houston	1	13	0	.071	199	447

Western Division
	W	L	T	Pct.	Pts.	OP
Oakland	9	4	1	.679	292	175
Denver	7	5	2	.571	354	296
Kansas City	7	5	2	.571	231	192
San Diego	2	11	1	.179	188	386

NATIONAL CONFERENCE

Eastern Division
	W	L	T	Pct.	Pts.	OP
Dallas	10	4	0	.714	382	203
Washington*	10	4	0	.714	325	198
Philadelphia	5	8	1	.393	310	393
St. Louis	4	9	1	.321	286	365
N.Y. Giants	2	11	1	.179	226	362

Central Division
	W	L	T	Pct.	Pts.	OP
Minnesota	12	2	0	.857	296	168
Detroit	6	7	1	.464	271	247
Green Bay	5	7	2	.429	202	259
Chicago	3	11	0	.214	195	334

Western Division
	W	L	T	Pct.	Pts.	OP
Los Angeles	12	2	0	.857	388	178
Atlanta	9	5	0	.643	318	224
New Orleans	5	9	0	.357	163	312
San Francisco	5	9	0	.357	262	319

*Wild Card qualifier for playoffs
Divisional playoffs: Oakland 33, Pittsburgh 14; Miami 34, Cincinnati 16
AFC Championship: Miami 27, Oakland 10
Divisional playoffs: Minnesota 27, Washington 20; Dallas 27, Los Angeles 16
NFC Championship: Minnesota 27, Dallas 10
Super Bowl VIII: Miami (AFC) 24, Minnesota (NFC) 7

1974

AMERICAN CONFERENCE

Eastern Division
	W	L	T	Pct.	Pts.	OP
Miami	11	3	0	.786	327	216
Buffalo*	9	5	0	.643	264	244
New England	7	7	0	.500	348	289
N.Y. Jets	7	7	0	.500	279	300
Baltimore	2	12	0	.143	190	329

Central Division
	W	L	T	Pct.	Pts.	OP
Pittsburgh	10	3	1	.750	305	189
Cincinnati	7	7	0	.500	283	259
Houston	7	7	0	.500	236	282
Cleveland	4	10	0	.286	251	344

Western Division
	W	L	T	Pct.	Pts.	OP
Oakland	12	2	0	.857	355	228
Denver	7	6	1	.536	302	294
Kansas City	5	9	0	.357	233	293
San Diego	5	9	0	.357	212	285

NATIONAL CONFERENCE

Eastern Division
	W	L	T	Pct.	Pts.	OP
St. Louis	10	4	0	.714	285	218
Washington*	10	4	0	.714	320	196
Dallas	8	6	0	.571	297	235
Philadelphia	7	7	0	.500	242	217
N.Y. Giants	2	12	0	.143	195	299

Central Division
	W	L	T	Pct.	Pts.	OP
Minnesota	10	4	0	.714	310	195
Detroit	7	7	0	.500	256	270
Green Bay	6	8	0	.429	210	206
Chicago	4	10	0	.286	152	279

Western Division
	W	L	T	Pct.	Pts.	OP
Los Angeles	10	4	0	.714	263	181
San Francisco	6	8	0	.429	226	236
New Orleans	5	9	0	.357	166	263
Atlanta	3	11	0	.214	111	271

*Wild Card qualifier for playoffs
Divisional playoffs: Oakland 28, Miami 26; Pittsburgh 32, Buffalo 14
AFC Championship: Pittsburgh 24, Oakland 13
Divisional playoffs: Minnesota 30, St. Louis 14; Los Angeles 19, Washington 10
NFC Championship: Minnesota 14, Los Angeles 10
Super Bowl IX: Pittsburgh (AFC) 16, Minnesota (NFC) 6

1975

AMERICAN CONFERENCE
Eastern Division
	W	L	T	Pct.	Pts.	OP
Baltimore	10	4	0	.714	395	269
Miami	10	4	0	.714	357	222
Buffalo	8	6	0	.571	420	355
New England	3	11	0	.214	258	358
N.Y. Jets	3	11	0	.214	258	433

Central Division
	W	L	T	Pct.	Pts.	OP
Pittsburgh	12	2	0	.857	373	162
Cincinnati*	11	3	0	.786	340	246
Houston	10	4	0	.714	293	226
Cleveland	3	11	0	.214	218	372

Western Division
	W	L	T	Pct.	Pts.	OP
Oakland	11	3	0	.786	375	255
Denver	6	8	0	.429	254	307
Kansas City	5	9	0	.357	282	341
San Diego	2	12	0	.143	189	345

NATIONAL CONFERENCE
Eastern Division
	W	L	T	Pct.	Pts.	OP
St. Louis	11	3	0	.786	356	276
Dallas*	10	4	0	.714	350	268
Washington	8	6	0	.571	325	276
N.Y. Giants	5	9	0	.357	216	306
Philadelphia	4	10	0	.286	225	302

Central Division
	W	L	T	Pct.	Pts.	OP
Minnesota	12	2	0	.857	377	180
Detroit	7	7	0	.500	245	262
Chicago	4	10	0	.286	191	379
Green Bay	4	10	0	.286	226	285

Western Division
	W	L	T	Pct.	Pts.	OP
Los Angeles	12	2	0	.857	312	135
San Francisco	5	9	0	.357	255	286
Atlanta	4	10	0	.286	240	289
New Orleans	2	12	0	.143	165	360

Wild Card qualifier for playoffs
Divisional playoffs: Pittsburgh 28, Baltimore 10; Oakland 31, Cincinnati 28
AFC Championship: Pittsburgh 16, Oakland 10
Divisional playoffs: Los Angeles 35, St. Louis 23; Dallas 17, Minnesota 14
NFC Championship: Dallas 37, Los Angeles 7
Super Bowl X: Pittsburgh (AFC) 21, Dallas (NFC) 17

1976

AMERICAN CONFERENCE
Eastern Division
	W	L	T	Pct.	Pts.	OP
Baltimore	11	3	0	.786	417	246
New England*	11	3	0	.786	376	236
Miami	6	8	0	.429	263	264
N.Y. Jets	3	11	0	.214	169	383
Buffalo	2	12	0	.143	245	363

Central Division
	W	L	T	Pct.	Pts.	OP
Pittsburgh	10	4	0	.714	342	138
Cincinnati	10	4	0	.714	335	210
Cleveland	9	5	0	.643	267	287
Houston	5	9	0	.357	222	273

Western Division
	W	L	T	Pct.	Pts.	OP
Oakland	13	1	0	.929	350	237
Denver	9	5	0	.643	315	206
San Diego	6	8	0	.429	248	285
Kansas City	5	9	0	.357	290	376
Tampa Bay	0	14	0	.000	125	412

NATIONAL CONFERENCE
Eastern Division
	W	L	T	Pct.	Pts.	OP
Dallas	11	3	0	.786	296	194
Washington*	10	4	0	.714	291	217
St. Louis	10	4	0	.714	309	267
Philadelphia	4	10	0	.286	165	286
N.Y. Giants	3	11	0	.214	170	250

Central Division
	W	L	T	Pct.	Pts.	OP
Minnesota	11	2	1	.821	305	176
Chicago	7	7	0	.500	253	216
Detroit	6	8	0	.429	262	220
Green Bay	5	9	0	.357	218	299

Western Division
	W	L	T	Pct.	Pts.	OP
Los Angeles	10	3	1	.750	351	190
San Francisco	8	6	0	.571	270	190
Atlanta	4	10	0	.286	172	312
New Orleans	4	10	0	.286	253	346
Seattle	2	12	0	.143	229	429

Wild Card qualifier for playoffs
Divisional playoffs: Oakland 24, New England 21; Pittsburgh 40, Baltimore 14
AFC Championship: Oakland 24, Pittsburgh 7
Divisional playoffs: Minnesota 35, Washington 20; Los Angeles 14, Dallas 12
NFC Championship: Minnesota 24, Los Angeles 13
Super Bowl XI: Oakland (AFC) 32, Minnesota (NFC) 14

NFL STANDINGS

1977

AMERICAN CONFERENCE

Eastern Division

	W	L	T	Pct.	Pts.	OP
Baltimore	10	4	0	.714	295	221
Miami	10	4	0	.714	313	197
New England	9	5	0	.643	278	217
N.Y. Jets	3	11	0	.214	191	300
Buffalo	3	11	0	.214	160	313

Central Division

	W	L	T	Pct.	Pts.	OP
Pittsburgh	9	5	0	.643	283	243
Houston	8	6	0	.571	299	230
Cincinnati	8	6	0	.571	238	235
Cleveland	6	8	0	.429	269	267

Western Division

	W	L	T	Pct.	Pts.	OP
Denver	12	2	0	.857	274	148
Oakland*	11	3	0	.786	351	230
San Diego	7	7	0	.500	222	205
Seattle	5	9	0	.357	282	373
Kansas City	2	12	0	.143	225	349

NATIONAL CONFERENCE

Eastern Division

	W	L	T	Pct.	Pts.	OP
Dallas	12	2	0	.857	345	212
Washington	9	5	0	.643	196	189
St. Louis	7	7	0	.500	272	287
Philadelphia	5	9	0	.357	220	207
N.Y. Giants	5	9	0	.357	181	265

Central Division

	W	L	T	Pct.	Pts.	OP
Minnesota	9	5	0	.643	231	227
Chicago*	9	5	0	.643	255	253
Detroit	6	8	0	.429	183	252
Green Bay	4	10	0	.286	134	219
Tampa Bay	2	12	0	.143	103	223

Western Division

	W	L	T	Pct.	Pts.	OP
Los Angeles	10	4	0	.714	302	146
Atlanta	7	7	0	.500	179	129
San Francisco	5	9	0	.357	220	260
New Orleans	3	11	0	.214	232	336

*Wild Card qualifier for playoffs

Divisional playoffs: Denver 34, Pittsburgh 21; Oakland 37, Baltimore 31, sudden-death overtime
AFC Championship: Denver 20, Oakland 17
Divisional playoffs: Dallas 37, Chicago 7; Minnesota 14, Los Angeles 7
NFC Championship: Dallas 23, Minnesota 6
Super Bowl XII: Dallas (NFC) 27, Denver (AFC) 10

1978

AMERICAN CONFERENCE

Eastern Division

	W	L	T	Pct.	Pts.	OP
New England	11	5	0	.688	358	286
Miami*	11	5	0	.688	372	254
N.Y. Jets	8	8	0	.500	359	364
Buffalo	5	11	0	.313	302	354
Baltimore	5	11	0	.313	239	421

Central Division

	W	L	T	Pct.	Pts.	OP
Pittsburgh	14	2	0	.875	356	195
Houston*	10	6	0	.625	283	298
Cleveland	8	8	0	.500	334	356
Cincinnati	4	12	0	.250	252	284

Western Division

	W	L	T	Pct.	Pts.	OP
Denver	10	6	0	.625	282	198
Oakland	9	7	0	.563	311	283
Seattle	9	7	0	.563	345	358
San Diego	9	7	0	.563	355	309
Kansas City	4	12	0	.250	243	327

NATIONAL CONFERENCE

Eastern Division

	W	L	T	Pct.	Pts.	OP
Dallas	12	4	0	.750	384	208
Philadelphia*	9	7	0	.563	270	250
Washington	8	8	0	.500	273	283
St. Louis	6	10	0	.375	248	296
N.Y. Giants	6	10	0	.375	264	298

Central Division

	W	L	T	Pct.	Pts.	OP
Minnesota	8	7	1	.531	294	306
Green Bay	8	7	1	.531	249	269
Detroit	7	9	0	.438	290	300
Chicago	7	9	0	.438	253	274
Tampa Bay	5	11	0	.313	241	259

Western Division

	W	L	T	Pct.	Pts.	OP
Los Angeles	12	4	0	.750	316	245
Atlanta*	9	7	0	.563	240	290
New Orleans	7	9	0	.438	281	298
San Francisco	2	14	0	.125	219	350

*Wild Card qualifier for playoffs

First-round playoff: Houston 17, Miami 9
Divisional playoffs: Houston 31, New England 14; Pittsburgh 33, Denver 10
AFC Championship: Pittsburgh 34, Houston 5
First-round playoff: Atlanta 14, Philadelphia 13
Divisional playoffs: Dallas 27, Atlanta 20; Los Angeles 34, Minnesota 10
NFC Championship: Dallas 28, Los Angeles 0
Super Bowl XIII: Pittsburgh (AFC) 35, Dallas (NFC) 31

1979

AMERICAN CONFERENCE

Eastern Division

	W	L	T	Pct.	Pts.	OP
Miami	10	6	0	.625	341	257
New England	9	7	0	.563	411	326
N.Y. Jets	8	8	0	.500	337	383
Buffalo	7	9	0	.438	268	279
Baltimore	5	11	0	.313	271	351

Central Division

	W	L	T	Pct.	Pts.	OP
Pittsburgh	12	4	0	.750	416	262
Houston*	11	5	0	.688	362	331
Cleveland	9	7	0	.563	359	352
Cincinnati	4	12	0	.250	337	421

Western Division

	W	L	T	Pct.	Pts.	OP
San Diego	12	4	0	.750	411	246
Denver*	10	6	0	.625	289	262
Seattle	9	7	0	.563	378	372
Oakland	9	7	0	.563	365	337
Kansas City	7	9	0	.438	238	262

NATIONAL CONFERENCE

Eastern Division

	W	L	T	Pct.	Pts.	OP
Dallas	11	5	0	.688	371	313
Philadelphia*	11	5	0	.688	339	282
Washington	10	6	0	.625	348	295
N.Y. Giants	6	10	0	.375	237	323
St. Louis	5	11	0	.313	307	358

Central Division

	W	L	T	Pct.	Pts.	OP
Tampa Bay	10	6	0	.625	273	237
Chicago*	10	6	0	.625	306	249
Minnesota	7	9	0	.438	259	337
Green Bay	5	11	0	.313	246	316
Detroit	2	14	0	.125	219	365

Western Division

	W	L	T	Pct.	Pts.	OP
Los Angeles	9	7	0	.563	323	309
New Orleans	8	8	0	.500	370	360
Atlanta	6	10	0	.375	300	388
San Francisco	2	14	0	.125	308	416

Wild Card qualifier for playoffs
First-round playoff: Houston 13, Denver 7
Divisional playoffs: Houston 17, San Diego 14; Pittsburgh 34, Miami 14
AFC Championship: Pittsburgh 27, Houston 13
First-round playoff: Philadelphia 27, Chicago 17
Divisional playoffs: Tampa Bay 24, Philadelphia 17; Los Angeles 21, Dallas 19
NFC Championship: Los Angeles 9, Tampa Bay 0
Super Bowl XIV: Pittsburgh (AFC) 31, Los Angeles (NFC) 19

1980

AMERICAN CONFERENCE

Eastern Division

	W	L	T	Pct.	Pts.	OP
Buffalo	11	5	0	.688	320	260
New England	10	6	0	.625	441	325
Miami	8	8	0	.500	266	305
Baltimore	7	9	0	.438	355	387
N.Y. Jets	4	12	0	.250	302	395

Central Division

	W	L	T	Pct.	Pts.	OP
Cleveland	11	5	0	.688	357	310
Houston*	11	5	0	.688	295	251
Pittsburgh	9	7	0	.563	352	313
Cincinnati	6	10	0	.375	244	312

Western Division

	W	L	T	Pct.	Pts.	OP
San Diego	11	5	0	.688	418	327
Oakland*	11	5	0	.688	364	306
Kansas City	8	8	0	.500	319	336
Denver	8	8	0	.500	310	323
Seattle	4	12	0	.250	291	408

NATIONAL CONFERENCE

Eastern Division

	W	L	T	Pct.	Pts.	OP
Philadelphia	12	4	0	.750	384	222
Dallas*	12	4	0	.750	454	311
Washington	6	10	0	.375	261	293
St. Louis	5	11	0	.313	299	350
N.Y. Giants	4	12	0	.250	249	425

Central Division

	W	L	T	Pct.	Pts.	OP
Minnesota	9	7	0	.563	317	308
Detroit	9	7	0	.563	334	272
Chicago	7	9	0	.437	304	264
Tampa Bay	5	10	1	.343	271	341
Green Bay	5	10	1	.343	231	371

Western Division

	W	L	T	Pct.	Pts.	OP
Atlanta	12	4	0	.750	405	272
Los Angeles*	11	5	0	.688	424	289
San Francisco	6	10	0	.375	320	415
New Orleans	1	15	0	.063	291	487

Wild Card qualifier for playoffs
First-round playoff: Oakland 27, Houston 7
Divisional playoffs: San Diego 20, Buffalo 14; Oakland 14, Cleveland 12
AFC Championship: Oakland 34, San Diego 27
First-round playoff: Dallas 34, Los Angeles 13
Divisional playoffs: Philadelphia 31, Minnesota 16; Dallas 30, Atlanta 27
NFC Championship: Philadelphia 20, Dallas 7
Super Bowl XV: Oakland (AFC) 27, Philadelphia (NFC) 10

NFL STANDINGS

1981

AMERICAN CONFERENCE
Eastern Division

	W	L	T	Pct.	Pts.	OP
Miami	11	4	1	.719	345	275
N.Y. Jets*	10	5	1	.656	355	287
Buffalo*	10	6	0	.625	311	276
Baltimore	2	14	0	.125	259	533
New England	2	14	0	.125	322	370

Central Division

	W	L	T	Pct.	Pts.	OP
Cincinnati	12	4	0	.750	421	304
Pittsburgh	8	8	0	.500	356	297
Houston	7	9	0	.438	281	355
Cleveland	5	11	0	.313	276	375

Western Division

	W	L	T	Pct.	Pts.	OP
San Diego	10	6	0	.625	478	390
Denver	10	6	0	.625	321	289
Kansas City	9	7	0	.563	343	290
Oakland	7	9	0	.438	273	343
Seattle	6	10	0	.375	322	388

NATIONAL CONFERENCE
Eastern Division

	W	L	T	Pct.	Pts.	OP
Dallas	12	4	0	.750	367	277
Philadelphia*	10	6	0	.625	368	221
N.Y. Giants*	9	7	0	.563	295	257
Washington	8	8	0	.500	347	349
St. Louis	7	9	0	.438	315	408

Central Division

	W	L	T	Pct.	Pts.	OP
Tampa Bay	9	7	0	.563	315	268
Detroit	8	8	0	.500	397	322
Green Bay	8	8	0	.500	324	361
Minnesota	7	9	0	.438	325	369
Chicago	6	10	0	.375	253	324

Western Division

	W	L	T	Pct.	Pts.	OP
San Francisco	13	3	0	.813	357	250
Atlanta	7	9	0	.438	426	355
Los Angeles	6	10	0	.375	303	351
New Orleans	4	12	0	.250	207	378

*Wild card qualifier for playoffs

First-round playoff: Buffalo 31, N.Y. Jets 27
Divisional playoffs: San Diego 41, Miami 38 (OT); Cincinnati 28, Buffalo 21
AFC Championship: Cincinnati 27, San Diego 7
First-round playoff: N.Y. Giants 27, Philadelphia 21
Divisional playoffs: Dallas 38, Tampa Bay 0; San Francisco 38, N.Y. Giants 24
NFC Championship: San Francisco 28, Dallas 27
Super Bowl XVI: San Francisco (NFC) 26, Cincinnati (AFC) 21

*1982

AMERICAN CONFERENCE

	W	L	T	Pct.	Pts.	OP
L.A. Raiders	8	1	0	.889	260	200
Miami	7	2	0	.778	198	131
Cincinnati	7	2	0	.778	232	177
Pittsburgh	6	3	0	.667	204	146
San Diego	6	3	0	.667	288	221
N.Y. Jets	6	3	0	.667	245	166
New England	5	4	0	.556	143	157
Cleveland	4	5	0	.444	140	182
Buffalo	4	5	0	.444	150	154
Seattle	4	5	0	.444	127	147
Kansas City	3	6	0	.333	176	184
Denver	2	7	0	.222	148	226
Houston	1	8	0	.111	136	245
Baltimore	0	8	1	.063	113	236

NATIONAL CONFERENCE

	W	L	T	Pct.	Pts.	OP
Washington	8	1	0	.889	190	128
Dallas	6	3	0	.667	226	145
Green Bay	5	3	1	.611	226	169
Minnesota	5	4	0	.556	187	198
Atlanta	5	4	0	.556	183	199
St. Louis	5	4	0	.556	135	170
Tampa Bay	5	4	0	.556	158	178
Detroit	4	5	0	.444	181	176
New Orleans	4	5	0	.444	129	160
N.Y. Giants	4	5	0	.444	164	160
San Francisco	3	6	0	.333	209	206
Chicago	3	6	0	.333	141	174
Philadelphia	3	6	0	.333	191	195
L.A. Rams	2	7	0	.222	200	250

Top eight teams in each Conference qualified for playoffs under format necessitated by strike-shortened season

First-round playoffs: Miami 28, New England 13; L.A. Raiders 27, Cleveland 10; N.Y. Jets 44, Cincinnati 17; San Diego 31, Pittsburgh 28
Second-round playoffs: N.Y. Jets 17, L.A. Raiders 14; Miami 34, San Diego 13
AFC Championship: Miami 14, N.Y. Jets 0
First-round playoffs: Green Bay 41, St. Louis 16; Washington 31, Detroit 7; Minnesota 30, Atlanta 24; Dallas 30, Tampa Bay 17
Second-round playoffs: Washington 21, Minnesota 7; Dallas 37, Green Bay 26
NFC Championship: Washington 31, Dallas 17
Super Bowl XVII: Washington 27, Miami 17

John Elway cocks the arm that launched 77 touchdowns.

JOHN ELWAY CALLS HIS SHOT

You're John Elway, All-American quarterback at Stanford and major-league baseball prospect, and you've called the option play. Do you pass footballs or run down fly balls?

The NFL wants you, the USFL wants you and the Yankees want you. You're the No. 1 pick in the NFL draft and you've got $140,000 already in the till after playing a summer in right field for the Yankee's Oneonta (N.Y.) farm club.

You've set NCAA records for passing attempts (1,243) and completions (774). You've thrown for 9,349 yards and 77 touchdowns and you're the most heralded college quarterback since Joe Willie Namath.

As a football player, you're projected as an instant pro superstar. A scout for BLESTO, one of the NFL's scouting combines, says of you: "He has the touch, the feel, the accuracy, and all the intangibles one looks for in a quarterback."

As a baseball player, the jury is out. At Oneonta, you hit .318 with four homers, 25 RBI and 13 stolen bases in 42 games. Jeff Scott, the Seattle Mariners' assistant director of player development, says of you: "He has some baseball ability, but not enough to knock your eyes out."

That same arm made Yanks covet him for right field.

Nonetheless, you're being wooed by George Steinbrenner. You and your agent, Marvin Demoff, have had provisional contract talks with the Yankees and they've reportedly offered you a five-year contract for an average of $500,000 a year, with an escape clause after each of the first three seasons.

You're a California boy and you've made it clear that, if it's football, you prefer to play for a West Coast team and not Frank Kush and the Baltimore Colts, the team that has first shot at you in the draft.

The Colts turn down impressive pre-draft offers from the San Diego Chargers and the Los Angeles Raiders and you're shocked and defiant. The Colts choose you and say they'll try to sign you. You say, "The Colts knew I had a royal flush, but they still called me on it."

The Colts have painted themselves into a corner. You announce that you're oiling your glove and getting ready to play baseball. You know you can try your hand in the minors for a couple of years and, if the future doesn't look bright in baseball, you can come back to the NFL as a free agent, able to name your club. After all, Roger Staubach had a four-year layoff between Annapolis and Dallas and it didn't hurt him.

You're in the best possible bargaining position and you're playing with a winning hand. You force the Colts to trade your rights to quarterback-hungry Denver in exchange for the Broncos' top pick, offensive lineman Chris Hinton, backup quarterback Mark Herrmann and a No. 1 draft choice in 1984.

You sign five one-year contracts for $1 million a year. And all the world finds out that your best game isn't baseball or football. It's poker.

1983 NFL DRAFT

Player	Order No.	Pos.	College	Club	Round
Abramowitz, Sid	113	T	Tulsa	Baltimore	5
Achica, George	57	DT	Southern California	Baltimore	3
Achter, Rod	239	WR	Toledo	Minnesota	9
Allen, Anthony	156	WR	Washington	Atlanta	6
Anderson, Gary	20	WR	Arkansas	San Diego	1
Arbubakrr, Hasson	238	DT	Texas Tech	Tampa Bay	9
Arnold, Jim	119	P	Vanderbilt	Kansas City	5
Ashley, Walker Lee	73	LB	Penn State	Minnesota	3
Austin, Cliff	66	RB	Clemson	New Orleans	3
Bailey, Don	283	C	Miami	Denver	11
Baldwin, Bruce	125	DB	Harding, Ark.	Denver	5
Bass, Mike	155	K	Illinois	New England	6
Belcher, Jack	227	C	Boston College	Los Angeles Rams	9
Belcher, Kevin	153	G	Texas-El Paso	New York Giants	6
Belk, Rocky	176	WR	Miami	Cleveland	7
Benson, Charles	76	DE	Baylor	Miami	3
Bird, Steve	130	WR	Eastern Kentucky	St. Louis	5
Black, Mike	181	P	Arizona State	Detroit	7
Blackledge, Todd	7	QB	Penn State	Kansas City	1
Blaylock, Billy	314	DB	Tennessee Tech	San Diego	12
Bortz, Mark	219	DT	Iowa	Chicago	8
Bostic, Keith	42	DB	Michigan	Houston	2
Bouier, Lorenzo	331	RB	Maine	Dallas	12
Bowyer, Walt	254	DE	Arizona State	Denver	10
Branton, Rheugene	148	WR	Texas Southern	Tampa Bay	6
Briscoe, Carlton	216	DB	McNeese State	Green Bay	8
Britt, James	43	DB	Louisiana State	Atlanta	2
Brown, Gurnest	180	DT	Maryland	Buffalo	7
Brown, Mark	250	LB	Purdue	Miami	9
Brown, Melvin	255	DB	Mississippi	Minnesota	10
Brown, Norris	213	TE	Georgia	Minnesota	8
Brown, Otis	242	RB	Jackson State	St. Louis	9
Brown, Ron	41	WR	Arizona State	Cleveland	2
Brown, Steve	83	DB	Oregon	Houston	3
Brown, Todd	154	WR	Nebraska	Detroit	6
Browner, Joey	19	DB	Southern California	Minnesota	1
Bryant, Kelvin	196	RB	North Carolina	Washington	7
Butcher, Brian	298	G	Clemson	Minnesota	11
Byrd, Gill	22	DB	San Jose State	San Diego	1
Caldwell, Bryan	77	DE	Arizona State	Dallas	3
Caldwell, Tony	82	LB	Washington	Los Angeles Rams	3
Camp, Reggie	68	DE	California	Cleveland	3
Capers, Wayne	52	WR	Kansas	Pittsburgh	2
Carter, Anthony	334	WR	Michigan	Miami	12
Casper, Clete	311	QB	Washington State	Los Angeles Rams	12
Castille, Jeremiah	72	DB	Alabama	Tampa Bay	3
Castor, Chris	123	DB	Duke	Seattle	5
Charles, Mike	55	DT	Syracuse	Miami	2

No. 2 in draft, SMU's Eric Dickerson is a rookie Ram.

334 THE COMPLETE HANDBOOK OF PRO FOOTBALL

Seattle got Penn State's Curt Warner, No. 3 overall.

NFL DRAFT 335

Player	Order No.	Pos.	College	Club	Round
Chickillo, Tony	131	DT	Miami	Tampa Bay	5
Christensen, Jeff	137	QB	Eastern Illinois	Cincinnati	5
Clark, Jessie	188	RB	Arkansas	Green Bay	7
Clasby, Bob	236	T	Notre Dame	Seattle	9
Clayton, Mark	223	WR	Louisville	Miami	8
Cofer, Mike	67	DE	Tennessee	Detroit	3
Collier, Reggie	162	QB	Southern Mississippi	Dallas	6
Contz, Bill	122	T	Penn State	Cleveland	5
Cooper, Mark	31	T	Miami	Denver	2
Covert, Jim	6	T	Pittsburgh	Chicago	1
Craig, Roger	49	RB	Nebraska	San Francisco	2
Creswell, Smiley	118	DE	Michigan State	New England	5
Crum, Stu	328	K	Tulsa	New York Jets	12
Curley, August	94	LB	Southern California	Detroit	4
Darby, Byron	120	DT	Southern California	Philadelphia	5
Dardar, Ramsey	71	DT	Louisiana State	St. Louis	3
Dawkins, Julius	320	WR	Pittsburgh	Buffalo	12
De Ayala, Kiki	152	LB	Texas	Cincinnati	6
Dent, Richard	203	DE	Tennesee State	Chicago	8
Dickerson, Eric	2	RB	Southern Methodist	Los Angeles Rams	1
Dotterer, Mike	222	RB	Stanford	Los Angeles Raiders	8
Dow, Don	317	T	Washington	Seattle	12
Drechsler, Dave	48	G	North Carolina	Green Bay	2
Dressel, Chris	69	TE	Stanford	Houston	3
Duda, Mark	96	DT	Maryland	St. Louis	4
Duerson, Dave	64	DB	Notre Dame	Chicago	3
Dunaway, Craig	218	TE	Michigan	Pittsburgh	8
Dunsmore, Pat	107	TE	Drake	Chicago	4
Dupree, Myron	172	DB	No. Carolina Central	Denver	7
Durham, Darius	270	WR	San Diego State	Tampa Bay	10
Durham, James	207	DB	Houston	Buffalo	8
Eason, Calvin	294	DB	Houston	New England	11
Eason, Tony	15	QB	Illinois	New England	1
Eatman, Irv	204	T	UCLA	Kansas City	8
Edgar, Anthony	174	RB	Hawaii	Philadelphia	7
Ehin, Chuck	329	DT	Brigham Young	San Diego	12
Ekern, Andy	326	T	Missouri	New England	12
Elko, Bill	192	DT	Louisiana State	San Diego	7
Ellard, Henry	32	WR	Fresno State	Los Angeles Raiders	2
Elway, John	1	QB	Stanford	Baltimore	1
Fada, Bob	230	G	Pittsburgh	Chicago	9
Farren, Paul	316	T	Boston University	Cleveland	12
Faulkner, Chris	108	TE	Florida	Dallas	4
Feasel, Grant	161	C	Abilene Christian	Baltimore	6
Fernandez, Mervyn	277	WR	San Jose State	Los Angeles Raiders	10
Fike, Dan	274	T	Florida	New York Jets	10
Foster, Jerome	139	DT	Ohio State	Houston	5
Gandy, Geff	279	LB	Baylor	Washington	10
Gardner, Ellis	146	T	Georgia Tech	Kansas City	6
Garrity, Greg	140	WR	Penn State	Pittsburgh	5
Gault, Willie	18	WR	Tennessee	Chicago	1
Giacomarro, Ralph	268	P	Penn State	Atlanta	10
Gilbert, Marcus	251	RB	Texas Christian	Washington	9
Gipson, Reginald	150	RB	Alabama A&M	Seattle	6
Grant, Otis	134	WR	Michigan State	Los Angeles	5
Gray, Riki	117	LB	Southern California	San Francisco	5
Green, Boyce	288	RB	Carson-Newman	Cleveland	11
Green, Darrell	28	DB	Texas A&I	Washington	1

336 THE COMPLETE HANDBOOK OF PRO FOOTBALL

San Diego made Arkansas' Billy Ray Smith a first-rounder.

A Bear of a tackle is Pitt's Jimbo Covert, the sixth pick.

338 THE COMPLETE HANDBOOK OF PRO FOOTBALL

Kansas City tagged Penn State's Todd Blackledge No. 7.

NFL DRAFT 339

Player	Order No.	Pos.	College	Club	Round
Green, Mike	245	LB	Oklahoma State	San Diego	9
Greenwood, David	206	DB	Wisconsin	New Orleans	8
Griffin, James	193	DB	Middle Tennessee	Cincinnati	7
Grimes, Randy	45	C	Baylor	Tampa Bay	2
Gross, Al	246	DB	Arizona	Dallas	9
Haddix, Michael	8	RB	Mississippi State	Philadelphia	1
Haji-Sheikh, Ali	237	K	Michigan	New York Giants	9
Hallstrom, Todd	224	T	Minnesota	Washington	8
Ham, Robin	243	C	West Texas State	Green Bay	9
Harmon, Mike	301	WR	Mississippi	New York Jets	11
Harper, John	102	LB	Southern Illinois	Atlanta	4
Harris, Bob	211	DB	Auburn	St. Louis	8
Harris, George	116	LB	Houston	Denver	5
Harvey, John	327	DT	Southern California	Green Bay	12
Hawkins, Brian	228	DB	San Jose State	Denver	9
Haworth, Steve	142	DB	Oklahoma	Houston	6
Headen, Andy	205	LB	Clemson	New York Giants	8
Hector, Johnny	51	RB	Texas A&M	New York Jets	2
Heflin, Victor	143	DB	Delaware State	Denver	6
Hernandez, Matt	210	T	Purdue	Seattle	8
Higginbotham, John	324	DT	N.E. Oklahoma	Tampa Bay	12
Hill, Greg	86	DB	Oklahoma State	Houston	4
Hinton, Chris	4	G	Northwestern	Denver	1
Holmoe, Tom	90	DB	Brigham Young	San Francisco	4
Hopkins, Thomas	262	T	Alabama A&M	Cleveland	10
Hopkins, Ronald	252	DB	Murray State	Baltimore	10
Hopkins, Wes	35	DB	Southern Methodist	Philadelphia	2
Horton, Ray	53	DB	Washington	Cincinnati	2
Howell, Wes	105	TE	California	New York Jets	4
Humphrey, Bobby	247	WR	New Mexico State	New York Jets	9
Hunter, Tony	12	TE	Notre Dame	Buffalo	1
Hutchison, Anthony	256	RB	Texas Tech	Chicago	10
Jackson, DeWayne	284	DE	South Carolina State	Kansas City	11
Jackson, Ernest	202	RB	Texas A&M	San Diego	8
James, Craig	187	RB	Southern Methodist	New England	7
Jeffcoat, Jim	23	DE	Arizona State	Dallas	1
Jenkins, Lee	281	DB	Tennessee	New York Giants	11
Johnson, Demetrious	115	DB	Missouri	Detroit	5
Johnson, Trumaine	141	WR	Grambling	San Diego	6
Joiner, Tim	58	LB	Louisiana State	Houston	3
Jones, James	13	RB	Florida	Detroit	1
Jones, Ken	315	T	Tennessee	Kansas City	12
Jones, Mike	159	WR	Tennessee State	Minnesota	6
Jones, Robbie	309	LB	Alabama	New York Giants	12
Jordan, Kent	249	TE	St. Mary's Cal.	Los Angeles Raiders	9
Junkin, Trey	93	LB	Louisiana Tech	Buffalo	4
Kaplan, Ken	158	T	New Hampshire	Tampa Bay	6
Kearse, Tim	303	WR	San Jose State	San Diego	11
Keel, Mark	240	TE	Arizona	New England	9
Kelly, Jim	14	QB	Miami	Buffalo	1
Kelly, Waddell	319	RB	Arkansas State	New England	12
Kinard, Terry	10	DB	Clemson	New York Giants	1
Kinnebrew, Larry	165	RB	Tennesee State	Cincinnati	6
Kirchner, Mark	191	G	Baylor	Pittsburgh	7
Korte, Steve	38	G	Arkansas	New Orleans	2
Kowalski, Gary	144	T	Boston College	Los Angeles Rams	6
Kraynak, Rich	201	LB	Pittsburgh	Philadelphia	8
Krumrie, Tim	276	DT	Wisconsin	Cincinnati	10
Kubiak, Gary	197	QB	Texas A&M	Denver	8

340　THE COMPLETE HANDBOOK OF PRO FOOTBALL

A Houston first-rounder is USC's Bruce Matthews.

The Giants' first pick was Clemson's Terry Kinard.

The Raiders' top choice was USC's Don Mosebar.

NFL DRAFT 343

Player	Order No.	Pos.	College	Club	Round
Lane, James	323	LB	Alabama State	St. Louis	12
Lane, Jimm	321	C	Idaho State	Detroit	12
Laube, Dave	261	G	Penn State	Detroit	10
Laufenberg, Babe	168	QB	Indiana	Washington	6
Ledbetter, Weldon	185	RB	Oklahoma	Tampa Bay	7
Lee, Carl	186	DB	Marshall	Minnesota	7
Lewis, Albert	61	DB	Grambling	Kansas City	3
Lewis, Darryl	128	TE	Texas-Arlington	New England	5
Lewis, Gary	98	NT	Oklahoma State	New Orleans	4
Lewis, Tim	11	DB	Pittsburgh	Green Bay	1
Lindquist, Scott	333	QB	Northern Arizona	Los Angeles Raiders	12
Lingner, Adam	231	C	Illinois	Kansas City	9
Lippett, Ronnie	214	DB	Miami	New England	8
Lucas, Tim	269	LB	California	St. Louis	10
Lukens, Joe	306	G	Ohio State	Miami	11
Lutz, Dave	34	T	Georgia Tech	Kansas City	2
Mack, Cedric	44	DB	Baylor	St. Louis	2
Magwood, Frank	318	WR	Clemson	New York Giants	12
Maidlow, Steve	109	LB	Michigan State	Cincinnati	4
Mangrum, David	312	QB	Baylor	Philadelphia	12
Mann, Charles	84	DE	Nevada-Reno	Washington	3
Marino, Dan	27	QB	Pittsburgh	Miami	1
Marshall, Leonard	37	DT	Louisiana State	New York Giants	2
Martin, Mike	221	WR	Illinois	Cincinnati	8
Mathews, Allama	322	TE	Vanderbilt	Atlanta	12
Mathison, Bruce	272	QB	Nebraska	San Diego	10
Matthews, Bruce	9	T	Southern California	Houston	1
Maxwell, Vernon	29	LB	Arizona State	Baltimore	2
Mayberry, Bob	290	G	Clemson	Seattle	11
McAdoo, Howard	305	LB	Michigan State	Cleveland	11
McCall, Jeff	194	RB	Clemson	Los Angeles Raiders	7
McClearn, Mike	209	G	Temple	Cleveland	8
McCloskey, Mike	88	TE	Penn State	Houston	4
McSwain, Chuck	135	RB	Clemson	Dallas	5
Mecklenburg, Karl	310	DT	Minnesota	Denver	12
Merrell, Jeff	259	DT	Nebraska	San Francisco	10
Merriman, Sam	177	LB	Idaho	Seattle	7
Metcalf, Bo Isaac	106	DB	Baylor	Pittsburgh	4
Miller, Brett	129	T	Iowa	Atlanta	5
Miller, Mike	104	WR	Tennessee	Green Bay	4
Mills, Jim	225	T	Hawaii	Baltimore	9
Montgomery, Blanchard	59	LB	UCLA	San Francisco	3
Moore, Alvin	169	RB	Arizona State	Baltimore	7
Moore, Steve	80	G	Tennessee State	New England	3
Moran, Eric	273	T	Washington	Dallas	10
Moriarty, Larry	114	RB	Notre Dame	Houston	5
Mosebar, Don	26	T	Southern California	Los Angeles Raiders	1
Moten, Gary	175	LB	Southern Methodist	San Francisco	7
Mott, Steve	121	C	Alabama	Detroit	5
Mularkey, Mike	229	TE	Florida	San Francisco	9
Mullen, Davlin	217	DB	Western Kentucky	New York Jets	8
Nelson, Chuck	87	K	Washington	Los Angeles Rams	4
Nelson, Karl	70	T	Iowa State	New York Giants	3
Newbold, Darrin	190	LB	S.W. Missouri	New York Jets	7
Newsome, Vince	97	DB	Washington	Los Angeles Rams	4
Oatis, Victor	147	WR	N.W. Louisiana	Philadelphia	6
O'Brien, Ken	24	QB	Cal-Davis	New York Jets	1
Odom, Henry	199	RB	South Carolina State	Pittsburgh	8
Parker, George	234	RB	Norfolk State	Buffalo	9

344 THE COMPLETE HANDBOOK OF PRO FOOTBALL

Detroit's first selection was Florida's Jim Jones.

NFL DRAFT

Player	Order No.	Pos.	College	Club	Round
Parker, Steve	292	WR	Abilene Christian	New England	11
Patterson, Darrell	151	LB	Texas Christian	New York Giants	6
Payne, Jimmy	112	DE	Georgia	Buffalo	4
Pelzer, Rich	232	T	Rhode Island	Philadelphia	9
Pickel, Bill	54	DT	Rutgers	Los Angeles Raiders	2
Pierson, Clenzie	291	DT	Rice	New York Giants	11
Pitts, Mike	16	DE	Alabama	Atlanta	1
Posey, Daryl	179	RB	Mississippi College	Kansas City	7
Potter, Kevin	226	DB	Missouri	Houston	9
Provence, Andrew	75	DE	South Carolina	Atlanta	3
Puzzuoli, Dave	149	DT	Pittsburgh	Cleveland	6
Rade, John	215	LB	Boise State	Atlanta	8
Ramsey, Tom	267	QB	UCLA	New England	10
Raugh, Mark	302	TE	West Virginia	Pittsburgh	11
Reed, Anthony	278	RB	South Carolina State	Miami	10
Reed, Doug	111	DT	San Diego State	Los Angeles Rams	4
Rembert, Johnny	101	LB	Clemson	New England	4
Richardson, Mike	33	DB	Arizona State	Chicago	2
Ricks, Lawrence	220	RB	Michigan	Dallas	8
Rimington, Dave	25	C	Nebraska	Cincinnati	1
Rivera, Gabriel	21	DT	Texas Tech	Pittsburgh	1
Roby, Reggie	167	P	Iowa	Miami	6
Rose, Chris	241	T	Stanford	Baltimore	9
Rush, Mark	100	RB	Miami	Minnesota	4
Salem, Harvey	30	T	California	Houston	2
Salley, John	295	DB	Wyoming	Atlanta	11
Sampson, Clinton	60	WR	San Diego State	Denver	3
Sams, Ron	160	G	Pittsburgh	Green Bay	6
Samuelson, John	212	LB	Azusa Pacific	Tampa Bay	8
Sapolu, Jesse	289	G	Hawaii	San Francisco	11
Schmitt, George	157	DB	Delaware	St. Louis	6
Schultheis, Jon	182	G	Princeton	Philadelphia	7
Schultz, Chris	189	T	Arizona	Dallas	7
Schulz, Jody	46	LB	East Carolina	Philadelphia	2
Scott, Carlos	184	C	Texas-El Paso	St. Louis	7
Scott, Malcolm	124	TE	Louisiana State	New York Giants	5
Scribner, Bucky	299	P	Kansas	Green Bay	11
Seabaugh, Todd	79	LB	San Diego State	Pittsburgh	3
Sebahar, Steve	285	C	Washington State	Philadelphia	11
Shumate, Mark	257	DT	Wisconsin	Kansas City	10
Simmons, Jeff	171	WR	Southern California	Los Angeles Rams	7
Skansi, Paul	133	WR	Washington	Pittsburgh	5
Smith, Billy Ray	5	LB	Arkansas	San Diego	1
Smith, Leonard	17	DB	McNeese State	St. Louis	1
Smith, Phil	85	WR	San Diego State	Baltimore	4
Spencer, Tim	307	RB	Ohio State	San Diego	11
Speros, Pete	263	G	Penn State	Seattle	10
Stapleton, Bill	208	DB	Washington	Detroit	8
Starring, Stephen	74	WR	McNeese State	New England	3
Stewart, Mark	127	LB	Washington	Minnesota	5
Stracka, Tim	145	TE	Wisconsin	Cleveland	6
Straughter, Roosevelt	275	DB	N.E. Louisiana	Pittsburgh	10
Strauthers, Thomas	258	DE	Jackson State	Philadelphia	10
Strenger, Rich	40	T	Michigan	Detroit	2
Talley, Darryl	39	LB	West Virginia	Buffalo	2
Tate, Ben	287	RB	No. Carolina Central	Detroit	11
Tate, Walter	266	C	Tennessee State	Minnesota	10
Taylor, Dan	300	T	Idaho State	Dallas	11
Taylor, Jim Bob	280	QB	Georgia Tech	Baltimore	11

346   THE COMPLETE HANDBOOK OF PRO FOOTBALL

Miami took Pitt's Dan Marino, 27th in first round.

NFL DRAFT 347

Player	Order No.	Pos.	College	Club	Round
Tharpe, Richard	260	DT	Louisville	Buffalo	10
Thayer, Tom	91	C	Notre Dame	Chicago	4
Thomas, Bryan	132	RB	Pittsburgh	Green Bay	5
Thomas, Jimmy	271	DB	Indiana	Green Bay	10
Thomas, Kelly	99	T	Southern California	Tampa Bay	4
Thomas, Ken	173	RB	San Jose State	Kansas City	7
Thompson, Robert	198	LB	Michigan	Houston	8
Tice, John	65	TE	Maryland	New Orleans	3
Townsell, JoJo	78	WR	UCLA	New York Jets	3
Townsend, Greg	110	DE	Texas Christian	Los Angeles Raiders	4
Triplett, Danny	282	LB	Clemson	Los Angeles Rams	11
Tuggle, John	335	RB	California	New York Giants	12
Turk, Jeff	183	DB	Boise State	Atlanta	7
Turner, Jim	81	DB	UCLA	Cincinnati	3
Turner, Maurice	325	RB	Utah State	Minnesota	12
Vandenboom, Matt	126	DB	Wisconsin	Buffalo	5
Walker, John	136	DT	Nebraska-Omaha	New York Jets	5
Walls, Herkie	170	WR	Texas	Houston	7
Walter, Mike	50	DE	Oregon	Dallas	2
Walters, Danny	95	DB	Arkansas	San Diego	4
Warner, Curt	3	RB	Penn State	Seattle	1
Washington, Lionel	103	DB	Tulane	St. Louis	4
West, Troy	200	DB	Southern California	Los Angeles	8
Wetzel, Ron	92	TE	Arizona State	Kansas City	4
White, Larry	293	DE	Jackson State	Buffalo	11
White, Vincent	163	RB	Stanford	New York Jets	6
Wilcher, Mike	36	LB	North Carolina	Los Angeles	2
Wiley, Roger	330	RB	Sam Houston	Pittsburgh	12
Williams, Aaron	296	WR	Washington	St. Louis	11
Williams, Byron	253	WR	Texas-Arlington	Green Bay	10
Williams, Carl	308	WR	Texas Southern	Baltimore	12
Williams, Dokie	138	WR	UCLA	Los Angeles Raiders	5
Williams, Eric	164	DB	North Carolina State	Pittsburgh	6
Williams, Gary	304	WR	Ohio State	Cincinnati	11
Williams, James	264	TE	Wyoming	New England	10
Williams, Jamie	63	TE	Nebraska	New York Giants	3
Williams, Michael	89	RB	Mississippi College	Philadelphia	4
Williams, Oliver	313	WR	Illinois	Chicago	12
Williams, Perry	178	DB	North Carolina State	New York Giants	7
Williams, Richard	56	RB	Memphis State	Washington	2
Williams, Ricky	233	RB	Langston	New England	9
Williams, Toby	265	DE	Nebraska	New England	10
Wilson, Darryal	47	WR	Tennessee	New England	2
Wilson, Stanley	248	RB	Oklahoma	Cincinnati	9
Winckler, Bob	166	T	Wisconsin	Washington	6
Wingle, Blake	244	G	UCLA	Pittsburgh	9
Witte, Mark	297	TE	North Texas State	Tampa Bay	11
Woetzel, Keith	195	LB	Rutgers	Miami	7
Worthy, Gary	286	RB	Wilmington	Chicago	11
Young, Andre	332	LB	Bowling Green	Cincinnati	12
Young, Glen	62	WR	Mississippi State	Philadelphia	3
Zavagnin, Mark	235	LB	Notre Dame	Chicago	9

348 THE COMPLETE HANDBOOK OF PRO FOOTBALL

1983 NFL SCHEDULE

*NIGHT GAME

SUNDAY, SEPT. 4
Atlanta at Chicago
Baltimore at New England
Denver at Pittsburgh
Detroit at Tampa Bay
Green Bay at Houston
L.A. Raiders at Cincinnati
L.A. Rams at New York Giants
Miami at Buffalo
Minnesota at Cleveland
New York Jets at San Diego
Philadelphia at San Francisco
St. Louis at New Orleans
Seattle at Kansas City

MONDAY, SEPT. 5
*Dallas at Washington

THURSDAY, SEPT. 8
*San Francisco at Minnesota

SUNDAY, SEPT. 11
Buffalo at Cincinnati
Cleveland at Detroit
Dallas at St. Louis
Denver at Baltimore
Houston at L.A. Raiders
New England at Miami
New Orleans at L.A. Rams
New York Giants at Atlanta
Pittsburgh at Green Bay
Seattle at New York Jets
Tampa Bay at Chicago
Washington at Philadelphia

MONDAY, SEPT. 12
*San Diego at Kansas City

THURSDAY, SEPT. 15
*Cincinnati at Cleveland

SUNDAY, SEPT. 18
Atlanta at Detroit
Baltimore at Buffalo
Chicago at New Orleans
Kansas City at Washington
L.A. Rams vs. Green Bay
  at Milwaukee
Minnesota at Tampa Bay
New York Giants at Dallas
New York Jets at New England
Philadelphia at Denver
Pittsburgh at Houston
San Diego at Seattle
San Francisco at St. Louis

MONDAY, SEPT. 19
*Miami at L.A. Raiders

SUNDAY, SEPT. 25
Atlanta at San Francisco
Chicago at Baltimore
Cincinnati at Tampa Bay
Cleveland at San Diego
Detroit at Minnesota
Houston at Buffalo
Kansas City at Miami
L.A. Raiders at Denver
L.A. Rams at New York Jets
New England at Pittsburgh
New Orleans at Dallas
St. Louis at Philadelphia
Washington at Seattle

MONDAY, SEPT. 26
*Green Bay at New York Giants

SUNDAY, OCT. 2
Baltimore at Cincinnati
Dallas at Minnesota
Denver at Chicago
Detroit at L.A. Rams
Houston at Pittsburgh
L.A. Raiders at Washington
Miami at New Orleans
Philadelphia at Atlanta
St. Louis at Kansas City
San Diego at New York Giants
San Francisco at New England
Seattle at Cleveland
Tampa Bay at Green Bay

MONDAY, OCT. 3
*New York Jets at Buffalo

NFL SCHEDULE 349

SUNDAY, OCT. 9
Buffalo at Miami
Denver at Houston
Green Bay at Detroit
Kansas City at L.A. Raiders
L.A. Rams at San Francisco
Minnesota at Chicago
New England at Baltimore
New Orleans at Atlanta
New York Jets at Cleveland
Philadelphia at New York Giants
Seattle at San Diego
Tampa Bay at Dallas
Washington at St. Louis

MONDAY, OCT. 10
*Pittsburgh at Cincinnati

SUNDAY, OCT. 16
Atlanta at L.A. Rams
Buffalo at Baltimore
Chicago at Detroit
Cincinnati at Denver
Cleveland at Pittsburgh
Dallas at Philadelphia
Houston at Minnesota
L.A. Raiders at Seattle
Miami at New York Jets
New York Giants at Kansas City
St. Louis at Tampa Bay
San Diego at New England
San Francisco at New Orleans

MONDAY, OCT. 17
*Washington at Green Bay

SUNDAY, OCT. 23
Atlanta at New York Jets
Chicago at Philadelphia
Cleveland at Cincinnati
Detroit at Washington
Kansas City at Houston
*L.A. Raiders at Dallas
Miami at Baltimore
Minnesota at Green Bay
New England at Buffalo
New Orleans at Tampa Bay
Pittsburgh at Seattle
San Diego at Denver
San Francisco at L.A. Rams

MONDAY, OCT. 24
*New York Giants at St. Louis

SUNDAY, OCT. 30
Baltimore at Philadelphia
Dallas at New York Giants
Detroit at Chicago
Green Bay at Cincinnati
Houston at Cleveland
Kansas City at Denver
L.A. Rams at Miami
Minnesota at St. Louis
New England at Atlanta
New Orleans at Buffalo
New York Jets at San Francisco
Seattle at L.A. Raiders
Tampa Bay at Pittsburgh

MONDAY, OCT. 31
*Washington at San Diego

SUNDAY, NOV. 6
Atlanta at New Orleans
Baltimore at New York Jets
Buffalo at New England
Chicago at L.A. Rams
Cincinnati at Houston
Cleveland vs. Green Bay
  at Milwaukee
Denver at Seattle
L.A. Raiders at Kansas City
Miami at San Francisco
Philadelphia at Dallas
St. Louis at Washington
San Diego at Pittsburgh
Tampa Bay at Minnesota

MONDAY, NOV. 7
*New York Giants at Detroit

SUNDAY, NOV. 13
Buffalo at New York Jets
Cincinnati at Kansas City
Dallas at San Diego
Denver at L.A. Raiders
Detroit at Houston
Green Bay at Minnesota
Miami at New England
New Orleans at San Francisco
Philadelphia at Chicago
Pittsburgh at Baltimore
Seattle at St. Louis
Tampa Bay at Cleveland
Washington at New York Giants

MONDAY, NOV. 14
*L.A. Rams at Atlanta

SUNDAY, NOV. 20
Baltimore at Miami
Chicago at Tampa Bay
Cleveland at New England
Detroit vs. Green Bay
  at Milwaukee
Houston at Cincinnati
L.A. Raiders at Buffalo
Kansas City at Dallas
Minnesota at Pittsburgh
New York Giants at Philadelphia

350 THE COMPLETE HANDBOOK OF PRO FOOTBALL

San Diego at St. Louis
San Francisco at Atlanta
Seattle at Denver
Washington at L.A. Rams

MONDAY, NOV. 21
*New York Jets at New Orleans

THURSDAY, NOV. 24
Pittsburgh at Detroit
St. Louis at Dallas

SUNDAY, NOV. 27
Baltimore at Cleveland
Buffalo at L.A. Rams
Denver at San Diego
Green Bay at Atlanta
Houston at Tampa Bay
Kansas City at Seattle
Minnesota at New Orleans
New England at New York Jets
New York Giants at L.A. Raiders
Philadelphia at Washington
San Francisco at Chicago

MONDAY, NOV. 28
*Cincinnati at Miami

THURSDAY, DEC. 1
*L.A. Raiders at San Diego

SUNDAY, DEC. 4
Atlanta at Washington
Buffalo at Kansas City
Chicago at Green Bay
Cincinnati at Pittsburgh
Cleveland at Denver
Dallas at Seattle
L.A. Rams at Philadelphia
Miami at Houston
New Orleans at New England
New York Jets at Baltimore
St. Louis at New York Giants
Tampa Bay at San Francisco

MONDAY, DEC. 5
*Minnesota at Detroit

SATURDAY, DEC. 10
Atlanta at Miami
Pittsburgh at New York Jets

SUNDAY, DEC. 11
Baltimore at Denver
Chicago at Minnesota
Cleveland at Houston
Detroit at Cincinnati
Kansas City at San Diego
New England at L.A. Rams
New Orleans at Philadelphia
St. Louis at L.A. Raiders
San Francisco at Buffalo
Seattle at New York Giants
Washington at Dallas

MONDAY, DEC. 12
*Green Bay at Tampa Bay

FRIDAY, DEC. 16
*New York Jets at Miami

SATURDAY, DEC. 17
Cincinnati at Minnesota
New York Giants at Washington

SUNDAY, DEC. 18
Buffalo at Atlanta
Denver at Kansas City
Green Bay at Chicago
Houston at Baltimore
L.A. Rams at New Orleans
New England at Seattle
Philadelphia at St. Louis
Pittsburgh at Cleveland
San Diego at L.A. Raiders
Tampa Bay at Detroit

MONDAY, DEC. 19
*Dallas at San Francisco

Nationally Televised Games

(CBS and NBC also will televise a national doubleheader game each Sunday during the regular season. All games carried on CBS Radio Network.)

REGULAR SEASON

Monday, Sept. 5—Dallas at Washington (night, ABC)
Thursday, Sept. 8—San Francisco at Minnesota (night, ABC)
Monday, Sept. 12—San Diego at Kansas City (night, ABC)
Thursday, Sept. 15—Cincinnati at Cleveland (night, ABC)
Monday, Sept. 19—Miami at Los Angeles Raiders (night, ABC)
Monday, Sept. 26—Green Bay at New York Giants (night, ABC)
Monday, Oct. 3—New York Jets at Buffalo (night, ABC)
Monday, Oct. 10—Pittsburgh at Cincinnati (night, ABC)
Monday, Oct. 17—Washington at Green Bay (night, ABC)
Sunday, Oct. 23—Los Angeles Raiders at Dallas (night, ABC)
Monday, Oct. 24—New York Giants at St. Louis (night, ABC)
Monday, Oct. 31—Washington at San Diego (night, ABC)
Monday, Nov. 7—New York Giants at Detroit (night, ABC)
Monday, Nov. 14—Los Angeles Rams at Atlanta (night, ABC)
Monday, Nov. 21—New York Jets at New Orleans (night, ABC)
Thursday, Nov. 24—(Thanksgiving) Pittsburgh at Detroit (day, NBC)
                                 St. Louis at Dallas (day, CBS)
Monday, Nov. 28—Cincinnati at Miami (night, ABC)
Thursday, Dec. 1—Los Angeles Raiders at San Diego (night, ABC)
Monday, Dec. 5—Minnesota at Detroit (night, ABC)
Saturday, Dec. 10—Atlanta at Miami (day, CBS)
                  Pittsburgh at New York Jets (day, NBC)
Monday, Dec. 12—Green Bay at Tampa Bay (night, ABC)
Friday, Dec. 16—New York Jets at Miami (night, ABC)
Saturday, Dec. 17—Cincinnati at Minnesota (day, NBC)
                  New York Giants at Washington (day, CBS)
Monday, Dec. 19—Dallas at San Francisco (night, ABC)

POSTSEASON

Saturday, Dec. 24—AFC First Round Playoff (NBC)
Monday, Dec. 26—NFC First Round Playoff (CBS)
Saturday, Dec. 31—AFC and NFC Divisional Playoffs (NBC and CBS)
Sunday, Jan. 1—AFC and NFC Divisional Playoffs (NBC and CBS)
Sunday, Jan. 8—AFC and NFC Championship Games (NBC and CBS)
Sunday, Jan. 22—Super Bowl XVIII at Tampa Stadium, Tampa, Florida (CBS)
Sunday, Jan. 29—AFC-NFC Pro Bowl at Honolulu, Hawaii (ABC)

MONDAY NIGHT GAMES (ABC)

Sept. 5—Dallas at Washington
Sept. 12—San Diego at Kansas City
Sept. 19—Miami at Los Angeles Raiders
Sept. 26—Green Bay at New York Giants
Oct. 3—New York Jets at Buffalo
Oct. 10—Pittsburgh at Cincinnati
Oct. 17—Washington at Green Bay
Oct. 24—New York Giants at St. Louis
Oct. 31—Washington at San Diego
Nov. 7—New York Giants at Detroit
Nov. 14—L.A. Rams at Atlanta
Nov. 21—N.Y. Jets at New Orleans
Nov. 28—Cincinnati at Miami
Dec. 5—Minnesota at Detroit
Dec. 12—Green Bay at Tampa Bay
Dec. 19—Dallas at San Francisco

SUNDAY, THURSDAY, FRIDAY NIGHT GAMES (ABC)

Thursday, Sept. 8—San Fran. at Minn.
Thursday, Sept. 15—at Cleveland
Sunday, Oct. 23—L.A. Raiders at Dallas
Thursday, Dec. 1—L.A. Raiders at SD
Friday, Dec. 16—N.Y. Jets at Miami

THE OFFICIAL NFL ENCYCLOPEDIA OF PRO FOOTBALL

THE ULTIMATE REFERENCE AND SOURCE BOOK FOR PRO FOOTBALL FANS OF ALL AGES

• Over 1,000 photos, plus 16 full-color pages of all-time record holders • Chronological team histories • Team vs. Team scores • Stars—statistics and biographies of Hall of Famers, prominent players, and coaches • NFL chronology from 1920 to today • Games—line-ups, scoring, summaries, and statistics • Roots of Pro Football • Equipment, rules, game language, and stadium data • And much more

(#H431—$27.95) hardbound volume

Buy it at your local bookstore or use this convenient coupon for ordering.

THE NEW AMERICAN LIBRARY, INC.
P.O. Box 999, Bergenfield, New Jersey 07621

Please send me _____ hardbound copies of THE OFFICIAL NFL ENCYCLOPEDIA OF PRO FOOTBALL (#H431—$27.95, in Canada $33.95). I am enclosing $_____ (please add $1.50 to this order to cover postage and handling). Send check or money order—no cash or C.O.D.'s. Price and number are subject to change without notice.

Name_____

Address_____

City _____ State _____ Zip Code _____

Allow 4-6 weeks for delivery.
This offer is subject to withdrawal without notice.